New Waves in Philosophy
Series Editors: **Vincent F. Hendricks** and

Titles include:
Jesús H. Aguilar, Andrei A. Buckareff and Keith Frankish (*editors*)
NEW WAVES IN PHILOSOPHY OF ACTION

Michael Brady
NEW WAVES IN METAETHICS

Otavio Bueno and Oystein Linnebo (*editors*)
NEW WAVES IN PHILOSOPHY OF MATHEMATICS

Boudewijn DeBruin and Christopher F. Zurn (*editors*)
NEW WAVES IN POLITICAL PHILOSOPHY

Allan Hazlett (*editor*)
NEW WAVES IN METAPHYSICS

Vincent F. Hendricks and Duncan Pritchard (*editors*)
NEW WAVES IN EPISTEMOLOGY

P.D. Magnus and Jacob Busch (*editors*)
NEW WAVES IN PHILOSOPHY OF SCIENCE

Yujin Nagasawa and Erik J. Wielenberg (*editors*)
NEW WAVES IN PHILOSOPHY OF RELIGION

Jan Kyrre Berg Olsen, Evan Selinger and Søren Riis (*editors*)
NEW WAVES IN PHILOSOPHY OF TECHNOLOGY

Thomas S. Petersen, Jesper Ryberg and Clark Wolf (*editors*)
NEW WAVES IN APPLIED ETHICS

Sarah Sawyer (*editor*)
NEW WAVES IN PHILOSOPHY OF LANGUAGE

Kathleen Stock and Katherine Thomson-Jones (*editors*)
NEW WAVES IN AESTHETICS

Cory D. Wright and Nikolaj J. L. L. Pedersen (*editors*)
NEW WAVES IN TRUTH

Forthcoming:
Thom Brooks (*editor*)
NEW WAVES IN ETHICS

Maksymilian Del Mar
NEW WAVES IN PHILOSOPHY OF LAW

Greg Restall and Gillian Russell
NEW WAVES IN PHILOSOPHICAL LOGIC

Future Volumes
NEW WAVES IN PHILOSOPHY OF MIND
NEW WAVES IN FORMAL PHILOSOPHY

New Waves in Philosophy
Series Standing Order ISBN 978–0–230–53797–2 (hardcover)
Series Standing Order ISBN 978–0–230–53798–9 (paperback)
(outside North America only)

You can receive future titles in this series as they are published by placing a standing order. Please contact your bookseller or, in case of difficulty, write to us at the address below with your name and address, the title of the series and the ISBN quoted above.

Customer Services Department, Macmillan Distribution Ltd, Houndmills, Basingstoke, Hampshire RG21 6XS, England

New Waves in Philosophy of Action

Edited by

Jesús H. Aguilar
Rochester Institute of Technology, USA

Andrei A. Buckareff
Marist College, USA

Keith Frankish
The Open University, UK

First published 2011 by
PALGRAVE MACMILLAN

Palgrave Macmillan in the UK is an imprint of Macmillan Publishers Limited, registered in England, company number 785998, of Houndmills, Basingstoke, Hampshire RG21 6XS.

Palgrave Macmillan in the US is a division of St Martin's Press LLC, 175 Fifth Avenue, New York, NY 10010.

Palgrave Macmillan is the global academic imprint of the above companies and has companies and representatives throughout the world.

ISBN 978–0–230–58060–2 hardback
ISBN 978–0–230–23060–6 paperback

This book is printed on paper suitable for recycling and made from fully managed and sustained forest sources. Logging, pulping and manufacturing processes are expected to conform to the environmental regulations of the country of origin.

A catalogue record for this book is available from the British Library.

Library of Congress Cataloging-in-Publication Data

New waves in philosophy of action/edited by Jesús H. Aguilar, Andrei A. Buckareff, Keith Frankish.
p. cm. — (New waves in philosophy)
Includes bibliographical references and index.
ISBN 978–0–230–23060–6
1. Act (Philosophy) I. Aguilar, Jesús H. (Jesús Humberto), 1962– II. Buckareff, Andrei A., 1971– III. Frankish, Keith.
B105.A35.N49 2011
128'.4—dc22

2010027480

10 9 8 7 6 5 4 3 2 1
20 19 18 17 16 15 14 13 12 11

Printed and bound in Great Britain by
CPI Antony Rowe, Chippenham and Eastbourne

Contents

List of Figures

Series Editors' Preface

New Waves in Philosophy Series

The aim of this series is to gather the young and up-and-coming scholars in philosophy to give their view of the subject now and in the years to come, and to serve a documentary purpose, that is, "this is what they said then, and this is what happened." It will also provide a snapshot of cutting-edge research that will be of vital interested to researchers and students working in all subject areas of philosophy.

The goal of the series is to have a New Waves volume in every one of the main areas of philosophy. We would like to thank Palgrave Macmillan for taking on this project in particular, and the entire *New Waves in Philosophy* series in general.

Vincent F. Hendricks and Duncan Pritchard

Notes on Contributors

Tim Bayne is University Lecturer in the Philosophy of Mind at the University of Oxford and a Fellow of St. Catherine's College. He is the author of a number of articles on consciousness, and is an editor of *The Oxford Companion to Consciousness*. His book *The Unity of Consciousness* is shortly to be published by Oxford University Press.

Lisa Bortolotti is Senior Lecturer in Philosophy at the University of Birmingham (UK). Her main research interests are in the philosophy of the cognitive sciences, with a particular focus on irrationality, self-knowledge, and agency. She is the author of *Delusions and Other Irrational Beliefs* (Oxford University Press, 2009) and the editor of *Philosophy and Happiness* (Palgrave Macmillan, 2009). She also writes about biomedical ethics, especially in the context of scientific research and reproduction.

Sara Rachel Chant is Assistant Professor of Philosophy at the University of Missouri-Columbia. Her main areas of research include metaphysics and philosophy of action, with special concern paid to the methodological approach taken towards classical problems in these areas. She has published her work in journals such as *Pacific Philosophical Quarterly, Philosophical Explorations, Studia Logica, and Philosophical Studies*. Chant is currently completing a book with Zachary Ernst on the epistemology of collectivity.

Neil Levy is Director of Research at the Oxford Centre for Neuroethics and Head of Neuroethics at the Florey Neuroscience Institutes (Melbourne, Australia). He is the author of five books, including *Neuroethics* (Cambridge University Press, 2007) and around 100 articles in applied ethics, philosophical psychology, and free will and moral responsibility. He is currently writing a book on luck and free will.

Dylan Murray Dylan Murray is a PhD student in the Department of Philosophy at the University of California, Berkeley. He was previously a Brains & Behavior Fellow in the Philosophy Department and Neuroscience Institute at Georgia State University. His research focuses on action theory, moral psychology, and philosophy of mind.

Thomas Nadelhoffer is Assistant Professor of Philosophy at Dickinson College. His research focuses on action theory, moral psychology, and the philosophy of law. He has published his work in journals such as *Analysis, Midwest Studies in Philosophy, Mind & Language*, and *Philosophy and Phenomenological Research*.

Eddy Nahmias is Associate Professor in the Philosophy Department and the Neuroscience Institute at Georgia State University. He specializes in philosophy of mind/cognitive science, free will, moral psychology, and experimental philosophy. He has published numerous chapters and articles in these areas, is co-editor of *Moral Psychology: Classic and Contemporary Readings* (Wiley-Blackwell), and is writing *Rediscovering Free Will* (Oxford University Press), which examines potential threats to free will from research in the mind sciences.

Bill Pollard is an Honorary Research Fellow at the University of Edinburgh. He has taught at the universities of Edinburgh, Warwick and York in the UK, and Dartmouth College in the USA. His main research interests are in the philosophy of action, with particular focus on the habits, their rationality and explanatory role. He is the author of *Habits in Action* (VDM Verlag Dr. Mueller e.K., 2008) and a number of articles on habits.

Carolina Sartorio is Associate Professor of Philosophy at the University of Arizona. Her main research interests are in metaphysics, ethics, and their intersection. She has published articles on the topics of causation, moral responsibility, agency, and free will.

Markus Schlosser is a Research Fellow at the University of Leiden. His main research area is the philosophy of action, with a focus on metaphysical issues. He has published his work in journals such as *Analysis*, and *Philosophical Explorations*. Currently, he is working on a philosophical evaluation of empirical claims concerning mental causation and free will.

Yonatan Shemmer is a Lecturer of Philosophy at The University of Sheffield, UK. His main interests are in practical reason and normative psychology. He has recently spent time thinking about constructivist views of practical reason and is co-editing a volume on Constructivism in practical philosophy. He is the author of "Desires as Reasons" (2007) as well as some other articles on Humeanism in practical reason.

Matthew Soteriou is Reader in Philosophy at the University of Warwick. His main research interests are in the philosophy of mind and action, and epistemology, with a particular focus on perception, mental action and the ontology of mind.

Manuel Vargas is Associate Professor of Philosophy at the University of San Francisco. His main areas of interest include the philosophy of agency, moral psychology, and Latin American philosophy. He is one of the authors (along with John Martin Fischer, Robert Kane, and Derk Pereboom) of *Four Views on Free Will* (Blackwell, 2007), and has written articles on such topics as free will, practical reason, evil, Eurocentrism, and the undead. He is currently working on a book on moral responsibility.

Acknowledgments

A volume such as this is the result of the hard work of a number of people. The editors would first like to thank the authors of the essays for their exceptional contributions to this volume. A debt of gratitude is also due to the editors of the *New Waves in Philosophy* series, Vincent F. Hendricks and Duncan Pritchard, for their support of this project. We are also grateful to Evan Selinger for putting us into contact with Vincent and encouraging us to contribute a volume to the series. Our contacts at Palgrave Macmillan, Priyanka Gibbons and Melanie Blair, deserve special thanks for their patience with us and willingness to be accommodating when we requested extra time to work on the manuscript. From Macmillan Publishing Solution Limited, we would like to thank Imran Shahnawaz and his production team for their editorial work.

The task of putting this volume together was greatly facilitated by the work of the many referees who were willing to review the articles for us. These included Kent Bach, John Bishop, Ish Haji, Bennett Helm, Terry Horgan, Ron Mallon, Michael McKenna, Alfred R. Mele, Shaun Nichols, Lucy O'Brien, Joëlle Proust, and Christine Tappolet. We are grateful to them all for their hard work.

We also wish to thank our home institutions for support. In particular, Andrei is grateful to Marist College for giving him a course release that allowed him extra time to work on this and other projects. Jesús is very thankful for the support received from the Rochester Institute of Technology in the form of course releases as the recipient of the Paul A. and Francena L. Miller Faculty Fellowship. Keith is grateful to The Open University for support during some difficult personal times, and to the Department of Philosophy and Social Studies at the University of Crete for welcoming him as a Visiting Researcher. In particular, he would like to thank Maria Venieri for helping him feel part of the philosophy community in Crete.

Finally, all three editors are especially grateful to their loved ones. Jesús wishes to thank Amy Wolf for her unfaltering support and loving understanding during his work on this volume. Andrei is grateful to his spouse, Lara E. Kasper-Buckareff for her encouragement, loving support, and legal advice. Keith wishes to thank his wife, Maria Kasmirli, for her patience, support, and excellent advice on philosophical matters.

Introduction

Jesús Aguilar, Andrei Buckareff, and Keith Frankish

1 Philosophy of action

This volume contains a set of cutting-edge essays by younger philosophers on various topics in what can broadly be characterized as the philosophy of action. Some of the essays are about the metaphysics of action and agency; some consider the nature of autonomy and free agency; some explore conceptual and normative issues; some draw on data from psychology and psychopathology. But what all of them have in common is that they address some problem related to our existence as human agents.

The range of topics covered in this collection is broad. This is intentional. Rather than focus on one narrow topic, we have chosen to collect papers that, taken together, introduce readers to some key debates in contemporary philosophy of action. Of course, exactly how broad a range of issues one will expect to find in such a volume will depend on how one characterizes the field of philosophy of action, and we shall begin by saying something about how we characterize it.

So what is the philosophy of action? One view treats it as either a narrow sub-discipline of philosophy or as a proper part of another sub-discipline or set of sub-disciplines, primarily metaphysics and the philosophy of mind. On this view, philosophy of action is focused on the conceptual, epistemological, and metaphysical issues surrounding the nature of action and its explanation (action-individuation, the nature of intentions and their role in intentional action, the nature of the will, reasons and their role in explaining action, and so on).

A problem with this characterization is that it winds up separating a host of closely related issues, excluding certain problems (for example, *akrasia* and *enkrasia*, free will, motivation) from the field simply because they do not concern foundational issues about the nature and explanation of human action. To illustrate what is wrong with this approach, we may make a comparison with epistemology. Much of the work on topics such as epistemic *akrasia*, epistemic virtue, and reasonable disagreements does not bear directly on questions about the nature of knowledge itself. (For example, one can theorize about the epistemic virtues but endorse a theory of knowledge that dispenses with any role whatsoever for epistemic virtues.) Do these topics belong outside epistemology? Since they all bear on issues related to the broader interests of epistemologists, including the nature of epistemic evaluations, they belong in epistemology. Something similar is the case with respect to the philosophy of action, where it is hard to make a clean separation between foundational issues about intentional action and wider issues about, for example, the nature of free agency. Indeed, one's view about a foundational issue may directly affect how one thinks about a non-foundational issue, and vice versa.

Another way of characterizing the philosophy of action is as a broad sub-discipline of philosophy. On this view, which is the one taken in this volume, the philosophy of action is a wide field that overlaps with other areas in important ways, but has its own distinctive set of questions and problems, all of which are *broadly* related to questions about the nature, explanation, and scope of our agency and action. So conceived, philosophy of action embraces not only traditional concerns about the nature and explanation of intentional action, but also a host of other issues, including, among others, the problems of *akrasia* and *enkrasia*, free will and moral responsibility, mental agency, motivation, omissions, practical reason, and social action. Of course, philosophy of action is closely related to other philosophical sub-disciplines. For instance, philosophy of mind and philosophy of action both address questions about mental action, mental causation, and reasons-explanations. This should not be surprising, however. As in other areas of philosophy, the boundaries between the various sub-disciplines are vague, relating to each other like the intersecting circles of a Venn diagram.

One objection to this view of the field is that the philosophy of action lies at the intersection of so many disparate sub-disciplines that there is very little glue to hold it together, so to speak. After all, in the course of their career, a philosopher may become an expert on the ontological issues in the philosophy of action without developing the same sophisticated understanding of the normative debates (which require a level of expertise in ethics that an ontologist may lack). Indeed, very few philosophers (Alfred Mele being a rare example) have proved able to move with ease among the various topics gathered under the banner of philosophy of action. So perhaps we should reject the idea that there is a unified sub-discipline identifiable as the philosophy of action. Rather, there are just problems about action and agency in the myriad sub-disciplines of philosophy that bear a family resemblance to each other. And—the objection goes—such a family resemblance is not enough to constitute the philosophy of action as a distinct sub-discipline in its own right.

However, this objection ignores the fact that, once again, philosophy of action is not unique in this respect. Compare the philosophy of mind.

Here, too, a philosopher may spend most of their career focusing on a narrow set of issues that do not bear directly on debates elsewhere in the field. One researcher might work on the problem of mental causation while another focuses almost entirely on the nature of phenomenal consciousness. Although there is some overlap between these two areas, the two researchers would need to undertake substantial retraining and scholarship if they suddenly decided to swap topics. The point is that philosophy of mind is not defined by a core body of knowledge and expertise shared by all practitioners. Rather, it is constituted by a set of linked problems, to which *different* bodies of knowledge and expertise need to be applied. In short, philosophy of mind, too, is unified only by a family resemblance among the various problems it encompasses—and is none the worse for that.

An advantage of characterizing the philosophy of action as a broad sub-discipline is that it puts pressure on philosophers of action to pay attention to work done in other areas of the field, which, they may find, bears directly on their own. To give just one example, if one concludes that there is nothing more to an agent's exercise of executive control than that the right type of mental states non-deviantly cause their behavior, then one may find that certain theories of autonomous control and free agency are no longer viable options. Of course, philosophers of action also need to pay attention to work in other philosophical sub-disciplines and in the relevant sciences. Indeed, recent years have seen increasing collaboration between philosophers, psychologists, and neuroscientists with respect to the study of agency and action, and many philosophers have made it a point to do work that is empirically informed (Myles Brand, Alfred Mele, Fred Adams, and Timothy O'Connor all come to mind). But the importance of such interdisciplinary connections does not weaken the case for treating philosophy of action as a broad sub-discipline within philosophy—the opposite, if anything.

Of course, in this short introduction we can only sketch the case for our view of the philosophy of action, and some readers may be unconvinced. Still, even if the philosophy of action is not an independent sub-discipline, there is no doubt that there are problems about human action and agency to be found in all of the major sub-disciplines of philosophy. The essays in this volume address many of these problems. And, though the coverage is not exhaustive, readers new to the field should come away from the volume with a good sense of current thinking about human action and agency. For their part, established researchers in the field will, we believe, find the essays to be original contributions that substantially advance many debates about action and agency.

2 The essays

The essays in this volume are divided between four parts. Those in the first part address issues at the foundation of theorizing about action and agency.

Those in the second and third parts relate to autonomy and free agency respectively, and those in the final part address issues which in various ways extend the boundaries of traditional philosophy of action.

2.1 Foundations of action and agency

The essays in Part I look at foundational issues in the philosophy of action, using both traditional methods and new approaches.

In "Agency, Ownership, and the Standard Theory," Markus Schlosser defends the Causal Theory of Action (CTA), according to which an agent-involving event counts as an action if it is caused in the right way by appropriate agent-involving mental states. The CTA is considered the standard theory of action, and Schlosser shows why it has retained this status, presenting its main features and arguing that it offers the only viable account of the metaphysics of agency. A major challenge to the CTA is that it is unable to provide an account of the role of the *agent*. On one version of the objection, the CTA reduces activity to mere happenings, and thus fails to capture the phenomenon of agency. On another, weaker, version of the objection, the CTA fails to capture the role played by the human agent in certain higher forms of action. In response, Schlosser argues that the CTA does support a robust notion of agency, especially when fleshed out with a feedback-comparator model of motor control, and that higher kinds of agency can be accounted for by supplementing the CTA in various ways.

In her contribution, "Failing to do the Impossible," Carolina Sartorio considers the relationship between intentional omissions and alternative possibilities. Specifically, she considers whether an agent's intentionally omitting to do something requires that the agent could have intentionally acted otherwise. Engaging with related work on moral responsibility and on omissions (including Harry Frankfurt's work on both), she provides an account of intentional omissions that can handle challenging cases that evoke competing intuitions. She contends that an agent can intentionally omit to act even if it is *impossible* for them to have acted otherwise. While this result may be welcome to those who contend that morally responsible agency does not require the ability to act contrary to how one actually acted, the same people may not welcome Sartorio's conclusion that there is an important asymmetry between the conditions for intentionally acting and for intentionally omitting to act.

In the final chapter in Part I, "Experimental Philosophy of Action," Thomas Nadelhoffer surveys work in the experimental philosophy of action. Many philosophers make claims about our everyday "folk" intuitions and judgments, and seek to develop theories that are broadly compatible with them. However, they have traditionally made these claims from the comfort of their armchairs, assuming that their own intuitions coincide with those of folk in general. Philosophers working in the new and rapidly developing field of experimental philosophy aim to correct this by conducting systematic surveys of people's intuitions on matters relevant to philosophical problems. This experimental approach has been particularly influential within philosophy of action, and Nadelhoffer argues for its importance in exploring the nature of intentional action. He focuses on Joshua Knobe's "side effect" findings, which indicate that our judgments about whether or not an action is intentional are influenced by our moral evaluation of the action's outcome—a view that runs counter to most traditional philosophical accounts of intentional action. Nadelhoffer reviews the key models that have been proposed to explain Knobe's data and introduces some recent work that may shape the debate in the future. His overall aim is to provide the reader with a framework for understanding the field of experimental philosophy of action and encouragement to contribute to it.

2.2 Autonomy

In the recent literature on the philosophy of action, a distinction has arisen between two different ways in which agents exercise control over their actions, which François Schroeter has christened *basic executive control* and *autonomous control* respectively (Schroeter, 2004). Basic executive control is manifested whenever an agent exercises whatever sort of guidance is necessary to ensure the successful execution of their actions, and it is arguable that when we theorize about run-of-the-mill intentional action, we are concerned with basic executive control. Autonomous control, on the other hand, is a species of control that manifests our capacity for self-governance ("autonomous" literally means *self-governed*), and many writers claim that basic executive control, while necessary for autonomous control, is not sufficient for it. If that is right, then we shall need to supplement our theories of intentional action in order to get an account of autonomous control and, hence, of what J. David Velleman calls "full-blooded-action" (Velleman, 1992).

One of the most popular strategies here is to appeal to "endorsement" or "identification" as the necessary addition to executive control that will deliver autonomous control. According to this view, variants of which have been offered by, among others, Michael Bratman, Harry Frankfurt, and J. David Velleman, an agent exercises autonomous control over an action if the action issues from motivational states with which they identify or which they have endorsed. Although it is not the only strategy for accounting for autonomy, the identification strategy is one of the most popular. Still, there are problems with it, and other accounts of autonomy have been proposed, including ones that take basic executive control to be sufficient for autonomous control. The essays in Part II of the volume adopt varying approaches to autonomy while also exploring other issues.

The first essay, Bill Pollard's "Identification, Psychology and Habits," takes up the search for a theory of identification, which (following Frankfurt) he understands as an account of the difference between motives that are external to the agent, such as drug cravings or sudden emotional impulses, and internal motives, with which the agent is identified. Pollard notes that existing accounts assume that for a motive to be internal it is necessary that it be suitably related to aspects of the agent's psychology—whether psychological states, such as higher-order desires, or psychological actions, such as decisions or judgments. Pollard rejects these accounts, arguing that they are subject to a regress, and proposes that for a motive to be internal it is sufficient that it expresses one of the agent's *habits*. If this is correct, then a theory of identification need not make reference to the agent's psychological states at all. Pollard also offers a definition of "habit" and defends a conception of agency according to which an agent is partly constituted by their habits.

Yonatan Shemmer's chapter "Mass Perverse Identification: An Argument for a Modest Concept of Autonomy" continues the themes of identification and autonomy. Shemmer notes that many philosophers subscribe to the so-called dependence thesis, according to which an agent performs an action autonomously only if they identify with the desire that motivates it. However, as Shemmer stresses, we very often act in ways that are not in accord with our value judgments—failing to donate to charity, shunning voluntary work, and so on. In such cases, he argues, we do not identify with the desires that motivate our actions, but the actions are autonomous all the same. Shemmer concludes that we must challenge the dependence thesis and accept that an action may be autonomous even if the agent does not identify with it. An action is autonomous, Shemmer proposes, provided it is part of a life that is composed of actions *most of which* the agent identifies with. Thus, ascriptions of autonomy, whether to agents or their actions, are always sensitive to global considerations. Shemmer defends this proposal from objections and argues that it comports with our core intuitions.

In his chapter "Cartesian Reflections on the Autonomy of the Mental," Matthew Soteriou turns to the role of mental agency in autonomy. Taking his lead from remarks in Descartes's *Mediations*, Soteriou focuses on two central but relatively neglected aspects of conscious thinking: *supposition*, in which a proposition that is not believed is temporarily adopted as a premise for the sake of argument, and *bracketing*, in which a proposition that is believed is temporarily excluded from use as a premise for the purpose of its epistemic evaluation. These acts, Soteriou argues, are not one-off events, but function as self-imposed constraints on our future reasoning, and in acknowledging and respecting them we manifest a distinctively human form of agency and autonomy.

2.3 Free agency

Part III of the volume is devoted to one of most prominent debates in the philosophy of action, and indeed in philosophy generally: the debate about free agency. There has been a resurgence of interest in this topic in recent years, which has contributed to a growth of interest in a range of related issues in philosophy of action. In many respects, debates over free agency have proved more tractable than was previously expected, with concessions being made by various parties. What has happened, especially since the 1980s, is that there has been a shift in emphasis from the debate over the question of the compatibility of free will with determinism (although this is still prominent) to debates over competing models of free agency. At the same time, a stronger sense is emerging of how issues about the explanation of action and questions about the nature of free agency hang together, even it if not always explicitly acknowledged in the literature.

In the opening essay of Part III, "The Revisionist Turn: A Brief History of Recent Work on Free Will," Manuel Vargas focuses on the recent history of the free will debate, locating it within the context of metaphilosophical debates among analytic philosophers regarding the methods and goals of philosophical inquiry. In particular, Vargas examines the differences between those who see the free will problem as primarily a metaphysical issue and those whose work on the problem is motivated primarily by ethical concerns. The metaphysicians' approach has elevated the role of intuitions in theorizing about free agency, whereas the ethicists have been more willing to adopt theories that are counter-intuitive but preferable on other grounds. Vargas sides with the ethicists, arguing that intuitions are a source of data when theorizing about free agency, but are not sacrosanct. Finally, as a way of highlighting some of the methodological challenges and options in theorizing about free agency, Vargas presents his own revisionist, responsibility-centric theory of free agency. He urges greater attention to the methodological matters he takes up in his essay in future theorizing about free will and moral responsibility.

In his essay, "Luck and Free Will," Neil Levy focuses on the role of the notion of luck in the free will debate. Traditionally, the notion has been invoked in an argument against the libertarian view that free actions are undetermined. It is argued that an undetermined event is a matter of luck, and that actions that are a matter of luck do not manifest control or, consequently, freedom, on the part of the agent. Unlike many working in the field, who treat luck as a primitive notion or provide anemic accounts of it, Levy develops a robust analysis of luck, and he goes on to argue that it poses a challenge for all theories of free agency, be they libertarian or compatibilist.

Another recent development in the free will debate is the application of the methods of experimental philosophy, discussed previously in Thomas Nadelhoffer's chapter. In their essay for this volume, "Experimental Philosophy on Free Will: An Error Theory for Incompatibilist Intuitions," Eddy Nahmias and Dylan Murray survey recent work in this area and present a new study of their own. Their results point to an error theory for incompatibilist intuitions among ordinary folk. Laypeople, they argue, confuse causal determinism with fatalism. In particular, most people who think causal determinism is incompatible with free will do so because they think it involves bypassing the means whereby agents exercise control. People who correctly understand causal determinism tend to regard it as compatible with free will and moral responsibility. This obviously poses a challenge for incompatibilists who hold that the folk are natural incompatibilists.

2.4 Action and agency in context

This final part includes three essays which in different ways push the boundaries of traditional philosophy of action and illustrate how issues of action and agency link up with wider concerns in philosophy of mind and cognitive science.

Tim Bayne's paper "Agentive Experiences as Pushmi-pullyu Representations," looks at the experience of agency—a topic that was, until recently, relatively neglected by both philosophers of action and philosophers of mind. In particular, Bayne asks how we should characterize the intentional structure and function of agentive experience. There are two established analyses here, thetic and telic. On the thetic analysis agentive experiences are descriptive, like beliefs; they represent how things are, and serve to track states of the world. On the telic analysis they are directive, like desires and intentions; they represent how we want things to be, and serve to direct action. Bayne examines both analyses before going on to propose a third, hybrid account, according to which agentive experiences are "pushmi-pullyu" representations, which have both thetic and telic structure. Bayne defends this view on empirical grounds, arguing that it best captures our current understanding of the cognitive role of agentive experiences.

In her paper, "Double Bookkeeping in Delusions: Explaining the Gap Between Saying and Doing," Lisa Bortolotti considers the role of psychotic delusions in the guidance of action—an issue that lies at the intersection of philosophy of action and the rapidly developing field of philosophy of psychopathology. The standard view of delusions is that they are instances of belief—a view known as the doxastic account. However, delusions sometimes fail to guide action in the way that beliefs do (a phenomenon referred to as "double bookkeeping"), and this suggests that their contents are not objects of genuine belief. Bortolotti defends the doxastic account, arguing, first, that many delusions do guide action, at least some of the time; second, that ordinary beliefs, too, sometimes fail to guide action; and, third, that failures to act upon delusions may be due to lack of motivation rather than to lack of commitment to their truth. Thus Bortolotti emphasizes the continuities between normal and abnormal cognition, shedding light on the roles of both belief and delusion.

The final paper in the volume, Sara Rachel Chant's "The Limits of Rationality in Collective Action Explanations," explores the nature of actions performed by more than one agent. Analyses of such actions traditionally proceed by identifying a set of reasons possessed by each of the participating individuals which justify their taking part in the collective action. Chant agrees that many cases fit this model. However, she also identifies a set of "difficult cases" where, for structural reasons, no such rational choice explanation is available. She explores these cases in detail and suggests that, in order to explain them, we may have to accept that people have an innate propensity to cooperate in certain circumstances. In studying some kinds of collective action, Chant concludes, we may need to adopt a similar approach to that taken in research on anomalous cooperative and altruistic behavior, where rational choice explanations are likewise unavailable.

3 Conclusion

As noted earlier, we do not pretend to have collected a group of essays that addresses all the issues in the philosophy of action. In fact, there are prominent perennial debates that are not taken up in any of the essays collected here. To attempt to cover every important debate would require a much larger volume, and one that would not obviously do what this collection is meant to do—namely expose readers to the work of some younger, up-and-coming philosophers of action on both ancient debates and new ones. The contributors to this volume will be leaders in the field for years to come. And this volume will have served its purpose if it allows both those new to the philosophy of action and seasoned veterans in the field to become acquainted with the work of these exceptional philosophers.

References

Schroeter, F. (2004), "Endorsement and Autonomous Agency," *Philosophy and Phenomenological Research*, 69, 633–59.

Velleman, J. D. (1992), "What Happens when Someone Acts?" *Mind*, 101, 461–81.

Part I
Foundations of Action and Agency

1
Agency, Ownership, and the Standard Theory

Markus E. Schlosser

The causal theory of action has been the standard view in the philosophy of action and mind. In the philosophy of mind, it is a piece of orthodoxy that is widely taken for granted and hardly ever questioned. In the philosophy of action, it has always had its critics. In this chapter, I will present responses to two challenges to the theory. The first says, basically, that there is no positive argument in favour of the causal theory, as the only reason that supports it consists in the apparent lack of tenable alternatives. The second challenge says that the theory fails to capture the phenomenon of agency, as it reduces activity to mere happenings (events and event-causal processes). This is often referred to as the problem of *disappearing agency*. A full defence of the causal theory should address both challenges. In the first part of this chapter, I will present what I take to be the core of the causal theory. In the second and the third part, I will then offer my responses to the two challenges. I will present a positive argument for the causal theory on the basis of considerations concerning the metaphysics of agency, and I will suggest that we *own* the agency that springs from our mental states and events *by default*.

My main aim is to show that there is no problem of disappearing agency, and we will see that my response to the first challenge will be conducive to this end. Let me point out, right at the start, that there are many controversial issues concerning the metaphysics of action and causation that are beyond the scope of this chapter. This means that I will have to make some substantial assumptions, especially in the first and second part.

1.1 Part 1: The standard theory

The causal theory of action, as I understand it, consists of two parts: a causal theory of the nature of actions and a causal theory of reason explanation. The former says, basically, that actions are events with a certain causal history (they are actions *in virtue of* this history). The latter is often stated by reference to Davidson's claim that reason explanation is a "species of causal explanation" (1980, p. 3). The core of the causal theory can then be unpacked as follows:

> Causal theory of the nature of action (CTA): An agent-involving event is an action just in case it is caused by the right agent-involving mental states and events in the right way.
>
> Causal theory of reason explanation (CTR): Reason explanations of actions are explanations in terms of the agent's mental states and events that rationalize and causally explain their performance. In particular, a reason explanation of an action in terms of the agent's mental states and events is true only if those states and events causally explain the action.

The *right* mental states and events, which CTA refers to, are mental attitudes that *rationalize* the performance of the action (such as desires, beliefs and intentions). The right way of causation is *non-deviant* causation. We will return to the issue of non-deviant causation in the third part. For now, consider the following clarifications.

Firstly, it is plausible to think that CTA and CTR stand or fall together, because it is plausible to assume that the mental states and events that CTA refers to are the same mental states and events that feature in reason explanations according to CTR. I will assume, throughout, that CTA and CTR do stand or fall together.[1]

Secondly, the conjunction of CTA and CTR is only the skeleton of the causal theory. It is supposed to capture the common core of causal theories of action or, more generally, the core of the causal approach to agency. In the following, I will nevertheless refer to this core as a *theory*, for the sake of convenience.

Thirdly, the view is usually referred to as the causal theory of action. Strictly speaking, it is an *event*-causal theory. There are alternative causal theories of agency, and I shall refer to it as the event-causal theory, or the event-causal approach, in order to avoid misunderstanding. As I understand it, an event-causal theory is not committed to the claim that only events are causally efficacious entities. It may allow for the causal efficacy or relevance of states, dispositions and other standing conditions, and it may construe events as particulars or instantiations of properties. But it is committed to the claim that at least one event is among the causes of every effect. Events are thought to play a central role in every causal transaction, because events are the entities that initiate or trigger the occurrence of the effect. Another way of characterizing the kind of causation in question would be to say that it is efficient causation by events, states or property-instantiations (by substances) as opposed to both teleological causation and causation by substances (*qua* substances).

Fourthly, CTR makes no claims concerning the nature of *reasons*. In particular, it does not claim that reasons are identical with mental states or events, and it is compatible with the view that reasons are facts or states of affairs (see Dancy 2000, for instance). CTR says that reason explanations are given in terms of mental states and events that rationalize the action. If reasons are facts, CTR can accommodate this by construing their role in reason explanations as the contents (or as what is being represented by the contents) of rationalizing mental states and events (in true and justified reason explanations). In order to avoid misunderstanding, I will call mental attitudes that rationalize actions *reason-states*, rather than reasons. Given this, any attempt to reject the event-causal theory by objecting to the claim that reasons are mental attitudes is simply missing its target.

Finally, the theory is sometimes referred to as the desire-belief theory of action. This is misleading insofar as the event-causal approach is by no means committed to the claim that all actions are caused and explained by desires and beliefs. Most proponents of the view hold now that intentions, construed as a genuine type of mental attitude, play a central role in the causation and explanation of action.[2] In principle, proponents of the view may refer to all kinds of mental entities that qualify as an agent's mental states, mental events, and to relationships between them. My aim here is to defend the event-causal approach to agency in general, rather than a particular version of the view.

1.2 Part 2: Why believe it?

Is the event-causal theory a plausible and intuitively attractive position? It is, I think, neither particularly plausible nor particularly implausible on the grounds of commonsense intuition. The reason for this is that commonsense is silent about most of the issues involved. It seems very plausible to say that the explanation of an action in terms of the agent's desires, beliefs and intentions is true only if the cited mental states motivated the agent to perform the action. But does this mean that the agent's mental states must have *caused* the action? Does this commit us to the claim that actions are *events*? Commonsense holds no answers, let alone conclusive reasons in favour of a particular causal or non-causal position.

What, then, is to be said in favour of the event-causal theory on the grounds of philosophical argument? Many proponents of the view think that the best argument is provided by Davidson's challenge from reason explanation. Davidson pointed out that it is possible to rationalize the performance of an action in the light of some of the agent's reason-states irrespectively of whether or not the agent acted *for* them. The agent may not have performed the action *because of having* those reason-states. In other words, reason explanation cannot be reduced to rationalization. Something else is needed.

This point is particularly salient in cases in which an agent has more than one set of reason-states that would rationalize the performance of an action, but in which there is reason to think that the agent acted only because of *one* set of reason-states. What explains the fact that the agent acted for one rather than another set of reason-states? In general, and to use Davidson's expression, what is the "mysterious connection" between reasons and actions? Davidson suggested that this can only be a causal connection. What else could it be? This, in short, is Davidson's challenge. (Davidson 1980, especially pp. 8–11. Compare also Ginet 2001.)

It has been pointed out that the core of this challenge is a metaphysical rather than an epistemological point (Child 1994, for instance). It is not about how we can know that an agent acted for a reason, but about what makes this true. Causal connections can ground the truth of reason explanations, and they can, in general, explain the metaphysical connections between an agent's reason-states and actions.

Opponents have responded by pointing out that this challenge provides at best an indirect and negative argument for the event-causal approach. We can distinguish two points here. First, as an inference to the *only* explanation, the argument lends merely *negative* support. It supports the view only on the assumption that there are no viable alternative accounts of reason explanation that can meet Davidson's challenge. Secondly, it is only an *indirect* argument insofar as it gives no direct and positive argument for the metaphysical framework of the event-causal approach. In particular, it offers no direct support to CTA. It provides negative support to CTR, and gives indirect support to CTA only insofar as CTA and CTR stand or fall together.

Given all this, it seems that one can undermine the force of the argument simply by presenting an alternative theory of reason explanation that meets Davidson's challenge. Wilson (1989), Sehon (2000), Ginet (1990 and 2001) and Schueler (2003) have pursued this line of argument, and they have offered alternative non-causal accounts of reason explanation. Proponents of the event-causal theory have responded by criticizing the offered non-causal alternatives, and they have argued, convincingly I think, that Davidson's challenge is very much alive (compare Mele 1992 and Clark 2003, for instance). But I do not think that the case for the event-causal approach rests on Davidson's challenge alone. In the remainder of this part, I will present a direct argument from the metaphysics of agency.

1.2.1 Naturalism and the event-causal order

Many philosophers, I suspect, would not agree with the suggestion that Davidson's challenge provides the only argument in support of the event-causal theory. For many, the best reason to endorse the view consists in its apparent compatibility and congeniality with naturalism. According to a fairly widespread form of philosophical naturalism, all particular occurrences, processes, and changes are to be understood and explained in terms of event-causation. In particular, any appeal to substance-causation, irreducible teleology or *sui generis acts* would constitute a violation of naturalism.

Given a strong commitment to this kind of naturalism, one has, it seems, a strong reason to endorse the event-causal approach to agency, because this view *locates* or *situates* agency within the event-causal order, as it were. Opponents of the view will point out, rightly, that this does not give *them* any reason to endorse the event-causal theory, simply because they reject this *kind* of naturalism. (This does not commit them to some kind of anti-naturalism. The term *naturalism* has been used in many different ways. Rejecting the outlined kind of event-causal naturalism, opponents of the event-causal theory need not reject naturalism as such.)

However, if the characterization of naturalism is weakened, in the right way, we can construct an argument for the event-causal theory that does not beg the question. Or so I will argue now. It should, I think, be uncontroversial that human agents are part of the event-causal order in the following weak sense. Our bodily movements are events that are part of the event-causal order in the sense that their occurrence and execution can be explained in terms of event-causation only—in terms of muscle contractions, motor commands, neural activity in the motor cortex and areas of the prefrontal cortex, and so on. This claim is clearly weaker than the claim that all occurrences, including actions, must be explained in terms of event-causation, and I suspect that only very few non-causalists, if any, would object to this weak or minimal version of naturalism. It is undeniable, I think, that we (or our *living bodies*, if you like) are part of the event-causal order in this weak or minimal sense. I will assume, from now on, that this is the case, and I will express this by saying that human agency is *minimally part* of the event-causal order. This is the first of two main assumptions for my argument.

Non-causalists often point out that we are primarily interested in *actions*, rather than bodily movements, when we are interested in human agency. When we give a reason explanation, for instance, we explain the performance of an action, rather than the mere occurrence of a movement. This, they rightly point out, is often overlooked due to the close relationship between bodily movements and basic actions. Roughly, a *basic action* is something an agent can do without doing anything else.[3] It is widely agreed that every action of ours is *either* a basic action *or* brought about by the performance of a basic action (perhaps via a chain or tree of non-basic actions). To take a standard example, you can give a signal by raising your arm. If you do so, you perform a non-basic action (giving a signal) by performing a basic action (raising an arm). The basic action is not performed by doing something else. It is, in particular, not performed by performing a bodily movement (the rising of your arm). But the basic action is also not identical with the bodily movement. Not every movement of this type constitutes or realizes the raising of an arm. They may be token-identical, but they are not type-identical.

Proponents of the event-causal theory can agree with all this, and I think they should agree. We are interested primarily in intentional behaviour, not bodily movement. We perform all non-basic actions by performing basic actions, and basic actions are not type-identical with bodily movements. Nevertheless, it seems obvious that basic actions stand in some intimate relationship with bodily movements. Should they not be token-identical, basic actions are at the very least partly constituted or realized by bodily movements.[4] This appears to be obvious, and I will assume that this is the case. That gives us the second assumption for my argument.

Taken together, the two assumptions give rise to the following central question in the metaphysics of agency: how can human agency be part of the event-causal order at all? Given that overt actions are constituted or realized by movements, and given that bodily movements can be explained in terms of neuro-physiological events, how can agents exercise their agency? How can agents, who are minimally part of the event-causal order, exercise control over their actions?

To make this question clearer, let us briefly consider the case of actions that are done for reasons (in the broad sense of being rationalized and motivated by reason-states). We can distinguish here between four things: actions, an agent's reason-states, bodily movements, and the causes of bodily movements. On the one hand, these actions are done for reasons. They are performed because their agents have certain reason-states. On the other hand, they are at least partly constituted or realized by bodily movements, which can be explained by reference to neuro-physiological events alone. Given the constitutive relationship between actions and movements, we need an explanation of how the influence of reason-states on the agent's actions is related to the causal efficacy of the neuro-physiological causes of the agent's bodily movements.

Agential and rational control *is* in need of explanation. In the following section, I will introduce what I take to be the basic options in the metaphysics of action, and we will assess them in light of the task that has just been outlined.

1.2.2 The metaphysics of agency

What is an agent? What is agency? First, let me restrict our considerations to overt actions (that is, roughly, actions that involve bodily movement).[5] A good starting point is to think of overt agency in terms of self-movement. Agents are beings or systems that can bring about change in their environment by bringing about change in themselves (by moving in a certain way). Agency is an exercise of this ability.

What is self-movement? Intuitively, it is movement that is brought about or initiated by oneself (by the agent or the system itself). What does this mean? We can distinguish here between three main options in the metaphysics of agency, which give three different answers to this question.

According to the first, self-movement is initiated by the self in the sense that it is caused by salient features of the agent, which are themselves caused by other features of the agent or the agent's environment. According to the second, self-movement is initiated, literally, by the agent (by the persisting being that is the agent, rather than features of that being). According to the third option, self-movement is initiated by a mental act of the will, often called *volition*, which is not itself caused by anything else.

Those, I think, are the three main options in the metaphysics of agency. The first is a reductive approach. It reduces an agent's role or power to the causal roles or powers of agent-involving states and events. Paradigm instances of this approach are event-causal theories, which provide a metaphysical account of agency in terms of event-causal relations between reason-states and actions.[6] The second approach is a non-reductive approach. It construes an agent's role or power as irreducible. Paradigm instances of this approach are agent-causal theories of action.[7] The third approach is also non-reductive in the sense that it rejects the reduction proposed by the first approach. Paradigm instances of this approach are volitional theories of action.[8]

A fourth possibility is to reject the project of giving a metaphysical account of agency as misguided. On this view, the notion of agency is essentially *normative*, and it can be captured and understood only from a normative or practical *standpoint*. The phenomenon of human agency is thought to *disappear* from any metaphysical, naturalistic or otherwise theoretical point of view. Let us call this the dual standpoint view.[9]

1.2.3 Dual standpoint theories

Our question is how human agency can be minimally part of the event-causal order. In particular, how can agents, who are minimally part of this order, exercise control over their actions? In order to give an answer to this question, one must provide a metaphysical account of human agency. The dual standpoint view does not acknowledge that there is a need for an explanation, and it rejects the metaphysical quest as misguided. It is, for this very reason, unsatisfactory, as it leaves one of the fundamental questions about human agency unanswered.

This dismissal of the dual standpoint view would be unjustified, if it could be shown that a metaphysics of agency *cannot* be given. But I have not seen any good argument to this conclusion. On the face of it, a metaphysics of agency is worth wanting, and different proposals are on offer. Given this, I see no reason to adopt the dual standpoint view. (We will return to the charge that agency disappears from a naturalistic standpoint further below.)

1.2.4 Volitionism

Volitionism is widely rejected, mostly due to internal problems with the theory. I will not summarize the most common objections here.[10] Let us consider, instead, whether the view can give an answer to our question.

According to volitionism, all actions originate from uncaused mental acts (acts of the will or volitions). No one, I assume, would wish to deny that mental acts are realized, partly at least, by events in the brain. But for all we know, there are no uncaused neural events. This alone, I think, renders the position very problematic and unpromising. Given that there are no uncaused neural events, neither at macro nor at micro levels of description, how could uncaused mental acts possibly be realized by neural events that are caused by other neural or physiological events?[11]

Furthermore, it remains a mystery just how the view can account for an agent's control at all. Volitions are neither caused by the agent, nor by the agent's reason-states. They are uncaused acts, and the agent appears to be a mere subject or bearer of volitions. Proponents of the view might say that this misrepresents their position, as volitions are necessarily *willed*, but not caused, *by the agent*—spontaneously, intentionally, and freely. But to say this is just to reaffirm the assumption that agents have control. What is needed, however, is an *explanation* of how agents can have control over actions that are constituted or realized by movements that have event-causal explanations.

1.2.5 The agent-causal approach

Some libertarians have tried to revive the agent-causal approach in the more recent debate on free will, because they think that only an agent-causal theory can account for the kind of power or control that is required for free will. But the agent-causal approach is still widely rejected, mainly because it is based on the very controversial notion of substance-causation (compare Clarke 2003). It has also been argued that the view is untenable in the light of empirical considerations (Pereboom 2001, for instance). In my opinion, the agent-causal approach fails more fundamentally as a theory of agency, because it fails to account for agential control. I have argued for this elsewhere (Schlosser 2008). In a nutshell, my argument goes as follows.

Both the event-causal and the agent-causal theory seek to explain agency and agential control in terms of causation. Of course, not every instantiation of a causal relation constitutes an exercise of control (or the instantiation of a relation of control). If a certain causal relation constitutes control, it must be in virtue of some further fact. According to the event-causal theory, control consists in non-deviant causation by reason-states. Crucial to this account are the causal roles of mental states and events, and, in particular, the causal and explanatory roles of their intentional contents. Nothing plays a similar role in the agent-causal theory. Nothing can possibly play this role, because the theory refers to agents *qua* substances as the causes of actions. On the agent-causal view, the causation of actions is not guided by any properties of the agent. But because of this, it remains obscure why we should think that instantiations of the agent-causal relation constitute exercises of control at all. Like volitionism, it does not explain agential control, but merely reaffirms the assumption that agents have control. Note that, according to this objection, the problem with the agent-causal theory is not that it construes agents as substances. The problem, rather, is that it does not *explain* how agents exercise control over their actions.[12]

1.2.6 The event-causal approach

Proponents of the event-causal theory may identify the agent with a substance (with the living organism, for instance). But within that framework, the agent's role, or the agent's control, is reduced to the causal roles of agent-involving mental states and events. Agential control is construed as non-deviant causation by reason-states. And the relationships between actions, bodily movements, reason-states and neural events are usually construed as intra-level and inter-level relations within a model of levels of explanation: the causal relationships at the level of mental description between reason-states and actions *depend on* and are *realized by* the causal relationships between the neural events and bodily movements that are identified at lower levels of description. In this way, the theory not only locates or situates agency within the event-causal order, but it gives an account of control and agency in terms of non-deviant causation by mental states and events. This shows how agents, who are minimally part of the event-causal order, can have and exercise control.

This account, of course, gives rise to various questions and problems. The most pressing are the problem of deviant causal chains and the problem of mental causation (in particular, the problem of causal exclusion).[13] I believe that the former problem has a solution, and we will return to this below. Various solutions to the problem of mental causation have been proposed.[14] Let me point out here only that it is not inherently a problem of *mental* causation. It is, more generally, a problem that concerns the relationships between causation and causal explanation at different levels of explanation. In particular, it is not a problem that arises especially for the event-causal theory of action. Unlike the problems for the other options in the metaphysics of agency, it is a problem that arises for all theories that assume the causal relevance of higher-level entities (including all the entities that are stipulated by the special sciences).

This completes my case in support of the event-causal approach to agency.[15] There is reason to endorse the metaphysical framework of the event-causal theory, because it is the only theory that can explain how human agency can be minimally part of the event-causal order. It might be objected that this is also merely a negative argument, as it promotes the view only by arguing that there are no viable alternatives. But we do not have to see it that way. There is, I submit, reason to endorse the event-causal theory because it gives a *good* explanation, and this explanation also happens to be the *only* explanation. More importantly, there is a significant difference to the way in which Davidson's challenge is merely negative.

My argument provides reason to adopt the metaphysical framework that is implicit in CTR and CTA, whereas Davidson's challenge lends direct support only to CTR.

1.3 Part 3: Disappearing agency and disappearing agents

In this final part, I will offer a response to the challenge of disappearing agency. My response comes in two parts, which correspond to the following two versions of the challenge. According to the first, the event-causal theory altogether fails to capture the phenomenon of agency, as it reduces activity to mere happenings. Understood in this way, it is a fundamental challenge to the event-causal approach as such. Statements of this first challenge can be found in Melden (1961) and Nagel (1986), for instance. A weaker objection has been raised in the more recent debate. According to this second version, the standard event-causal theory fails to capture important aspects of human agency, because it fails to account for the proper role of the human *agent* in the performance or exercise of certain *kinds* of agency. This challenge grants that the event-causal theory can account for some basic kinds of human agency (and animal behaviour). But it calls for a substantial revision or supplementation of the view in order to account for the more refined or higher kinds of human agency. In this version, the challenge has been acknowledged even by many proponents of the event-causal approach, including Velleman (1992), Bratman (2001), Enç (2003), and Schroeter (2004). In the following, I will refer to the first challenge as the challenge of disappearing *agency*, indicating that it is a fundamental challenge to the event-causal approach to agency. And I will refer to the second challenge as the challenge of disappearing *agents*, indicating that it is a challenge concerning the role of agents in the performance of actions.

1.3.1 Disappearing agency

Both challenges have been presented by means of spurious metaphors and rhetoric. According to the event-causal theory, it has been claimed, the agent is a *mere locus* in which events take place, a *mere bystander* or *victim* of causal pushes and pulls. Proponents of the fundamental challenge have sometimes used such metaphors in order to make the point that agency *disappears* within an ontology of events and event-causation.

One can acknowledge that this challenge has some intuitive force. But it is more important to note that its proponents have not produced a single *argument* to support their case, and they have certainly not identified a philosophical *problem*.[16] Their case is entirely based on intuition, and in some cases on mere metaphor and rhetoric.

However, having said this, and having acknowledged that the objection has some intuitive force, proponents of the event-causal theory should also be able to say something in response. It is not obvious that agency cannot be understood in terms of event-causal processes. But it is also not obvious that agency *can* be understood in terms of event-causation. What can we say in response?

A first thing to point out is that some of the rhetoric is not just misleading, but false. The agent is certainly not a *victim* or a *helpless bystander* only in virtue of being a subject of events (in virtue of being a substance that is involved in events). Events may be called *happenings* in virtue of the fact that they *occur* in time. But the fact that events are occurrences does not entail or show that an agent's mental events and movements are things that *happen to* the agent, in the sense that they assail or befall the agent, or in the sense in which we say that a bad or unjust thing happened to us. When I remember something, for instance, I am a constitutive part of an event, but I am no victim or helpless bystander.

Secondly, we must remember that the event-causal theory is *intended* to be a reductive theory. Its proponents aim to provide necessary and sufficient conditions for agency, and they propose to do this without any kind of circularity by way of providing a reductive *explanation* of agency in terms of event-causal processes. But, as every proponent of a reductive explanation would insist, a reduction is a form of vindication rather than elimination. The theory does not eliminate agency, nor does it eliminate agents. Rather, it provides a vindication by giving an account of how agency can be minimally part of the event-causal order.

Thirdly, and most importantly, there is a constructive response to the challenge. The challenge says, basically, that the event-causal approach fails to capture agency. We can interpret this as saying that it fails to capture the fact that agents can exercise control over their behaviour. Construed in this way, proponents of the event-causal theory can respond by showing that the view has the resources to distinguish between event-causal processes that constitute agential control and event-causal processes that do not. If this can be achieved within the event-causal framework, then the challenge is mistaken.

1.3.2 Event-causation and agential control

The event-causal theory construes control in terms of event-causation and rationalization. It says that an agent exercises control only if the behaviour in question is caused by mental states and events that rationalize its performance (we call such rationalizing attitudes *reason-states*). But causation by reason-states is not sufficient for control and agency. This is highlighted by examples involving deviant or wayward causal chains.

In all standard examples of causal deviance, the causal chain that connects the agent's reason-states and the action runs through some state or event that undermines the agent's control. Typically, this is some state of nervousness or agitation.[17] Consider, for instance, Davidson's climber example.

> A climber might want to rid himself of the weight and danger of holding another man on a rope, and he might know that by loosening his hold on the rope he could rid himself of the weight and danger. This belief and want might so unnerve him as to cause him to loosen his hold [...].
>
> (Davidson 1980, p. 79)

Examples of this kind raise a problem for the event-causal theory. The behaviour is caused and rationalized by mental states, but it seems clear that the agent is not performing an action at all. It is, rather, a sheer accident that the state of nervousness causes precisely that type of movement that is rationalized by the reason-states. In order to provide a satisfactory account of agency, the theory must exclude deviant causal chains in event-causal terms (in particular, without presupposing an irreducible notion of control or agency).

The interesting point for us here is that deviant causal chains are *control-undermining* chains. If the theory can exclude deviant causal chains, it can, *ipso facto*, exclude control-undermining chains. And if it can exclude control-undermining chains, it can distinguish between event-causal chains that constitute agential control and ones that do not.

I think that the problem of deviant causal chains can be solved, and I have proposed a solution elsewhere (Schlosser 2007b). In broad outline, I have argued that deviant causal chains are excluded if the theory requires that the agent's reason-states must be causally efficacious and explanatory *in virtue of their intentional contents*. This requirement is violated in the standard cases of causal deviance. Given this, we get a straightforward response to the challenge of disappearing agency. The event-causal theory can capture agency, because it has the resources to distinguish between event-causal chains that constitute agential control and ones that do not.

1.3.3 Ownership of agency

In response, opponents might argue that the problem is not that causal chains can be deviant, but that the constituents of those chains are mere states and events. Let us assume, for the sake of argument, that actions are non-deviantly caused by the agent's mental states and events. The objection says that this still does not guarantee agency, because the agent may not identify with being moved by those states and events. Being non-deviantly caused by mental states and events, the resulting behaviour may still not be a true and proper expression of the *agent's own* agency. Let us call this the challenge from *ownership* (ownership of agency).

Many will associate this challenge with the issues raised by Harry Frankfurt's influential article on free will and personhood (1988, chap. 2, originally published in 1971). Following Frankfurt, one might be tempted to give a response to the objection by appealing to a notion of identification or endorsement within a so-called hierarchical theory of agency. This route has been taken by some philosophers in response to the problem of disappearing *agents*. The central idea here is to distinguish between desires or motives that *speak for* or *stand for* the agent by means of an account of identification or endorsement (compare Korsgaard 1996 and Bratman 2001, for instance). On this approach, an agent acts from desires that are truly his or her *own* just in case the agent *endorses* the desires as motives for action. Let us call this the *endorsement strategy*.

I shall not attempt here to assess the endorsement strategy as such. Nor will I go into the details of particular versions of this approach. I want to argue, rather, that the endorsement strategy would not give us a convincing response to the objection from ownership.

To begin with, let us consider Frankfurt's main example of the unwilling addict. He is moved by a desire to acquire and take drugs, but he does not want to be motivated in this ways—he does not endorse being moved by those desires. We can agree with Frankfurt and his followers that cases of this kind highlight important and interesting aspects of human agency. But we must be careful to interpret them in the right way.

Frankfurt says that the unwilling addict is a "passive bystander to the forces that move him" (ibid. p. 22). Elsewhere he talks about desires that are "rejected" as "external" (1988, chap. 5, for instance). David Velleman and Michael Bratman have suggested that examples of this kind show that the event-causal theory "leaves out" the agent. The unwilling addict performs an action when he acts on the desire, but this falls short of "agency *par excellence*" (Velleman 1992) or "full-blooded" human agency (Bratman 2001). Construed in this way, the example can be used to raise the challenge of disappearing agents (to which we will turn below). But I think that this reading can and should be resisted here.

Firstly, it should be uncontroversial that the unwilling addict is not a mere bystander or locus in the flow of events. He is capable of a good degree of control and agency, and he exercises this ability in the pursuit of drugs, an endeavour which requires some planning and practical reason.

Secondly, it should also be uncontroversial that the addict's desire and the resulting behaviour is his *own* in some basic or minimal sense. In order to see this, compare the unwilling addict with serious cases of schizophrenia, where patients report that their actions are under the control of some external agent or force, or with cases of the "anarchic hand syndrome," where patients report that one of their hands moves on its own (compare Frith et al. 2000, for instance).

Third, proponents of the event-causal theory should seek to respond to the challenge at the most fundamental level. The endorsement strategy can be pursued in order to account for a *kind* of ownership that is characteristic of *autonomous* agency, for instance. But this would leave more basic kinds of agency unaccounted for. We can agree that the unwilling addict falls short of autonomous agency (or agency *par excellence*). But, on the other hand, he is not like the schizophrenic patient who feels as if alien forces are acting through him. What is required in order to meet the objection at the fundamental level is an account of the basic kind of ownership and agency that is exhibited even by the unwilling addict.

I propose the following response to the objection from ownership. In normal instances of human agency, including basic cases of minimally rational planning agency, actions that are non-deviantly caused by the agent's mental states and events are an expression of the agent's own agency *by default*: our agency springs from our mental states and events, unless defeating conditions obtain. Ownership of agency, in other words, does not have to be conferred by endorsement and it does not depend on it. It is a given, unless things go wrong.

But what are *normal* instances? In order to get a viable response, we must have an answer to this question. Fortunately, there is a computational model of the sense of agency that provides a good answer. In broad outline, the model is this. Whenever a motor command for the performance of a bodily movement is sent from premotor areas to the motor control system, a copy of this command is used to produce a prediction of the movement (a so-called *forward model*). This prediction is then sent to a comparator where it is compared with incoming visual and proprioceptive information concerning the actual movement. The main purpose of this sub-personal system is to monitor, correct, and fine-tune movements. But it is now widely assumed that this system is also responsible for a sense of the ownership of agency. This is the sense that the movements are our own doing, initiated and guided by us, and it is assumed that this sense or feeling is the result of a match between the prediction and the feedback (the match, of course, need not be perfect, as the function of the system is to correct and fine-tune).[18]

There is good empirical support for this model, and it is now widely deployed by psychologists and cognitive scientists working on human action. Given this model, we can say what normal instances are. They are cases in which the feedback-comparison system performs its function, producing a sense of the ownership of agency. This sub-personal mechanism may fail to produce a sense of agency for various reasons. It may be interfered with or break down in various ways that correspond to a variety of abnormal cases and defeating conditions. What the defeating conditions are is largely an empirical question. It has been argued that the model can explain a wide range of deficiencies and abnormalities, each highlighting ways in which the mechanism may break down or fail to perform its function (Frith et al. 2000).

It would be implausible, I think, to suggest that the ownership of agency is in all cases conferred by the agent's endorsement. The correct reading of Frankfurt's unwilling addict supports this. There is a basic or minimal sense in which the addict's desire for the drug is his own and in which his own agency springs from it (in combination with other mental states and events).

It should be noted that the proposed default view is fully compatible with an endorsement theory, as I have argued only that the endorsement strategy should not be deployed in response to the challenge from ownership. So, the default view may well be supplemented with an endorsement theory of autonomous agency, for instance.

1.3.4 Disappearing agents

Let us now turn to the challenge of disappearing *agents*, and let us assume that the outlined feedback-comparator model can account for a basic and default sense of the ownership of agency. What about the more refined and higher kinds of human agency, such as autonomous agency? Even *proponents* of the event-causal theory have conceded that the view fails to account for the agent's participation or proper role in the performance of higher kinds of agency.

I accept the point that the basic version of the event-causal theory has to be refined or supplemented in order to account for higher kinds of agency. But I do not accept all the claims made and implied by the challenge. In particular, I do not accept the suggestion that the event-causal theory fails to include the *agent* or fails to account for the *agent's* role and participation—a point that has been conceded even by some proponents of the event-causal approach.

Firstly, putting things in terms of the *agent's* role or participation creates a false dichotomy. Throughout this chapter, we distinguished between more *basic* and *higher* kinds of agency. It is very plausible to think that the aspects or kinds of human agency form a spectrum, or a hierarchy, from lower and basic to higher and more refined kinds of agency. At the bottom of this hierarchy one finds behaviour that is purposeful but to a high degree driven by environmental stimuli (such as instinctive, automatic or highly habitual reactions). Moving up the hierarchy we get intentional, rational, deliberative, reflective and self-controlled agency, and towards the top we find autonomous and free agency. For our purposes, the details and the exact order do not matter. The important point is that agency comes in shades of grey, as it were, not as an all-or-nothing phenomenon. Whenever human agency is exercised, some but not necessarily all kinds of human agency are instantiated.

This is why I find talk about the *agent's* role or participation unhelpful. If we say that the agent's participation is characteristic of autonomous agency, does that mean that the agent does not participate in lower kinds of behaviour? This would be rather odd, to say the least. If we want to capture the important aspects of human agency, we better begin with a framework of *kinds of agency*. Talk about the agent's role and the agent's participation creates a bipartition that does not match up with the varieties of human behaviour.

Secondly, as just pointed out, it is rather implausible to suggest that the agent does not participate in lower kinds of agency. The most natural thing to say, and the most natural assumption to begin with, is that all instances of agency involve an agent. Wherever there is agency, there is an agent participating, playing a role as the agent. As explained in part two, the event-causal theory provides a reductive explanation of the agent's role. It does not eliminate the agent. Given that, there is simply no room for an additional role of the agent in higher kinds of agency. The agent is already there, from the start, and the agent does play a role in all kinds of agency.

In other words, to ask for *further* participation of the agent is to miss the point of the reductive approach to agency. Higher kinds of agency do not spring from the participation of the agent. They spring, rather, from certain *features of the agent*. They spring from properties that are instantiated only in cases of autonomous agency, for instance. We may *say* that the agent participates more, or to a higher degree, in some instances of agency. But this is metaphorical. It should be taken to mean that the agent instantiates certain properties or exercises certain abilities, which are not instantiated or exercised in lower kinds of agency, and in virtue of which the agent exercises the higher kind of agency in question.

What should we make, then, of the challenge of disappearing agents? Is it an empty challenge? Construed, literally, as a challenge of disappearing *agents* it is an empty challenge, as I have just suggested. But that does not mean that it is empty altogether. I acknowledge that the event-causal theory must be supplemented and refined. But not by bringing the *agent* back into the picture. The agent was never absent. The right way to respond, rather, is to show how the theory can distinguish between the various kinds of agency within the event-causal framework (without, in particular, presupposing some kind of agent-causation). This task is beyond the scope of this chapter. But I shall briefly indicate two directions that proponents of the causal theory may take. One possible starting point for an account of higher kinds of agency is Frankfurt's (1988) hierarchical model. In order to solve the well-known regress problems that plague this approach, one may appeal to special types of mental attitudes, such as the motive to be governed by reasons (Velleman 1992) or higher-order policies that provide cross-temporal continuity and stability (Bratman 2001). Alternatively, one can appeal to historical conditions on the way in which agency-relevant attitudes, such as desires, beliefs and intentions, must have been formed or acquired (Mele 1995). I tend to favour this second approach, as I think that higher-order attitudes play a less significant role in human agency than Frankfurt and his followers assume.

More recently, François Schroeter (2004) argued that we must refer to the role of the *conscious self* in the initiation and guidance of autonomous action. In my view, this is not an option for the committed proponent of the event-causal approach. Schroeter insists that reference to the role of the conscious self is *not* a covert evocation of some kind of agent-causation, and he claims that the view is consistent with naturalism (p. 650). I understand

Velleman's and Bratman's views, for instance, which account for the agent's role by reference to some of the agent's mental states. According to Schroeter, however, the conscious self cannot be reduced to conscious mental states and events, nor does he want to say that the self must therefore be a substance. But it seems clear that the self must be some kind of entity, in a metaphysically robust sense, as it is supposed to be causally relevant in the initiation and guidance of action. Schroeter does not say what kind of thing it is, and I fail to see what it could possibly be.

Perhaps the role of the conscious self goes beyond the role of conscious mental states and events due to the *unity* of the self. The question of what this unity might consist in is, of course, also beyond the scope of this chapter. I should point out, though, that proponents of the event-causal approach are not restricted to explanations in terms of *collections* of mental states and states. They may, rather, refer to the agent's mental states, mental events, and the *relationships* that hold between them. Given this, it is, I think, far from obvious that the role of a conscious and unified self cannot be captured and reductively explained by an event-causal theory of agency.

Acknowledgements

I would like to thank John Bishop for very helpful comments on an earlier version of this chapter, which was written when I was a post-doc fellow at the University of Bristol with a research project on the causal theory of action. This project was funded by the Austrian Science Fund (FWF).

Notes

1. This claim will appear to be rather weak if one thinks that CTR and CTA are essentially or necessarily connected. But it seems that one can coherently hold one without the other. One may, for instance, hold CTR in conjunction with a substance-causal view on the nature of actions.
2. This is usually credited to Bratman 1987. Compare also Brand 1984, Bishop 1989, Mele 1992, and Enç 2003.
3. For a recent discussion of the notion of basic action see Enç 2003.
4. I am restricting my considerations here to *overt* behaviour. But I think that similar claims hold with respect to the relationship between basic *mental* acts and neural events.
5. For an application of the event-causal approach to mental action see, for instance, Mele 1997.
6. Davidson 1980, Brand 1984, Bishop 1989, Mele 1992, and Enç 2003, for instance.
7. Chisholm 1964 and O'Connor 2000. Compare also Clarke 2003.
8. Ginet 1990 and McCann 1998, for instance.
9. Proponents include Nagel 1986, Korsgaard 1996, and Bilgrami 2006.
10. See, for instance, Brand 1984, Enç 2003, and Clarke 2003.
11. Jonathan Lowe (1993) argued that the causal relevance of volitions is compatible with the causal closure of the physical, if volitions are construed as *enabling* or

structuring causes rather than triggering causes. But this fails to capture the proper role of volitions. They are supposed to *initiate* actions. To construe them as enabling or structuring causes does not account for their efficacy as volitions.

12. Strictly speaking, the agent-causal approach is a *version* of the non-reductive approach to agency. I have argued that the case against the agent-causal approach generalizes to a case against the non-reductive approach (Schlosser 2008).
13. Roughly, the problem of causal exclusion is that the causal sufficiency of physical events (or, more generally, the causal closure of the physical) appears to exclude the causal relevance of mental events (see Crane 1995, for instance). This problem arises only if one assumes that mental causation requires the downward causation of physical events. Elsewhere I have argued that the mental causation of actions does not require downward causation (Schlosser 2009).
14. For instance Yablo 1997 and Gibbons 2006, among many others.
15. An earlier but more detailed version of this argument can be found in Schlosser 2007a.
16. In contrast to that, the challenge from deviant causal chains *does* raise a genuine problem. Virtually all proponents of the event-causal approach have acknowledged this. Compare Davidson 1980, Bishop 1989, and Enç 2003, for instance.
17. I am restricting my considerations here to the most problematic type of causal deviance, which has been called *basic* or *primary* deviance. Compare Bishop 1989 and Schlosser 2007b.
18. This is the most basic version of the model. For more advanced and more detailed accounts see Frith et al. 2000 and Pacherie 2007, for instance. For an application of this model to the case of mental agency see Campbell 1999.

References

Bilgrami, A. (2006), *Self-Knowledge and Resentment*. Cambridge: Harvard University Press.

Bishop, J. (1989), *Natural Agency: An Essay on the Causal Theory of Action*. Cambridge: Cambridge University Press.

Brand, M. (1984), *Intending and Acting*. Cambridge: MIT Press.

Bratman, M. E. (1987), *Intention, Plans, and Practical Reason*. Cambridge: Harvard University Press.

———. (2001), "Two Problems about Human Agency,' *Proceedings of the Aristotelian Society* 2000–2001: 309–26.

Campbell, J. (1999), "Schizophrenia, the Space of Reasons, and Thinking as a Motor process," *The Monist* 82: 609–25.

Child, W. (1994), *Causality, Interpretation and the Mind*. Oxford: Oxford University Press.

Chisholm, R. (1964), "Human Freedom and the Self," Reprinted in G. Watson (2003) (ed.), *Free Will*. Oxford: Oxford University Press, 26–37.

Clarke, R. (2003), *Libertarian Accounts of Free Will*. Oxford: Oxford University Press.

Crane, T. (1995), "The Mental Causation Debate," *Proceedings of the Aristotelian Society*, supplementary volume 69: 211–36.

Davidson, D. (1980), *Essays on Action and Events*. Oxford: Oxford University Press.

Dancy, J. (2000), *Practical Reality*, Oxford: Oxford University Press.

Enç, B. (2003), *How We Act: Causes, Reasons, and Intentions*. Oxford: Oxford University Press.

Frankfurt, H. (1988), *The Importance of What We Care About*. Cambridge: Cambridge University Press.

Frith, C. D., Blakemore, S. and Wolpert, D. M. (2000), "Abnormalities in the Awareness and Control of Action," *Philosophical Transactions of the Royal Society* 355: 1771–88.

Gibbons, J. (2006), "Mental Causation without Downward Causation," *Philosophical Review* 115: 79–103.

Ginet, C. (1990), *On Action*. Cambridge: Cambridge University Press.

———. (2001), "Reasons Explanations of Action: Causalist versus Noncausalist Accounts," in R. Kane (ed.), *Oxford Handbook on Free Will*. Oxford: Oxford University Press, 386–405.

Korsgaard, Ch. (1996), *The Sources of Normativity*. Cambridge: Cambridge University Press.

Lowe, E. J. (1993), "The Causal Autonomy of the Mental," *Mind* 102: 629–44.

McCann, H. (1998), *The Works of Agency*. Ithaca: Cornell University Press.

Melden, A. I. (1961), *Free Action*. London: Routledge and Kegan Paul.

Mele, A. R. (1992), *Springs of Action*. Oxford: Oxford University Press.

———. (1995), *Autonomous Agents*. Oxford: Oxford University Press.

———. (1997), "Agency and Mental Action," *Philosophical Perspectives* 11: 231–49.

Nagel, T. (1986), *The View from Nowhere*. New York: Oxford University Press.

O'Connor, T. (2000), *Persons and Causes: The Metaphysics of Free Will*. Oxford: Oxford University Press.

Pacherie, E. (2007), "The Sense of Control and the Sense of Agency," *Psyche* 13: 1–30.

Pereboom, D. (2001), *Living Without Free Will*. Cambridge: Cambridge University Press.

Schlosser, M. E. (2007a), *The Metaphysics of Agency* (Doctoral dissertation, University of St. Andrews). *Research Repository* (http://hdl.handle.net/10023/163).

———. (2007b), "Basic Deviance Reconsidered," *Analysis* 67: 186–94.

———. (2008), "Agent-Causation and Agential Control," *Philosophical Explorations* 11: 3–21.

———. (2009), "Non-Reductive Physicalism, Mental Causation and the Nature of Actions," in H. Leitgeb and A. Hieke (eds), *Reduction: Between the Mind and the Brain*. Frankfurt: Ontos, pp. 73–89.

Schueler, G. F. (2003), *Reasons and Purposes: Human Rationality and the Teleological Explanation of Action*. Oxford: Oxford University Press.

Schroeter, F. (2004), "Endorsement and Autonomous Agency," *Philosophy and Phenomenological Research* 69: 633–59.

Sehon, S. R. (2000), "An Argument Against the Causal Theory of Action Explanation," *Philosophy and Phenomenological Research* 60: 67–85.

Velleman, D. (1992), "What Happens when Someone Acts?" Reprinted in his (2000) *The Possibility of Practical Reason*, Oxford: Oxford University Press, pp. 123–43.

Wilson, G. M. (1989), *The Intentionality of Human Behaviour*. Stanford: Stanford University Press.

Yablo, S. (1997), 'Wide Causation'. *Philosophical Perspectives* 11: 251–81.

2
Failing to Do the Impossible

Carolina Sartorio

2.1 The billionaire puzzle

A billionaire tells you: "That chair is in my way; I don't feel like moving it myself, but if you push it out of my way I'll give you $100." You decide you don't want the billionaire's money and you'd rather have him go through the trouble of moving the chair himself, so you graciously turn down the offer and go home. As it turns out, the billionaire is also a stingy old miser; he was never willing to let go of $100. Knowing full well that the chair couldn't be moved due to the fact that it was glued to the ground, he simply wanted to have a laugh at your expense.

This is a case of omission: you expressed your agency mainly by what you intentionally omitted to do, not by what you did. But what exactly did you intentionally omit to do in this case? There is no question that you intentionally omitted to *try* to move the chair. But did you also intentionally omit to *move the chair*? On the face of it, it seems that you didn't. Even if not moving the chair was something that you wanted to do, and even if, as a matter of fact, you didn't move the chair, it seems that you didn't intentionally omit to move the chair. For, contrary to what you were led to believe, you couldn't move it, and the fact that you couldn't move it seems to preclude your having intentionally omitted to move it. (Of course, this is not to say that you shouldn't be commended for failing to comply with the billionaire's whimsical wants. You should still be commended for that, but not by virtue of having intentionally omitted to move the chair; only by virtue of having intentionally omitted to try to move it. After all, that's what he wanted you to do: he wanted you to try to move the chair motivated by the desire to get $100.)

Note that the claim is that you didn't *intentionally omit* to move the chair. Perhaps there is some ordinary or theoretically useful sense of the word "omission" in which there is an omission here (and, in fact, sometimes I will talk as if this were true). Still, what's important for our purposes is that this isn't an intentional omission. For example, if omissions were mere non-doings, then, clearly, there would be an omission even in this case. If omissions were mere non-doings, it would be very easy to omit to do the impossible: all of us would always omit to do the impossible, since it's impossible. But there would still be restrictions on what we can intentionally omit to do. In other words, even if omitting to do the impossible were easy (as easy as it can get), intentionally omitting to do the impossible would still be hard, and for what is apparently the same reason: because the act in question is impossible.

Examples like the billionaire case suggest that intentional omissions can be importantly subject to *counterfactual constraints*, that is, constraints that have to do with what the agent could have done, or with what the agent does in other possible worlds different from the actual world. Moreover, these seem to be constraints that only omissions are subject to (unlike actions of the positive kind) or, at the very least, that mainly omissions are subject to. For (positive) actions don't seem to be subject to the same kind of constraints: on the face of it, whether an agent acts intentionally is wholly dependent on the actual facts; it is not determined by what happens in other possible worlds. Compare: what prevents me from intentionally jumping to the moon if I try to jump to the moon is whatever actually stops me when I try (say, the gravitational field). By contrast, what prevents me from intentionally failing to jump to the moon if I intend not to jump to the moon is the fact that I wouldn't have been able to jump to the moon even if I had tried. In other words: I cannot intentionally jump to the moon, and I cannot intentionally fail to jump to the moon either. But the reason I cannot do the latter is grounded in the counterfactual facts in a way that the reason I cannot do the former is not.

Now, what exactly is the role of counterfactual constraints in intentional omissions? For some theories, that role is straightforward: an agent intentionally omits to act *only if* it was possible for him to perform the act in question (see, for example, Zimmermann (1981), Ginet (2004), and Bach (2010)). In other words, according to these theories, intentional omissions require "the ability to do otherwise" (or "alternative possibilities"). But, is the ability to do otherwise truly a necessary condition of intentional omissions? Is it really impossible to omit (intentionally) to do the impossible?

Interestingly, other examples suggest otherwise: they suggest that it *is* possible for agents to omit (intentionally) to do the impossible. Consider the following scenario:

> *The Child and the Neuroscientist*: You see a child drowning in the water, you deliberate about whether to jump in to save him and, as a result of your own free deliberation, you decide not to do so. Unbeknownst to you, there was an evil neuroscientist closely monitoring your brain. Had you shown any signs that you were about to decide to jump in, the neuroscientist would have intervened by making you decide not to jump in and, as a result, you would still have failed to rescue the child.

This is a "Frankfurt-style" scenario. In a Frankfurt-style scenario, an agent makes a decision to act or not act completely on his own, and then acts or doesn't act based on that decision. Unbeknownst to the agent, the evil neuroscientist has been waiting in the wings to make sure that he makes the relevant decision but, given that the agent arrives at it on his own, the neuroscientist never has to intervene. Frankfurt famously used these scenarios to show that moral responsibility for actions or omissions doesn't require the ability to do otherwise (the claim about actions appears in Frankfurt (1969); he then extended the claim to omissions in (Frankfurt (1994)), as a reaction to a paper by Fischer and Ravizza (Fischer and Ravizza (1991)). In The Child and the Neuroscientist, Frankfurt would argue, you are morally responsible for your not saving the child despite the fact that you couldn't have saved him (you couldn't have saved the child, in this case, because you couldn't even have decided to save him). It is equally clear (if not clearer), Frankfurt would presumably say, that you intentionally omit to save the child in this case. You intentionally omit to save to him because you failed to save him on the basis of your own decision not to save him. Again, this is so even if you couldn't have saved him.[1]

In other words, The Child and the Neuroscientist seems to be a counterexample to *both* of the following principles:

> PPA ("Principle of Possible Action" (for moral responsibility), van Inwagen (1978)): An agent is morally responsible for omitting to perform a given act only if he could have performed that act.
> PPA-IO ("Principle of Possible Action for Intentional Omissions"): An agent intentionally omits to perform a given act only if he could have performed that act.

So, this is how things stand. On the one hand, in the billionaire case, we want to say that the agent doesn't intentionally omit to act because he couldn't have done otherwise. However, on the other hand, it seems that we cannot say this because, as The Child and the Neuroscientist scenario suggests, agents can intentionally omit to act even when they couldn't have done otherwise. Hence there is a puzzle. I will call this puzzle "the billionaire puzzle."

How should we try to solve the puzzle? One way to solve it would be to endorse a form of skepticism about Frankfurt-style cases. My own view is that there are good reasons to resist the argument against PPA based on Frankfurt-style cases, and that, similarly, there are good reasons to resist the parallel argument against PPA-IO.[2] Still, in this paper I will assume that Frankfurt is right in believing that Frankfurt-style omission cases are counterexamples to both of these principles. I will do this for two reasons. First, there is no denying that Frankfurt-style cases have intuitive appeal, and that they show that principles like PPA and PPA-IO are, at least, debatable.

In fact, most people who have contributed to the literature on moral responsibility for omissions seem to agree with Frankfurt about PPA (even Fischer and Ravizza, who changed their minds after their (1991) paper; see their (1998), ch. 5).[3] And I take it that most people would also agree that PPA-IO fails, for similar reasons. So the question arises: what *could* the connection between intentional omissions and alternative possibilities *be*, if it's not that intentionally omitting to act requires alternative possibilities? There surely seems to be some connection (otherwise, why did it seem so plausible to say, in the billionaire case, that the reason you didn't intentionally omit to move the chair is that you couldn't have moved the chair?). But what is this connection, if it's not that you cannot intentionally omit to do what you couldn't have done? Secondly, even if intentional omissions did require alternative possibilities, there would still be some explaining to do as to *why* it is that they do. Why is PPA-IO true, if it is true? This seems to call for an explanation (in particular, an explanation would be most pressing if it turned out that omissions behave in this way but actions don't—why is there such an asymmetry?). As we will see, reflecting about what the relation between intentional omissions and alternative possibilities could be if it's not PPA-IO would also help us find such an explanation.

Hence the billionaire puzzle is the puzzle that arises if one believes that PPA-IO is false, or if one is unsure whether it is true. The challenge is to explain the sense in which your inability to move the chair in the billionaire case is accountable for your not having intentionally omitted to move the chair, without appealing to the claim that intentional omissions require alternative possibilities. My main aim in this paper is to solve the billionaire puzzle. Of course, there is a similar puzzle that arises about moral responsibility: What is the connection between moral responsibility for omissions and alternative possibilities, if it's not that moral responsibility for an omission requires alternative possibilities? Although this question is not my main concern here, we will touch on it too. In fact, my strategy will be to examine the relationship between intentional omissions and alternative possibilities in light of the debate about moral responsibility and alternative possibilities. As we will see, that debate can shed important light on our topic. I turn to this in the next section.

2.2 Frankfurt's revised principle of alternative possibilities

When Frankfurt rejected the principle that an agent's moral responsibility for an action requires the agent's ability to do otherwise (the "Principle of Alternate Possibilities," or PAP), he put forth a different principle about the connection between moral responsibility and alternative possibilities (one that he considered to be friendly to a compatibilist view about determinism and the freedom of the will). Although this principle was originally intended as a claim about (positive) actions, a question that naturally arises given our topic in this paper is whether it could apply to omissions in the same way. In this section I will first argue that it doesn't: that Frankfurt's principle fails to capture the relationship between moral responsibility and alternative possibilities in cases of omission. However, even if the principle fails for omissions, it will be enlightening for our purposes to see *how* it fails. As we will see, looking at the way in which Frankfurt's principle fails will give us the key to solving the billionaire puzzle.

Frankfurt's revised principle about the relationship between moral responsibility and alternative possibilities (for actions) says:

> PAP-revised (revised version of the Principle of Alternate Possibilities, Frankfurt (1969)): An agent is not morally responsible for performing an action if he did it *only because* he could not have done otherwise.

For example, Frankfurt argues, when you are coerced into doing something you are not morally responsible for your act to the extent that you did it only because of the (irresistible) threat that was made. If the threat, and only the threat, moved you to act, then you are not morally responsible for your act. This case should be contrasted with a Frankfurt-style case. In a Frankfurt-style case, what actually causes the agent to act are the agent's own reasons. So, Frankfurt thinks, even if the agent couldn't have done otherwise, he is morally responsible for his act in that case, because he acted for his own reasons.

Let's call the factors in virtue of which an agent couldn't have done otherwise *inevitability factors*. Frankfurt's idea is that inevitability factors can only reduce the agent's moral responsibility when they actually move the agent to act (and when they are the only thing that moves the agent to act, in particular, when the agent doesn't act for his own reasons). According to Frankfurt, then, PAP-revised captures the truth, and the *only truth*, behind the idea that moral responsibility for acts and alternative possibilities are linked. As Frankfurt-style cases show, one can be morally responsible for acting even if one couldn't have done otherwise. But when what actually moves one to act are the inevitability factors, and only those factors, one is not morally responsible. Thus, whereas PAP is false, PAP-revised is true: moral responsibility for an act doesn't require having the ability to do otherwise, but it does require not acting as a result of (only) the inevitability factors.

Let's assume that Frankfurt is right and PPA-revised is the true principle governing the relationship between moral responsibility and alternative possibilities in cases of action. Could it also be the true principle regarding such a relationship in cases of omission? This is what one would expect if, as Frankfurt seems to believe, the conditions of moral responsibility for actions and omissions (or at least those that have to do with the kind of "control" the agent must have to be morally responsible) are perfectly symmetrical.[4] The revised principle for omissions would read:

> PPA-revised (revised version of the Principle of Possible Action): An agent is not morally responsible for omitting to perform an act if he omitted to perform it *only because* he could not have done otherwise, i.e. only because he could not have performed the relevant act.

Now, what does it mean to say that an agent omitted to perform an act *only because he couldn't have performed the relevant act*? By analogy with the case of actions, we should take it to mean that the agent omitted to act moved only by inevitability factors—those factors in virtue of which he couldn't have performed the relevant act. In other words, the inevitability factors, and those factors only, caused him to omit to act. So we should take PPA-revised to be the claim that an agent is not morally responsible for omitting to perform an act if he omitted to perform the act moved only by inevitability factors, that is, if inevitability factors, and those factors only, caused him to omit to act.

Note that here we are assuming that omissions can be caused just like actions can, in particular, we are assuming that an agent's omitting to act can be the causal output of different things, including inevitability factors. I will go along with that assumption (although, as will be apparent later, I think that such an assumption is not ultimately essential to the views put forth in this paper). And recall: Frankfurt's claim would be that PPA-revised is the only truth, or the whole truth, behind the idea that responsibility for omissions and alternative possibilities are connected: an agent is not morally responsible for an omission when he is caused to omit to act by inevitability factors, and this is the only significant connection between moral responsibility for omissions and alternative possibilities.

Now, *is* PPA-revised the truth, and the complete truth, behind the idea that responsibility for omissions and alternative possibilities are connected? Although Frankfurt in fact seems to think so,[5] I'll argue that it isn't. Consider an example where the agent's inability to perform the relevant act seems to relieve him of moral responsibility for his omission. Here is a paradigm example from the literature (Fischer and Ravizza (1991), p. 261, and Fischer and Ravizza (1998), p. 125):

> *Sharks*: You see a child drowning in a pond and you decide against jumping in to save him. Unbeknownst to you, you couldn't have saved the child: if you had jumped into the water, some hungry sharks would have attacked you and prevented you from saving him.

As Fischer and Ravizza claim, you are not morally responsible for not saving the child in this case (only for not trying to save him). Frankfurt agrees (Frankfurt (1994), p. 622). Moreover, the fact that you are not morally responsible for your not saving the child seems to have something to do with your inability to save the child (in fact, intuitively we would say that you are not morally responsible for not saving him because you couldn't have saved him). But in this case you were *not* moved to omit to act by the inevitability factors. The inevitability factors in this case are the sharks. Clearly, the sharks didn't move you to omit to act in this case. You weren't even aware of their presence![6]

It is not completely clear what Frankfurt would say about this. There is one point in his paper that suggests that he might want to insist that the sharks are operative in the relevant sense. He writes:

> The sharks operate both in the actual and in the alternative sequences, and they see to it that the child drowns no matter what John [the agent in the situation he describes] does.
>
> (Frankfurt (1994), p. 623).

The sharks certainly operate in the sense that they *guarantee* that the agent will not save the child. But so does the neuroscientist in a Frankfurt-style case, where (we are assuming) the presence of the neuroscientist bears no relevance to the agent's moral responsibility. So this cannot be the relevant sense of "operate": for the sharks to operate in the relevant sense, they must *cause* the agent's omission, they must be the reason (and the only reason) the agent didn't save the child. I think it's clear that the sharks play no such causal role in the actual sequence of events, given how the case is set up.

Of course, there are other possible scenarios where the sharks (and only the sharks) do cause you to refrain from jumping into the water and saving the child. In those scenarios you omit to act because you couldn't have done otherwise, in Frankfurt's sense. Of course, in those scenarios you are not morally responsible for not saving the child either. But recall that PPA-revised is supposed to capture the *whole* truth about the relationship between moral responsibility for omissions and alternative possibilities. Scenarios like Sharks show that it fails to do so. For you are not morally responsible for your omission in Sharks, your lack of moral responsibility is in some important way connected to your inability to do otherwise, but PPA-revised fails to explain why you are not morally responsible for your omission in that case.

By the way, this is interesting because it suggests that, even if Frankfurt were right that actions and omissions are symmetrical in that being morally responsible for them doesn't require having the ability to do otherwise, that is, they are symmetrical with respect to what the relationship between responsibility and alternative possibilities *isn't*, an asymmetry would still crop up between them when trying to explain what the relationship between responsibility and alternative possibilities *is* (given that it's not that responsibility requires the ability to do otherwise). Let's say that Frankfurt is right and, in cases of action, the relationship consists in the fact that responsibility requires not acting only because one couldn't have done otherwise. It would seem that, in cases of omission, the relationship does not consist in this fact, or is not exhausted by this fact. You fail to be morally responsible if the sharks cause you to omit to act, but you *also* fail to be morally responsible if the sharks just happen to be there and don't cause you to omit to act. In other words, the connection between moral responsibility and alternative possibilities is particularly robust in the case of omissions, in a way that escapes Frankfurt's principle.[7]

2.3 The phenomenon of mutual causal cancellation

So let's ask once again: Why aren't you morally responsible for not saving the child in Sharks? As we have seen, it won't help to say that the inevitability factors made you not save the child: the inevitability factors didn't actually make you do (or not do) anything, because they were causally inoperative. But they still seemed to play *some* role. What role did they play? As we will see, reflecting on the role played by the sharks will help us solve the billionaire puzzle.

Here's an idea about the sharks' role that seems, on the face of it, more promising. Despite their being causally inefficacious (or, maybe: in addition to their being themselves causally inefficacious), the sharks were responsible for the fact that *another* factor was also causally inefficacious. Which other factor? Assuming a broadly causalist framework of agency, one could say: whichever factor is the cause of an agent's not acting when the agent intentionally omits to act. Presumably, this will be some mental event or state concerning the agent. Following many causalists, let's say that it's the agent's having formed an intention, such as the intention to omit to perform the act in question.[8] Then the relevant factor in Sharks is your having formed the intention not to save the child. Had it not been for the fact that the sharks were present, you would have been able to carry out your intention not to save the child: your intention not to save the child would have then accounted for, or it would have caused, your not saving the child, and thus you would have been morally responsible for not saving him. But, in fact, given the presence of the sharks, your intention not to save the child didn't account for, or didn't cause, your not saving the child. As a result, you weren't morally responsible for not saving him.

In other words, according to this proposal, the role played by the sharks is that the sharks severed the causal relationship that would otherwise have existed between your intention and your omission, without themselves causing your omission. It will be useful to distinguish *three* different features that the sharks have vis-à-vis the causal history of your omission to save the child. First, an actual (negative) causal feature: the sharks are in fact *not* a cause of your not saving the child. Second, a counterfactual (positive) causal feature: the sharks *would* have been a cause of your not saving the child if you had intended to perform the relevant act (if you had formed a different intention). And third, a feature that determines the (negative) causal role of other factors: the sharks are the reason your intention not to act isn't a cause of your not saving the child *either*.

The role played by the sharks is analogous to the role that certain factors play in a particular kind of causal structure that has been recently discussed in the literature on causation. Here is an example of it:

> *The Catcher and the Wall*: Someone throws a baseball and you catch it. Behind you there is a solid brick wall, which would have stopped the ball if you hadn't caught it. Behind the wall, there is a window, which remains intact throughout that time.[9]

Consider the question: What role does *the wall* play in this case? The first thing to note is that, given that you caught the ball and thus it never touched the wall, it seems wrong to say that the wall is responsible for the window's remaining intact in this case (or that the wall actively prevents the window from breaking). The wall never gets to do anything, in particular, it never gets to deflect the ball away from the window.

But, then, what role does the wall play in this situation? It is plausible to say the following: the wall "protected" the window but only in the sense that, due to its existence, the window was never in danger of breaking. As a result, other things *also* failed to cause the window's remaining intact. In particular, *your catch* failed to cause the window to remain intact. In other words: the wall rendered your catch causally inefficacious, and it rendered your catch causally inefficacious by making the window "unbreakable."

Again, we can distinguish three different features that the wall has concerning the causal history of the outcome of the window remaining intact. First, the wall didn't cause the window to remain intact. Second, the wall would have caused the window to remain intact if you hadn't caught the ball (since, if you hadn't caught the ball, the window's remaining intact would have depended on the wall's presence). And, third, the wall is the reason that your catch didn't cause the window to remain intact either (if the wall hadn't been there, your catch would have been a cause of the window's remaining intact). So the wall in this case is the analogue of the sharks in Sharks; it plays exactly the same kind of role vis-à-vis the causal history of the outcome in question.

The structure of The Catcher and the Wall is usually called "preemptive prevention" in the literature on causation. However, this isn't a good label, at least not in this particular case. "Preemptive prevention" suggests that there is an outcome that is being prevented, a preempting factor that actually does the preventing, and a preempted factor that would have done the preventing in the absence of the preempting factor. The Catcher and the Wall would be a case of preemptive prevention in this sense if the catcher were the preempting factor and the wall were the preempted factor with respect to the prevention of the window shattering. But, as we have seen, this is not what happens: the wall isn't what prevents the window from shattering, and the catcher isn't what prevents the window from shattering either. "Mutual causal cancellation (neutralization)" or perhaps, more specifically, "mutual prevention cancellation (neutralization)," are more appropriate labels in this case, since they capture the fact that neither is a cause of the relevant non-occurrence (neither is a "preventor") and that this is so due to each other's presence (the wall isn't a preventor given what the catcher does and, vice-versa, the catcher isn't a preventor given the wall's existence). So these are the labels I will use.[10]

2.4 Solving the billionaire puzzle

Now let us return to our puzzle about intentional omissions. How can the preceding discussion help us solve the billionaire puzzle?

Basically, the proposal has two parts. The first part is to suggest that the glue tying the chair to the ground in the billionaire case is like the sharks in Sharks and like the wall in The Catcher and the Wall. Although the glue didn't itself account for, or didn't cause, your not moving the chair (it would have, if you had tried to move the chair, but it didn't in the actual scenario), it was responsible for the fact that the relevant mental events/states concerning you (for example, your having formed the intention not to move the chair) weren't causally connected to your not moving the chair. This would be yet another illustration of the phenomenon of mutual causal cancellation or neutralization: the glue didn't cause your not moving the chair because you didn't intend to move it, but, also, the relevant mental items concerning you didn't cause your not moving the chair because of the glue. In other words, the inevitability factors and the relevant mental items concerning the agent render each other causally inefficacious, in that they deny each other the opportunity to be active preventors. Then the second part of the proposal is to suggest that this explains why your not moving the chair wasn't intentional. For, again, following a broadly causalist perspective of agency, one could suggest that an omission is not intentional unless it was (suitably) caused by the relevant mental items concerning the agent. For example, one could suggest that, even if you formed the intention not to move the chair, and even if you didn't move the chair, you couldn't carry out your intention not to move the chair because the intention didn't cause your not moving the chair. And this was due to the presence of the inevitability factors. Hence, to the extent that the inevitability factors are responsible for severing that causal relationship, they are responsible for the fact that the non-doing isn't an intentional omission.[11]

Now, before we take this idea any further, let me make one important clarification. As it should be clear by now, I think that the reason why you don't intentionally omit to move the chair in the billionaire case is basically the same reason why you are not morally responsible for your not saving the child in Sharks. But I don't thereby mean to suggest that the relationship between moral responsibility for omissions and alternative possibilities is *exactly the same relationship as* that between intentionally omitting to act and alternative possibilities (in fact, I think it's probably not, as I explain momentarily). All I mean to say is that sometimes the fact that an agent isn't morally responsible for an omission and the fact that an agent doesn't intentionally omit to act can have the same source. Intuitively, this is true of Sharks and the billionaire case: intuitively, the reason you don't intentionally omit to move the chair in the billionaire case is the same kind of reason why you fail to be morally responsible for your omission in Sharks, namely, that you wouldn't have been able to perform the relevant act even if you had tried. There could be other kinds of cases where an agent fails to be morally responsible for an omission in virtue of his inability to do otherwise but where he still intentionally omits to act. This might be true, for example, of a scenario of coercion. Imagine that someone issues a powerful threat against my saving the child (a threat that any reasonable person would succumb to, for example, he threatens to kill my family if I do), but I can save him if I decide to do so. Imagine that I omit to save the child as a result of the threat (and only as a result of the threat). In this case, I intentionally omit to save the child, but (at least Frankfurt would say) I am not responsible for omitting to save him. Moreover, my lack of moral responsibility in this case too seems to be importantly tied to my inability to do otherwise. Scenarios of this kind suggest that the relationship between moral responsibility for omissions and alternative possibilities is probably not the same as the relationship between intentionally omitting to act and alternative possibilities. But this isn't a problem for our argument here.[12]

Now we are ready to state the solution to the billionaire puzzle in more precise terms. Part of the solution consists in the formulation of a new principle about the connection between intentionally omitting to act and alternative possibilities. This principle is:

> PMCC-IO ("Principle of Mutual Causal Cancellation for Intentional Omissions"): An agent does not intentionally omit to perform an act (even if he doesn't perform the act, and even if he has the relevant desires, intentions, etc. not to act) if inevitability factors and the relevant mental items enter in a relation of mutual causal cancellation with respect to the agent's not acting.

The other part of the solution is the claim that the billionaire case is a scenario of mutual causal cancellation of the relevant kind. The key to solving the puzzle, then, is to switch the focus from what *moves* the agent to omit to act to what *doesn't* move the agent to omit to act. As suggested by PMCC-IO, inevitability factors can play a role in rendering the omission non-intentional even if they don't themselves move the agent to omit to act: in particular, they are responsible for the omission's not being intentional when it's in virtue of *them* that the relevant mental items concerning the agent don't result in the agent's omission.[13]

I will end this section by making two remarks about PMCC-IO: one of them is friendly to Frankfurt's ideas and the other one isn't. First, the Frankfurt-friendly remark: It is important to see that PMCC-IO is consistent with the claim that an agent can intentionally omit to act when he couldn't have done otherwise (in other words, PMCC-IO is not PPA-IO). According to PMCC-IO, agents cannot intentionally omit to do the impossible when the inevitability factors and the relevant mental items render each other causally inefficacious. But, of course, for all PMCC-IO says, agents *can* intentionally omit to do the impossible to the extent that this isn't the case. In particular, PMCC-IO is consistent with the claim that, in a Frankfurt-style omission case, the agent intentionally omits to act even if he couldn't have done otherwise. Note that the structure of a Frankfurt-style omission case is such that the agent freely comes to form an intention and then omits to act, based on that intention. The counterfactual intervener is situated, so to speak, "before the intention" rather than "after the intention": he would have prevented the agent from forming a different intention, rather than preventing him from doing anything different *once* he had formed a different intention. So in a Frankfurt-style omission case there is no temptation to say that the inevitability factors sever the link between the agent's intention and his omission (and thus there is no temptation to say that the intention and the inevitability factors render each other causally inefficacious). Although the agent couldn't have formed a different intention, arguably, (if intentions to omit to act ever result in agents' omissions) the intention that the agent formed did result in his omission. For example, an advocate of Frankfurt-style cases would claim that, in The Child and the Neuroscientist case (our Frankfurt-style omission scenario from section 1), you freely form the intention not to jump in to save the drowning child, and the child drowns as a result of your forming that intention. Although the existence of the neuroscientist makes it impossible for you to decide to save the child, it doesn't cut off whatever connection exists between your intention not to save the child and your not saving him (and nothing else does, in particular, there are no sharks).[14]

Here is another way to see this: an advocate of Frankfurt-style cases could argue that The Child and the Neuroscientist doesn't have the structure of a mutual causal cancellation scenario, like The Catcher and The Wall. Instead, an advocate of Frankfurt-style cases could argue that it has the structure of a scenario like the following:

> *The Catcher and the Neuroscientist*: Someone throws a baseball and you catch it. Behind you there is a window, which would have shattered if the

> ball had reached it. This time there is no brick wall or any other obstacles to the ball's reaching the window. But, as it turns out, you couldn't have failed to catch the ball. A neuroscientist has been closely monitoring your movements: if you hadn't instinctively placed your glove in the right place a few seconds before the ball got there, he would have sent some signals to your brain that would have resulted in your catching the ball all the same.

Here we don't hesitate to think that your catch caused the window to remain intact. Of course, you couldn't have failed to catch the ball, but this is no objection to the claim that your catch prevented the shattering. Similarly, in The Child and the Neuroscientist you couldn't have formed the intention to jump in, but, it could be argued, this is no objection to the claim that your intention not to jump in caused your omission to save the child.

Now for the remark about PMCC-IO that is not Frankfurt-friendly: PMCC-IO is consistent with there being an asymmetry between actions and omissions concerning the conditions for acting/omitting to act intentionally.[15] For all PMCC-IO says, inevitability factors might sever the link between the relevant mental items and the agent's behavior in cases of omission but not in cases of action. Or they might sever that link much more often in cases of omission than in cases of action. That is, it might be that, although both acting intentionally and omitting intentionally to act require that the relevant mental items cause the behavior, the conditions under which the relevant mental items cause the behavior are different for actions and omissions, given the different role played by inevitability factors in each case. Elsewhere I have argued that there is, in fact, a causal asymmetry between actions and omissions concerning the role of inevitability factors.[16] If so, this fact, together with PMCC-IO, would entail that the relationship between intentional omissions and alternative possibilities is ultimately different from the relationship between actions and alternative possibilities.

2.5 Final remarks

According to PMCC-IO, *if* and *when* there is mutual causal cancellation between inevitability factors and the relevant mental items concerning the agent, the agent doesn't intentionally omit to act. Although PMCC-IO doesn't specify any particular conditions under which there is mutual causal cancellation between the inevitability factors and the relevant mental items, I have argued that there are at least some paradigmatic cases where this happens. In particular, I have argued that this is what happens in the billionaire case and in other scenarios with the same structure. So PMCC-IO, in conjunction with the claim that the billionaire case is a scenario of mutual causal cancellation, provides a solution to the billionaire puzzle.

I said at the outset that reflecting about the billionaire puzzle would be enlightening even if it turned out that intentional omissions do require alternative possibilities (in particular, even if Frankfurt-style cases failed to show that they don't). Now we can see why. Reflecting about the billionaire puzzle led us to the formulation of PMCC-IO, an alternative principle concerning the relationship between intentional omissions and alternative possibilities (one that doesn't presuppose that intentional omissions require alternative possibilities). As I noted at the outset, even if intentional omissions did require alternative possibilities, that is, even if PPA-IO were, after all, true, there would still be a question as to why it is true. And it seems that, if PPA-IO were true, we could appeal to PMCC-IO to explain why it is true. For, given PMCC-IO, if PPA-IO were true, this would have to be because in *all* cases of omission where inevitability factors are present, the inevitability factors and the relevant mental items enter in a relation of mutual causal cancellation. If this were true, it would explain why intentional omissions require alternative possibilities: they would require alternative possibilities because they would require the absence of inevitability factors, and they would require the absence of inevitability factors because, were there to exist any inevitability factors, they would (by means of entering in a relation of mutual causal cancellation with the relevant mental items) break off the causal links that are essential for an intentional omission to obtain).[17]

Let me conclude by describing one important way in which I think that the project in this paper might be incomplete, or might need some more pruning. I take it that the billionaire case (and other scenarios with a similar structure) are paradigm examples of omission where the agent's inability to act precludes his having intentionally failed to act. I've offered an account of this in terms of the phenomenon of mutual causal cancellation. Now, on the face of it, there could be other examples that fall out of this account because they don't involve causal connections (or the lack thereof). Imagine, for instance, an arrogant mathematician who believes that a certain mathematical claim is a theorem but doesn't bother to try to prove it. Imagine that the claim isn't really a theorem (it cannot be proved from the axioms). Does the mathematician intentionally omit to prove it? Presumably not, since he couldn't have proved it. So the mathematician's not proving the theorem fails to be an intentional omission, just like your not moving the chair in the billionaire case does. Could we tell the same kind of story I've told about the billionaire case in the mathematician case? Arguably, it couldn't be exactly the same story. One feature of the billionaire case, in virtue of which I have claimed there is mutual causal cancellation in that case, is that the inevitability factor in question (the glue tying the chair to the ground) would have been causally responsible for your not moving the chair if you had tried to move it. But in the mathematician case the inevitability factor is a mathematical fact: the fact that a particular mathematical claim doesn't follow from certain axioms. Presumably, a mathematical fact couldn't have been *causally* responsible for the mathematician's failure to prove the theorem, if he had tried to prove it. If so, there isn't mutual causal cancellation in this case.

I see two main ways to go about addressing this problem. First, one could argue that what's at issue here is a broader kind of mutual cancellation: mutual *explanatory* cancellation, which needn't be of the causal kind. On this view, had the mathematician tried to prove the claim, the fact that the claim isn't a theorem would still (non-causally) explain why he fails to do so. (Note that this is what one would be tempted to say anyway if one believed, contrary to what I have assumed in this paper, that omissions cannot be caused by anything or be causes of anything; in that case, omissions couldn't give rise to situations of mutual causal cancellation, but they would still likely give rise to situations of mutual explanatory cancellation.) Second, one could argue that (at least sometimes) agents cannot genuinely try to bring about states of affairs that are logically impossible, for example, I cannot try to bring it about that p & not-p.[18] If so, perhaps the fact that I cannot even try to bring it about that p & not-p more directly explains why I cannot intentionally fail to bring it about that p & not-p. Either way, the story would have to be modified or complemented accordingly, if we wanted to account for these kinds of cases. At any rate, I suspect that cases of this kind are somewhat special and out of the ordinary, and thus they probably deserve a special treatment, which I cannot give them here.

Notes

* I am grateful to Kent Bach, Juan Comesaña, Dan Hausman, Ori Simchen, and audiences at the University of North Carolina-Chapel Hill, the University of British Columbia, and Torcuato Di Tella University for helpful comments on earlier versions of this paper.

1. The reason I say that it might seem even clearer that you intentionally omit to save the child in this case (than that you are morally responsible for your omission) is that, one could argue, you would have intentionally omitted to save the child *even if* the neuroscientist had intervened. For, given the way the case is set up, even if the neuroscientist intervenes, he intervenes by causing you to decide not to save the child; as a result, you still fail to save the child based on your decision not to save him. For our purposes, we don't need to settle the question whether your not saving the child would be intentional in that case too; all that is needed is the claim that your omission is intentional in the scenario where the neuroscientist doesn't intervene.
2. See Sartorio (2005) (and see Sartorio (2009) for complementary arguments).
3. See also, for example, Clarke (1994) and McIntyre (1994).
4. Frankfurt writes: "In my view, there is every reason to prefer an account that is straightforwardly symmetrical." And: "The two cases [the relevant omission and action cases under his consideration] are, in any event, perfectly symmetrical. If there is any discordance in holding John [the agent in a given omission case] morally responsible for refraining from saving the child, it is equally discordant

to regard Matthew [the agent in the parallel action case] as morally responsible for saving him." (Frankfurt (1994), pp. 622–3.)

5. He writes: "Now it seems to me that when we turn from cases of action to cases of omission, we find the very same possibility. In the actual sequence of events, the fact that someone could not have performed a certain action—and hence could not have avoided omitting it—may have no causal influence on his behavior. It may play no role whatsoever in accounting for his omitting to perform the action." (Frankfurt (1994), p. 621) Here Frankfurt is thinking of cases where the agent is morally responsible for an omission even if he couldn't have performed the relevant act. He seems to think that part of the explanation of why an agent is responsible in these cases is that he doesn't omit to act *because* he couldn't have done otherwise.
6. Ginet makes a similar point about a different example in his (2006), pp. 82–3. See also Widerker (2000), pp. 189–90.
7. Compare with a parallel case of action: The child is placidly napping on a raft in the water. You want the child to drown so you create waves by violently moving your body in the water. The child falls off the raft and drowns. Had you not independently decided to create the waves, you would have noticed the sharks in the water, which would have resulted in your swimming quickly towards the shore, which would have, again, resulted in the waves and the child drowning. In this case the mere presence of the sharks doesn't get you off the hook: you would have failed to be morally responsible for making the child drown if the sharks had caused you to create the waves, but you are morally responsible given that they didn't.

   A different possible response by Frankfurt is suggested in his (2006), pp. 341–2. The response consists in saying that the agent in Sharks is not morally responsible for the omission to save the child simply because there is no such omission: there is no such omission on the part of the agent since saving the child wasn't in his control. I think that this response would only push the problem back one step. For then the question would be: Why is there no omission in Sharks for the agent to be morally responsible for, but there is one in a Frankfurt-style case, if in both cases the agent couldn't have performed the relevant act?
8. Contrary to what many causalists seem to believe, I don't think that intentions not to act are the relevant mental causes in cases of intentional omission (see Sartorio (2009); the view that I favor thus ends up being an unorthodox version of causalism, and only if one understands "causalism" very broadly, as I am understanding it here). But I still think that the sharks render the relevant mental items causally inefficacious in this case. So what exactly one takes the relevant mental items to be in this case is not essential for the point about Sharks to hold.
9. The example is originally by McDermott (1995)). I am interested in the treatment given of it by Collins (2000), which differs to an important extent from McDermott's.
10. Thanks to Kent Bach for an illuminating discussion of the appropriate labels to use in these cases. The reason this type of structure is usually called "preemptive prevention" is that there are other examples with apparently the same basic structure where it seems more plausible to say that one of the factors preempts the other factor by actually doing the preventing (for example, if we replace the solid brick wall with another human catcher; in that case it seems more plausible to say that the agent who catches the ball prevents the shattering—see Collins (2000) for the contrast between the two cases). Unlike genuine scenarios of preemptive prevention, mutual causal cancellation scenarios seem to give rise to

a puzzle. In the Catcher and the Wall, had both the catcher and the wall been absent, the window would have shattered. So it seems that the catcher and the wall "together" prevented the shattering. But how can this be, if neither was a preventor? A possible answer is to say that a disjunctive fact (the fact that either was present) did the preventing. Notice that a similar puzzle would arise for Sharks: if the sharks didn't cause the child's death, and neither did I, then what did? For more reasons to believe in disjunctive causes, see Sartorio (2006).

11. The same can be said about Locke's famous example of the man who stays inside a room talking to someone he likes, although, unbeknownst to him, the door has been locked from the outside so that he cannot get out (Locke (1975), bk. 2, ch. 21, sect. 10). It seems to me that, although the man intentionally omits to *try* to leave the room, he doesn't intentionally omit to leave the room, for the same reason you don't intentionally omit to move the chair in the billionaire case.
12. Another kind of scenario where the agent is not morally responsible for his omission because he couldn't have done otherwise but where, it could be argued, he still intentionally omits to act is a Frankfurt-style scenario where the neuroscientist intervenes by causing the agent to decide not to act in the relevant way (see note 1 above). In light of cases like these, a tentative way to formulate the principle about the connection between moral responsibility for omissions and alternative possibilities could be: one is not morally responsible for an omission *either* if one's intention not to act was caused by inevitability factors *or* if inevitability factors and one's intention rendered each other causally inefficacious with respect to the fact that one didn't act.
13. A similar shift in focus would help explain why the agent isn't morally responsible in Sharks. As I pointed out in section 2, Frankfurt's guiding thought about the connection between moral responsibility and alternative possibilities was that inevitability factors can only reduce the agent's moral responsibility for his act/omission if they play an actual role in making the agent act/omit to act. In light of our preceding discussion, I think we should say that inevitability factors can also reduce the agent's responsibility if they cut off the connection between the relevant mental items concerning the agent and his act/omission *without themselves making him act/omit to act*. This is so because, in that kind of case too, the agent doesn't act/omit to act *for his own reasons*.
14. Clarke (1994) and McIntyre (1994) suggest something along these lines as part of their justification for the claim that the agent is morally responsible for his omission in cases with this structure. Note that the claim that the agent's intention results in his omission in these cases could still fail if it were *generally* false that the intention results in the omission in cases of intentional omission. But what we cannot say, it seems to me, is that *the inevitability factors* are the reason the intention doesn't result in the omission in these cases.
15. This shouldn't be surprising, given the divergence between PMCC-IO and Frankfurt's own principle (PPA-revised), discussed in section 2.
16. See Sartorio (2005). There I draw attention to a moral asymmetry that results between actions and omissions as a result of the causal asymmetry, not to an asymmetry concerning the conditions for acting/omitting to act intentionally.
17. Notice that the claim would have to be that Frankfurt-style cases are scenarios of mutual causal cancellation too, just like Sharks or the billionaire case. But how could this be, if, as we have seen, it is not plausible to say that in Frankfurt-style cases the inevitability factors sever the link between the agent's intention not to act and his failing to act? As suggested above (see notes 8 and 14), one would have to

say that the agent's intention not to act is not the relevant mental item, in this or other omission cases. I have argued for this in Sartorio (2009). As I explain there, I take this to be a rather surprising fact about omissions, and one that is definitely not immediately obvious. The fact that it's not immediately obvious could be used to "explain away" the initial appearance that an agent intentionally omits to act in a Frankfurt-style case.

18. Albritton defends a view of this kind in his (1985).

References

Albritton, R. (1985), "Freedom of Will and Freedom of Action," Presidential Address, American Philosophical Association (Pacific Division), reprinted in G. Watson (ed.) (2003), *Free Will*, Oxford University Press, second edition, 408–23.

Bach, K. (2010), "Refraining, Omitting, and Negative Acts," in T. O'Connor and C. Sandis (eds), *Companion to the Philosophy of Action*, Oxford: Wiley-Blackwell.

Clarke, R. (1994), "Ability and Responsibility for Omissions," *Philosophical Studies* 73: 195–208.

Collins, J. (2000), "Preemptive Prevention," *Journal of Philosophy* 97, 4: 223–34.

Fischer, J. and M. Ravizza (1991), "Responsibility and Inevitability," *Ethics* 101: 258–78.

Fischer, J. and M. Ravizza (1998), *Responsibility and Control*, Cambridge: Cambridge University Press.

Frankfurt, H. (1969), "Alternate Possibilities and Moral Responsibility," *Journal of Philosophy* 66, 23: 829–39.

Frankfurt, H. (1994), "An Alleged Asymmetry Between Actions and Omissions," *Ethics* 104, 3: 620–3.

Frankfurt, H. (2006). "Some Thoughts Concerning PAP," in D. Widerker and M. McKenna (eds). *Moral Responsibility and Alternative Possibilities*, Ashgate, Aldershot (UK) 339–45.

Ginet, C. (2004), "Intentionally Doing and Intentionally Not Doing," *Philosophical Topics* 32, 1–2: 95–110.

Ginet, C. (2006). "In Defense of the Principle of Alternative Possibilities: Why I Don't Find Frankfurt's Argument Convincing," in D. Widerker and M. McKenna (eds). *Moral Responsibility and Alternative Possibilities*, Ashgate, Aldershot (UK) 75–90.

Locke, J. (1975). *An Essay Concerning Human Understanding*, ed. P. Niddich, Oxford University Press, Oxford.

McDermott, M. (1995). "Redundant Causation," *British Journal for the Philosophy of Science* 46: 523–44.

McIntyre, A. (1994). "Compatibilists Could Have Done Otherwise: Responsibility and Negative Agency," *Philosophical Review* 103: 453–88.

Sartorio, C. (2005). "A New Asymmetry between Actions and Omissions," *Noûs* 39, 3: 460–82.

Sartorio, C. (2006). "Disjunctive Causes," *Journal of Philosophy* 103, 10: 521–38.

Sartorio, C. (2009). "Omissions and Causalism," *Noûs* 43, 3: 513–30.

van Inwagen, P. (1978). "Ability and Responsibility," *Philosophical Review* 87: 201–24.

Widerker, D. (2000). "Frankfurt's Attack on the Principle of Alternative Possibilities: A Further Look," *Philosophical Perspectives* 14: 181–201.

Zimmermann, M. (1981). "Taking Some of the Mystery out of Omissions," *Southern Journal of Philosophy* 19: 541–54.

3
Experimental Philosophy of Action

Thomas Nadelhoffer

3.1 Introduction

When it comes to determining how responsible an agent is for her actions, it matters a great deal whether she acted intentionally rather than unintentionally. As Oliver Wendell Holmes Jr. once remarked, "even a dog distinguishes between being stumbled over and being kicked" (Holmes 1963, 7). Given the central role that ascriptions of intentional action play in our everyday moral and legal practices, it is no surprise that the concept of intentionality[1] has historically received a lot of attention in the philosophical literature. Moreover, until quite recently, philosophers have been content to rely on their own *a priori* intuitions about particular cases in trying to trace the contours of the concept of intentional action. However, exclusive reliance on this traditional approach to action theory has been called into question as of late by researchers working in the nascent field of experimental philosophy.[2]

The primary goal of the present essay is to provide the reader with an overview of the work that has been done in the past few years in experimental philosophy of action. In doing so, I first briefly argue for the relevance of data on folk intuitions to the philosophical project of exploring the concept of intentionality (§3.2). Then, I survey some of the salient research that has recently been done. At this stage, I begin with the early ground-breaking work by Bertram Malle and Joshua Knobe (§3.2). Next, I discuss the surprising results from Knobe's later attempts to probe folk intuitions concerning side effects and intentionality, and I show why these results put prima facie pressure on traditional philosophical accounts of intentional action (§3.3). Having discussed Knobe's controversial so-called side effect findings, I go on to examine five of the explanatory models that have been put forward thus far in the literature that have either already been widely discussed or that are likely to shape the debate in the months and years ahead (§3.4). At the end of the day, my aim is to provide the reader with a framework for approaching and understanding the growing field of experimental philosophy of action. Hopefully, my efforts on this front will encourage more people to join in the interdisciplinary task of trying to better understand the nature of agency and responsibility.

3.2 The standard model of intentionality

As we saw in the introduction, in the event that someone accidentally or unintentionally harms you, this usually mitigates how much blame you think the person deserves. If, on the other hand, someone purposely and intentionally harms you under normal circumstances, this is grounds for judging the person to be fully blameworthy. In short, judgments about intentional action lie at the heart of the sphere of our ascriptions of responsibility. Moreover, a standard direction of fit is commonly assumed to exist between the two—namely, judging whether an agent is fully responsible for *x-ing* requires one to first decide whether she *x-ed* intentionally.

For present purposes, I am going to call this the standard model of intentionality and blame. In short, it is a *uni-directional* view whereby judgments about intentionality serve as inputs to judgments concerning responsibility, but not the other way around.[3] However, as intuitive as the standard model may appear at first, it has been called into question by recent data on folk ascriptions of intentional action. But before I examine the gathering evidence for the competing *bi-directional* model—that is, the view that judgments concerning the moral badness of an action (or the blameworthiness of an agent) sometimes influence judgments of intentionality—I first want to briefly discuss the relevance of folk intuitions to the philosophy of action more generally.

The first thing worth pointing out is that there is a rich philosophical tradition whereby philosophers are in the business of analyzing folk beliefs, judgments, and concepts. Frank Jackson has arguably put forward the most thorough and persuasive recent defense of this position. On his view, "our subject is really the elucidation of the situations covered by the *words* we use to ask our questions—concerning free action, knowledge . . . or whatever" (Jackson 1998, 33). And given that ordinary language is often the proper subject matter of philosophy, "consulting intuitions about possible cases" is the proper method (Jackson 1998, 33). While I entirely agree with Jackson's contention that philosophers should often focus on our ordinary beliefs and judgments,[4] his view is nevertheless based on the questionable assumption that the intuitions of analytic philosophers are representative of those of laypersons.

This is a problem that Jackson acknowledges when he says that he is "sometimes asked—in a tone that suggests that the question is a major objection—why, if conceptual analysis is concerned to elucidate what governs our classificatory practice, don't I advocate doing serious opinion polls on people's responses to various cases? My answer is that I do—when it is necessary" (Jackson 1998, 36–37). Many experimental philosophers would agree with Jackson that when it comes to issues such as free will, moral responsibility, and intentional action, people's ordinary intuitions are the appropriate starting point for philosophical investigation while nevertheless questioning the validity of Jackson's method of getting at them—namely, armchair reflection coupled with *informal* polls of students and friends.[5] To the extent that philosophers are going to continue making claims concerning the contours of folk intuitions, the task of testing these claims should be attended to with the same carefulness and rigor one finds in psychology and cognate fields. In light of this concern, experimental philosophers have recently begun using techniques borrowed from the social sciences to get at folk judgments concerning a wide variety of philosophical issues.

One topic that has received a lot of attention among experimental philosophers is intentionality.[6] After all, as Alfred Mele has correctly pointed out, any adequate philosophical analysis of intentional action should be "anchored by common-sense judgments" about particular cases (Mele 2001, 27)—even if it admittedly need not capture or reflect *all* of these judgments. On this view, one way of testing an analysis of intentional action would be to see whether it agrees with people's actual pre-theoretical intuitions. Having done so, if we find that an analysis of intentional action is entirely inconsistent with folk intuitions, we will be in a good position to suggest that it "runs the risk of having nothing more than a philosophical fiction as its subject matter" (Mele 2001, 27).

Data about folk intuitions become all the more important for philosophers such as Hugh McCann who explicitly claim to be interested in the ordinary concept of intentional action and not its philosophical counterparts (McCann 1998, 210). So, while those philosophers who are merely interested in technical concepts and other so-called terms of art may dismiss empirical data concerning folk intuitions *tout court*, philosophers such as Jackson and McCann, who are explicitly interested in analyzing our everyday concepts, are beholden to the results of the kind of research being done by experimental philosophers. As such, even if experimental philosophy is admittedly not relevant to *all* philosophical projects, it is inescapably relevant to *some* of them. Unfortunately, until fairly recently, there was a dearth of controlled and systematic research concerning how people actually think and talk about intentionality. It is now time to examine the attempts by experimental philosophers to address this empirical lacuna.

3.3 The birth of experimental philosophy of action

While it should come as no surprise that philosophers have not traditionally spent much time exploring folk ascriptions of intentional action in a controlled and systematic way, it is surprising that many of the early psychological models of intentional action (for example, Heider 1958; Jones & Davis 1965)—and even some of the recent ones (for example, Fiske 1989; Fleming & Darley 1989; Shaver 1985)—simply assume that intentionality plays an important role in social perception without studying the precise nature of this role. Malle and Knobe tried to address this gap with their groundbreaking research on intentional action (Malle & Knobe 1997). Their main goal was to investigate the folk concept of intentionality and examine its "implications for social perception, attribution, and development" (1997, 3). In order to get at the folk concept of intentional action, Malle and Knobe ran a series of studies.

In the first study, 159 undergraduates were given a questionnaire and asked to answer the following question: "When you say that somebody performed an action intentionally, what does that mean? Please explain." All of the participants' answers were then transcribed into another booklet and then coded. The four most common features of intentional action that were identified by participants were:

Component:	**Frequency:**
Desire	27%
Belief	39%
Intention	51%
Awareness	23%

Because these four components accounted for 96 percent of the findings, Malle and Knobe conclude that "the folk concept of intentional action includes: (a) a desire for an outcome, (b) beliefs about the action leading to that outcome, (c) an intention to perform that act, and (d) awareness of performing that act" (1997, 8–9).

As Malle and Knobe point out, none of the past psychological models of intentional action capture all of the elements of their own four-component model. Whereas Jones and Davis (1965), Ossorio and Davis (1968), and Shaver (1985) all identified the belief and desire components, they overlooked the importance of intention and awareness. Similarly, Heider's (1958) model of intentional action had both an intention and a desire component, but it lacked belief and awareness components. Nevertheless, Malle and Knobe point out that all of these models also postulated something that their own four-component model lacks—namely, an ability or skill component. Surprisingly, this component was absent from the participants' definitions—which explains why Malle and Knobe do not include it in their model. But given that it is intuitively plausible that ability or skill are necessary for intentional action, Malle and Knobe concluded that they should examine the issue more carefully.

To see whether considerations of ability or skill have an effect on folk ascriptions of intentional action, Malle and Knobe ran a preliminary study that involved the following vignette:

> Jerry is a novice at darts. He has never played darts before and is not particularly talented at games like this. Surprisingly, he hits triple 20 (a very difficult throw) on his first try. A friend dismisses the throw as a fluke, so Jerry tries again, missing badly.
>
> (1997, 8)

The results of the study were as follows: 77 percent of the participants judged that Jerry wanted to hit a triple 20, but only 16 percent said that he hit triple 20 intentionally. In a second condition, participants were told that Jerry hit triple 20 twice in a row. This time, 55 percent judged that he hit triple 20 intentionally. Presumably, the difference in participants' judgments in these two conditions is the result of the fact that hitting triple 20 twice in a row demonstrates more skill or ability than successfully hitting it only once.

In light of their overall findings, Malle and Knobe expanded upon their original model by adding a skill condition. Their revised five component model took the following form:

Belief Desire

⇘ ⇙

Intention Skill Awareness

⇘ ⇓ ⇙

Intentionality

On Malle and Knobe's view, performing an action intentionally "requires the presence of five components: a desire for an outcome; beliefs about an action that leads to that outcome; an intention to perform the action; skill to perform the action; and awareness of fulfilling the intention while performing the action" (1997, 12). Moreover, they suggest that these five components are "hierarchically arranged, such that belief and desire are necessary conditions for attributions of intention and, given an *intention*, skill and awareness are necessary conditions for attributions of *intentionality*" (1997, 15).

Despite the obvious advantages provided by Malle and Knobe's five-component model,[7] it does not appear on the surface to be able to accommodate the results of subsequent findings. For instance, as we are about to see in the following section, Knobe has shown that when participants are given vignettes that involve agents who knowingly bring about morally negative side effects, intentionality is ascribed to these side effects even though some of the conditions of Malle and Knobe's five-component model have not been satisfied. These side effect findings further complicate the traditional philosophical project of spelling out the folk concept of intentional action in terms of necessary and jointly sufficient conditions. Minimally, this subsequent research forces us to think more carefully about what we take to be both the *actual* and the *proper* relationship between moral judgments and ascriptions of intentionality. That being said, it is now time to examine the side effect findings and consider their implications for the philosophy of action.

3.4 Knobe's side effect findings

In a series of studies that set the stage for much of the recent work in experimental philosophy of action, Knobe explored whether folk intuitions about the intentionality of foreseeable yet undesired side effects are influenced by moral considerations (Knobe 2003a & 2003b). Each of the 78 participants in the first of these side effect experiments was presented with a vignette involving either a "harm condition" or a "help condition." Those who received the harm condition read the following vignette:

> The vice-president of a company went to the chairman of the board and said, "We are thinking of starting a new program. It will help us increase profits, but it will also harm the environment." The chairman of the board answered, "I don't care at all about harming the environment. I just want to make as much profit as I can. Let's start the new program." They started the new program. Sure enough, the environment was harmed.
>
> (Knobe 2003a, 191)

They were then asked to judge how much blame the chairman deserved for harming the environment (on a scale from 0 to 6) and to say whether they thought the chairman harmed the environment intentionally. 82 percent of the participants claimed that the chairman harmed the environment intentionally. Participants in the help condition, on the other hand, read the same scenario except that the word "harm" was replaced by the word "help." They were then asked to judge how much praise the chairman deserved for helping the environment (on a scale from 0 to 6) and to say whether they thought the chairman helped the environment intentionally. Only 23 percent of the participants claimed that the chairman intentionally helped the environment (Knobe 2003a, 192).

Needless to say, philosophers and psychologists alike found these side effect findings to be both surprising and puzzling. If nothing else, Knobe's studies provided support for the aforementioned bi-directional model of intentionality while at the same time putting pressure on the more "valence neutral" models that have traditionally populated the action theory literature.[8] Keep in mind that at least according to the aforementioned philosophical approach to action theory that is espoused by Jackson, McCann, and others, an adequate theory of intentionality will be one that comports with the salient folk intuitions and judgments. As such, if it turns out that whether someone is judged to have done something intentionally depends not only on her mental states at the time but also on the moral valence of the outcome, then the standard model of intentionality falls short as a complete analysis of the folk concept of intentional action. Unsurprisingly, defenders of the more traditional valence neutral model have not taken Knobe's findings lying down. Indeed, as we will see in what follows, recent studies suggest that perhaps the conclusions drawn by Knobe and others have been premature. But before we examine some of the criticisms of Knobe's findings, we should first discuss his own preferred model for explaining them.

3.5.1 Explaining the side effect findings

3.5.1.1 The core competency view

As we saw in the previous section, there is gathering evidence that "people's beliefs about the moral status of a behavior have some influence on their intuitions about whether or not the behavior was performed intentionally" (Knobe 2006, 205). However, even if it is true that moral judgments do have this effect on ascriptions of intentionality—which is itself a hotly contested claim—it is nevertheless an open question whether they should. In short, we must be careful to distinguish the descriptive issue concerning how people's intentionality judgments are *actually formed* from the normative issue concerning how these judgments *ought to be formed*. While some researchers have traditionally suggested that the concept of intentionality is intimately bound up with moral considerations (for example, Bratman 1987; Duff 1982; 1990; Harman 1976), others have claimed that moral judgments should not influence our ascriptions of intentional action (Butler 1978; Katz 1987; Mele and Sverdlik 1996).

When considered in light of the aforementioned side effect findings, the key issue on the normative front is whether Knobe's participants' responses reflect their underlying competence with the concept of intentional action or whether these responses amount to performance errors. Knobe places himself in the core competency camp. On his view, the existing data suggest that the concept of intentional action is inherently evaluative—that is, judgments about badness both *do and should* affect our ascriptions of intentional action. As such, his view can be broken down into the following two central claims:

1. The Badness but not Blame Hypothesis: Judgments concerning the moral badness of an action (or side effect) influence ascriptions of intentionality but judgments concerning the blameworthiness of the agent do not.

2. The Competency Hypothesis: Judgments concerning the moral badness of an action (or side effect) properly influence ascriptions of intentionality.

The first hypothesis speaks to the kinds of moral considerations that affect our intentionality judgments, whereas the second one speaks to whether the judgments we arrive at in light of these considerations are legitimate. On Knobe's view, they are. As he says:

> This chief contribution of this new model is the distinctive status it accords to moral considerations. Gone is the idea that moral considerations are 'distorting' or 'biasing' a process whose real purpose lies elsewhere. Instead, the claim is that moral considerations are playing a helpful role in people's underlying competence itself. They make it possible for people to generate intentional action intuitions that prove helpful in the subsequent process of assessing praise and blame.
>
> (Knobe 2006, 226

Unsurprisingly, both elements of Knobe's view have come under recent attack. While some action theorists have challenged the descriptive claim that badness but not blame influences judgments of intentionality, others have granted that moral considerations have an effect but denied the normative claim that this influence is legitimate.

One thing worth pointing out is that while it is easy to envision how one might put the Badness but not Blame Hypothesis to the test, the Competency Hypothesis is much more difficult to pin down empirically. After all, one could test the former claim by running studies designed to explore (a) whether you find the side effect findings even in cases not involving moral considerations, or (b) whether both blame and badness can have similar effects on ascriptions of intentional action. However, the same cannot be said for the Competency Hypothesis. After all, even if all of the data show that moral considerations do influence ascriptions of intentional action, how would one test to see whether this influence is normatively appropriate?

Edouard Machery has recently suggested that the debate about conceptual competence is unlikely to be resolved anytime soon (2008). On his view, settling this normative issue would require us to first have an agreed upon account of what it means to be competent with a concept—a consensus that he correctly points out is presently lacking. As he says:

> The controversy can be resolved only if there is a principled distinction between what constitutes our competence with a given concept and what results merely from the multitude of factors that affect our use of this concept at a given time on a given occasion. Unfortunately, the literature on

> concepts has not converged and does not seem to be converging on such a principled distinction. Barring such a distinction, however, the controversy about whether the Knobe effect bears on our conceptual competence with the concept of intentional action cannot be properly resolved.
>
> (Machery 2008, 172–73)

Machery goes on to point out that while there are several competing accounts of conceptual competence in the philosophical literature, there is no consensus concerning which one is correct nor does it appear that any is forthcoming. As such, the question that underlies the so-called competency problem will purportedly remain unanswered indefinitely.

Machery's criticisms of the debate about conceptual competence are both important and far-reaching. Fortunately, for the purposes of the present essay, I do not need to address his otherwise well-placed concerns. My goal is simply to provide an overview of the web of complex issues that have arisen thus far in the literature on folk ascriptions of intentional action. So, while those of us who have a stake in the competency debate need to take Machery's objections seriously, now is neither the time nor the place to try to resolve the issue. Instead, I merely wanted to alert the reader to Machery's worries before further exploring the data that prompted him to voice his concern in the first place. And for that, there is no better place to begin than with the very first competing model that was put forward in the wake of Knobe's early findings—namely, the pragmatic implicature view developed by Fred Adams and Annie Steadman.

3.5.1.2 The pragmatic implicature view

In the first published commentary on the side effect findings, Adams and Steadman suggested that Knobe's studies merely get at the "pragmatic dimension of intentional talk" rather than getting at what they call the "core concept" of intentional action (2004a, 174). On their view, understanding the concept of intentional action requires both an understanding of the "cognitive machinery that underlies intentional action" and a grasp of the type of counterfactual dependency that necessarily holds between intentions and intentional action (2004a, 174). And to the extent that laypersons purportedly lack an understanding of these underlying concepts and causal relationships, "folk notions of intentional action are not clearly articulated" (2004a, 173). Hence, Adams and Steadman conclude that rather than accessing a core concept of intentional action, Knobe's experiments are merely getting at participants' grasp of the pragmatic features of intentional language—features that include the types of judgments that people make that depend more on social context than on the "semantic content of a sentence or judgment" (2004a, 174).

As such, Adams and Steadman do not contest the truth of the Badness but not Blame Hypothesis. Instead, they attempt to repudiate the Competency

Hypothesis by providing a rival explanation for Knobe's findings. By their lights, when we normally say that an agent is blameworthy for *x-ing*, the conversational implication is that she intentionally *x-ed*. This implicature notwithstanding, Adams and Steadman do not think that blame is part of the semantic content of intentional language. As such, they believe that the aforementioned implicature and not the semantic content of intentional action is driving Knobe's results. To support this latter claim, they suggest that, "the truth conditions for 'S did A intentionally' do not include praise or blame. It is not necessary for act A to be good or bad for the action to be intentional" (Adams and Steadman 2004a, 178). Hence, according to Adams and Steadman, this sort of conversational implicature—and not an underlying folk concept of intentional action—must have been driving the participants' judgments in Knobe's experiments. So, for instance, because the participants disapproved of the CEO's indifference to harming the environment, they wanted to blame him. Moreover, since to say that the CEO is blameworthy for harming the environment is to conversationally imply that he intentionally did so, the participants judged that his harming the environment was intentional. But given that blame does not constitute part of the semantic meaning of the core concept of intentional action, the results of Knobe's experiment purportedly only give us insight into the pragmatic features of intentional language.

For now, I want to set aside the question of whether pragmatic (especially moral), rather than semantic, features of intentional language best explain the existing data. Instead, I want to discuss a separate objection that Adams and Steadman have put forward—namely, that nothing in Knobe's first side effect studies justifies the assumption that participants were not judging that the CEO intended to harm the environment. On their view, "if Knobe were to put on his questionnaire 'Is it possible to do A intentionally without intending to do A?' the folk would experience cognitive dissonance. They would likely hesitate to embrace both that the chairman intentionally harmed the environment and that he did not intend to harm the environment" (2004b, 276). In defending the so-called Simple View[9]—that is, the view that intending to *x* is necessary for intentionally *x-ing*—Hugh McCann has subsequently objected to Knobe's side effect findings on similar grounds (McCann 2005). As he says:

> Defenders of the simple view have reason, however, to call for further evidence. An interesting fact about the second of the above experiments is that none of the subjects was asked to pronounce on *both* the issue of intentionality and that of intention. That is, none were tested on their willingness to make the pair of statements that, according to the simple view, would be implicitly contradictory: namely, that the chair in either vignette had acted intentionally, yet lacked the corresponding intention. (McCann 2005, 739)

To his credit, McCann decided to put his objections to the test. In the study that is most salient to our present discussion, Knobe's earlier CEO harm vignette was once again used, except this time (a) a quarter of the participants were asked whether the CEO *intentionally* harmed the environment, (b) a quarter of the participants were asked whether he had the *intention* to harm the environment, and (b) the other half of the participants were asked *both* questions. The results were as follows:

	One question	**Both questions**
Intentional	63%	80%
Intention	27%	12%

As you can see, the results displayed in the left column are roughly in line with the results of Knobe's earlier experiment. The results displayed in the right column, on the other hand, appear to falsify McCann's prediction—something he acknowledges with the following remarks:

> Indeed, they seemed to welcome the opportunity to understand the case in just this way, with those ascribing intentionality to the chairman increasing, and those imputing intending/intention decreasing. This appears to be the precise opposite of shying away from any contradiction implicit in such a pair of verdicts, and so may be thought to finish off the simple view once and for all.
>
> (McCann 2005, 742)

But rather than conceding defeat, McCann surprisingly goes on to claim that, "perversely enough, it is in fact the simple view that is behind the phenomenon" (2005, 742). I have argued that McCann's response is untenable (Nadelhoffer 2006c), but fully exploring either of our views on this front would take us too far afield. So, for now I want to turn our attention away from the pragmatic implicature view put forward by Adams, Steadman, and McCann and look instead at my own preferred explanation of the side-effect findings—a view that has been subjected to several penetrating criticisms of its own as of late.

3.5.1.3 The blame plus affective bias view

In a series of early papers, I tried to show that not only was Knobe right that the moral badness of an action or side effect could influence folk ascriptions of intentionality, but that judgments concerning the moral *blameworthiness* of agents can have a similar effect (Nadelhoffer 2004a; 2004b; 2004c). On my view, while Knobe was correct that moral considerations can influence intentionality judgments, he was wrong about the scope of these moral considerations. Whereas he wanted to limit the scope to judgments concerning badness, I wanted to expand it to include judgments about blameworthiness. But our disagreement is not limited to this descriptive issue. It turns out we also disagree about the fundamental normative issues as well. Whereas Knobe thinks that the participants in his studies are using the concept of intentional action competently, I think they are making performance errors. On my view, when people's moral intuitions lead them to judge that the CEO intentionally harms the environment, they are making a mistake.

In this respect, I side with Adams, Steadman, McCann and others on the normative question, even if we provide divergent accounts of what leads participants astray. Rather than appealing to the alleged pragmatic implicatures embedded in the scenarios, I suggest instead that participants' judgments concerning the blameworthiness of the CEO in both the harm and help cases bias their judgments concerning intentionality. In short, the negative affect elicited by the vignettes leads participants to mistakenly ascribe intentionality in ways that run counter to how they would ordinarily use the concept of intentional action in non-moral cases. In motivating my affect performance error model, I have drawn on recent developments in moral psychology that provide a useful framework for understanding and interpreting the side effect findings.

One of the key notions underlying much of the recent work in moral psychology is "automaticity" (Bargh & Chartrand 1999)—that is, "the mind's ability to solve many problems, including high-level social ones, unconsciously and automatically" (Greene & Haidt 2002, 517). The seeming ubiquity of these automatic mental processes has led some researchers to reject rationalist models of moral psychology in favor of non-rationalist affective models. According to these affective models, "moral judgment is more a matter of emotion and affective intuition than deliberative reasoning" (Greene & Haidt 2002, 517). And while these new explanatory models make room for certain types of higher cognition, they nevertheless suggest that emotional and non-rational processes, rather than deliberative and rational ones, are primarily responsible for our moral judgments.

One view that is particularly salient for our present purposes is Mark Alicke's Culpable Control Model (CCM) of blame attribution—which he describes in the following way:

> When blame-validation mode is engaged, observers review structural linkage evidence in a biased manner by exaggerating the actor's volitional or causal control, by lowering their evidential standards for blame, or by seeking information to support their blame attribution. In addition to spontaneous evaluation influences, blame-validation processing is facilitated by factors such as the tendencies to over ascribe control to human agency and to confirm unfavorable expectations.
>
> (Alicke 2000, 558)

According to Alicke, judgments concerning personal control—and hence of moral blameworthiness—are unwittingly influenced by spontaneous affective reactions to the agents and actions involved. In extending this model of blame attribution to the side effect findings, I have suggested that participants' prepotent negative responses to the CEO in the harm case cause them to go into blame-validation mode, which in turn colors their subsequent assessment of the intentionality of his actions. Because participants think that the CEO is a blameworthy character who knowingly brings about a harmful side effect, they are mistakenly led to conclude that he intentionally harms the environment. In the help case, on the other hand, because participants are once again presented with a unsavory CEO who doesn't care about the environment, they are loathe to judge that he helped the environment since this would suggest that they viewed the CEO favorably. In both cases, participants are not so much *using* the concept of intentional action as they are *misusing* it as the result of being biased by a spontaneous desire to blame the CEO for being utterly indifferent towards the environment.

By my lights, the affect-driven performance error model has two main strengths. First, it is entirely consistent with the standard model of intentionality whereby ascriptions of intentional action properly serve as inputs to moral judgments but not the other way around. Second, the explanation it provides for Knobe's side effect findings is congruent with work being done in social and moral psychology on blame attribution, automaticity, social intuitionism, and so on. Unfortunately, it has also subsequently been shown to have two potentially serious shortcomings. But before we will be in the position to adequately assess the main criticisms that have been put forward thus far, we must first be careful to distinguish the following three distinct components of my view:

1. The Blame Validation Hypothesis: Judgments concerning an agent's blameworthiness sometimes influence folk ascriptions of intentionality.
2. The Negative Emotion Hypothesis: The blame validation thesis is best explained in terms of participants' spontaneous negative affective responses to the vignettes.
3. The Performance Error Hypothesis: When blame validation leads people to ascribe intentionality in side effect cases, these ascriptions are mistaken.

To date, most of the criticisms of my view have focused on the first two theses, so I am going to follow suit for the purposes of this paper.[10] The first thing worth pointing out is that since the blame validation thesis does not commit me to the view that blame validation is either necessary or sufficient for ascriptions of intentionality in side effect cases, simply pointing to cases where people judge that an agent brought about a side effect intentionally in a non-blame case is not enough to undermine this component of my view. Instead, one would need to show that blame doesn't influence ascriptions of intentionality even in the cases where the agents are blameworthy. To my knowledge, no one has yet produced the kind of disconfirming evidence needed to falsify the claim that blame validation partly explains some of the existing data. As such, I think this component of my view could still have some explanatory role to play when it comes to the side effect findings. However, in light of an exciting recent study by Liane Young and colleagues, I am less sanguine about the future of my Negative Emotion Hypothesis.

In an effort to test the affective component of my view, Young et al. administered the original Knobe effect vignettes to several patients with damage to their ventromedial prefrontal cortex (VMPFC)—a region of the brain that has been "implicated in emotional processing across a wide range of tasks in both functional imaging and neuropsychological studies" (Young et al. 2006, 267). If my views about affective bias were correct, then patients with damage to their VMPFC should not make the same mistaken ascriptions of intentionality in cases involving negative side effects. After all, according to my model, negative emotion triggers the blame validation, which in turn leads people's intuitions astray when it comes to the intentionality of side effects. Much to my dismay, the results of Young et al.'s study do not appear to support my hypothesis. As they say:

> Contrary to the emotion hypothesis, we found that the intentional attributions made by the VMPC participants conformed to the same basic pattern of intentional attributions made by normal participants. All seven VMPC participants judged that the chairman intentionally harmed the environment, whereas only two out of the seven judged that the chairman intentionally helped the environment. These proportions were significantly different . . . Not only did patients show the asymmetry between help and harm cases, virtually identical proportions of patients and normal subjects showed the asymmetry. Five out of seven lesion cases, that is, 71.4%, showed the effect, while 72.1% of the normal participants showed the effect; the difference between these proportions was not significant.
>
> (Young et al. 2006, 271)

However, even if their study "refutes the strong hypothesis that the asymmetry in intentional attributions can be explained entirely by the emotional responses we have to actions with moral value" (Young et al. 2006, 274), it is unclear that anyone holds such a view. My own view, for instance, can be cast along much weaker lines.

Rather than being committed to the strong hypothesis, I am merely wed to the weaker view that negative affect partly explains the side effect findings—a claim that I do not believe has been refuted by the otherwise illuminating research by Young et al. On the one hand, as they concede, "the VMPC is not the only brain region involved in processing emotion, as borne out by the fact that individuals with lesions to the VMPC are certainly not devoid of all emotion. Thus, it is possible that aspects of emotional processing that operate independently of the VMPC play some role, for example, along the lines suggested by the emotion hypothesis" (2006, 273). On the other hand, it may be that only a minimal amount of affect is required to trigger the bias that I suggest partly explains the side effect findings. If this is the case, then the fact that the VMPC patients have severe affective deficits is not enough to show that affect doesn't nevertheless partly explain their asymmetrical intuitions. Luckily, this, too, is a testable claim. So, hopefully, more work will be done on this front in the future. In the meantime, my own view will admittedly remain on a much shakier empirical footing than I would prefer. That being said, I would now like to turn our attention to the very promising work being done on individual differences and folk judgments of intentionality.

3.5.1.4 The interpretive diversity view

As we have seen thus far, most of the commentary on the side effect findings has focused on (a) explaining why it is that most participants deem that foreseen but undesired negative side effects are brought about intentionally whereas most participants think that foreseen but undesired positive side effects are not brought about intentionally, and (b) trying to ascertain whether the asymmetrical intuitions elicited by side effect cases are normatively appropriate. However, in the wake of Knobe's early studies, while much attention was paid to the intuitional differences exhibited *between* the harm and help conditions, the curiously stable intuitional differences *within* the conditions were largely ignored. After all, even if we manage to explain why the majority of participants judge that the CEO harmed but did not help the environment intentionally, it is unclear why such a stable minority have the opposite intuition. By my lights, the attempt to shed light on this issue has led to one of the more promising lines of research in experimental philosophy of action.

The first researchers to identify and attempt to address the variability of intuitions within conditions were Shaun Nichols and Joe Ulatowski (2007). The central issue they set out to explore is the curious fact that, "while the effects on the CEO case are statistically quite large, the experiments consistently reveal nontrivial minority responses, and those responses require some explanation too ... If the concept of *intentional* really is as Knobe suggests, why is there always a significant minority that maintains that the CEO didn't harm the environment intentionally?" (Nichols & Ulatowski 2007, 354). To see just how important this observation is to the debate about the side effect findings, consider it in light of the three models we discussed earlier. If the majority of participants' responses are to be explained in terms of their judgments concerning (a) the badness of the side effect, (b) the blameworthiness of the agent, or (c) the pragmatic implicatures of the scenarios, then what explains the diverging intuitions within the conditions? Is there a subset of individuals who are simply insensitive to moral considerations or blind to the subtle semantic ambiguities of the scenarios? Given that all of the participants are fluent English speakers, why would there be such stable disagreement between participants who read the same scenarios?

While analyzing the results of their own study, Nichols and Ulatowski discovered the following "surprising pattern":

> In our experiment, we found pronounced systematic individual differences. The minority who said that the CEO didn't intentionally harm the environment in Harm *also* said that the CEO didn't intentionally help the environment in Help. And the minority who said that the CEO intentionally helped the environment in Help also said that the CEO intentionally harmed the environment in Harm. What do we say in light of the consistent responses of these two minorities? Our hypothesis is that 'intentional' exhibits *interpretive diversity,* i.e. it admits of different interpretations. Part of the population, when given these sorts of cases, interpret 'intentional' one way; and part of the population interpret it in another way. On one interpretation both cases are intentional and on the other interpretation, neither is.
> (Nichols & Ulatowski 2007, 356)

By my lights, the importance of the interpretive diversity hypothesis cannot be overstated. If nothing else, Nichols and Ulatowski focused attention on a feature of the side effect findings that had been entirely neglected by previous researchers. Having done so, they then set out to explain the between subject disagreement that had been part of the findings from the start.

In order to shed light on the interpretive diversity hypothesis, Nichols and Ulatowski asked participants to explain why they judged the CEO's actions to be either intentional or not intentional. In light of this simple methodological twist, an interesting pattern appeared. The minority of participants who judged that the CEO did not intentionally harm the environment were more focused on the CEO's desires and intentions than they were on the fact that he foresaw that adopting the program would harm the environment. Conversely, the most common explanations provided by the majority who deemed that the CEO did harm the environment intentionally focused on foresight rather than intention. The help case produced similar results. Whereas the minority of participants who judged that the CEO intentionally helped the environment appealed to the fact that CEO knowingly helped the environment, the majority claimed that the CEO did not intentionally help the environment because he neither intended nor desired to do so. In light of these results, Nichols and Ulatowski suggest that:

> "Intentional" gets interpreted differently in Harm and Help. We will not attempt to give precise characterizations of the two interpretations. But

> the lay explanations suggest that something like *foreknowledge* and *motive* are at the heart of the two different interpretations of "intentional." Henceforth we will refer to these two interpretations as "foreknowledge" and "motive," though of course that is a very rough approximation.
> (2007, 358)

On their view, the most parsimonious explanation of the interpretive diversity hypothesis is that there are two different concepts of intentionality—one that is based on foresight and one that is based on motive.

This multiple concepts hypothesis has subsequently been advanced by another pair of researchers who are broadly operating within the same interpretive diversity framework—namely, Fiery Cushman and Alfred Mele (2007; 2008). Picking up where Nichols and Ulatowski left off, Cushman and Mele further explored the intuitional asymmetry of the side effect findings. More specifically, they ran a series of interesting new studies aimed at identifying the criteria that participants rely on in arriving at intentionality judgments. In light of their results, Cushman and Mele were able to ferret out the following three rules that different participants seem to be relying on (2008, 182–3):

1. Rule B: An action is intentional if it is performed with belief.
2. Rule D: An action is intentional if it is performed with desire, given the necessary background conditions.
3. Rule MB: Belief is a sufficient condition only in cases of morally bad actions.

On Cushman and Mele's view, it is the fact that different participants use these competing rules that explain why some participants respond NN to the harm and help cases while others respond either YY or YN. Minimally, they believe that rule B and rule D suggest that there are at least two concepts of intentional action that get implicated by the participants in the side effect cases. However, Cushman and Mele are unsure what to make of rule MB. As they say:

> The responses of groups NN, YY, and YN may seem to be the product of three distinct concepts of intentional action—namely, one that makes desire a necessary condition of intentional action, one that makes belief a sufficient condition, and one that includes Rule MB. However, it may be that, in fact, there are just two concepts of intentional action at work and rule MB captures a qualitatively different effect of moral judgment. Now, one of us is less confident than the other about the nature of concepts and more willing not to stop at two folk concepts and go all the way to three (the third being a concept of intentional action that includes MB). Splitting the difference, we get two and half folk concepts.
> (Cushman & Mele 2008, 177)

By my lights, the work done by both Nichols and Ulatowski and Mele and Cushman has advanced the debate about the nature of folk ascriptions of intentionality. Minimally, they have collectively put pressure on the traditional philosophical project of providing an analysis of "the" folk concept of intentional action. After all, there is gathering evidence that there is not a monolithic concept of intentionality but rather several closely related but distinct concepts—some of which focus on cognitive considerations and others of which focus on conative or moral considerations. Of course, even if this is true, it is still an open question why some people use one concept whereas others use a different concept in assessing the same scenario.

In a series of novel papers, Adam Feltz and Edward Cokely have tried to shed light on precisely this issue (Cokely & Feltz 2009; Feltz & Cokely 2007). In their efforts to explain the interpretive diversity identified by both Nichols and Ulatowski and Mele and Cushman, Feltz and Cokely have approached the issue through the lens of the existing literature in psychology on individual differences. One of the issues they explore is whether differences in participants' personality traits might explain the interpretive diversity one finds in the results. More specifically, they suggest that the personality trait extraversion might have an important explanatory role to play. In order to test their hypothesis, Feltz and Cokely had participants complete a brief Big Five personality instrument before presenting them with Knobe's CEO vignettes. The results were as follows:

> Individuals low in extraversion often did not agree that the chairman intentionally harmed the environment while more extraverted participants showed firm agreement. Thus, we seem to have identified a personality trait that largely accounts for the judgment asymmetry.
>
> (Feltz & Cokely 2007, 20)

In light of their research, Feltz and Cokely follow both Nichols and Ulatowski and Mele and Cushman in claiming that there is not one folk concept but many. As they say:

> The observed judgment asymmetry appears to be multiply determined resulting from the interplay of judgment biases and individual differences. The influence of both general personality and specific conceptual individual differences demonstrates that there is not necessarily a homogenous "the folk" whose judgment can be assessed at the level of group means. In contrast, as different people have different goals, sensitivities, and experiences, their judgments and biases can be expected to vary in systematic, adaptive, and theoretically interesting ways.
>
> (Feltz and Cokely 2007, 23)

This is an important insight that helps set the stage for future research on the interpretive diversity model of intentionality. That being said, I now want to shift gears and examine what I take to be the most serious challenge to the gathering data on the side effect findings. After all, one could respond to these findings in one of two ways. On the one hand, one could take the findings at face value and simply try to provide an explanation for them. On the other hand, one could attempt instead to explain away the data by rejecting the experimental designs that have been used to generate them. As we are about to see, Steve Guglielmo and Bertram Malle have opted for this latter approach.

3.5.1.5 The forced dichotomy view:

In a pair of recent papers, Guglielmo and Malle set out to put pressure on Knobe's side effect findings and thereby vindicate the standard view of intentionality (n.d. A; n.d. B). But since discussing all of the data they marshal forward is beyond the scope of the present essay, I will simply focus on the two studies that I take to pose the greatest potential threat to the explanatory models we have discussed thus far. In the first study, Guglielmo and Malle presented participants with versions of Knobe's harm vignettes. However, unlike Knobe's earlier studies, which forced participants to make simple dichotomous intentionality judgments, Guglielmo and Malle provided participants with more answer choices in the hopes that this would yield greater insight into how they actually viewed the CEO's primary actions. Upon reading a version of Knobe's CEO harm vignette, participants were first once again forced to make a yes/no intentionality judgment. Having done so, they were then provided with multiple action descriptions to choose from and asked to select "the most accurate description of what the CEO did." The choices were as follows:

1. "The CEO willingly harmed the environment."
2. "The CEO knowingly harmed the environment."
3. "The CEO intentionally harmed the environment."
4. "The CEO purposely harmed the environment."

Unsurprisingly, 73 percent of the participants answered the dichotomous intentionality question in the affirmative—which is roughly what one would expect based on Knobe's earlier findings. Surprisingly, however, across all four conditions of the study, only 1 percent of the participants deemed that "intentionally harmed the environment" was the most accurate description of what the CEO did. By contrast, 82 percent selected "knowingly harmed the environment," and 14 percent selected "willingly harmed the environment." On the surface, these results put serious pressure on the side effect findings. After all, if the bi-directional model were correct, one would expect that the participants in these studies would find it most correct to say that the CEO "intentionally" or "purposely" harmed the environment. But contrary to this expectation, these were the two *least* popular options.

As Guglielmo and Malle point out, "this finding is particularly noteworthy because the same participants who first provided the forced-choice intentionality response afterwards picked a different label as the most accurate behavior description" (n.d. A). On their view, these results suggest that when participants "are freed from the forced dichotomous choice and have a chance to select a more subtle interpretation of the situation at hand," their answers no longer undermine the standard model of intentionality (n.d. A). In light of these findings, Guglielmo and Malle believe they have both undermined the bi-directional model while at the same time vindicating the aforementioned valence-neutral five-component model. By their lights, people do not normally conceptualize the CEO as having intentionally harmed the environment. Instead, when people are given the choice, they view his behavior as "the intentional action of adopting a profit-raising program while fully knowing (and not preventing) that it would harm the environment." But insofar as this is the case, the side effect findings begin to look like little more than artifacts of an impoverished experimental design. Indeed, the results of a follow up study appear to further undermine the purported evidence for the bi-directional model of intentionality.

In this second study, participants were once again presented with Knobe's CEO harm vignette. They were then told that "this situation has certain ambiguities and leaves some questions open. How can we best describe what the CEO did? Please pick the most accurate description . . . then pick the second-most accurate description" (n.d. A). The action descriptions available to participants this time around were as follows:

1. "The CEO intentionally harmed the environment."
2. "The CEO intentionally adopted an environment harming program."
3. "The CEO intentionally adopted an environment-harming program and a profit-raising program."
4. "The CEO intentionally adopted a profit-raising program that he knew would harm the environment."
5. "The CEO intentionally adopted a profit-raising program."

As Guglielmo and Malle once again correctly point out, if the bi-directional model of intentionality were correct, one would expect participants to select the first and second action descriptions as the most accurate. However, as was the case in the earlier study, only a minority of participants found these to be the "most accurate descriptions." In fact, the first two descriptions were selected as either the most or second most accurate by only 16 percent of the participants. Conversely, 83 percent of the participants deemed the fourth action description to be either the most or the second most accurate, while 20 percent selected the third description. In short, the results of this study provide evidence that "when people were asked to indicate which action the CEO performed intentionally, they showed striking agreement: He intentionally adopted a profit-raising program that he knew would harm the environment; he did not intentionally harm the environment" (n.d. A). Guglielmo and Malle believe these findings lay to rest the bi-directional model of intentionality favored by Knobe and others. On their view, participants in earlier studies only judged that the CEO harmed the environment intentionally because they were forced to give a dichotomous intentionality judgment. However, once participants are given more choices, their intuitions no longer seem to provide any evidence for the bi-directional model.

When viewed collectively, the results of Guglielmo and Malle's recent studies appear to pose a serious challenge to the side effect findings. However, things are arguably less straightforward than they have assumed. By my lights, more work needs to be done before they "disconfirm" the claim that moral considerations sometimes influence folk ascriptions of intentional action. Of course, determining whether I am right is an empirical affair. As such, I have recently run some studies to put my worries to the test (Nadelhoffer forthcoming). For present purposes, however, examining the results would take us too far afield. Given the breadth and sophistication of the challenge put forward by Guglielmo and Malle, it will take more than a handful of studies to lay all of their objections to rest. So, while I humbly believe that my follow-up studies establish that the side effect findings have not yet been fully explained away, it is nevertheless clear that Guglielmo and Malle have thrown down the gauntlet in defense of the standard model of intentionality. As such, any subsequent work on the folk concept(s) of intentional action must carefully take Guglielmo and Malle's insightful criticisms into account. I have admittedly only been able to scratch the surface of their important work in this paper. In the future, researchers working on experimental philosophy of action will hopefully give Guglielmo and Malle's recent multi-pronged attack on the side effect findings the full attention it deserves.

3.7 The future of experimental philosophy of action

At this point, I have now (a) tried to establish the relevance of folk intuitions to the philosophical project of exploring the nature of intentionality, (b) discussed the standard model of intentional action, (c) explored the challenges posed to this traditional model by the side effect findings, and (d) examined several of the key models that have been advanced thus far in the debate to explain the gathering data. As such, I hope that you now have a firm grasp of the recent historical roots of experimental philosophy of action. Unfortunately, I was only able to cover a small fraction of the views that have been advanced in the literature. Given space limitations, I focused on the views that have either had the biggest impact on the debate thus far or which I believe will shape the debate in the years ahead. But since I am also confident that future research in this area will also be influenced by several of the models and positions that I was lamentably unable to discuss along the way, I would be remiss if I did not at least provide a brief sketch of a few of the myriad views that have recently been put forward:

1. The Trade-Off View (Machery 2008): On this view, the side effect findings are not being driven by moral considerations at all. Instead, they are being driven by the fact that in the harm cases, the agent is making a trade off whereas in the help cases, the agent is not. According to Machery, this asymmetry can explain participants' asymmetrical intuitions without needing to appeal to the moral valence of the scenarios.[11]
2. The Modality View (Nanay 2010): Much like Machery's trade off hypothesis, Bence Nanay's view tries to explain the data without appealing to the moral valence of the actions (or side effects). By his lights, "the attribution of intentionality has little to do with morality, but a lot to do with modality: with what would have happened if the agent had not ignored some of her reasons" (Nanay 2010, 38).
3. The Responsibility View (Wright and Bengson 2009): Jen Wright and John Bengson try to explain the side effect findings in terms of two factors—namely, (a) "judgments of positive/negative responsibility are asymmetrical," and (b) "the intentionality of actions commonly connects the evaluative status of actions to the responsibility of actors, the latter of which alone typically implies intentionality" (2009, 25). Once again, we find a model that attempts to account for the side effect findings without appealing to moral judgments concerning badness or blame. Instead, the claim is that asymmetrical judgments of "positive/negative responsibility"—both moral and non-moral—are really doing all of the work.
4. The Motivating Reasons View (Hendriks 2009): According to Frank Hendriks, the side effect findings can be "explained in terms of the considerations which an agent takes or should take into account when thinking about what to do, that is, in terms of motivating and normative reasons" (2009, 631). On this view, participants ought to have asymmetrical intuitions in the praise and harm cases because there is a principled difference between the two—namely, "people need to be motivated appropriately in order to be praiseworthy, but not to be blameworthy" (2009, 632).[12]
5. The Deep Self View (Sripada 2009): Chandra Sripada adopts a Humean approach to the side effect findings whereby the asymmetrical intuitions are to be explained in terms of participants' judgments about the CEO's psychology. On this view, participants' ascriptions of intentional action are partly driven by what Sripada calls the Concordance Principle—that is, "an agent brings about an outcome intentionally or is responsible for bringing about an outcome only if that outcome is concordant with the agent's underlying Deep Self" (n.d.). In short, the side effect findings are ultimately explicable in terms of judgments about an agent's deep vs. her superficial self.
6. The Moral Mechanism Interference Model (Nado 2008): In her attempts to explain the side effect findings, Jennifer Nado develops a novel performance

error model. Rather than appealing to pragmatic implicatures or affective biases, Nado appeals to a "tacit moral mechanism" that "uses a variety of inputs, many from the theory of mind mechanism, in order to produce moral judgments—and the mechanism is sometimes capable of going back and overwriting those inputs after its judgment has been made" (Nado 2008, 714). In distinguishing her model from my own affect driven view, she points out that "the proposed moral mechanism is a *reasoning* system, employing a body of facts including theory of mind information, information about local norms, etc. Moral emotions, if they play any role in such moral reasoning, play a supporting role at best" (Nado 2008, 717).

These are just a few of the growing number of rival explanations of the side effect findings that researchers working on experimental philosophy of action must take into consideration.

Hopefully, as psychologists and philosophers continue to work together, they will find themselves moving toward a consensus view. In the meantime, there are several other avenues of potentially fruitful research that merit mention. For instance, some exciting work has already been done on the intentionality judgments of children (Leslie et al. 2006; Pellizoni et al. 2009) as well as people with autism (Zalla & Machery n.d.) and brain damage (Young et al. 2006). Hopefully, this trend will continue as we move forward. By probing the intuitions of people with a wide variety of developmental or cognitive differences, we should be able to shed new and interesting light on the nature of intentionality. Similarly, it would be very helpful if more cross-cultural studies were run. As it stands, Knobe has once again been a trail blazer on this front Knobe & Burra (2006a). I strongly encourage others to follow in his footsteps.

In addition to looking for both group and individual differences when it comes to intentionality judgments, researchers in experimental philosophy of action should also continue to explore and utilize new methodologies. From reaction time studies and mock jury simulations to neuroimaging studies that examine the neural correlates of ascriptions of intentional action, there are a number of potentially fruitful empirical avenues to pursue.[13] In light of these exciting possibilities, it is clear that at this point we have just begun to scratch the surface when it comes to unlocking the secrets surrounding how humans go about making complicated judgments about responsibility and agency. It is also clear that the future of experimental philosophy of action is an open sea—pregnant with the potential for further interdisciplinary research at the cross roads of psychology and philosophy. And while the winds are constantly shifting and the ultimate destination is still unclear, there are grounds for optimism that the researchers working in this exciting new field will continue to forge ahead in their attempts both to resolve long-standing philosophical puzzles about intentional action and to tear down the disciplinary boundaries that have traditionally impeded progress on this front.[14]

Notes

1. In this paper, when I use the term "intentionality" I am using it as shorthand for "intentional action." My usage is not to be confused with Brentano's notion of intentionality as the mind's "direction towards an object" (Brentano 1874) even if the two are admittedly related in some respects.
2. For an in-depth introduction to experimental philosophy, see Nadelhoffer & Nahmias (2007) and Knobe & Nichols (2008).
3. See, for example, Malle & Knobe (1997); Mele (1992); Mele & Moser (1994); and Mele & Sverdlik (1996).
4. Two points of clarification are in order at this point. First, just because someone claims that data concerning folk intuitions are relevant to *some* philosophical debates, it does not follow that she is committed to the view that these data are relevant to *all* philosophical debates. Second, just because someone claims that folk intuitions are *relevant* to some philosophical problems, it does not follow she believes they *solve* these problems. To my knowledge, no experimental philosopher tries to move from "the folk think that *x* is the case" to "*x* is the case." Instead, to the extent that the folk intuitions are philosophically relevant, they serve as starting points and constraints to philosophical investigation and not final arbiters of philosophical truth.
5. It is worth pointing out that experimental philosophy is not a homogenous field. While experimental philosophers do admittedly share a methodological commitment to using controlled and systematic studies to shed light on philosophical problems, both the focus and the purpose of these studies widely vary. See Nadelhoffer & Nahmias (2007) for a taxonomy of the different branches of experimental philosophy.
6. See, for example, Adams & Steadman (2004a); (2004b); Cokely & Feltz (2009); Cushman & Mele (2007); (2008); Feltz & Cokely (2007); Guglielmo & Malle (n.d.); Hindriks (2008); Knobe (2003a); (2003b); (2004a); (2004b); (2005a); (2005b); (2006); Knobe & Burra (2006a); (2006b); Knobe & Mendlow (2004); Lanteri (2009); Leslie et al. (2006); Machery (2008); Malle (2001); (2006); Malle & Knobe (1997); Mallon (2008); McCann (2005); Meeks (2004); Nadelhoffer (2004a); (2004b); (2004c); (2005); (2006a); (2006b); (2006c); (forthcoming); Nado (2008); Nanay (2010); Nichols & Ulatowski (2007); Pellizoni et al. (2009); Phelan & Sarkissian (2008); (2009); Sripada (2009); Turner (2004); Wiland (2007); Wright and Bengson (2009); Young et al. (2006).
7. For instance, by purportedly identifying all of the necessary components of the folk concept of intentional action, Malle and Knobe's model not only integrates a number of the past analyses of intentional action that have been put forward by both psychologists and philosophers, but it also reveals precisely where these previous analyses went wrong.
8. According to proponents of valence neutral models, a proper analysis of the concept of intentional action won't have any moral components—that is, whether an agent *x-ed* intentionally won't depend on the moral status of *x*. See, for example, Malle & Knobe (1997); Mele (1992); Mele & Moser (1994); and Mele & Sverdlik (1996).
9. For more on the simple view, see Adams (1986); Bratman (1984); (1987); and McCann (1998).
10. See the aforementioned discussion by Machery of the "competence problem" for a criticism of my Performance Error Hypothesis.

11. For criticisms of Machery's view, see Mallon (2008) and Phelan and Sarkissian (2009).
12. For a response to Hendriks' view, see Lanteri (forthcoming).
13. For instance, Guglielmo and Malle have recently run some studies that collect data on participants' reaction times. By my lights, more of this kind of research is called for if we are ever to develop a complete understanding of the nature of intentionality. Relatedly, I am presently working on a series of studies with Owen Jones, Joshua Greene, and others that explore folk intuitions concerning the differences between the legal *mens rea* concepts *purposely, knowingly, recklessly*, and *negligently*. Depending on the results of our pilot studies, we will be using fMRI downstream in an effort to shed more light on the neural underpinnings of our folk psychological judgments.
14. I would like to thank Ron Mallon and Keith Frankish for very helpful comments on an earlier draft of this paper. I would also like to thank the MacArthur Foundation for funding my research this year as part of the MacArthur Law and Neuroscience Project.

References

Adams, F. (1986), "Intention and Intentional Action: The Simple View," *Mind & Language*, 1, 281–301.

Adams, F. and Steadman, A. (2004a), "Intentional Action in Ordinary Language: Core Concept or Pragmatic Understanding," *Analysis* 74, 173–81.

———. (2004b), "Intentional Actions and Moral Considerations: Still Pragmatic," *Analysis* 74, 264–7.

Alicke, M. D. (2000), "Culpable Control and the Psychology of Blame." *Psychological Bulletin*, vol. 126, no. 4: 556–74.

Bargh, J. A. and Chartrand, T. L. (1999), "The Unbearable Automaticity of Being." *American Psychologist*, 54: 462–79.

Bratman. M. (1984), "Two Faces of Intention," *Philosophical Review*, 93, 375–405.

———. (1987), *Intention, Plans, and Practical Reason*. Cambridge, MA: Harvard University Press.

Brentano, F. (1874), *Psychologie vom empirischen Standpunkt*, Leipzig: Duncke & Humblot.

Butler, R. (1978), "Report on *Analysis* 'Problem' no. 6," *Analysis* 38: 113–14.

Cokely, E. and Feltz, A. (2009), "Individual Differences, Judgment Biases, and Theory-of-Mind: Deconstructing the Intentional Action Side Effect Asymmetry," *Journal of Research in Personality*, 43, 18–24.

Cushman, F. and Mele, A. R. (2007), "Intentional Action, Folk Judgments, and Stories: Sorting Things Out," *Midwest Studies in Philosophy* 31, 184–201.

———. (2008), "Intentional Action: Two-and-a-Half Folk Concepts?" In J. Knobe and S. Nichols (eds), *Experimental Philosophy*. New York: Oxford University Press.

Duff, R. A. (1982), "Intention, Responsibility, and Double Effect." *The Philosophical Quarterly*, vol. 32, no. 126: 1–16.

———. (1990), *Intention, Agency, and Criminal Liability*. Oxford: Basil Blackwell.

Feltz, A. and Cokely, E. (2007), "An Anomaly in Intentional Action Ascription: More Evidence of Folk Diversity." *Proceedings of the Cognitive Science Society*.

Fiske, S. T. (1989), "Examining the Role of Intent: Toward Understanding its Role in Stereotyping and Prejudice." In J. S. Uleman, J. S., and J. A. Bargh (eds), *Unintended Thought: Limits of Awareness, Intention, and Control*. New York: Guilford Press, 253–83.

Fleming, J. H. and J. M. Darley. (1989), "Perceiving Choice and Constraint: The Effects of Contextual and Behavioral Cues on Attitude Attribution," *Journal of Personality and Social Psychology*, 56: 27–40.
Greene, J. and J. Haidt. (2002), "How (and Where) Does Moral Judgment Work?" *Trends in Cognitive Science*, 6: 517–23.
Guglielmo, S. and Malle, B. F. (n.d. A.), "Can Unintended Side Effects Be Intentional? Solving a Puzzle in People's Judgments of Intentionality and Morality."
———. (n.d. B.), "Enough Skill to Kill: Intentional Control and the Judgment of Immoral Actions." University of Oregon.
Harman, G. (1976), "Practical Reasoning." *Review of Metaphysics* 79: 431–63.
Heider, F. (1958), *The Psychology of Interpersonal Relations*. New York: Wiley.
Hindriks, F. (2008), "Intentional Action and the Praise-Blame Asymmetry," *The Philosophical Quarterly*, 58, 630–41.
Holmes, O. W., Jr. 1963. *The Common Law*. Boston: Little, Brown
Katz, L. (1987), *Bad Acts and Guilty Minds*. Chicago: University of Chicago Press.
Jackson, F. (1998), *From Metaphysics to Ethics: A Defense of Conceptual Analysis*. Oxford University Press.
Jones, E. E. and K. E. Davis. (1965), "From Acts to Dispositions: The Attribution Process in Person Perception." In L. Berkowitz (ed.), *Advances in Experimental Social Psychology*. Hillsdale, NJ: Erlbaum, 371–88.
Knobe, J. (2003a), "Intentional Action and Side-Effects in Ordinary Language," *Analysis*, 63, 190–3.
———. (2003b), "Intentional Action in Folk Psychology: An Experimental Investigation," *Philosophical Psychology*, 16(2), 309–23.
———. (2004a), "Folk Psychology and Folk Morality: Response to Critics," *Journal of Theoretical and Philosophical Psychology*, 24(2), 270–9.
———. (2004b), "Intention, Intentional Action and Moral Considerations." *Analysis*, 64, 181–7.
———. (2005a), "Theory of Mind and Moral Cognition: Exploring the Connections," *Trends in Cognitive Sciences* 9, 357–9.
———. (2005b), "Cognitive Processes Shaped by the Impulse to Blame," *Brooklyn Law Review*, 71, 929–37.
———. (2006), "The Concept of Intentional Action: A Case Study in the Uses of Folk Psychology," *Philosophical Studies*. 130: 203–31.
Knobe, J. and Burra, A. (2006a), "The Folk Concept of Intention and Intentional Action: A Cross-Cultural Study," *Journal of Cognition and Culture*, 6(1–2), 113–32.
———. (2006b), "Experimental Philosophy and Folk Concepts: Methodological Considerations," *Journal of Cognition and Culture*, 6(1–2), 331–42.
Knobe, J. and Mendlow, G. (2004), "The Good, the Bad, and the Blameworthy: Understanding the Role of Evaluative Reasoning in Folk Psychology," *The Journal of Theoretical and Philosophical Psychology* 24.
Knobe, J. and Nichols, S. (2008), "An Experimental Philosophy Manifesto." In Knobe, J. and Nichols, S. (ed.), *Experimental Philosophy*. New York: Oxford University Press, 3–14.
Lanteri, A. (2009), "Judgments of Intentionality and Moral Worth: Experimental Challenges to Hindriks," *Philosophical Quarterly*, 59, 713–20.
Leslie, A., Knobe, J., and Cohen, A. (2006), "Acting Intentionally and the Side-Effect Effect: 'Theory of Mind' and Moral Judgment," *Psychological Science*, 17, 421–7.
Machery, E. (2008), "The Folk Concept of Intentional Action: Philosophical and Experimental Issues," *Mind & Language*, 23, 165–89.

Malle, B. (2001), "Folk Explanations and Intentional Action." In L. Moses B. Malle, & D. Baldwin (Ed. *Intentions and Intentionality: Foundations of Social Cognition* (265–86), Cambridge: MIT Press.

———. (2006), "Intentionality, Morality, and their Relationship in Human Judgment," *Journal of Cognition and Culture*, 6(1–2), 87–112.

Malle, B. and Knobe, J. (1997), "The Folk Concept of Intentional Action." *Journal of Experimental Social Psychology*, 33, 101–21.

Mallon, R. (2008), "Knobe vs. Machery: Testing the Trade-Off Hypothesis," *Mind and Language*, 23(2), 247–55.

McCann, H. (1998), *The Works of Agency: On Human Action, Will and Freedom*. Cornell: Cornell University Press.

———. (2005), "Intentional Action and Intending: Recent Empirical Studies," *Philosophical Psychology*, 18, 737–48.

Meeks, R. (2004), "Unintentionally Biasing the Data: Reply to Knobe," *Journal of Theoretical and Philosophical Psychology*, 24, 220–3.

Mele, A. R. (1992), *Springs of Action: Understanding Intentional Behavior*. New York: Oxford University Press.

———. (2001), "Acting Intentionally: Probing Folk Notions." In B. F. Malle, L. J. Moses, and D. A. Baldwin (eds), *Intentions and Intentionality: Foundations of Social Cognition* (27–43), Cambridge, MA: MIT Press.

Mele, A. R. and Moser, P. K. (1994), "Intentional Action." *Noûs*, 28, 39–68.

Mele, A. R. and Sverdlik, S. (1996), "Intention, Intentional Action, and Moral Responsibility." *Philosophical Studies*, 82, 265–87.

Nadelhoffer, T. (2004a), "The Butler Problem Revisited," *Analysis* 64(3), 277–84.

———. (2004b), "Praise, Side Effects, and Intentional Action," *The Journal of Theoretical and Philosophical Psychology* 24, 196–213.

———. (2004c), "Blame, Badness, and Intentional Action: A Reply to Knobe and Mendlow," *The Journal of Theoretical and Philosophical Psychology* 24, 259–69.

———. (2005), "Skill, Luck, Control, and Intentional Action," *Philosophical Psychology* 18(3), 343–54.

———. (2006a), "Bad Acts, Blameworthy Agents, and Intentional Actions: Some Problems for Jury Impartiality," *Philosophical Explorations* 9(2), 203–20.

———. (2006b), "Foresight, Moral Considerations, and Intentional Actions," *The Journal of Cognition and Culture*, 6(1), 133–58.

———. (2006c), "On Trying to Save the Simple View," *Mind & Language* 21:5, 565–86.

———. (2010), "The Causal Theory of Action and the Still Puzzling Knobe Effect." In A. Buckareff (ed.), *The Causal Theory of Action*, MIT University Press, 277–95.

Nadelhoffer, T. and Nahmias, E. (2007), "The Past and Future of Experimental Philosophy." *Philosophical Explorations*, 10(2), 123–49.

Nado, J. (2008), "Effects of Moral Cognition on Judgments of Intentionality," *British Journal for the Philosophy of Science*, 59, 709–31.

Nanay, B. (2010), "Morality or Modality? What Does the Attribution of Intentionality Depend On?" *Canadian Journal of Philosophy*, 40, 28–40.

Nichols, S. and Ulatowski, J. (2007), "Intuitions and Individual Differences: The Knobe Effect Revisited," *Mind & Language*, 22(4), 346–65.

Ossorio, P. G. and K. E. Davis. (1968), "The Self, Intentionality, and Reactions to Evaluations of the Self." In C. Gordon and K. J. Gergen (eds). *The Self in Social Interaction*. New York: Wiley.

Pellizoni, S., Siegal, M., and Surian, L. (2009), "Foreknowledge, Caring and the Side-Effect Effect in Young Children," *Developmental Psychology*, 45: 289–95.

Phelan, M. and Sarkissian, H. (2008), "The Folk Strike Back: Or, Why You Didn't Do it Intentionally, Though it Was Bad and You Knew it," *Philosophical Studies*, 138(2), 291–8.

———. (2009), "Is the 'Trade-Off Hypothesis' Worth Trading For?" *Mind and Language*, 24, 164–80.

Shaver, K. G. (1985), *The Attribution of Blame*. New York: Springer-Verlag.

Sripada, C. (2009), "The 'Deep Self' Model and Asymmetries in Folk Judgments about Intentionality and Responsibility," *Philosophical Studies*.

Turner, J. (2004), "Folk Intuitions, Asymmetry, and Intentional Side Effects," *Journal of Theoretical and Philosophical Psychology*, 24, 214–19.

Wiland, E. (2007), "Intentional Action and 'In Order To'," *Journal of Theoretical and Philosophical Psychology*. 27, 113–18.

Wright, J. and Bengson, J. (2009), "Asymmetries in Folk Judgments of Responsibility and Intentional Action," *Mind & Language*, 24:1, 24–50.

Young, L., Cushman, F., Adolphs, R., Tranel, D., and Hauser, M. (2006), "Does Emotion Mediate the Relationship between an Action's Moral Status and its Intentional Status? Neuropsychological Evidence," *Journal of Cognition and Culture*, 6(1–2), 291–304.

Zalla, T. and Machery, E. (n.d.), "The Concept of Intentional Action in Asperger Syndrome."

Part II
Autonomy

4
Identification, Psychology, and Habits

Bill Pollard

4.1 Identification

In his 1971 paper "Freedom of the Will and the Concept of a Person" Harry Frankfurt raises a question about the nature of identification. In his pursuit of an account of free action, Frankfurt notices that the motives that may or may not lead us to act fall into two importantly distinct categories. On the one hand there are motives which are somehow alien, or external, to an agent. Examples given include the craving of the unwilling addict, the "jealously spiteful desire to injure" an acquaintance, and an overwhelming "spasm of emotion."[1] On the other hand, there are motives which are not alien, but are internal to agency, which is to say that the agent is, in some sense, "identified" with them.[2] For Frankfurt, these are the motives that are associated with free action. The question is how we should distinguish motives of the first sort from motives of the second. An account of identification will answer this question.

Talk of 'motives' here should not be over-interpreted. The assumption is that every action is preceded by a motive, but not all motives lead to action. Beyond that there need be no ontological commitment to what a motive is. It is not necessary, for instance, that a motive be felt, so one should not be tempted to think that the debate can be resolved by pointing to a characteristic feeling that might accompany external motives—a feeling of alienation perhaps—which is absent from the internal ones.[3] And in deference to current debates about the nature of reasons, motives might be conceived as psychological states like beliefs, desires, or combinations of these, or conceived externally as states of the world within the agent's purview.[4] And we can be similarly neutral about the relations which might be said to hold between motives and actions.[5]

There is a lot at stake. In a more recent paper Frankfurt claims that this notion of identification "is fundamental to any philosophy of mind and action" (1991, p. 103). And David Velleman claims that without an account of identification we can only have an account of "what happens when someone acts halfheartedly, or unwittingly," and not an account of what happens in what he calls "human action *par excellence*" (1992, p. 124). The thought seems to be that if we don't have an account of identification we don't have an account of how agents are genuinely the authors of what they do, since for all we know, they might be acting from external motives.

But I don't think any of the accounts of identification that have been put forward are adequate to capture the idea.[6] These accounts wrongly assume that the internality of a motive is to be understood solely in terms of the motive's relation to elements in the agent's psychological make-up. These might be psychological states of a certain sort, such as higher-order desires, or sets of beliefs and desires. Or they may be psychological performances, such as decisions or judgments, made by the agent. Either way, I think these accounts, which I call "psychological accounts", are open to serious objections. Or so I shall argue.

My proposal is that the idea of identification can, at least on some occasions, be understood without reference to the agent's psychology at all. For I think that reference to the familiar patterns of behavior known as the agent's habits can be sufficient to determine whether a particular motive is internal. Specifically, I shall argue that *for an agent to identify with a motive, it is sufficient for that motive to express one of her habits*. If this is right, and habits are non-psychological, it follows that psychology is not necessary for identification, and psychological accounts of identification fail.

I don't mean to be marking out the psychological in a controversial way here. I am content with a characterization which maintains that psychological phenomena—beliefs, desires, decisions, and the like – are those which exhibit an epistemic asymmetry between the first-person on the one hand, and the second- and third-person on the other, when this asymmetry favors the first-person. In other words, I have a privileged perspective on my psychology compared with any of you. This broad characterization leaves open whether a given psychological item is conscious or non-conscious, propositional or non-propositional, as well as whether one could be mistaken about it.[7]

By this standard, habits are not psychological. This becomes clear if we understand habits as, roughly, patterns of repeated, automatic behavior.[8] Being behavioral, then, habits do not exhibit the asymmetry characteristic of psychological phenomena. Indeed, if anything, we might say that habits exhibit the opposite asymmetry, in which the second-person perspective, of those that know us well, has a privilege over the first. It is a sometimes disturbing fact that your partner often knows your habits better than you do yourself—especially the irritating ones.

In §4.2 I survey psychological accounts of identification, and I raise some quite general concerns about the adequacy of such accounts. In §4.3 I give my definition of habit and locate it in contemporary philosophy of action. In §4.4 I explicate the relation between agency and habits. In §4.5 I consider and answer an objection raised by "external habits." And I finish in §4.6 with some brief remarks on the implications for agency.

4.2 Psychological accounts

The classic psychological account is that given by Frankfurt himself in the 1971 paper that started all the fuss. Frankfurt proposes that what distinguishes the internal motives from the external ones is the possession or absence of a "second-order volition". Such a volition is a second-order desire with a special content, namely, that a first-order desire (or motive) be her "will." As Frankfurt puts it, when the agent has a second-order volition she "identifies [her]self *decisively* with one of [her] first-order desires" (p. 21, original italics).

The crucial feature that Frankfurt hopes to have discerned in these second-order volitions is that they themselves are necessarily internal to agency. But as Gary Watson first pointed out, we can also question the internality of second-order volitions:

> the notion of orders of desires or volitions ... does not tell us why or how a particular want can have, among all of a person's "desires," the special property of being peculiarly his "own."
>
> (Watson 1975, 218–9)

In other words, if we can raise the question about the internality of a first order desire, we ought to be able to raise it about a higher order desire. Unless we have some non-question-begging way of stopping the threatening regress, the account must fail. In a later paper Frankfurt (1987) takes this challenge seriously and offers an alternative.

All this is standard fare. For my purposes what is important about this failed account is that first, the account is psychological, since identification relies on nothing more than relations to other items in the agent's psychology; and that second, the relation to psychology is supposed to be a necessary condition. After all, if it were not supposed to be necessary, there would be no inevitable regress, because there would at least be logical space for an alternative sufficient condition.

Since Frankfurt's paper, there have been many more attempts to stop the regress. A popular option is to appeal not to a single psychological state, but to a larger set of them, which is supposed to be somehow less susceptible to externality. Watson (1975), for instance, proposes an account of identification based on the idea of the agent's "evaluational system" consisting of the agent's "ends and principles" (p. 216). However, Watson later rejects this view on the basis of it's susceptibility to a set of counterexamples which he calls "perverse cases":

> When it comes right down to it, I might fully "embrace" a course of action I do not judge best; it may not be thought best, but is fun or thrilling; one loves doing it, and it's too bad it's not also the best thing

> to do, but one goes in for it without compunction. ... one needn't see it as expressing or even conforming to a general standpoint one would be prepared to defend.
>
> (1987, p. 150)

Watson takes perverse cases to demonstrate that one can have an internal motive to do something other than what one's evaluational system recommends, and as a result, he abandons this account of identification. I think Watson is right to do so. Again we see that the account is psychological (one must have a grasp of one's ends and principles to defend them), and the relation to psychology must be a necessary condition for the counterexample to work at all.

Appeals to other sets of psychological states can be found in the literature. In his most recent contribution to the topic, Frankfurt proposes that "identification is constituted ... by an endorsing higher-order desire with which the person is satisfied" (1992, p. 105), and satisfaction is in turn to be understood in terms of the agent's "understanding and evaluation of how things are with him" (p. 105). Nomy Arpaly and Timothy Schroeder (1999a) propose that internal motives must be more or less "well-integrated" into the rest of the agent's psychology. And David Shoemaker (2003) has suggested that it is the agent's "nexus of cares" which cannot be dissociated from who she is.

I take it that all of these accounts posit psychology as necessary for identification, and they are accordingly going to fall prey to broadly the same sort of counterexample as Watson's account. Put very simply, the problem is that if we can question the internality of the original motive, we should be able to do the same for each of the psychological items which together are supposed to be necessarily internal. Whatever relation or relations might be supposed to hold between the motive and these items, or between the items themselves, it seems highly implausible that internality will consist in relations to items whose internality is in question.

To illustrate this in the case of Frankfurt's (1992) theory, an agent might be satisfied with a certain second-order desire, but it might still be the case that the psychological states that jointly constitute her being in a state of satisfaction are external to her. Certainly no desire is in any better shape regarding its internality than the first order motive itself. And since beliefs can be deluded, wishful, or in other ways questionably connected to the agent, and perhaps en-masse, we won't find guarantees of internality there either. So we have no reason to think that any given set of states is internal to agency.

So, for example, I might be satisfied with my desire to have a motive to give to charity, which is to say that I have all the right thoughts and feelings about it (or at least lack the negative thoughts and feelings, to be totally fair to Frankfurt). But there is still room for doubt about whether these thoughts and feelings (or their absences) are really me. And the doubt is I think well illustrated if we learn that it is also the case that I have never actually given to charity before and I never will again. This gives us a strong intuition that this motive, however laudable it might be, is not really "me," no matter how much I may think it is.

Or again, in Arpaly and Schroeder's terms, a motive might be very well integrated into my overall psychology, but it's my overall psychology that is out of kilter with the agent I really am.[9] And the same could be said of Shoemaker's nexus of cares. The best my psychology can guarantee is that it represents the agent I think I am, and if we follow through on the hypothesized doubt about internality, that can fall short of the agent I really am.

For completeness I should also mention another sort of account in the literature which is still psychological, but does not on the face of it depend on the motive's relation to psychological states, but instead on its relation to a psychological performance; specifically, a decision with a certain sort of content. This has been suggested by Frankfurt (1976, 1987) and more recently endorsed by Michael Bratman (1996). The idea is that decisions about motives are immune to externality. After all, who else but the agent makes decisions? But it doesn't take too much thought to see that this won't work. There is David Velleman's (1992) example of the unwitting decision to use insults to sever a friendship, following which, Velleman thinks, it is true to say "it was my resentment speaking, not I" (p. 127). If this is right, we can legitimately question the internality of decisions.[10] Even if you don't share Velleman's intuition (which I don't), there is another route which does not rely on it. The argument is that insofar as a decision is an action (and what else can it be if it is necessarily internal to agency?), then we should be able to inquire about the motive for that action, and we are once again in a position to question that motive's internality. Whichever way we go, without an alternative sufficient condition for identification, we have a vicious regress.[11]

By way of diagnosis I think that what may be at work in all of the accounts of identification on offer is a contemporary version of that time-honored Cartesian myth: that psychology exhausts the self. Why else would all accounts of identification make psychology necessary? But if that assumption was ever justified, it seems particularly out of place in this debate. In a context in which we are trying to understand agency, whose paradigm expression is overt action, then surely there are other resources we can appeal to which are both familiar and non-psychological. Resources which, perhaps together with psychology, combine to make up a necessarily practical, as opposed to a merely thinking, self. And I think habits provide some of these resources.

4.3 Habits

Habits have had some bad press in analytic philosophy. This is not only due to a prevailing intellectualism about what can count as an action in the first place, but also due to misunderstandings of what habits are. Among other things, acceptance of the position on offer will depend on our being free from such prejudicial preconceptions.

The intellectualism regarding actions, which has perhaps surprisingly taken hold largely independently of the issue of identification, has it that to make the distinction between action or what we do on the one hand, and mere behavior or what happens to us on the other, we must appeal to states or operations of the agent's intellect. These might be reasons, perhaps understood as suitably related beliefs and desires (Davidson 1980; Smith 1987), or states of the world (Collins 1997, Dancy 2000); intentions, where these aren't reducible to reasons (Bratman 1988); or acts of will of some sort (Ginet 1990; O' Shaughnessy 1973).

The problem here is that if we simply assume the correctness of a conception of action which need only draw on psychology, there will seem to be no interesting place for non-psychological *explanantia*. Insofar as habits are explanatory of actions at all, they would not be needed for understanding activity itself. I think these intellectualist accounts of activity are at best only partially right. But I won't argue for that controversial view here, nor indeed assume it.[12] The important thing here is to note that understanding the active-passive distinction and understanding the internal-external distinction are different tasks. So even if the former distinction could be made without reference to habits, we shouldn't assume the same for the latter.

Another set of prejudices concerns our conception of habit itself, and regards habits as little more than reflexes, or bodily processes of some sort, and as a result, they have as little to do with agency as these classes of behavior. Of course conceiving habits as physiological was part of their attraction for the likes of Skinner and Watson and their doomed version of behaviorism. And perhaps unsurprisingly philosophers were keen to distance themselves from any such reductive conception of agency. So we find Ryle (1949) arguing that habits cannot be the right sorts of items to exorcize the Cartesian ghost, and Winch (1958) rejecting the view that habitual behavior could be meaningful. Little more has been said in habits' defense since, at least by analytic philosophers.[13]

But I suggest that the problem is not with the concept of habit, but with the particular conception of habits against which there is an understandable reaction. Other less prejudicial notions are available, which bear a closer resemblance to our everyday conception, and allow us to see habits, and agency itself, in a new light. In particular, I believe that the right conception of habit can provide non-psychological materials for a sufficient condition for identification. What then is this conception?

As I shall understand it, a habit is *a pattern of repeated behavior which has become automatic for an agent as a result of that repetition, and over which she has intervention control*. A habitual action is an *automatic manifestation of a habit*. Some of this will be familiar enough; some of it needs elucidation.

I take it nobody will question the requirement that for a behavior to count as a habit it must have been repeated in the past, and probably more than once. I take this to be a conceptual truth about habit. If you haven't done it before, it's not your habit. And this is one of the ways in which habits differ from the sorts of dispositions that often occupy philosophical attention, such as fragility or elasticity, which can be correctly ascribed independently of the bearer's history.

Stipulating that habits are automatic captures our intuition that when we have a habit of doing something, we do whatever it is without thinking. Automaticity consists in at least the following two features. Most obviously, an automatic behavior lacks preceding thought, or at least any thought of which the agent is immediately aware, with the action in question as its content. On the face of it, when one has a habit of doing something, one doesn't think about whether to do it, or why; one just does it. This is illustrated when one finds oneself acting habitually, independently of what one might be thinking at the time, though one may of course reflect upon why one did it afterwards.

The second aspect of automaticity is perhaps best characterized as a certain sort of bodily proficiency with the sort of behavior in question. We find ourselves able to perform that kind of behavior more easily, and this is not just explained by the lack of thought. Every musician and sportsperson recognizes this not least because they have cultivated habits in order to achieve this proficiency. But everybody has such proficiency in less exotic activity. One's behavior is in a certain sort of harmony with one's environment or equipment, there is a smoothness and immediacy to one's movements which would simply be impossible were it not for the prior repetition. This proficiency in acquired habits is revealed when we force ourselves to think about some behavior we normally do habitually when we do it, and the proficiency disappears, as when one thinks about the movements involved in walking and one moves mechanically or stumbles.

So if a kind of behavior has become both possible without conscious thought, and also proficient, it is automatic in the sense that could qualify it as habitual. Not only does this capture a familiar feature of habits, but it also serves to mark them out from behaviors which are merely repeated by co-incidence, like walking across the same point on the kitchen floor once a day.

We also have the materials for distinguishing habits from other phenomena which might easily be confused with them. Here we see the significance of that aspect of the definition which states that the automaticity of habits results from prior repetition. Instincts, addictions, phobias and compulsions, then, might all have been repeatedly manifested, and might all be manifested automatically, but the automaticity did not result from the repetition. For example, the automaticity of an instinctive behavior could be explained by referring simply to innate capacities; an addictive behavior could make reference only to the agent's relation to a particular substance to explain the automaticity, and so on. But with habits, repetition is essential to explaining the automaticity, since the automaticity of habits results from the repetition. And that allows us to distinguish habits from these other sorts of repeated, automatic behaviors.

Intervention control is the other term of art in the definition of habit. This is the familiar idea that when we act habitually we are always able to stop ourselves from doing it, either before we do it, or while we are doing it, and do something else or nothing at all. This ability will sometimes be very important, as when exercising a habit would get us into trouble of some sort, perhaps because we are in an unusual situation. But we can also opt out of a habitual action for any reason, however whimsical, or for no reason at all.

One might be concerned here about the internality of the motives to intervene. If interventions must arise from internal motives, and those motives must themselves be associated with habits, don't we have another kind of vicious regress threatening? The answer is no. After all, I am not offering a necessary condition for identification, only a sufficient one. So I can allow that there may be other sources of internal motives which are not underwritten by habits, and such motives might be operative in the interventions.

The idea of intervention control provides another way of distinguishing habits from other often assimilated behavior types. Most obviously we don't enjoy intervention control over reflexes or bodily processes. A reflex such as a leg extension can't be stopped unless by tensing the muscles, or physically restraining it. Harder cases are reflexes like eye blinks over which we have intervention control for at least short periods of time, but not for too long (as demonstrated in the child's game). Turning to bodily processes, one has no control over one's digestion, say, except by eating more or less. Slightly trickier are processes like breathing or the heartbeat, over which we have some control. But while we might be able to control the way we breathe, or even the rate of the heartbeat, we can't control whether we breathe or whether our heart beats. Such cases show why it's right to say that insofar as we have intervention control over a putative repeated behavior type, it is a habit (assuming the other parts of the definition are met), and insofar as we lack it, it is not.

The idea of intervention control also allows us to distinguish habits from more subtly distinct behavior types like addictions or phobias, which might be said to have a hold over us. For we can find ourselves indulging these sorts of behaviors despite decisions to the contrary. The will alone is simply not enough to stop us taking the drug, or fleeing from the spider. In a very real sense then we are victims of these conditions, as they are appropriately termed, rather than willing participants. But this is not the case with habits which can always be interrupted on a whim.

That's not to say that habits aren't hard to break. They typically are. But that's not because it's impossible to intervene; but because it's hard to pay sufficient attention to intervene on every occasion in such a way that the behavior type ceases to be automatic, though of course there are never guarantees that it will.

Including the idea of intervention control in the definition of habit provides us with one route to explaining how exercises of habits can be actions. For we are responsible for those behaviors over which we have intervention control, and there is at least an intuitive sense in which we can say that actions are those behaviors for which we are responsible.[14] For it is always true to say we could have done otherwise.[15] This intuition is enough to license, at least provisionally, the terminology which says that exercises of habits are habitual *actions*.

But we are unlikely to be convinced that these exercises of habits are full-blown actions unless we can make some sense of how their performance originates in the agent herself. For I have so far said nothing about the source of habitual actions, and surely the mere absence of intervention by an agent is insufficient for a piece of behavior to be attributed to that agent, in the sense that she is it's author. When there is no intervention, that is, in the normal case, where does the agent come in?

A working assumption of this paper is that every action is preceded by a motive, so we should allow for present purposes that this assumption applies to habitual actions too, notwithstanding the fact that such motives are never conscious. But even if we make this allowance, we won't of course find the agent in the motive, or not at least until we have an account of identification. So are we stuck? I don't think so.

For what I want to suggest is that elsewhere in the notion of habit I have proposed are the materials we need to say that we have enough for identification already in the very idea that the motive expresses (or equivalently, typically issues in an action which exemplifies) one of the agent's habits.

4.4 The agent and her habits

The claim of this paper is that if an agent has a habit of Φ-ing and a motive to Φ, that motive is necessarily internal. Very simply this is because a habit partly constitutes the agent who has that habit. This associated claim about agency is that to be the agent that one is, is at least to have all of the habits one has.

The idea that we are our habits is not a new one. William James suggested that we are "bundles of habits" (1890, p. 104), and John Dewey wrote that "[a]ll habits ... constitute the self" (1922, p. 25). And a number of continental thinkers have also identified the self with habits.[16]

My claim is less radical. I don't claim that an agent is nothing but her habits. All I claim is that an agent's habits partly constitute her. So there may be more to the agent than her habits. I do not want to deny, for instance, that at least some non-habitual behaviors can be attributed to the agent. There may be, for instance, a strong case for thinking that important life choices of the sort that interested Sartre, are attributable to the agent, even though they are only made once. And contemporary philosophy of action characteristically privileges behaviors which issue from the agent's thought, and certainly when that thought is conscious we intuitively attribute it to the agent (though we may lack an account of this). Both sorts of case presuppose notions of agency which are non-habitual. There may well be other constituents to agents besides.

Indeed, for the purposes of the present argument it is helpful that habits do not exhaust agency. After all, my notion of intervention control depends upon the possibility that the intervener is the agent herself. And it would be implausible to insist that any interventions must themselves be habitual. Typically conscious thought of some sort will play a role in the interruption. One might, for example, notice things are different from normal, or make the decision to do something different this time. So it would be unhelpfully dogmatic to deny the agent is manifest in such optings-out.

The main question, however, is why should we think habits constitute the agent, even partially?

One answer that I often hear is that the agent intentionally acquires her habits. After all, we often do intentionally cultivate habits that will help us in our daily lives. Many of us have cultivated habits of taking exercise, eating at the same time every day, routines of getting up and going to bed, as well as the habits associated with skills such as playing the guitar, sculling or speaking another language. The tempting thought here is that what makes habits part of the agent is that the agent had a role in acquiring the habit, namely, at some point in the past she decided to acquire it. Of course practice was also necessary, but practice follows from the initial decision. In other words, habits are only part of agency insofar as the agent chose to acquire that habit. While this approach potentially provides an account of how some habits can be said to be part of the agent, it falls short of the claim that all an agent's habits constitute her agency. For on this account, the habits that are not chosen are not part of the agent at all.

I challenge people who articulate this position with the fact that many of the habits that intuitively make up our identities are acquired quite unintentionally. I point to all those they acquired during their childhood, idiosyncrasies and mannerisms, and many of the habits connected with getting used to living in a new environment. A typical reply is to weaken the claim. They will say that as long as the agent has at some stage reflected upon a given habit, and has decided she is contented enough with it, then that is enough for it to be part of who she is. Presumably then, some habits are still left out of the agent's identity; those that have not been somehow touched by the agent's intellect. I am yet to hear a convincing account of this intellectual ceremony, and how it is supposed to effect a change in identity when the manifestations of the habit are indistinguishable before and after. But I doubt we need such an account anyhow.

What is at work in both strengths of the claim is a version of the intellectualism I am opposing. It says that the real agent is the thinking agent. Admittedly such views represent a considerable move away from the orthodox picture which requires that agency is conferred by thought for each and every action. Here it is allowed that an agency-conferring thought could have happened long ago, and prior to habit acquisition. Nevertheless the intellectualism is still there in the assumption that an essential ingredient of agency is psychological. And that was what caused all the problems with the accounts of identification canvassed in §4.2.

I propose instead a de-intellectualized explanation of how habits count as constituents of agency, which draws on two features of habits. And since these features are shared by all habits, this supports the claim that all an agent's habits constitute her agency, as opposed to some subset of them. I call the features success and naturalness.

The feature I call success refers to the fact that these past repetitions are nothing short of overt behaviors. That is to say, in the past the agent didn't merely have a motive to behave in this way and didn't in fact go through with it, perhaps deciding better of it. Rather, the motive made it all the way to action. And what is more, this same sort of thing happened a number of times, not just once. It is in this sense that having a habit counts as a success.

Success is significant in disclosing the agent because the habit consists in not merely a history of thought, but a history of behavior, that is, in what the agent actually does. Insofar as we are interested in the agent's identity, as opposed to the thinker's identity, or some other sort of identity, this is where we should look: at what she does. Imagine the person who, despite having never read a philosophical book or engaged in philosophical discussion, claims she is a philosopher—though she has often thought about doing these things. I suspect we would say that until she does these things she is not a philosopher. At best she is an aspiring philosopher. I am making the same point about habits in general; the history of repetition guarantees that these sorts of behaviors aren't merely aspirational.

This example also shows the significance of the number of times the agent has done this sort of thing before. If the person had read a philosophy book just once, we would hesitate to call her a philosopher. But if she had done it many times, there is a point at which we might be willing to say that she has made it part of the fabric of her life, part of who she is. This is an important fact about the connection between habits and the agent's identity: the more times someone has done this sort of thing before, the happier we are to say that doing this is part of who the person is.

The second feature of habits that explains their connection to the agent's identity is what I call naturalness. This is a deliberate allusion to the idea of "second nature," which captures the way in which some behaviors are so well practiced that the agent does them as a matter of course, or finds it easier to do them than not to do them.[17] That all habits are natural in this sense is guaranteed by the definition which says that the repeated behavior must have become automatic for the agent, which, as we saw in §4.3, entails proficiency and a lack of conscious thought.

The relation between naturalness and agency is familiar from at least the following three contexts. First, it is familiar from when we are learning some new skill, say in sport or music, and after practice the requisite movement eventually becomes easy to do; we can do it more quickly, reliably, and without thinking. I think it's right to say that at this point we extend our agency: new forms of actions become possible, and we can build on what is now natural to acquire new skills at a more sophisticated level. Second, when we have acquired a habit unconsciously we sometimes "find ourselves" now doing it. Sometimes this realization is a nuisance, because it reveals we were "on auto-pilot," as we call it, and this has led us to do something we didn't mean to do.[18] At other times, the realization is reassuring because we find ourselves doing what we would have chosen to do anyway. Either way, I want to suggest, at the point of realization, we learn something new about who we are as agents. And third, there are contexts of uninhibited behavior, when the agent's usual sensitivities to social constraints are absent. When we witness such behavior in others we tend to think that we witness something that is revealing of who the agent really is. After all, the agent has no reason to censor what comes most naturally. Here then are three illustrations of how the naturalness of a piece of behavior discloses the agent's identity. And since habitual actions are natural, they also disclose agency.

Since success and naturalness are shared by all habits, it follows that all habits partly constitute the agent. That may sound surprising when one considers habits which one may think rather unimportant to one's identity, such as the habit of putting one's left sock on before the right; or the habit of walking the same way to work every day. But I have not yet come across a principled way of ruling such habits out; and anyway, intuitions might be misleading here.

Note that neither of these features of habit presupposes a conception of agency which is psychological. Naturalness is not for instance understood as depending on psychological input any more than the blink of an eye is. And success is not itself a psychological matter, though the overt past behaviors might have originated from psychology.

The proposal then is that habits themselves partly constitute agency because they are all successful and natural. If this is right we have the resources for a non-psychological sufficient condition for identification. We can now say that *for an agent to identify with a motive, it is sufficient for that motive to express one of her habits.*

4.5 "External Habits"?

An important line of resistance denies that all habits constitute the self; there are, in other words, external habits, as we might call them. If there were such habits, motives which express them would not be internal. At first glance it may seem that there is a rich seam of external habits. Think of bad habits; and the habits one would rather not have; and Frankfurt himself seems to be referring to a habit of an external sort when he speaks of the craving of the unwilling addict as a paradigm of external motivation.[19] Let us consider these in turn.

First of all, bad habits. A habit might be deemed bad simply in view of the fact that its normal exercises are bad or wrong things to do, by some moral or other standard. An example would be the habit of taking a really long time in the only bathroom at peak time. A habit might also be deemed bad not just because its individual manifestations are bad (or wrong), which they may not be, but because it's bad (or wrong) to be in the habit of doing it. So for example there doesn't seem to be anything the matter with clearing one's throat after uttering a sentence just once. But somebody who was in the habit of doing so after every sentence (or even most of them), would drive everybody around them to distraction.

But however we characterize bad habits, I don't think they qualify as external. Whether she likes it or not, the agent has historically refrained from intervening in such behaviors, although that option was available to her. Perhaps indeed, the agent does not even realize that she has the habit in question. Were somebody to point it out to her, she might understandably be ashamed. But any shame would only serve to confirm her identification with that way of doing things, for it makes no sense to be ashamed of things over which one has no control.[20]

This brings us to the distinct class of habits that we would rather not have. This might be because we realize that they are bad in one of the ways described above. Or it might be because we realize for the first time that something has become a habit, and we would rather not have it, no matter how good or bad it might be. Here our normative assessment of our habit is in conflict with the fact of its possession. Presumably these, then, are good candidates for external habits.

But merely having made a negative assessment of a habit one has is not enough for it to be dissociated from oneself. One can't will away one's numerous previous exercises of it, and one can't will away the capacity to do it automatically. What one can do, of course, is to make arrangements to break the habit, which might involve avoiding the circumstances in which it is normally exercised, or setting in place strategies to ensure that whenever one is in such circumstances in the future, one does something else. One might just resolve not to exercise the habit when next in these circumstances, but given doing so is automatic, this strategy might be doomed. Other strategies include applying external constraints, such as a foul tasting substance on one's finger nails in an attempt to break the habit of nail biting. Notoriously, of course, these strategies may not succeed, especially with habits that have become entrenched over years.

I concede that we would have an example of an external habit if it could be argued that at some point between this period of negatively assessing the habit and successfully losing it, the habit could be said to be external. But I don't see how. While the agent still has a history of the relevant sort, and while she acts automatically because of that history, that habit remains part of her identity as an agent. Indeed, that is why successfully losing a habit is so momentous—for only at that point has one changed who one is.

Finally, let us turn to Frankfurt's example of the unwilling addict. If her craving is indeed an external motive as Frankfurt thinks it is, and the resulting action is habitual, that would suggest that the habit must be external. Fortunately however, there are grounds for denying that an addiction is a habit. As we saw in §4.3, if the automaticity of addictive behaviors can be explained without reference to repetition they don't count as habits. The addict's relation to the substance in question would seem to do the trick. What is more, if the addict is genuinely unwilling, and this manifests itself in conscious thought or some other sort of felt psychological tension at the time of action, that will disqualify it from being automatic, and hence disqualify it from being habitual, at least on this occasion. So if the craving is not an exercise of a habit, I am not committed to denying it is external, so there is no threat to my proposal.

So I don't think we have found an example of an external habit, and the claim stands.

4.6 Agency: Psychological or habitual?

The problem with existing accounts of identification is that they rely solely on psychology, and this generates regresses of various kinds. The main difficulty is that if we are allowed to question the internality of the original motive to action, there is little to stop us questioning the internality of the rest of the agent's psychology. I have suggested that to stop such regresses we need a non-psychological sufficient condition for identification, and I have proposed one that is based on habits. In order to defend this idea I have argued that habits are constituents of agency. If I am right, psychological accounts of identification fail.

The emerging conception of agency is richer than before. At the very least it consists of behavioral components extended over the agent's history. Psychological items may also have a role in constituting agency, but we will need a convincing account of that relation.

In this light it is tempting to suppose that habits might enjoy a certain sort of priority over psychology in the constitution of agency. For if the grounds I have given for agency being constituted by habits are right, this invites us to wonder if our intuitions about the role of thought in grounding agency are themselves well grounded. In particular, if we think of those actions without a history as the first manifestation of a possible future habit, we can see a quite general reason for thinking of such actions as only potentially connected to the agent. There will only be a fact of the matter in the context of the agent's developing practical life. Such first-time actions are hardly, then, examples of "agency *par excellence*," as Velleman might put it, no matter how well suited they might be to explanation in terms of psychological posits.[21] If agency has an "*excellence*" at all, it may more obviously appear in the well-practiced and automated routines that we call good habits.

Notes

1. The examples are, respectively, from Frankfurt (1971, pp. 17–19), and Frankfurt (1977, pp. 67 and 63).
2. This way of putting things is supposed to be neutral between being identified as an act, as when one has identified with a character in a play; and being identified as a fact, as when a suspect's true identity is revealed.
3. This point is well made by Arpaly & Schroeder (1999b).
4. Davidson (1980) is the most influential holder of the former sort of theory; Collins (1997) defends a version of the latter.
5. The standard choice is between causal and teleological relations.
6. Frankfurt himself has proposed no fewer than three accounts in published work, which depend upon the agent having respectively: a "second-order volition" that the motive form her "will" (1971); having made a "decision" to adopt a motive (1977, 1987); and having a "higher-order desire" with which the agent is reflectively "satisfied," to endorse the motive (1992). Gary Watson (1975) has proposed that identification is to be understood in terms of the agent's "evaluational system" comprising her "ends and principles"; a view that he later abandons (Watson 1987). David Velleman (1992), Michael Bratman (1996), Nomi Arpaly and Timothy Schroeder (1999a) and David Shoemaker (2003) also account for identification in terms of the agent's psychological states or performances.
7. It thus allows us to count "desires" as psychological even on Frankfurt's (1971) permissive characterization of them (p. 13).
8. See also Pollard (2006a & b) for this sort of characterization of habit.
9. It might be objected that Arpaly and Schroeder can avoid this criticism because their claim is that the states which are internal are "*deep*": "A belief or desire is *deep* insofar as it is a powerful force in determining the actor's behavior, deeply held, deep-rooted. Deep beliefs tend to resist revision ... and deep desires tend to be satisfied with preference over shallower desires in contexts where a choice is forced" (1999a, p. 173). But the most delusional beliefs can resist revision; and we are given no reason for thinking that the tendency of a desire to override others could possibly contribute to its internality, as compulsions, addictions and phobias show. I agree that behavioral patterns are important, but not because they disclose the mental locus of agency; because they *are* agency.

10. It is a disturbing fact that Bratman (1996) accepts this counterexample, concluding that "concerning any mental act or occurrence, even a decision, one can raise the question of whether or not the agent identifies with it" (p. 193), yet goes on to give an account based on decisions.
11. The same line of argument would apply to other psychological performances, such as processes of reasoning.
12. One reason this can't be assumed is that in this paper I don't question the idea of a "motive," a psychological item which precedes all actions, or so we can believe for the purposes of a paper on identification. On my view, there might be motiveless actions.
13. A notable exception is Brett (1981) who argues against both Ryle and Winch.
14. Here we are not restricting the notion of responsibility to moral responsibility, but to personal responsibility quite generally.
15. With due respect to Frankfurt, this capacity may not be necessary for responsibility, but he says nothing to suggest it is not sufficient.
16. For an excellent survey see Carlisle (2006).
17. Anthony Kenny: "If one has a habit of doing X, then it is harder not to do X than if one has not" (1989, p. 85).
18. This sort of "absent-minded" behaviour arguably represents an important, though neglected, variety of weakness of will. It is against the agent's best judgement, and, if the claim of this paper is right, is also a genuine action.
19. Frankfurt (1971, pp. 17–19).
20. Support for this view comes from Dewey: "A bad habit suggests an inherent tendency to action, and also a hold, command over us. It makes us do things we are ashamed of, things which we tell ourselves we prefer not to do. It overrides our formal resolutions, our conscious decisions. When we are honest with ourselves we acknowledge that a habit has this power because it is intimately part of ourselves. It has a hold upon us because we are the habit" (1922, p. 24).
21. Velleman (1992, p. 124).

Bibliography

Arpaly, N. and Schroeder, T. (1999a), "Praise, Blame and the Whole Self," *Philosophical Studies*, 93, 161–88.

———. (1999b), "Alienation and Externality," *Canadian Journal of Philosophy*, 29, 371–88.

Bratman, M. (1988), *Intentions, Plans and Practical Reason*. Cambridge: Harvard University Press.

———. (1996), "Identification, Decision, and Treating as a Reason," reprinted in Bratman (1999, 185–206.

———. (1999), *Faces of Intention*. Cambridge: CUP.

Brett, N. (1981), "Human Habits," *Canadian Journal of Philosophy*, 11, 357–76.

Carlisle, C. (2006), "Creatures of Habit: the Problem and the Practice of Liberation," *Continental Philosophy Review*, 38, 19–39.

Collins, A. C. (1997), "The Psychological Reality of Reasons," *Ratio*, 10, pp. 108–23.

Dancy, J. (2000), *Practical Reality*. Oxford: OUP.

Dewey, J. (1922), *Human Nature and Conduct*. New York: Henry Holt & Co.

Davidson, D. (1980), *Essays on Actions and Events*. Clarendon Press: Oxford.

Frankfurt, H. G. (1971), *Freedom of the Will and the Concept of a Person*, reprinted in Frankfurt 1988, 11–25.

———. (1976), *Identification and Externality*, reprinted in Frankfurt 1988, 58–68.
———. (1987), *Identification and Wholeheartedness*, reprinted in Frankfurt 1988, 159–76.
———. (1988), *The Importance of What We Care About*. Cambridge: CUP.
———. (1992), "The Faintest Passion," reprinted in Frankfurt 1999, 95–107.
———. (1999), *Necessity, Volition, and Love*. Cambridge: CUP.
Ginet, C. (1990), *On Action*. Cambridge: CUP.
James, W. (1890), *The Principles of Psychology, Vol. 1*. New York: Henry Holt and Company.
Kenny, A. (1989), *The Metaphysics of Mind*. Clarendon Press: Oxford.
O' Shaughnessy, B. (1973), "Trying (as the Mental 'Pineal Gland')," reprinted in Mele 1997, 53–74.
Pollard, B. (2006a), "Explaining Actions With Habits," *American Philosophical Quarterly*, 43, 57–68.
———. (2006b), "Actions, Habits and Constitution," *Ratio*, 19, pp. 229–48.
Ryle, G. (1949), *The Concept of Mind*. London: Penguin.
Shoemaker, D. W. (2003). "Caring, Identification, and Agency," *Ethics*, 114, 88–128.
Smith, Michael (1987), "The Humean Theory of Motivation," *Mind*, 96, 36–61.
Velleman, J. D. (1992), "What Happens When Someone Acts?," reprinted in Velleman (2000), 123–43.
———. (2000), *The Possibility of Practical Reason*. Clarendon Press: Oxford.
Watson, G. (1975), "Free Agency," *Journal of Philosophy*, 72, 205–20.
———. (1987), "Free Action and Free Will," *Mind*, 96, 145–72.
Winch, P. (1958), *The Idea of a Social Science and its Relation to Philosophy*. Oxford: Routledge.

5

Mass Perverse Identification: An Argument for a Modest Concept of Autonomy*

Yonatan Shemmer

We care deeply about the poor, the hungry children in Africa, and about those that are struck by cancer. We think we should do something to help them. We think we should do more than we actually do to help. We think we ought to give more money, spend more time informing ourselves, be more engaged in political activity that would affect change. We think doing more is important and valuable. We want to do more and we often resolve to do more. And then we don't.

When people do not or cannot act the way they want, when they do not or cannot act in accordance with what they value and care about we think that they are not autonomous. Autonomy requires being governed by one's own motives and values, by the motives and values that are central to one's identity. Yet we do not think that our failure to do as much as we deem we should for the poor or the hungry is a failure of autonomy.

Something must give. Either we should reconsider the view that our values and motives constitute our identity or we should rethink the relation between acting autonomously and being governed at the time of action, by the motives and values that are central to our identity. I argue for the latter option. In particular I argue that whether an action is autonomous or not depends, among other things, on the extent to which it is part of a network of actions that are governed by the values and motives central to the person. If we are autonomous when we fail to do as much as we think we should for the poor, it is because for the most part our actions are governed by desires and values that are central to our identity.

I will proceed as follows. The dependence thesis reflects a common understanding of the relation between autonomy and identification. I will explicate this thesis as well as some other central concepts needed for the discussion. I will then present a putative argument against both the traditional understanding of akrasia and against some alternative contemporary understandings of that notion. The argument is not conclusive. It leaves us with two options: reject many of the available theories of akrasia or reject the dependence thesis. The cost of the first option is too high. I will conclude by suggesting an alternative to the dependence thesis and discussing some problems this alternative faces.

Akrasia

The term akrasia has been most often understood as "action against the agent's better judgment." That is, action that conflicts with the agent's considered beliefs about what she should do. Let us dub this "the standard view." Literally the Greek word "akrasia" means "lack of command over oneself." The literal meaning of the word may be the basis for a broader understanding of the term. The idea of an agent who does not have command over herself, or who is not autonomous, may be interpreted in accordance with the standard view, but is also open to other understandings. What these would be depends first on who we think the commanding self is, or in other words, on what we think of as the "agent's position," and second, on what we understand by the notion of control. The two ideas, that of the agent's position, and that of being under the agent's control, are often seen as being related in the following way. An agent is under her own control if the forces that constitute the agent's position govern her actions. So to give a precise content to alternative understandings of akrasia we need to consider accounts that distinguish the agent's position from influences that are external to the agent. Theories of identification are well suited to provide such an account.

Identification

Sometimes we are moved by forces that are external to us. People push us, or we trip unintentionally. On other occasions our behavior is motivated by our desires but in ways that still seem beyond our control. We are motivated by unconscious desires, or by addictive desires or by desires that we have only because someone points a gun to our head. On these occasions (or at least on some of them) it seems appropriate to describe the desires that move us as forces that are external to us; forces that move us against our will. Yet on other occasions our actions are under our full control. We are motivated to act as we do by our desires and our desires themselves are desires that fully represent us. These are desires we identify with and cannot be described as forces that are external to us. Theories of identification aim to characterize the dividing line between our own desires, that is, those that speak for us, and those that are external to us.

Identification and self-control

"In autonomous action the agent herself directs and governs the action" says Michael Bratman in "Autonomy and Hierarchy."[1] Bratman expresses here a common view. On this view there is a tight connection between identification and autonomous action. There are many ways to specify this general claim. Not all of these will be accepted by everyone, but it seems to me that many would be willing to subscribe, at least, to the view that identification with the motives of action is a necessary condition for autonomous action.[2] An agent, it is often thought, cannot be self controlled if the forces that move her to action are forces external to her, forces that do not speak for her; are forces with which she does not identify.[3] The view is therefore a view about the dependence of autonomous action on the agent's identification at the time of decision making:

An agent performs an action autonomously only if she identifies with the desires that motivate the action.

Call this view The Dependence Thesis.

The dependence thesis needs to be clarified. Agents identify with a multiplicity of desires and these desires often conflict, or at least conflict in specific circumstances. In such conflict situations the agent is often happy to let the strength of the relevant desires determine her actions. Thus I may identify with my desire to eat chocolate ice cream and with my desire to eat vanilla ice cream. When I stand in front of the ice cream freezer in the supermarket I let the strength of these desires at the time of decision making determine my decision. If I feel a stronger desire to have chocolate, this is the one I am going to buy, otherwise I will buy the vanilla ice cream. Sometimes however I accept two desires as my own, that is, I identify with both of them, but I also have a preference about which one of them should prevail in circumstances of conflict. Moreover I identify with that preference. I may for example identify with my desire to watch the news all the way through and identify with my desire to pick my friend up on time from the train station. However when in the middle of watching the news I suddenly remember I have to leave for the train station to fetch my friend, I do not let the relative strength of my desires at the time determine my actions. Rather I have a (standing) preference about which desire should prevail in these circumstances—I prefer that my desire to get to my friend on time prevail - and I may on reflection be identified with that preference. The dependence thesis applies to these cases as well. If an agent is identified with a preference to be motivated in cases of conflict by one desire and not another then she will be autonomous only if she is motivated to act by the desire she prefers to be motivated by.[4]

Identifying with an akratic action

How should we treat action against one's better judgment that the agent identifies with? Assuming the standard view of akrasia, such action involves identifying with an akratic decision. Watson has called this sort of identification *"perverse identification"*—while not denying that it is possible to identify against one's better judgment, that is, on the standard view, to stand by your akratic action—he claimed that this phenomenon leaves us "with a rather elusive notion of identification and thereby an elusive notion of self-determination".[5] Watson is a proponent of the standard view concerning akrasia. He believes that an agent who acts against his better judgment is not self controlled. He also believes that the agent's judgment about what is right (usually) determines the agent's identification. However he thinks that on rare occasions it is possible for agents to defiantly position themselves against their normative judgments. Watson, that is, thinks it psychologically possible for an agent to believe that it is right not to perform an action, and nevertheless identify with that action, and be alienated from his belief. But it also seems to him that there is something wrong with this sort of psychological state, something that reveals improper functioning of one's psychological mechanisms.

Mass perverse identification

Many of us throughout our lives think that we do not do *enough*, do not contribute *enough*, to the promotion of various causes we believe in: we do not do enough to help the poor, the abused, animals, people in third world countries whose basic needs are not met, the environment and so on. Nothing prevents us from contributing *more* but in full knowledge of the options, time after time we decide to spend our money and time in different ways. We judge, we believe, we see it as central to our value system, that we should spend more time thinking about what we can do to fight child slavery, that we should spend more time in the soup kitchen, that we should give more money to cancer research, that we should go more often to political meetings. We believe we should do more when we reflect about our life as a whole and we believe we should do more in specific choice junctions. Nevertheless we end up not doing as much as we think we should. The phenomenon encompasses all walks of life—rich and poor, religious and secular, young and old, those who are otherwise easily driven by their appetites and those who are not, reflective and less reflective people, people who are otherwise self controlled and those who are not, those that do nothing to promote the causes they deem in need of promotion and those that already do quite a bit. We are surely morally responsible for our choice not to do more, and intuitively (though maybe not according to some theories of autonomy) are autonomous in this choice. Intuitively we are also identified with our actions. Unlike the drug addict we do not feel that a force that is external to us has compelled us to behave in a way that does not represent our true self—we do not feel alienated from our choices in these cases. We feel that the choice is ours—maybe not the best choice we have made—but ours nonetheless. Following Watson we might want to call this phenomenon Mass Perverse Identification or MPI. I will call instances of this type of identification "MPI-cases."

How often do we face decisions to which we respond in such perverse manner? Given the great number of occasions on which we are reminded of our insufficient contribution, the answer seems to be: quite often. We see advertisements on TV that remind us of child malnutrition in Africa, we read in the papers about disasters in various parts of the world, political campaigns are based on the plight of the poor, we see beggars and homeless people in the street and we receive mail asking us to contribute to causes we think we should contribute to. We often do give or help, or send money. But we rarely do as much as we think we should do. And as we have just seen we are not lacking reminders.

Part of the explanation for this phenomenon is the fact that there is no specific deadline by which we need to act in order to send money or join the soup kitchen. So it is easy to postpone the decision to act. But this cannot be the whole story. There is no deadline by which we need to buy new jeans and yet somehow this gets done.

You might think that MPI cases do not display any perverseness because our value judgments are not really in conflict with our choices or the desires that motivate these choices. We judge that we should do more for children in Africa, but our current desire when we decide not to help today, is not the desire *not* to do more for children in Africa. Rather it is the desire not to do something about it *right now* or even more plausibly the desire to sleep, or go shopping, or work, or any of the other things we do instead of helping children in Africa. Maybe then there is no straightforward conflict between our background value judgments and our current desire. I don't think so. While deciding not to do anything right now, we are often well aware of the fact that right now is exactly one of these times in which we should be doing more if we were to follow our value judgments. We often do not lie to ourselves. We do not say: I am not doing anything right now but it is OK, because I know that in the future I will satisfy the demand to do more. Rather we say to ourselves: I know I should be doing more *right now,* I know that if I don't send the money right now I will probably not send it later, and nevertheless I am deciding not to—again.[6]

Note how similar the situation is to the situation of the person who is getting drunk. He faces a choice of whether to drink another glass of wine or stop. He knows that drinking another glass is taking him on the path to getting drunk. He values staying sober. Is there a conflict between his value judgments and his decision to drink another glass? The person who is getting drunk could try to maintain that his decision is autonomous by claiming that there is no strict conflict. After all the glass he is about to drink is not by itself going to make him drunk. He could drink it and then stop. In fact, no particular glass is going to make him drunk. Therefore we could conclude: no particular decision to drink another glass is in conflict with his value judgment.

We usually reject that kind of defense in the case of the person who is getting drunk. He knows, we say, that if he wants to finish the evening sober he should not drink beyond the third glass. And when he makes the decision to drink the fourth or fifth glass he is acting against his value judgments, even if in theory he could have drunk them and then stopped. Similarly when we choose to go to the party and not to the soup kitchen for the 100th time, we know we act against our value judgments, even if in theory we could make up for that by an exemplary behavior in the following year.

MPI, self-control and, identification

Could a psychological phenomenon that so many of us throughout most of our adult life experience on a daily or weekly basis be deemed abnormal? The question is not primarily a statistical question. After all, actions we perform only seldom are considered normal. We sort the stuff we have accumulated in the depth of our cupboard once every few years (at best) but there is nothing abnormal about this action. Watson's dubbing of MPI cases as perverse was not based on the thought that these cases are rare; and the realization that they are not rare would not change his understanding. If identifying with an akratic decision is problematic or perverse it is not because it is rare but rather because in doing so we breach an ideal. What ideal? The most plausible answer is: "the ideal of autonomy." Autonomy requires that we control ourselves and we breach the ideal by failing to submit our actions to our governance. The prevalence of MPI-cases casts doubt on the thought that there is such an ideal not merely because those cases are common. Rather, it casts doubt on the thought that there is such an ideal because of the combination of their commonality and the fact that when we are confronted with the gap between our decisions and our value judgments we do not react with the appropriate concern—the seeming identification with the akratic decision comes easily to us; it does not initiate an inner struggle. The realization that we do not act on our values is not tortured, not even an occasion for self scrutiny. We accept it as natural.

Watson believed that our value judgments are central to our identity.[7] He was torn though, in his understanding of the proper theoretical analysis of their centrality. On the one hand he thought that the ideal that requires us to comply with our value judgments cannot be treated like one-among-many ideals; an ideal we might not follow yet still not lose a part of what makes us who we are. On the other hand he realized that we sometimes identify with actions we do not value. The term "perverse identification" captured his complex approach to these cases. Indeed he thought that cases of identifying against one's value judgments are perverse precisely because he thought that our value judgments are fundamental, if not constitutive, of our identity.

MPI cases suggest that our value judgments play a smaller or less central role in defining our identity or our selfhood than Watson thought. MPI cases thus also suggest that the more common, narrow, understanding of akrasia (as "action against one's better judgment") is not the best way to specify the broader more generic understanding one would get by taking seriously the literal meaning of the term: self-control. We are not less self-controlled because we are not controlling ourselves in accordance with our value judgments.[8]

MPI and other theories of identification

Other theories of identification such as those of Frankfurt and Bratman may be seen as better alternatives, as would a view of identification based on Arpaly and Schroeder's coherentist theory of responsibility. A coherentist view assigns value judgments a smaller, though un-eliminable, role in delineating the contours of the self. Both Bratman and Frankfurt claim that value judgments are not necessary for identification. These views suggest a different notion of identification and therefore a different account of self control. Since beliefs about values or about right action are not central, according to these theories, to our understanding of identification, the possibility that someone identifies against their beliefs need not be seen as perverse. One might therefore hope that on these views MPI cases are not perverse after all. But these theories as well seem to be challenged by MPI cases. A close analysis will show that—at least as long as we accept the Dependence thesis[9]—according to all three we are deviating from an ideal of self control in MPI cases; not merely some of us sometimes, but rather most of us, most of the time. So even if we "loosen" our definition of akrasia (that is, even if we stop seeing action in accordance with one's judgments as necessary for self control), in decisions in cases of MPI we may still be displaying, according to these theories, a lack of self-control or of autonomy. Yet intuitively, there seems to be no loss of control or of autonomy in our decision not to do more for our favorite causes. And our unconcerned reaction to this prevalent phenomenon challenges the thought that we are breaking some ideal of self control or autonomy.

Let us look at each one of these theories more carefully.

Coherentism (Arpaly & Schroeder)[10]

According to a coherentist view an agent identifies with an action to the extent that his beliefs in favor of the action and the desires that motivate the action are well integrated with his other beliefs and desires. A desire or belief is more integrated to the extent that it prevails in conflict with other desires or beliefs (respectively) and in inverse proportion to the number of conflicting desires and beliefs the agent has.

Consider cases of MPI in light of that view. Most of us believe that it would be good to do more for our favorite causes; when we think about it we do not find that we have many conflicting beliefs; and when we consider a conflicting belief—for example, the belief that we had had a hard year and we may be exempt this year—the belief that we should do more usually prevails.

Now consider our desires. We have many desires that accidentally conflict with the desire to do more for our favorite causes. Everything in our lives that requires time, attention or money *accidentally* conflicts with the desire to do more charitable work or to give more to charitable causes. However these are accidental conflicts. Desires always conflict with other desires accidentally: the desire to eat ice cream conflicts accidentally with the desire to drive to work, because you cannot do both at the same time. Such accidental conflict does not mean we are alienated from our desire to eat ice cream. What matters to identification is in-principle conflict. The desire to murder someone conflicts in principle with the desire to be moral. Most of us have no desires that in-principle conflict with the desire to do more for our favorite good causes.

Perhaps our desire to do more for charitable causes is an apparent desire. Perhaps it is not a real desire, perhaps we just pretend to ourselves and to others to care about non-profit work while not really caring about it. It is hard to measure whether a desire is real or only apparent but there are a few available signs. I will mention here two central ones:

1. When we desire something our attention to possible means for the satisfaction of the desire, or to information about the object of the desire, is heightened. When you want a new car you will notice car ads, and articles about new security features in cars will be at the center of your attention. Ads about sail boats and new regulations in the local marina, on the other hand, will go under your radar.

   I constantly think that I should be more politically engaged and though I do very little about it, my attention is always drawn to political activity that I could be involved in. I notice TV advertisements about hungry children in Africa and pay attention to them in a way that I never do to laundry detergent advertisements. And not only do I pay special attention to these advertisements or TV programs: each time I chastise myself for not doing anything about it.
2. It is not the case that the satisfaction of a real desire always brings us pleasure and that the satisfaction of apparent desire does not. But there is a correlation between these two factors. The achievement of goals we only say we care about, or think we care about when we really do not, will often bring no pleasure with it.

   Contributions in action or money to charitable or political causes are often very satisfying.

   We are not lying to others or to ourselves when we say that we want to do more, we really do.

It looks then that on a coherentist position we are identified with the desire to help more. A coherentist position fashioned after Arpaly and Schroeder's view would allow for degrees of identification. Even though our desires and beliefs in favor of charitable work are real and even though they fit well with our other desires and beliefs, the fact that in cases of conflict we do not act on them, indicates, on that view, that our identification with them is not complete. As opposed to a strict cognitivist view (such as Watson's), according to which the agent's value judgments are the only determinants of identification, a coherentist would not conclude that we are wholly identified with the desire to do more for charitable causes. Her view will lead to a moderate conclusion; perhaps, that we are mostly identified with the desire to help more. But even this moderate view conflicts with our intuitive understanding of MPI cases. Agents in MPI cases seem identified with the way they in fact act and more importantly they seem wholly autonomous in their actions. The problem is that you cannot both be wholly identified with not doing more for charitable causes and therefore be autonomous in your actions[11] while being—as a coherentist analysis suggests—mostly identified with the desire to do more for charitable causes.

In the case of a coherentist view the problem is not only with the conflict between the agent's value judgments and her action, rather the problem is with the gap between the combination of value judgments and desires that are central to the agent and the agent's action.

But is there such a conflict? The coherentist might claim that there isn't. An agent may be identified with the desire to do more for charitable or political causes, they might say, and also with the desire to go to a party right now. The two desires are not necessarily conflicting. It may simply be a case of selecting between two options both of which the agent identifies with. Therefore the agent's decision to satisfy the desire to go to the party and not to go to the organizational meeting is not an indication that the agent is acting in a way that conflicts with what she identifies with.

I think that this is not the case. My deliberation between going to the movies and going to the organizational meeting for a campaign against poverty in Africa is categorically different than my deliberation between a party and a movie. I often know full well that I have made too many decisions in favor of parties and against organizational meetings. I know full well that the balance of my decisions does not represent the balance of my preferences. And finally I often perform one more deliberation before deciding and in this final deliberation I often pose myself the question about my particular preferences concerning the current decision—and even then I realize that my preference is for the organizational meeting. And after all these background and foreground desires have been considered, I decide to go to the party. On the coherentist view my actions conflict with my identification. On that view, and given the Dependence thesis, what I am displaying is weakness of will, the forces that move me to action are alien to me; they do not constitute my identity. But this is not how it feels to me and how it seems to others. The decision seems to be my own, unforced and autonomous.

Frankfurt

Frankfurt's analysis of identification and weakness of will has changed over the years. For simplicity's sake I will work with the view he ended up with in one of his later articles on the topic, "The Faintest Passion".[12]

In this article Frankfurt claimed that to be identified with a desire the agent has to have a high order desire (of order($n>1$)) in favor of that first order desire being the desire that motivates her to action, and she must be satisfied with that high order desire; where being satisfied with a desire is on reflection having no higher order desires that conflict with the desire in question.

On this view in MPI-cases we are clearly identified with the desire to do more for our favorite non-profit causes and in particular with the preference that in this choice junction we select to spend time or money on charity and not on leisure or on work. When we reflect on our options[13] we desire that our desire to do more motivate us on this particular occasion. This is a high order desire to be motivated by the desire to do more. And when we survey our higher order preferences we find no conflicting desire. On similar grounds, according to Frankfurt's view, in MPI-cases when we deliberate whether to go to the party or the organizational meeting of a political campaign, we are not identified with the desire to go to the party. According to Frankfurt we are displaying weakness of will when we go to the party. And to the extent that identification is necessary for self control[14] then according to Frankfurt's view we are not self-controlled when we decide to go to the party.

Frankfurt's view, like the coherentist view, yields the wrong result. My decision to go to the party and not to the organizational meeting is as self-controlled as they come—or so we think when we are not in the grip of any philosophical theory.

An objector might point out the following feature of Frankfurt's theory in order to block this conclusion.

Frankfurt tells us that an agent is identified with a desire only when she has reflected on the desire and considered her higher order preferences with regard to this desire. But though many of us have reflected on the general desire to do more for non-profit causes, we often do not engage in such reflection in MPI-cases, that is, just before we choose to spend our time in a different way. So it is possible that according to Frankfurt in such cases though the agent is identified with the general desire to do more for non-profit causes, she is not identified with a preference to do more in this choice junction.

The claim that an agent can only be identified with a desire if she reflected on that desire is not a simple claim to defend. Indeed many authors who have written after Frankfurt have challenged it. There is however quite strong textual evidence in Frankfurt's writing that this was his position.[15] I assume that this was indeed his position.

However even if, following this interpretation, we cannot claim that the agent in MPI-cases is identified with the preference to spend her time on a non-profit project, it is still the case that, according to Frankfurt's theory, the agent in MPI-cases is also not identified with the alternative action. The agent is also not identified with the desire to go, say, to the party instead of the soup-kitchen. But if identification is a necessary condition for self control or autonomy then the agent is also not self-controlled in her decision to go to the party.

Frankfurt might deny that agents are necessarily not self controlled in those cases in which they are not reflective. He might claim that there are three possible kinds of status with respect to identification: being identified, being non-identified, and a third undetermined middle status.

He may also think that there are three statuses with respect to autonomy. Being autonomous, being non-autonomous and a third undetermined middle status. Finally he may think that an agent who occupies the middle status with respect to identification may also occupy the middle status with respect to autonomy.

On that view even though reflection is necessary for identification, when the agent is non-reflective we cannot conclude that she is not identified. In particular Frankfurt might contend that in cases in which the agent is not reflecting the question about her identification is meaningless or undetermined and therefore in these cases we cannot draw any clear conclusions about the agent's autonomy.[16] Finally he might contend that most MPI-cases are of that sort.

The view I have just explored entails the rejection of the Dependence thesis. However this rejection leaves us with a worry. Most of our actions are taken without reflection at the moment of decision making. This last view therefore implies that most of the time we are neither autonomous nor non-autonomous. But this is an odd view to hold. After all, the question about whether an agent is autonomous in her actions is a natural question, and we usually expect either a positive or a negative answer. This expectation would be surprising if it were so often frustrated. At the very least then, we can conclude that Frankfurt's view needs to be supplemented to give us an account of autonomy in cases of non-reflective decision making and in particular in MPI cases.

Like the other views we have discussed, Frankfurt's view will meet predictable challenges in trying to account for these cases. The theoretical resources available to Frankfurt are elements of the agent's mental life: desires, high order desires, beliefs, and emotions. In MPI-cases the preponderance of our desires, beliefs and emotions all suggest that what we really prefer is to spend more time promoting non-profit causes. However when we fail to do it time and again, our intuitions still tell us that our actions are self-controlled.

In the next section we will look at Bratman's theory of identification. Bratman has famously appealed to policies and plans to try to capture the difference between desires that the agent identifies with and those that she does not. Maybe his use of these additional resources allows him to better deal with MPI-cases.

Bratman

On Bratman's view an agent is identified with a desire if she has decided (or would have decided had she reflected on the matter) to adopt a self governing policy of treating that desire as reason giving in practical deliberation; and if that policy does not conflict (and would not conflict if she were to reflect upon it) with other self governing policies of the agent; and if the agent in fact would treat the desire as reason giving in actual deliberation.[17]

A self governing policy is a policy whose function is to control the agent's own processes of deliberation and decision making. A self governing policy of treating a desire as reason giving is a self governing policy of counting the desire as a relevant consideration when one deliberates whether to do something or not.

Let us check whether in MPI-cases the agent is identified with the desire to do more for a non-profit cause. Whether or not the agent has reflected on the matter, it is clear that in MPI-cases the agent would have formed a policy (if she were to reflect) in favor of doing more for charitable causes in cases of this very kind. It is also clear that the agent has no conflicting self-governing policies. However it is not clear whether in MPI-cases, and with regards to the desire to do more for one's charitable causes, Bratman's third condition for identification is satisfied or not. Does the agent in deliberation about action take into account as reason giving (or would take it into account if he were to reflect) his desire to do more for charitable causes but then fail to act in accordance with his deliberation? If this is the case then Bratman's model is also challenged by MPI cases. I suspect that this is often the case and therefore those occasions in which the agent fails to act on her policy supported deliberation are a problem for Bratman as well.

Bratman might claim, however, that though agents do form policies in favor of treating their desires to do more for charitable causes as reason giving, when it comes to actual deliberation they fail to treat their desire to do more as reason giving. Agents do not merely fail to act on this desire, but seem also not to take it into account in deliberation. When I am about to sign a check for a new pair of shoes, while knowing all too well that I could do without these and could instead donate the money to charity, and I deliberate about whether to buy them I do not treat my desire to do more for charitable causes as reason giving. If, or when, this is the case, then on Bratman's criteria I am not identified with the desire to do more for charity.

On the other hand, given Bratman's criteria, on these cases the agent is also not identified with the desire to do whatever she is doing instead of donating time or money to charity. The first criterion is not satisfied with regards to this desire. Agents in MPI-cases do not (and would not under reflection) have a policy in favor of treating the preference to do other than increase their contribution in time or money to charitable causes as reason giving.

So Bratman's account of identification is challenged by MPI-cases, but only partially. First it is challenged by those cases in which Bratman's analysis yields the conclusion that agent's are identified with the desire to do more for charitable causes. Second, in those cases in which according to Bratman's analysis we are not identified with the desire to do more for charitable causes Bratman's theory still faces a considerable problem: on his view the agent is also not identified with the actions they take instead of doing more for charitable causes and this conclusion is in tension with the intuition that agents are self controlled in MPI cases.[18]

Putting these challenges aside, MPI cases pose another problem for Bratman's account. On Bratman's view agents are not autonomous in MPI-cases even if they are identified with their actions, because in that case their identification conflicts with their value judgments. Although Bratman thinks that judging a desire valuable is neither sufficient nor necessary for identification, he thinks that identification that conflicts with the agent's value judgment cannot be autonomous because it displays an internal incoherence that is incompatible with autonomy.[19] Bratman is thus endorsing a stronger version of the dependence thesis. *An agent performs an action autonomously only if she identifies with the desires that motivate the action and these desires do not conflict with her value judgments.* So on Bratman's account agents in MPI-cases are not autonomous. As we have seen this view conflicts with our intuitive understanding of MPI-cases.

The ideal of autonomy

What should we do? One way to go is to try and amend our conditions for identification. To manipulate details of the criteria for identification so that it turns out that in MPI cases we are identified with the actions we end up taking and not with those suggested by our desires/beliefs/policies. But it's not clear to me how that could be done. As I said above the various potential mental states that could serve as components in these new criteria seem to point in one direction: what we do is not what we identify with and certainly not what we judge right. I think that in one way or another the various authors I have discussed above have gotten it right. To the extent that our intuitions about identification in MPI cases don't agree with the various theories of identification presented above, the problem is with those intuitions. I will explain later why I think our intuitions are misleading us. But first, to the main problem:

MPI cases do not challenge the existing accounts of identification, what they do challenge is our view of autonomy. What we face is a challenge to our understanding of self-control or autonomy as an ideal. More exactly MPI-cases challenge our common understanding of the way in which our ideal of autonomy imposes necessary conditions for autonomous action. We often think that a necessary condition for an agent being autonomous with respect to a particular action is that the agent is identified with the desires that motivate the action.[20] This is the Dependence thesis. As we have seen, some authors (all those I have discussed with the exception of Bratman) promote a view of identification according to which if we accept the Dependence thesis we are bound to conclude that in MPI cases agents are not self controlled in their actions. This conclusion flies in the face of our reaction to these cases. What therefore must be challenged is the Dependence thesis.

Depending on how we understand MPI cases, Bratman's analysis of identification may not lead us—given the Dependence thesis—to the conclusion that agents are not self controlled in those cases. But Bratman endorses a more demanding version of the Dependence thesis. On his view autonomy requires both that the agent identifies with her motives *and* that her identification coheres with her value judgments. Call this view Dependence +. As a result even on his analysis of identification and given Dependence + we must conclude that agents are not self controlled in MPI cases. Thus MPI cases challenge either Dependence or Dependence +. Dependence and Dependence + are not completely off-track; they should, however, be amended. For simplicity's sake I will focus henceforth on Dependence, though everything I say is also applicable to Dependence +. Before I explain how to amend Dependence and rethink our ideal of autonomy, some clarifications are in place.

Clarifications

The Dependence thesis claims that identification is a necessary condition for autonomous action. Many authors have argued that our mental states at the time of deliberation and action cannot provide us with *sufficient* conditions for autonomy. The view that previous choices or prior social conditions provide additional necessary conditions for autonomy with respect to a particular action is a good example for that position.[21] My challenge of Dependence is neutral with respect to these views. Others have argued for the inclusion of a different set of conditions in our analysis of autonomy, conditions that ensure that the agent has basic capacities, such as the ability to respond to reasons, that are deemed necessary for autonomous action.[22] Nothing I say here is in conflict with these claims. There may also be ways to challenge the Dependence thesis that do not rely on MPI-cases and therefore, that differ from the one I present here. I do not think that MPI-cases are the only way to challenge the Dependence thesis.

Autonomy as a flexible ideal

So how should we rethink our ideal of autonomy? There is a way to rethink this ideal, deal with MPI-cases and leave intact the Dependence thesis. We could say that compliance with the ideal of self control or autonomy only demands autonomy in the majority of cases. So even though we are not fully autonomous in MPI cases there is nothing wrong with that. It is enough if one is autonomous most of the time. Some lack of autonomy does not go against our ideals—this is why we are not troubled by MPI-cases. The Dependence thesis entails that in MPI-cases we are not autonomous. This is either because we do not identify with our motivating desires or (as Bratman thinks) because even if we do identify with our motivating desires, our deliberation conflicts with our value judgments. On this way of rethinking the ideal of autonomy, the Dependence thesis is right: we are not autonomous in MPI cases, but this is not a problem. Autonomy is like "being nice." We are not being nice when we lose our temper. But there is no ideal that requires that we be nice to everyone all the time. Sometimes it's OK to lose one's temper.

This relaxation of the ideal of autonomy is a step toward the solution. But we are not there yet. The current suggestion may explain why we do not feel bad in MPI cases but it does not explain why it seems to us that we are autonomous when we make the decision to go to the party instead of volunteering in a charitable organization. The current solution insists that we are not autonomous in MPI cases and this goes against our intuitions.

The correct solution does involve a relaxation of our ideal of autonomy but in a different way. To see how consider an analogy. We have an ideal of eating healthily. If we eat fruits and vegetables, use fresh ingredients, cook things instead of buying TV-dinners and buy organic food then we eat healthily. Call someone who eats that way someone with good eating habits. Eating lots of candies is not very good for your health. But if you are someone with good eating habits who eats lots of candies once in a while we will not say that you are therefore not eating healthily. Even while you eat the candies there is nothing unhealthy in your eating. Eating the candies is not only part of a life of eating healthily, rather it is itself an instance of eating healthily—for an agent with good eating habits. Autonomy, I think, works in the same way. We need to be identified with our actions and to act in ways that do not conflict with our value judgments most of the time—a large part of our actions need to be of that sort. To this extent the Dependence thesis is correct. But once we reach that level, the fact that even more actions of ours could be identified with does not mean that we have breached an ideal of autonomy and so when we perform actions we do not identify with these actions are not less autonomous.

When we are autonomous agents we act autonomously even when we do not identify with our action.

You might think that the solution I have just suggested is problematic. First you might claim that in MPI-cases we may be *autonomous agents*, but in acting against the motives we identify with and in not doing what we believe we should do we are not *acting autonomously*—that is, you might emphasize the distinction between autonomy as a property of the agent and autonomy as a feature of particular actions, and you might further claim that unidentified-with actions are not autonomous.[23] Second, you may claim that there is reason to think that the analogy with eating healthily is misleading. Some sugar in one's diet is not only OK, it's actually required. However it is not clear that some lack of identification is required in one's actions.

A different analogy might help us with both of these problems. Think of "keeping in shape." Sitting in front of the TV does not help you keep in shape. But if you run a marathon each week, then sitting in front of your TV for an hour does not make it the case that even there and then you are not keeping in shape. Autonomy is like "keeping in shape." It is primarily a feature of the agent and only in a derivative way a feature of particular actions. Particular actions contribute to our keeping in shape. We can say whether an action is of a type that contributes to us keeping in shape—when we run we contribute to keeping ourselves in shape. We can also say whether an action contributes to us being autonomous—when we identify with our actions we contribute to us being autonomous. But we keep in shape even when we don't exercise, if we are indeed keeping in shape; and we are autonomous, even when we do not identify with a specific action, if we are indeed autonomous. More important: if we are autonomous agents we are sometimes autonomous agents with respect to particular actions with which we are not identified and in which we decide against our value judgments. If we are autonomous agents then sometimes we *act* autonomously even in performing actions with which we do not identify.

On the view proposed in the previous paragraph autonomy is a matter of degree. This is not the first time philosophers suggest that autonomy comes in varying degrees. Others have suggested criteria for autonomy or for moral responsibility and claimed that one can satisfy these criteria more or less.[24] But the view I am suggesting here differs from these views. On the standard view that sees autonomy as a matter of degree, if a particular action satisfies the criteria of autonomy only to a very low degree we will not consider the action autonomous. On my view an action may not satisfy any of the criteria for identification or for acting on one's value judgments and we might nevertheless think of the agent who performs the action as someone who acts autonomously in performing that action—as long as overall the agent is an autonomous agent.

But now another objection may be raised against this view. If an action may be autonomous regardless of whether an agent identifies with the desires that motivated it, as long as the agent is autonomous overall, why is it that some actions are considered non-autonomous regardless of how autonomous the agent is in general? For example, why is it that even an agent that is autonomous overall will not be considered self-controlled when in the grip of heroin? In reply I suggest we go back to our analogy with eating healthily. If you have good eating habits you eat healthily even when you eat three pieces of cake one after the other. If you eat too much sugar and butter in general then you are not eating healthily when you eat three pieces of cake one after the other. However, even if you have good eating habits if you eat cyanide you are not eating healthily. Some foods are so damaging to your health that even overall good eating habits cannot confer on the action of eating them the status of "healthy eating." Similarly some activities are indicative of a significant collapse of our autonomous agency. When an agent takes drugs as a result of his addiction to heroin, his activity is indicative of a significant collapse of his ability to identify with his actions and therefore of his ability to perform autonomous actions.[25] Thus in these cases one could not claim that being autonomous overall confers the status of "being self-controlled" on the action one does not identify with, since that action raises doubts about the claim that the agent is indeed autonomous overall. Granted, more needs to be said in order to give a precise characterization of situations in which the features of a single action suffice to count it as non-autonomous. Such a characterization is a topic for a separate paper.

Let me summarize how I think we should view the relation between autonomy and identification in light of MPI-cases. Identifying with your motivating desires and/or[26] acting on your better judgments contribute to being autonomous. An autonomous agent may be autonomous even when she is not identifying with her motivating desire. She may be autonomous in two ways: first she may be an autonomous agent, but second, she may be performing this very action autonomously. There is nothing innovative about the first part of the view. Most of us think that an agent may be an autonomous agent, in general, even if she sometimes performs actions motivated by desires with which she does not identify. One way to put it is to say that on the standard view autonomy as a feature of the agent is global. On the standard view what counts toward being autonomous in general are instances of local autonomous actions. And what counts toward being non-autonomous in general are local non-autonomous actions. I have no quarrel with this part of the standard view. But it is also often thought that autonomy as a feature of particular actions is local. People have thought that whether you are autonomous with respect to a particular action does not depend on whether you are identified with some of your other actions.[27] This part of the standard view, I believe, should be rejected. Autonomy is global not only when we speak of it as a feature of agents but also when we speak of it as a feature of particular decisions or actions. Autonomy is always global.[28]

Autonomy, being in shape, eating healthily are not isolated examples of global predicates. Global predicates are pervasive. When you are "driving to LA" you are "driving to LA" even when you stop at a red light. It's not only that in general you are driving to LA during these hours. Rather we can say that stopping at the red light is part of your "driving to LA." The same goes for "cooking dinner." If I spend the afternoon in the kitchen "cooking dinner," then I am cooking dinner even when I stop for two minutes to read the paper. What I stop doing is not the cooking of dinner. Rather I stop mixing and stirring. If you enter the kitchen during the two minutes in which I am reading the paper and ask me what I'm doing I can certainly say that I am reading the paper, but I can also say that I am cooking dinner. And there will be nothing false or misleading in what I say. And finally the same goes for being happy at a certain time. Some events and activities are of a sort that contributes to your happiness; others are neutral or detract from your happiness. But it is not a necessary condition for being happy at a certain moment that you have an experience of the sort that contributes to your happiness. If you are happy during a certain period then even moments in which you have neutral experiences or ones that detract from your happiness may be experienced as happy moments. Happiness at a time is a global property.

In all these cases what you do at a moment inherits some of its properties from the network of actions that surround it. Even if the local properties of your actions are not typical, these uncharacteristic actions are not interruptions; their nature as actions of a certain sort is determined by their relative position in the surrounding scheme of actions. The same is true for certain experiences.

A normative objection

An objector might still be unsatisfied for a reason I have not hitherto considered. Autonomy, the objector might claim, is an ideal and you have given us no reason to think that the ideal is any less demanding than it was traditionally thought to be. We think that an agent should act on their better judgment on any particular occasion and we think that they should not act on desires that they do not identify with. So autonomy as an ideal is not relaxed one little bit—it is as demanding as it always was.

I have not explicitly considered this worry, but what I said above does answer it. The way we speak of autonomy is a reflection of our ideal of autonomy, of what we think is normatively required by that ideal. Let me rephrase that answer in the negative form. What reasons do we have for thinking that autonomy is, contrary to my claim, a local ideal with respect to specific actions? What reasons do we have for thinking that we ought to be identified with every single action of ours and that we always have to act on our better judgment? Why think that in MPI cases we ought to decide other than the way we in fact do—due to the ideal of autonomy? The answer cannot be that our decisions in MPI-cases are statistically abnormal. First, because they are not; and second, because even if they were statistically abnormal, such statistical abnormality would not be a basis for a normative ideal to act in the statistically normal way. The way we react to MPI-cases also makes the attempt to claim that our behavior is in breach of an ideal very hard: we are neither alarmed nor distraught when we realize we failed to act as we thought we should. A constitutive analysis is not going to explain the normative force of the putative ideal either. A constitutivist might claim that the requirement to do more in MPI-cases is constitutive of our agency or our identity. But as, David Enoch[29] suggested, this leaves open the question why we should care about agency/identity and not about shmagency/shmidentity. As far as I can see MPI cases make it very hard to justify a local ideal of autonomy with respect to specific actions.

From the view of autonomy presented here it does not follow that we should be satisfied with our current level of contribution to noble causes. We may still need to do more than we do. We may need to do more than what we in fact do because it would be good to do more, or because we have subjective reasons to do more. What we cannot say is that we need to contribute more to noble causes because our autonomy requires us to do so.[30]

Mass perverse identification?

Our intuitions about MPI cases are in conflict with some standard views about identification and autonomy. On most theories of identification we are not identified with our actions in MPI cases and on the standard view of autonomy we are not autonomous on these occasions. However, we ordinarily think that in these cases we are identified with our actions and that when we perform these actions we act autonomously. I have concluded above that we should reject the standard view of autonomy and accept our intuition that in MPI cases we act autonomously. But I have also maintained that we should accept some version or other of the standard views of identification. We should think that we are not indentified with our actions in MPI cases. How then shall we explain the intuition that we are identified with our actions in these cases?

Identification is a technical term. Intuitions about it should be suspect. Autonomy or self-control, though not as simple or common as, for example, the concept of pain, is understood and discussed by everyone. We all struggle to overcome temptation, we all wish we would stop procrastinating, we all dread the thought of being governed by substances, persons, or emotions external to us. Intuitions about self-control rightly carry much weight when we philosophize about this concept. This is why we should pay more attention to our intuitions about self-control than to our intuitions about identification. Still, why are our intuitions about identification so far off the mark? If I am right about what I have said so far, then identification and autonomy are tightly linked. Furthermore most agents in MPI cases are acting autonomously. It is not a surprise then, that our intuitions about autonomy affect our intuitions about identification. We think that we are autonomous in MPI cases and we think that autonomy is closely related to identification, so we also think—mistakenly—that we are identified with our motives in these cases.

"MPI cases" is therefore a misnomer. In those cases we are not, after all, perversely identified. We do not identify with the desire to stay home despite the fact that all the mental states that constitute where we stand endorse going to the charity event. In these cases we are rather identified with our desire to do more for, or give more to, the causes we deem important. But if we are autonomous enough, then even actions of ours that we are not identified with might nevertheless be self-controlled.

Watson thought that he located cases in which an agent realizes that the mental states that ought to constitute where she stands support one decision and she, the agent, defiantly (and maybe paradoxically) endorses another decision. Such endorsement seemed, rightly, perverse to him. Whether such perverse identification is possible or not, the view that it is a daily occurrence must be rejected.

Conclusion

To provide an analysis of autonomy, and therefore also of the collapse of autonomy, or akrasia, we need an analysis of the agent's position; an analysis of what philosophers call "identification." The best analyses of the idea of "the agent's position" understand that notion in terms of a structure of desires, policies and judgments. An agent is autonomous, in part, to the extent that her actions are guided by a structure of desires, policies and judgments that constitute her position. But an action may be autonomous even if it is motivated by desires that are rejected by the agent—as long as it is part of a network of actions we are identified with.

Notes

* Thanks to Christine Tappolet for detailed and very helpful comments on an early draft of this paper. Thanks also to Michael Bratman, Jenny Saul, Rosanna Keef, Jimmy Lenman and Steve Makin for very helpful discussions of the ideas presented here.

1. Michael Bratman, "Autonomy and Hierarchy," in his *Structures of Agency*, OUP, Oxford 2007, pp. 162–86.
2. Nomy Arpaly in *Unprincipled Virtue* (OUP, Oxford 2003) distinguishes 8 meanings of autonomy. Among these are "managing in the world without the help of others," "not being servile or submissive," "not being physically controlled by others" (pp. 117–26). Arpaly is certainly right about the fact that we use "autonomy" to mean different things. I think, however, that we have a general

notion of autonomy, captured by Bratman's characterization, that explains why we consider "servility," "lack of financial means," "physical coercion" . . . all to be failures of autonomy. My discussion here aims to better understand the relation between what Arpaly calls authenticity and our other uses of the word autonomy.

Arpaly also rightly warns us from the hasty thought that a theory of autonomy would give us, with no further work, conditions for moral responsibility (pp. 137–41). I have no such thought.

3. The move to a broader understanding of akrasia, one that is mediated by the appeal to identification may not free us from a dependence on the notion of value judgments. One important view in the debate about identification sees identification as determined by the agent's value judgments.
4. This extension of the notion of identification is discussed by some theorists of identification; others merely present the idea of identification with a desire for certain states of affairs. I nevertheless think it is a natural extension and need not be objected to by the authors I discuss below.
5. Gary Watson, "Free Action and Free Will," *Mind*, 96, 1987, pp. 150–1.
6. I make a similar comment later with respect to the possibility that there is no conflict between my current desire to do something other than acting for a charitable cause right now, and those desires, central to my identity, to do more for charitable causes.
7. Gary Watson, "Free Agency," *Journal of Philosophy*, 72, 1975, pp. 205–20.
8. The terminological question is of course of no importance. Many authors have used the term akrasia simply to mean "action against one's better judgment" (see, for example, Arpaly, *Unprincipled Virtues*, p. 35) and this is perfectly alright. My interest is neither in criticizing this (definitional) use of the term nor those who investigated the phenomenon of action against one's better judgment. My comments here merely bear on the relation between identification and our value judgments; though ultimately my interest will be in the relation between identification and autonomy.
9. It is not always clear whether these theorists accept the Dependence thesis. There is some textual evidence that all of them do, but it is not conclusive—I provide it in footnotes to the discussion of their views. In any case, as will become clear, my challenge is not to the views of these authors but rather to the Dependence thesis itself.
10. Nomy Arpaly and Timothy Schroeder, "Praise, Blame, and the Whole Self," *Philosophical Studies*, vol. 93, no. 2, February 1999, pp. 161–88. A few comments should be made with regards to my treatment of their view:

    The view is primarily presented as giving conditions for praiseworthiness and blameworthiness—it is not, explicitly at least, a theory of identification.
    Since the view was conceived as a view of moral responsibility and since later on Arpaly moved to reject the thought that there is a tight connection between identification and responsibility, it is hard to tell whether they would have welcomed a coherentist theory of identification fashioned after their view of responsibility.

    Despite 1 and 2 above I am here considering a challenge to Arpaly and Schroeder's view as a theory of identification that can ground our analysis of self-control. I am doing so, first, because I think that such a theory is an important alternative to existing views of identification—whether or not it was conceived as such; and second, since, at the end of the day, as we shall soon see, I think the problem is not with that view but rather with our understanding of the relation between autonomy and identification.

11. Arpaly and Schroeder present their view as a theory of responsibility; they seem, however, to accept the Dependence thesis—see their comment about Gobbles' self-control in p. 178.
12. Harry G. Frankfurt, "The Faintest Passion," *Proceedings and addresses of the American Philosophical Association* 66 (1992).
13. Most often we act without reflecting. I am here discussing those rare occasions in which we do reflect, I will address later the more common non-reflective cases.
14. To see the connection that exists according to Frankfurt between autonomy and identification consider the following series of quotes from "Autonomy, Necessity and Love" (in his *Necessity, Volition and Love,* Cambridge University Press, Cambridge 1999, pp. 132–6):

    "A person acts autonomously only when his volitions derive from the essential character of his will"
    "What autonomy requires is not that the essential nature of the will be a priori, but that the imperatives deriving from it carry genuine *authority.*"

    A few paragraphs down the same article in order to explain what authority is, Frankfurt distinguishes between jealousy and addiction on the one hand and love on the other.

    "When conditions like jealousy or addiction enslave us, they do so by virtue of their sheer overwhelming intensity or strength. .... In many circumstances we regard forces of these kinds as alien to ourselves. This is not because they are irresistible. It is because we do not identify ourselves with them and do not want them to move us."

    Thus according to Frankfurt identification is necessary for the essential nature of the will to have authority, and authoritative will is necessary for autonomy.
15. According to Frankfurt an agent who does not reflect about a specific decision is a wanton with respect to that decision—identification cannot be ascribed to wantons. See "The Faintest Passion," section 8 and Frankfurt's characterization of the relation between wantonness and the formation of second order volitions in his "Freedom of the Will and the Concept of a Person," *Journal of Philosophy*, 68, no. 1,1971.
16. If his view about the relation between wantonness and freedom of the will is any indication then Frankfurt did not hold the view I suggest here. In "Freedom of the Will and the Concept of a Person" he famously claimed that wantons cannot enjoy freedom of the will.
17. See Michael Bratman, "Identification, Decision, and Treating as a Reason.," *Philosophical Topics* 24 (1996), Section 8; and Michael Bratman, "Reflection, Planning, and Temporally Extended Agency," *The Philosophical Review*, 109, no. 1 (2000) pp. 55, 60.
18. In "Autonomy and Hierarchy" Bratman argues for the view that "central cases of autonomous action" are captured by his analysis of identification. He therefore doesn't see himself as providing necessary and sufficient conditions for

autonomous action. Though he expresses the hope that this analysis can be extended to capture all cases of autonomous action, his position as it stands, leaves open the possibility that MPI cases would not, in his final view, be seen as cases of non-autonomous action and therefore will not challenge his view of identification. Since on my final analysis MPI cases indeed do not challenge the various views of identification I consider, but rather pressure us to accept a more flexible view of the relation between identification and autonomy, the fact that Bratman is not committed to the claim that acting against one's identification always constitutes a breach of autonomy, is not a problem for what I say here.

19. Michael Bratman, "Planning Agency, Autonomous Agency," in his *Structures of Agency*, OUP, Oxford 2007, p. 213.
20. Christine Tappolet in her "Personal Autonomy, akrasia, and Self-control" (unpublished manuscript) raises similar worries about the relation between autonomy and self-control. However, Tappolet restricts her worries to the notion of self control as "action against one's better judgment".
21. See, for example, John Martin Fischer and Mark Ravizza, *Responsibility and Control: A Theory of Moral responsibility*, Cambridge University Press, New York, 2003. Fischer and Ravizza are concerned with moral responsibility but most of their arguments would be relevant to a discussion of autonomy as well.
22. See, for example, Bernard Berofsky, *Liberation from Self*, Cambridge University Press, New York 1995.
23. Dworkin thinks that autonomy is only a characteristic of the agent and not of particular actions, while Christman claims that it can be either a feature of the agent or a feature of particular actions. See Gerald Dworkin, *The Theory and Practice of Autonomy*, Cambridge University Press, New York 1988; John Christman, "Autonomy in Moral and Political Philosophy," *The Stanford Encyclopedia of Philosophy* (Fall 2009 Edition), Edward N. Zalta (ed.)
24. See for example Richard Arneson, "What, if Anything, Renders All Humans Morally Equal?" in D. Jamieson, ed. *Singer and his Critics*. Oxford: Blackwell Publ. 1999, pp. 103–28.
25. At the very least it is indicative of the collapse of his ability to identify with his actions from the moment the addiction has taken hold of him. Indeed if it weren't indicative of such collapse it is far from clear that we wouldn't count the activity of taking the drugs as autonomous.
26. "and/or" since I am not trying to arbitrate here between the various theories of identification and between Dependence and Dependence +.
27. Though, as I have mentioned above, some authors think that whether you are autonomous with respect to action x may depend on whether you were autonomous with respect to some particular actions that you performed prior to x.
28. One still needs to specify the way in which the autonomy of one action depends on the identification of the agent with other actions. The autonomy of any action may depend on the identification of the agent with her actions throughout her life or may depend on the identification of the agent with other actions during the same period or perhaps with other actions of the same kind. One also needs to say under what conditions lack of identification will render an action non-autonomous regardless of its surrounding actions. I did not suggest a specific view of these relations.
29. David Enoch, "Agency, Shmagency: Why Normativity Won't Come From What is Constitutive of Action," *Philosophical Review*, 115 (2), (2006).

30. In any case autonomy is probably best understood as what Broome has called a wide-scope ideal. It requires certain coherence between our beliefs and desires on the one hand, and our decisions on the other, but it is neutral with regards to what we have to change in order to achieve that coherence. For that reason as well autonomy alone will not require us to change our behavior in MPI-cases rather than our antecedent beliefs and desires.

6

Cartesian Reflections on the Autonomy of the Mental

Matthew Soteriou

In a recent paper Korsgaard (2009b) articulates and defends a claim that she notes is part of a venerable philosophical tradition: that "reason is what distinguishes us from other animals, and that reason is in some special way the active dimension of mind." Under this view, "the human mind is active in some way that the minds of the other animals are not, and ... this activity is the essence of rationality." Korsgaard cites as examples of philosophers belonging to this tradition Kant, in his association of reason with the mind's spontaneity, and Aristotle, in his doctrine of the active intellect, or *nous*. I think a case can also be made for regarding Descartes as belonging to this tradition.

Descartes is notorious for the way in which he downgrades the psychology of non-human animals, going so far as to deny them a mind in denying them a rational soul; and he also often places emphasis upon, and attaches significance to, active, agential aspects of the rational human mind. In the *Meditations* he alludes to the way in which the mind "uses its freedom" when engaged in the method of doubt. In the *Principles of Philosophy* Descartes states explicitly that it is our free will that allows us to withhold our assent in doubtful matters.[1] And the Fourth Meditation is largely devoted to arguing that the act of judgment involves not only the intellect but also the will.[2]

My principal concern in this paper, though, isn't that of defending a particular interpretation of Descartes' texts. The aim is simply to reflect on some remarks that Descartes makes in the *Meditations* as a springboard for a discussion of the role of agency in our conscious thinking—and in particular, the extent to which self-determination and self-governance may be involved in conscious reasoning and self-critical reflection. In fact the paper will largely be devoted to reflecting on two sentences that appear in the Synopsis of the *Meditations*, and discussing some issues that arise out them. These sentences introduce Descartes' summary of the Second Meditation.

> In the Second Meditation, the mind uses its own freedom and supposes the non-existence of all the things about whose existence it can have

even the slightest doubt; and in so doing the mind notices that it is impossible that it should not exist during this time. This exercise is also of the greatest benefit, since it enables the mind to distinguish without difficulty what belongs to itself, i.e., to an intellectual nature, from what belongs to the body.

Descartes claims here that the mind "uses its own freedom" in supposing something. The first question I shall be considering (in section 6.1) is the following. In what respect, if any, does the mind "use its own freedom" when engaged in supposition? In particular, what is the role of agency in supposing something for the sake of argument?

The specific description that Descartes offers of the mind's aim in the Second Meditation is that of supposing the non-existence of all the things "about whose existence it can have even the slightest doubt." Identifying the propositions one believes whose veracity there can be slightest reason to doubt is an exercise in self-critical reflection. In section 6.2 I shall be considering the extent to which agency is implicated in self-critical reflection. I shall be arguing that the capacity to engage in self-critical reflection involves the capacity to "bracket" one's beliefs, and that the capacity to bracket one's beliefs is related to the capacity to engage in suppositional reasoning. When one brackets a belief, and when one supposes something for the sake of argument, one imposes a constraint on one's own reasoning *by* reasoning in recognition of that self-imposed constraint. In both cases, I shall be suggesting, the conscious reasoning one engages in is both self-conscious and self-governed. I shall then briefly touch on the relevance of this view of supposition and self-critical reflection to Descartes' further claim that "the mind notices that it is impossible that it should not exist during this time."

Finally, in section 6.3, I shall be saying a bit more about how I think we should conceive of the role of agency in the reasoning one engages in when one engages in self-critical reflection. In particular, I shall do so by contrasting my proposal with a view according to which the role of agency in such reasoning, and indeed, all conscious reasoning, can at best be "merely catalytic" and "indirect."[3]

6.1

In what respect, if any, does the mind "use its own freedom," as Descartes suggests, when engaged in supposition? What is the role of agency in supposing? First we need to narrow down the notion of supposition that is our concern. The phrase "S supposes that *p*" is sometimes used to attribute to S the belief or opinion that *p*, or an unacknowledged commitment to the truth of *p*; whereas the sort of supposition I want to focus on is more like an exercise of the imagination. However, we shouldn't simply equate "supposing that *p*" with "imagining that *p*," for to do so might invite the following line of thought. A way of imagining that *p* is to imagine a situation in which *p* is true, and a way of imagining a situation in which *p* is true is by imagining (for example, visualizing) a scene in which *p* is true. Indeed, whenever one visualizes a scene one thereby imagines a situation in which certain propositions are true. So whenever one visualizes a scene one thereby imagines that such and such is the case; and since supposing that *p is* imagining that *p*, whenever one visualizes a scene one thereby supposes that such and such is the case.

The problem with the conclusion of this line of thought is that visualizing a scene isn't in itself sufficient for engaging in the kind of supposition that is our concern. For the notion of supposition that I want to focus on is the kind of supposition that is involved in assuming something for the sake of argument; and intuitively, visualizing something doesn't in itself amount to assuming something for the sake of argument. So what is involved in assuming something for the sake of argument? Perhaps just putting forth, or introducing, *p* as a premise in one's reasoning, or treating *p* as a premise in one's reasoning? But these descriptions can also apply to judging that *p* (and also to asserting that *p*). So what is the difference between judging that *p* and supposing that *p*?

Judging that *p* involves representing *p as true*. Representing *p* as true isn't simply equivalent to entertaining in thought the proposition that *p* is true, for one can entertain in thought the proposition that *p* is true without representing *p as true*, as when one judges that "either *p* is true or it isn't." But for the same reason, entertaining in thought the proposition that *p* is true isn't sufficient for supposing that *p*, for entertaining in thought the proposition that *p* is true is something that one can do when one supposes for the sake of argument that "*either p* is true or *q* is true."

If we hold that judging that *p* involves representing *p* as true, a temptation may be to think that supposing that *p* for the sake of argument is a matter of acting as if one is representing *p* as true—perhaps imagining or pretending to represent *p* as true. However, a problem with this proposal is that it suggests that supposing that *p* can be a stand-alone mental act—that is, it suggests that it might be possible for one to suppose that *p* for the sake of argument, without doing anything else. Since judging (or asserting) that *p* can be a stand-alone act, it should be possible for pretending or imagining that one is judging (or asserting) that *p* to be a stand-alone act too. However, supposing that *p* for the sake of argument is not a stand-alone mental act—it is not something one can do without doing anything else. And this is relevant to why visualizing something cannot in itself be sufficient for assuming something for the sake of argument.

The idea that supposing that *p* is not a stand-alone act is something that is touched upon by Dummett in his chapter on assertion in *Frege: Philosophy of Language*. There Dummett considers the question of whether there is a force that attaches to the proposition that *p* when one supposes that *p*, which is distinct from the force that attaches to the proposition that *p* when one asserts that *p*. At one point Dummett (1973) makes the following remark:

> In supposition a thought is expressed but not asserted: "Suppose..." must be taken as a sign of the force (in our sense) with which a sentence is uttered. (Certainly it is not logically an imperative: I could, having said, "Think of a number," ask "Have you done so yet?," but it would be a joke if I asked that question having said "Suppose the witness is telling the truth.")
>
> (p. 309)

If "suppose the witness is telling the truth" is understood as "suppose *for the sake of argument* that the witness is telling the truth," then there is an oddity in the question, "Have you done so yet?" As Dummett remarks, the oddity of the question wouldn't apply if one had said "Think of a number." And we can add, neither would the oddity apply if one had said "imagine a bowl of cherries," or "imagine asserting that the witness is telling the truth." This is connected, I suggest, with the idea that the latter can be, what I have been calling, stand-alone mental acts, whereas supposing that *p* for the sake of argument cannot.

The idea that supposing that *p* for the sake of argument cannot be a stand-alone mental act is also connected, I think, with Frege's stance on supposition.[4] Frege denies that in the case of supposing that *p* a force that is distinct from that of assertion attaches to the proposition that *p*. He holds instead that the force of assertion attaches to a sentence that has *p* as a constituent.[5] On Frege's view, in the case of supposition that *p*, "p" does not appear as a complete sentence at all, but only as a constituent in a more complex sentence—in particular, it features as the antecedent of a conditional that is asserted. So Frege does not make use of a distinct force of supposition in formalizing logic.

Gentzen later went on to do so.[6] As Dummett notes,

> [Gentzen] had the idea of formalizing inference so as to leave a place for the introduction of hypotheses in a manner analogous to that in which in everyday reasoning we say "suppose ..." We require no warrant for introducing any new hypothesis, and we reason from it with just the same rules as those governing inferences from premises which we assert outright: the point of the procedure being that from the fact that certain consequences follow from some hypothesis, we can draw a conclusion that no longer depends on that hypothesis.
>
> (p. 309)

This looks like an improvement on Frege's proposal. As Gentzen observed, it is closer to the modes of inference that occur in informal reasoning.[7] For our purposes, a point that might be made against Frege's view is that it fails to mark adequately the distinction between (a) a part, or constituent, of a thought one judges, and (b) a step taken in reasoning. However, Dummett suggests that there does seem to be *something* right in what Frege says, and here I agree with Dummett. He writes,

> Although we may, contrary to Frege's view, regard suppositions as complete sentences, still supposition is different from other linguistic acts in that it is possible only as a preparation for further acts of the same speaker: namely for a series of utterances not themselves assertions (but consequences of the supposition), which culminate in an assertion. I could not just say, "Suppose 2 has a rational square root," and then stop . . . I must go on to discharge the original supposition.
>
> (p. 313)

The idea here, I take it, is that one can only genuinely be said to have introduced a supposition into one's reasoning if one does things that count as discharging that supposition (or starting to discharge that supposition);[8] and furthermore, one can only discharge the supposition if it has been introduced. Frege captures this idea by holding that when one supposes that *p* a single force (that is, assertion) attaches to a complex hypothetical sentence that has *p* as a constituent. If we hold instead that when one supposes that *p* a distinct force attaches to the proposition that *p*, we should hold that the force that attaches to the proposition that *p* and the force that attaches to propositions one infers from *p* are, in a certain sense, interdependent. That is to say, the fact that the force of supposition attaches to a proposition that *p* depends upon the occurrence of acts that count as discharging that supposition. And furthermore, when one infers *q* from *p*, the force that attaches to one's inference that *q* depends upon the fact that it is made under the scope of a supposition.

This is a reflection of the idea that we do not capture adequately the attitudinative aspect of a subject's mental condition when he supposes that *p* if we allow that supposing that *p* can be a stand-alone mental act—that is, if we allow that a subject can be said to be supposing that *p* for the sake of argument without doing anything else. The fact that a subject has adopted a suppositional attitude toward the content that *p* depends upon the occurrence of acts that count as discharging the supposition. This is why we fail to capture adequately the attitudinative aspect of a subject's mental condition when he supposes that *p* if we say that the subject is merely pretending or imagining that he is representing *p* as true. When one supposes that *p* and infers *q* from *p*, one isn't imagining or pretending that one is representing those propositions as true; and this is connected with the fact that when one is engaged in supposition, one is engaged in *actual* reasoning, not pretend or imagined reasoning.[9]

We can capture the idea that supposing that *p* for the sake of argument is not a stand-alone mental act if we say that the subject who supposes that *p* for the sake of argument represents *p* as true *by* reasoning on the assumption that *p* (where reasoning on the assumption that *p* is genuine reasoning, not pretend or imagined reasoning). Not just any old reasoning counts as reasoning on the assumption that *p*. When one reasons on the assumption that *p* one reasons with certain constraints in play—for example, one reasons on the assumption that *p* by drawing inferences from *p* and/or by introducing other propositions as premises in one's reasoning that are not inconsistent with *p* (unless entailed by *p*). Of course these constraints on one's reasoning are also in play when one introduces *p* as a premise in one's reasoning by *judging* that *p*. So what is the difference between these cases?

When one reasons on the *supposition* that *p*, the relevant constraints on one's reasoning are self-imposed. They are not simply constraints on one's reasoning that are imposed by facts in the world whose obtaining one acknowledges. And furthermore, when one reasons on the supposition that *p* one *treats* the relevant constraints on one's reasoning as self-imposed. When one reasons on the supposition that *p* one recognizes that the constraint of treating *p* as true is a constraint on one's reasoning that one has imposed on oneself. One manifests this recognition in the way in which one reasons—for example, by discharging the supposition with an outright conditional judgment or assertion.

So when one supposes that *p* for the sake of argument one imposes a constraint on one's reasoning *by* reasoning in recognition of it. For the subject who supposes that *p* for the sake of argument represents *p* as true by reasoning on the assumption that *p*, where this involves reasoning in recognition of the self-imposed constraint of treating *p* as true. This is related to the respect in which the introduction of a supposition into one's reasoning and the occurrence of acts that count as discharging that supposition are interdependent—that is, the idea that one can only genuinely be said to have introduced a supposition into one's reasoning if one does things that count as discharging that supposition, and one can only discharge the supposition if it has been introduced.

We are now in a position to turn to the question of the role of agency and self-determination in suppositional reasoning. When one acts in recognition of a self-imposed constraint, one treats oneself as a source of constraint over that activity. This is one way of thinking of what is going on in cases of self-determined, self-governed behavior. Metaphorically speaking, there's a sense in which the self-governing agent must simultaneously occupy the role of legislator and legislatee. That is, in order for an agent to be capable of governing himself, he must be capable of both imposing obligations on himself, as legislator, and he must be capable of recognizing and acting on those obligations, as the one being legislated to. His authority as self-governing legislator depends upon his own recognition of that authority. In fact it is necessary and sufficient for it. If he doesn't recognize the authority of his own legislations, then he cannot be self-governing, for he will have no authority over himself, but if he does recognize the authority of his own legislations, then he has that authority, and so is self-governing. So all an agent needs to do in order to impose on himself an obligation to do something is to recognize the authority of that self-imposed obligation. In particular, all he needs to do is act in a way that manifests his recognition of that self-imposed obligation.

The self-governing agent takes himself to have authority over himself, and he manifests this stance toward himself in the way that he acts. That is to say, the self-governing agent can impose constraints on himself by simply behaving in a way that manifests his recognition of constraints that he has imposed on himself. He imposes a constraint on himself by behaving as though he has. In this way he acts "under the idea of freedom." Acting as if one has imposed a constraint on oneself, one thereby imposes the constraint on oneself. One treats oneself as a source of constraint on oneself, and thereby governs oneself.[10]

The suggestion that has been made is that when one supposes that *p* for the sake of argument one imposes on one's reasoning the constraint of treating *p* as true by reasoning in recognition of that self-imposed constraint. There is, then, a sense in which "the mind uses its own freedom" when engaged in suppositional reasoning. For the mental activity involved is self-determined, in the following respect: one treats oneself as a source of constraint over one's own thinking, and thereby makes oneself a source of constraint over one's own thinking.

The suggestion here is that the mental activity one engages in when supposing that *p* is activity that manifests an attitude toward oneself—an attitude of treating oneself as the source of that activity. The mental activity one engages in is, in this respect, *self-conscious* mental activity. When this kind of activity occurs, something imposes a constraint on itself by acting in recognition of it. The source of the constraint on the activity is that which is acting in a constrained manner. In acting in this way, that which is acting is aware of itself as imposing a constraint on its activity in so acting. So that which is acting is presented to itself, in so acting, under a reflexive mode of presentation.[11] The subject of the activity is presented, under reflexive guise, as that which is imposing constraints on the activity by acting in recognition of them—that which is governing the activity by performing it. In this respect, when such reasoning occurs the subject of that reasoning is presented, under reflexive guise, as locus of mental autonomy—as that which governs one's thinking and reasoning when it is self-governed.

I have tried to identify a respect in which Descartes is right to claim that the "mind uses its own freedom" when engaged in supposition. Descartes' more specific description of the mind's aim in the Second Meditation is that of supposing "the non-existence of all the things about whose existence it can have even the slightest doubt."

Identifying the propositions one believes whose veracity there can be slightest reason to doubt is an exercise in self-critical reflection. To what extent is agency implicated in self-critical reflection? Is the kind of suppositional reasoning we have just been concerned with necessarily involved in self-critical reflection? I turn to these questions in the next section.

6.2

Self-critical reflection can potentially result in a variety of belief loss that is subject to epistemic evaluation—that is, the withdrawal of assent. Not all belief loss is subject to epistemic evaluation, and not all belief loss that is subject to epistemic evaluation need be the result of self-critical reflection.

Belief is always subject to epistemic evaluation, no matter what its causal origin, but the same is not true of belief loss. The fact that one forgets propositions one used to believe is not generally thought of as subject to epistemic evaluation.[12] So whether or not an *event* of belief loss is subject to epistemic evaluation cannot be solely determined by the epistemic status of the subject's beliefs prior to and after the belief loss. Belief loss is subject to epistemic evaluation only if it is somehow guided by the aim of avoiding error, where belief loss that is aimed at error-avoidance can either be guided by a conscious intention to avoid error, or by a sub-personal cognitive system that has that function. Belief loss that is aimed at avoiding error need not be guided by error-avoiding mechanisms alone; and we can make sense of belief loss that is *mis*directed at error avoidance.[13] This seems to allow us to make sense of there being instances of belief loss that are subject to epistemic evaluation but which we regard as epistemically inappropriate.

Not all instances of belief loss aimed at avoiding error, so construed, are instances of a subject withdrawing assent from some proposition as a result of self-critical reflection. Belief revision that results from the acquisition of, and updating of, evidence need not involve anything as reflective as self-critical reflection. Self-critical reflection, as I am understanding that notion here, occurs only when a subject engages with the question of whether *p* with the aim of avoiding error when he already believes that *p*. We can regard withdrawal of assent that results from self-critical reflection as a variety of the more general notion of belief revision, and we can regard belief revision as a variety of the more general notion of belief loss.

One question that can be raised about this notion of self-critical reflection is the following: how are we to make sense of the idea of a subject being consciously engaged with the question of whether *p* when he already believes that *p*? One might think that when one believes that *p* one regards the question of whether *p* as settled, whereas the subject who raises the question of whether *p*, and attempts to answer it, does not regard the question of whether *p* as settled.[14] So as soon as one raises the question of whether *p* and attempts to answer it, hasn't one ceased to regard the question of whether *p* as settled, and so hasn't one surrendered one's belief that *p*? In which case, how is self-critical reflection possible?[15]

Consider a related case in which one attempts to come up with a proof for a proposition that one already knows to be true (for example, an arithmetical theorem that one knows, via testimony, to be true). It doesn't seem right to say that a subject engaged in such activity is attempting to determine/find out whether *p* is true, for he already knows that *p* is true. Nonetheless, there is an important sense in which the activity the subject is engaged in is epistemic and truth-directed. The subject is engaged in actual (and not pretend or imagined) reasoning, where such reasoning is subject to epistemic evaluation. Steps taken in such reasoning may be epistemically unjustified, and indeed the conscious judgment "therefore, *p*" that concludes such reasoning may be epistemically unjustified, despite the fact that the subject retains his knowledge (and hence justified belief) that *p* throughout such reasoning.

When one attempts to come up with a proof for the truth of *p* when one already believes (or knows) that *p* one *brackets* one's belief that *p*. Importantly, to bracket one's belief that *p* is not to withdraw assent from *p*. The bracketing of one's belief that *p* is not something that is subject to epistemic evaluation and it is not something that requires epistemic grounds, whereas withdrawing assent from *p* (or suspending judgment over *p*) is subject to epistemic evaluation, and does require epistemic grounds.

When one brackets one's belief that *p* one does not use *p* as a premise in the reasoning one is engaged in. Of course the fact that a subject engages in reasoning without using *p* as a premise in his reasoning does not in itself entail that the subject has bracketed a belief that *p*. Such a subject may not believe that *p*, and even if he does, the truth of *p* may not be relevant to the reasoning he is engaged in, and even if it is, he may not realize that it is. We have a case in which a subject is bracketing his belief that *p* only when the fact that the subject is not using *p* as a premise in the reasoning he is engaged in is a constraint on that reasoning that the subject has imposed on himself, and one which the subject treats as a constraint that he has imposed on himself.

What we have here is akin to the account of supposing that *p* for the sake of argument outlined in the previous section. One brackets one's belief that *p by* reasoning in recognition of a self-imposed constraint—where the relevant constraint in this case is that of *not* using *p* as a premise in one's reasoning. Agency is implicated in the bracketing of one's belief in just the same way in which it is implicated in suppositional reasoning. When one brackets one's belief that *p* one imposes a constraint on one's reasoning by reasoning in recognition of it. The mental activity involved is self-determined, in the following respect: one treats oneself as a source of constraint over one's own thinking, and thereby makes oneself a source of constraint over one's own thinking. The mental activity one engages in is *self-conscious* mental activity. The subject of the activity is presented, under reflexive guise, as that which is governing the activity by performing it—that which is imposing constraints on the activity by acting in recognition of them. In this respect, when such reasoning occurs the subject of that reasoning is presented, under reflexive guise, as locus of mental autonomy.

The suggestion here is that one brackets one's belief by reasoning in recognition of a self-imposed constraint; and importantly, the reasoning one thereby engages in is actual (and not pretend or imagined) reasoning—reasoning that is epistemic, that is truth-directed, and subject to epistemic evaluation, just as suppositional reasoning is. In the case of self-critical reflection, one brackets one's belief that *p* and attempts to rule out not-*p*, with the aim of avoiding error. This involves mental activity that is self-conscious and self-governed, but which is also epistemic, truth-directed, and subject to epistemic evaluation.

This leaves unspecified the conditions under which one is epistemically justified in suspending judgment over *p* (and hence epistemically justified in withdrawing assent from *p*) as a result of such self-critical reflection, and I don't propose to address that issue here. What's important for our purposes is the claim that the sort of self-critical reflection involved in searching for epistemic grounds for doubting propositions one believes to be true does involve a form a conscious reasoning very much like that involved in suppositional reasoning. It involves reasoning that is self-conscious and self-governed.

When such reasoning occurs, an aspect of oneself is presented, under reflexive guise, as locus of mental and epistemic autonomy—that is, as that which governs one's reasoning *by* reasoning, where the aim of such reasoning is to determine what to believe. When one engages in self-critical reflection there is a sense in which that aspect of oneself that is presented under reflexive guise is an aspect of oneself from which one cannot dissociate oneself. For example, when one considers the question "what am I?," and one questions one's beliefs about what one thinks one is, it is hard to conceive of how one might dissociate oneself from that which is presented under a reflexive guise in considering that question. Indeed, this aspect of oneself will necessarily be presented under reflexive guise whenever one engages in self-critical reflection in an attempt to dissociate or distance oneself from some aspect of oneself.

We can compare here some comments that Velleman makes about Aristotle's claim that each person seems to be his "Intellect" (sometimes translated as "Understanding"). Aristotle describes the Intellect as "that whereby the soul thinks and supposes."[16] Its activity is "reflective," and it is that element which is "naturally to rule and guide."[17] In the Nicomachean Ethics he claims of the Intellect that, "Each of us would seem actually to *be* this, given that each is his authoritative and better element," and "man is this most of all."[18] Commenting on this claim, Velleman (2000) writes,

> This part of your personality constitutes your essential self in the sense that it invariably presents a reflexive aspect to your thinking: it invariably appears to you as "me" from any perspective, however self-critical or detached. That's what Aristotle means, I think, when he says that each person seems to be his understanding. You can dissociate yourself from

> other springs of action within you by reflecting on them from a critical or contemplative distance. But you cannot attain a similar distance from your understanding, because it is something that you must take along, so to speak, no matter how far you retreat in seeking a perspective on yourself. You must take your understanding along, because you must continue to exercise it in adopting a perspective, where it remains identified with you as the subject of that perspective, no matter how far off it appears to you as an object... It's your inescapable self, and so its contribution to producing your behaviour is, inescapably, your contribution.

Now let us consider Descartes' claim that in supposing the non-existence of all things about whose existence it can have the slightest doubt, "the mind notices that it is impossible that it should not exist during this time." According to the account of suppositional reasoning outlined in the previous section, one makes such a supposition *by* reasoning on that assumption, and when one reasons on that assumption one thereby engages in self-conscious mental activity that presents an aspect of oneself under reflexive guise. One can of course reason on the assumption that one does not exist, but it is impossible to reason on the assumption that one does not exist without thereby engaging in mental activity that presents an aspect of oneself under reflexive guise during the time that one is engaged in such reasoning. And that which is presented under reflexive guise is presented as locus of mental autonomy—as that which governs one's thinking when it is self-governed.

Furthermore, when one engages in self-critical reflection and considers what one can have the slightest grounds to doubt, one may bracket one's belief that one exists, but when one does so, one thereby engages in self-conscious mental activity that presents an aspect of oneself under reflexive guise. In particular, one engages in self-conscious mental activity that presents an aspect of oneself, under reflexive guise, as locus of mental and epistemic autonomy. And furthermore, I have suggested, that which is thereby presented under reflexive guise is an aspect of oneself from which one cannot dissociate oneself. In that respect we might agree with Descartes that one cannot dissociate oneself from one's "intellectual nature" when engaged in such an exercise.

In the rest of the quote from the Synopsis of the *Meditations*, Descartes goes on to claim, "this exercise . . . enables the mind to distinguish without difficulty what belongs to itself, that is, to an intellectual nature, from what belongs to the body." On one reconstruction of Descartes' thinking, Descartes is alluding here to an epistemological criterion that enables the mind to distinguish what belongs to itself "from what belongs to the body." According to this interpretation, for Descartes, the application of this epistemological criterion is supposed to help protect the coherence of the notion of disembodied existence, which in turn is used as a step in an argument for substance dualism.

If we assume that, for Descartes, the application of such an epistemological criterion is supposed to help protect the coherence of the notion of disembodied existence, we should look to Descartes' conception of disembodied existence in order to get a clearer view of how the application of the epistemological criterion is to be understood. It is worth noting in this context that according to Descartes, the disembodied soul has the faculty of the intellect, but lacks the faculties of sensory perception and imagination.[19] Moreover, a point that is perhaps obvious, but one which I think is worth emphasizing, is that for Descartes the disembodied soul is a disembodied *agent*. Making coherent the notion of a disembodied intellectual *agent* would require making sense of the notion of an agent capable of action but incapable of bodily action. One might then wonder whether an epistemological criterion can be applied to mark a distinction between mental action and bodily action.[20] Can the latter be the subject of skeptical attack in a way in which the former cannot?[21] And if so, can this be used to make coherent the notion of such a disembodied agent?

It would take us too far afield to address these issues here, for as I mentioned at the outset, my principal concern here isn't that of offering any particular interpretation of Descartes' texts. For what remains of the paper I want to remain focused on the question of the role of agency in self-critical reflection.

At the start of the paper I cited Korsgaard's recent discussion of the claim that "reason is what distinguishes us from other animals, and that reason is in some special way the active dimension of mind." Korsgaard connects the idea that we have a distinctive, capacity for *active* reasoning with the idea that we have a form of "reflective" consciousness that allows us to engage in self-critical reflection. Some of Korsgaard's critics have objected to the idea (which they take to be part of her proposal) that our ability to reflect on our own beliefs somehow allows belief formation to be governable by such reflection. They argue that it is a mistake to think that we have "reflective *control*" over belief acquisition and revision. The fact that we have a reflective form of consciousness (for example, the fact that we know what we think), they object, does not thereby allow the notion of freedom to get a grip in the realm of belief, and so does not thereby provide us with a form of epistemic autonomy.[22]

The view I have been outlining is similar to Korsgaard's, insofar as I too have been suggesting that there is a form of reasoning implicated in our capacity to engage in self-critical reflection that is both self-conscious and self-governed. However, central to that view is the claim that the role of mental autonomy in self-critical reflection is to be understood in terms of our capacity to *bracket* our beliefs, and not merely in our capacity to know what we believe. I have suggested that our capacity to bracket beliefs is related to our capacity to engage in suppositional reasoning, which involves reasoning in recognition of a self-imposed constraint. In the final section of the paper I want to clarify further how I think we should conceive of the role of agency in self-critical reflection, given this emphasis on the notion of bracketing. In particular, I want to do so by contrasting my proposal with a view according to which the role of agency in such reasoning (and indeed, all conscious reasoning) can at best be "merely catalytic" and "indirect".[23]

6.3

Korsgaard connects the human capacity for self-awareness with the idea that "the human mind is active in some way that the minds of the other animals are not" (2009), which, in turn, she claims, provides us with a form of epistemic autonomy. O'Shaughnessy (2000) expresses a similar line of thought. He suggests that our capacity to know that we have thoughts, "together with the capacity to contemplate their denial as a possibility that is not in fact realized" provides us with a form of mental freedom that allows us to "transcend the condition of animal immersion":

> the animal merely has its beliefs, which are produced in it through sense, regularities in experience, desire, innate factors, etc. It does not know it has them, it has no hand in their installation, and it cannot compare them to the world. All it can do is harbour them and act upon them.
>
> In this special sense animals may be said to be *immersed* in the world in a way thinking beings are not . . . there can in their case be no *working toward* a belief, no believing through *cogitation*, no form of *responsibility* for belief, and in consequence no kind of *mental freedom*.
>
> . . . one of the primary uses of self-awareness in thinking creatures is in self-determination and mental freedom.
>
> (p. 110)

One difficulty with this sort of view, one might think, is that it leaves unclear how the mere capacity to become conscious of one's own beliefs, and their grounds, can provide one with the ability to "have a hand in their installation." According to Korsgaard, as self-conscious subjects, we have reflective awareness of our own mental states and activities as such, and this self-conscious form of consciousness opens up what she calls "a space of reflective distance." For she suggests, "our capacity to turn our attention onto our own mental activities is also a capacity to distance ourselves from them, and to call them into question."[24] This looks similar to O'Shaughnessy's suggestion that what allows us to 'transcend the condition of animal immersion', is our capacity to know that we have thoughts together with the capacity to contemplate their denial. Korsgaard then claims that this space of reflective distance ensures that "we are, or can be, active, self-directing, with respect to our beliefs." It "presents us with the possibility and the necessity of exerting a kind of control over our beliefs."[25] However, again, one might wonder how this "space of reflective distance" is supposed to allow us to "exert control over our beliefs." As Moran puts it, it is not as though, glancing inwards, we can simply manipulate our attitudes as so much mental furniture.[26] So how does agency figure in the exercise of self-critical reflection that is made possible by "the space of reflective distance?"

According to one way of regarding this issue, the role of mental agency in self-critical reflection can at best be rather limited. Here we might compare Galen Strawson's skepticism about the extent of the role of agency over our thinking and reasoning.[27] Thinking about something involves the occurrence of mental acts individuated, in part, by their propositional contents, and Strawson claims that these mental acts can be mental actions only if the particular contents that individuate them are ones that the subject intends to think. However, in the case of many such mental acts it seems that the content of the mental act cannot figure in the content of one's prior intention. Strawson has argued that no thinking of a particular thought-content is ever an action. This is because one's thinking of the particular content can only amount to an action if the content thought is already there, "available for consideration and adoption for intentional production" in which case, "it must already have 'just come' at some previous time in order to be so available" (p. 235). One way of putting this point is to say that when conscious reasoning occurs, there is no *attempt* to think a thought with a given content.[28] In the case of the sort of thinking that occurs when one reasons, what is important is that relevant changes to one's mind occur. Perhaps sometimes one also knows that such changes occur, but arguably the acquisition of such knowledge is itself simply a further change to one's mind. So agency is not, after all, implicated in the thinking of the particular thoughts that occur when one reasons. Strawson does not deny that mental actions do occur, but on his view, "Mental action in thinking is restricted to the fostering of conditions hospitable to contents' coming to mind" (p. 234).

Strawson claims that, "the role of genuine action in thought is at best indirect. It is entirely prefatory, it is essentially—merely—catalytic" (p. 231). It "is restricted to the fostering of conditions hospitable to contents' coming to mind," for according to Strawson, the component of agency in thinking and reasoning is restricted to that of setting the mind at a given topic, aiming or tilting the mind in a given direction, and waiting for contentful thoughts to occur—waiting "for the 'natural causality of reason' to operate in one" (p. 231). Once one has taken mental aim at a given topic, "the rest is a matter of ballistics, mental ballistics"—"as ballistic as the motion of the ball after it has ceased to be in contact with one's foot" (p. 239). Strawson writes, "There is I believe no action at all in reasoning... considered independently of the preparatory, catalytic phenomena just mentioned" (p. 232).[29] On this view the mental events involved in conscious reasoning are not in themselves agential, rather, they can (sometimes) be the effects of something agential.

I have offered a rather different proposal as to how we should conceive of the role of mental agency in the sort of conscious reasoning that occurs when one engages in self-critical reflection. On my view the notion of bracketing one's beliefs has a key role to play. I have argued that self-critical reflection involves a capacity to bracket one's beliefs, and agency is implicated in the bracketing of one's belief in just the same way in which it is implicated in suppositional reasoning.[30] In both cases the mental activity involved is self-determined, in the following respect: one treats oneself as a source of constraint over one's own thinking, and thereby makes oneself a source of constraint over one's own thinking. For in both cases one imposes a constraint on one's reasoning by reasoning in recognition of it. This leads to a rather different view of how we should conceive of the extent of the role of mental agency in such reasoning.

First, we can contrast the picture I have offered of the way in which agency is implicated in suppositional reasoning and self-critical reflection, with the conception of action that Frankfurt criticizes in his paper "The Problem of Action"[31]. In that paper Frankfurt targets a view of action that holds that the "essential difference between actions and mere happenings lies in their prior causal histories," and which thereby implies that, "actions and mere happenings do not differ essentially in themselves at all" (p. 69). According to the account of action that Frankfurt objects to, actions and mere happenings are "differentiated by nothing that exists or that is going on at the time those events occur, but by something quite extrinsic to them—a difference at an earlier time among another set of events entirely . . . they locate the distinctively essential features of action exclusively in states of affairs which may be past by the time the action is supposed to occur" (p. 70).

According to the accounts of suppositional reasoning and self-critical reflection I have been recommending, agency is implicated in the conscious mental events that constitute a subject's suppositional reasoning and self-critical reflection in so far as such events manifest the subject's recognition of a self-imposed constraint. For example, when a subject supposes that *p* for the sake of argument, the constraint of treating *p* as true is a constraint that the subject imposes on himself *by* reasoning in recognition of it. The constraint he imposes on himself is *sustained* by the occurrence of conscious mental events that manifest his recognition of that self-imposed constraint. So the agency that is implicated in such reasoning does not simply reside in its prior causal history—that is, in the fact that some appropriate, temporally prior, intention or belief/desire pair initiated it.

For this reason, the picture that I am suggesting of the way in which agency is implicated in suppositional reasoning and self-critical reflection can also be contrasted with Strawson's characterization of the role of agency in thinking and reasoning. Strawson's view suggests that the conscious mental events involved in suppositional reasoning, and the sort of reasoning that occurs when one engages in self-critical reflection, can in principle lack appropriate, agential, causal antecedents and thereby lack any aspect of agency whatsoever. In contrast, I have argued that in the cases of suppositional reasoning and self-critical reflection, the conscious reasoning one engages in manifests an attitude toward oneself—an attitude of treating oneself as the source of that activity. Acting as if one has imposed a constraint on oneself, one thereby imposes the constraint on oneself. One treats oneself as a source of constraint on oneself, and thereby governs oneself. So the forms of reasoning involved in suppositional reasoning and self-critical reflection—the forms of reasoning that allow us to 'transcend the condition of animal immersion'—are necessarily self-conscious and self-governed.[32]

Notes

1. For discussion of the role of the mind's freedom in the Method of Doubt see *Principles of Philosophy* Pt. I: 6, and 39.
2. In *Principles of Philosophy* Descartes also claims, "the supreme perfection of man" is that he acts freely, and in the Fourth Meditation Descartes writes, "it is above all in virtue of the will that I understand myself to bear in some way the image and likeness of God."
3. Strawson 2003.
4. See Frege 1906, 1918, and 1923.
5. An issue that is also relevant to Frege's view of supposition, which I don't discuss, is the suggestion that he commits to the view that one can make inferences only from *true* premises, and hence not from a mere hypothesis. On this issue, see Anscombe 1959. For a diagnosis of Frege's commitment to this claim, different from that offered by Anscombe, see Dummett 1973; and for skepticism about the claim that Frege should be interpreted as committing to this view, see Stoothoff 1963.
6. See also the system developed by Fitch (1952), discussed by Green (2000).
7. Gentzen 1969, p. 78.
8. One can of course express one's intention to suppose that *p* without discharging that supposition, and one can also issue an invitation to others to engage in that supposition, but an expression of an intention to suppose that *p* isn't in itself sufficient for supposing that *p*, and neither is the issuing of such an invitation. It might be held that in the case of a speech act, an utterance of 'suppose that *p*' can be regarded as having the force of supposition, whether or not one successfully begins to discharge that supposition, as long as the utterance is understood as carrying the normative requirement that one should attempt to discharge it. One might argue that in the case of thought, where this doesn't involve any overt speech acts, the decision to suppose that *p* brings with it a similar normative commitment. For example, in deciding to suppose that *p* one commits oneself to discharging that supposition. However, deciding to suppose that *p* isn't equivalent to supposing that *p*; and once a decision to suppose that *p* has been made, I suggest, one doesn't genuinely start supposing that *p* until one begins to discharge that supposition. It is thought, and not speech acts, that I am principally concerned with here.
9. Compare Anscombe's remark: "Aristotle rightly says that a conclusion is reached in just the same way in a 'demonstrative' and a 'dialectical' syllogism: if you say 'suppose p, and suppose q, then r'; or if, being given 'p', you say: 'suppose q, then r'; you are just as much inferring, and essentially in the same way, as if you are given 'p' and 'q' as true and say '*therefore* r'." (1959, p. 116).

10. These remarks on the notion of self-governance obviously ignore a number of important and substantive questions—for example, the question of the constraints that the *truly* self-governing should impose on himself when determining which constraints to impose on himself.
11. For a discussion of the notion of a "reflexive mode of presentation" that has influenced my thinking here, see Velleman 2006.
12. Compare Harman 1984, 1986 and 1995. See also Williamson 2000, p. 219.
13. Compare Velleman's discussion, in "On the Aim of Belief," of what makes an "acceptance" a belief (in Velleman 2000, pp. 252–4).
14. Compare the discussions of Levi 1980 in Adler 2002, Ch. 11, and in Roorda 1997.
15. Compare Adler 2002 on, what Adler calls, the "blindness problem": "The normal workings of belief is to 'blind' us to what might be described from the outside as clues to the contrary . . . The 'blindness' problem is deep because to solve it we cannot just attempt to remove the blinders, since they are a facet of the good workings of belief" (p. 286).
16. *De Anima* III.4, 429a, in Aristotle 1984.
17. *NE* X.7, 1177a, in Aristotle 1984.
18. *NE* X.7, 1177b, in Aristotle 1984.
19. In the Sixth Meditation the faculty of the intellect is distinguished from the faculties of sensory perception and imagination. There Descartes claims that the faculty of the intellect can exist without the latter two faculties, but these latter two faculties cannot exist without the faculty of intellect. See also *Principles of Philosophy* Pt. II: 3 and the letter to Gibieuf, 19 January 1642 (in Descartes 1985), where Descartes is explicit that the faculties of sensory perception and imagination belong to the soul only in so far as it is joined to the body.
20. For a brief discussion of this idea, see Soteriou 2009.
21. It seems clear that in the First Meditation, in attempting to undermine by skeptical argument the putative knowledge we acquire via the senses, Descartes takes himself to be undermining the knowledge we have of our own bodily actions: "I shake my head and it is not asleep; as I stretch out and feel my hand I do so deliberately and I know what I am doing... Suppose then that I am dreaming, and that these particulars—that my eyes are open, that I am moving my head and stretching out my hands—are not true." So one relevant consideration here is whether skeptical arguments that target the putative knowledge we acquire via the senses can be used to undermine our putative knowledge of our own bodily actions, in a way in which they cannot be used to undermine our putative knowledge of our own mental actions.
22. For this line of objection to Korsgaard see Owens 2000.
23. Strawson 2003.
24. Korsgaard 1996, p. 93.
25. Korsgaard 2009b. See also Korsgaard 2009a, pp. 115–16.
26. See Moran 1999 and 2001.
27. Strawson 2003.
28. Compare here Travis 2008: "Both thinking and saying represent something as so. Saying relies on means for representing to others. Thinking—representing to oneself—does not . . . So saying needs vehicles—incarnations of visible, audible, forms, recognizably doing what they do. Representing to myself works otherwise. One *chooses* what to say; not what to think. I judge *just* where I can judge no other. It need not be made recognizable to me what I am judging for me to do so . . . Judging needs no vehicles in *such* roles. Does it need vehicles at all?" (p. 4).

29. Strawson's view is criticized by Buckareff 2005, and discussed in Mele 2009. Compare also Dorsch's (2009) notion of the 'mediated' agency involved in certain varieties of thinking: we "trigger" some process (epistemic or merely causal) with some goal in mind, but recognize, and instrumentally rely on, the capacity of such a process to lead, *by itself,* to the desired outcome. For a rather different view of the role of agency in reasoning, see Gibbons 2009.
30. O'Shaughnessy seems to acknowledge the significance to our "mental freedom" of our ability to bracket our beliefs and engage in suppositional reasoning, although he doesn't put this in quite the terms I do. He writes, "cogitation entertains propositions under the heading 'not yet to be used', or 'may be rejected', it 'puts them on ice for the time being', whereas the 'practical immersion' of animals only entertains propositions as 'to be used here and now'"; and "Transcending the condition of 'animal immersion' is achieved through the linguistically assisted capacity to think in the modalities of the possible and the hypothetical, which is an exercise of the imaginative power" (2000, p. 110).
31. Reprinted in Frankfurt 1988.
32. Many thanks to Tom Crowther, Guy Longworth, and Lucy O'Brien for their comments on earlier drafts. For very helpful discussion of these issues, thanks also to Steve Butterfill, Bill Brewer, Quassim Cassam, Naomi Eilan, Christoph Hoerl, Hemdat Lerman, and Johannes Roessler.

References

Adler, J. (2002), *Belief's Own Ethics*. Cambridge, MA: MIT Press.

Anscombe, G. E. M. (1959), *An Introduction to Wittgenstein's Tractatus: Themes in the Philosophy of Wittgenstein*. St. Augustine's Press: Indiana.

Aristotle (1984), *The Complete Works of Aristotle; Revised Oxford Translation*. J. Barnes, ed., Bollingen Series, Princeton: Princeton University Press.

Buckareff, A. (2005), "How (not) to think about Mental Action," *Philosophical Explorations: An International Journal for the Philosophy of Mind and Action*, 1741–5918, vol. 8, no. 1, 2005: 83–9.

Descartes, R., (1985), *Philosophical Writings of Descartes*, Volumes I–III, (Translated by Cottingham, Stoothoff and Murdoch; Vol. III edited by Cottingham, Stoothoff, Murdoch and Kenny). Cambridge: Cambridge University Press.

Dorsch, F. (2009), "Judging and the Scope of Mental Agency," in O'Brien and Soteriou, eds, *Mental Actions*. Oxford: Oxford University Press.

Dummett, M. (1973), *Frege: The Philosophy of Language*. London: Duckworth.

Fitch, F. B. (1952), *Symbolic Logic*. New York: Ronald Press.

Frege, G. (1906), "On the Foundations of Geometry; Second Series," in, B. McGuinness, trans M. Black, *Collected Papers on Mathematics, Logic, and Philosophy* (Oxford: Blackwell, 1984).

Frege, G. (1918), "Negation," in, B. McGuinness, trans M. Black, *Collected Papers on Mathematics, Logic, and Philosophy* (Oxford: Blackwell, 1984).

Frege, G. (1923), "Compound Thoughts," in, B. McGuinness, trans by M. Black, *Collected Papers on Mathematics, Logic, and Philosophy* (Oxford: Blackwell, 1984).

Frankfurt, H. (1988), *The Importance of What We Care About*. New York: Cambridge University Press.

Gentzen, G. (1969), *The Collected Papers of Gerhard Gentzen*, ed. M. E. Szabo, Amsterdam.

Gibbons, J. (2009), "Reason in Action," in O'Brien and Soteriou, eds, *Mental Actions*. Oxford: Oxford University Press.

Green. M. (2000), "The Status of Supposition," *Nous* 34:3: 376–99.
Harman, G. (1984), "Positive versus Negative Undermining in Belief Revision," *Nous*, 18: 39–49.
Harman, G. (1986), *Change in View: Principles of Reasoning*. Cambridge, MA: MIT Press.
Harman, G. (1995), "Rationality," in E. E. Smith and D. N. Osherson, eds. *Thinking: Invitation to Cognitive Science*, vol. 3. Cambridge, MA: MIT Press. Also in his *Rationality, Meaning and Mind* (1999), Oxford University Press.
Korsgaard, C. (1996), *The Sources of Normativity*. Cambridge: Cambridge University Press.
Korsgaard, C. (2009a), *Self-Constitution: Agency, Identity, and Integrity*. Oxford: Oxford University Press.
Korsgaard, C. (2009b), "The Activity of Reason," Presidential Address of the Eastern Division of the American Philosophical Association, 2008. Forthcoming in *The Proceedings and Addresses of the American Philosophical Association*, vol. 83, no.2, November 2009.
Levi, I. (1980), *The Enterprise of Knowledge*. Cambridge, MA: MIT Press.
Mele, A. (2009), "Mental Action: A Case Study," in O'Brien and Soteriou, eds, *Mental Actions*. Oxford University Press.
Moran, R. (1999), "The Authority of Self-Consciousness," *Philosophical Topics*, vol. 26, nos 1 and 2: 179–200.
Moran, R. (2001), *Authority and Estrangement: An Essay on Self-Knowledge*. Princeton: Princeton University Press.
Owens, D. (2000), *Reason without Freedom*. London: Routledge.
O'Shaughnessy, B. (2000), *Consciousness and the World*. Oxford: Oxford University Press.
Roorda, J. (1997), "Fallibilism, Ambivalence and Belief," *The Journal of Philosophy* 94: 126–55.
Soteriou, M. (2009), "Mental Agency, Conscious Thinking, and Phenomenal Character," in O'Brien and Soteriou, eds, *Mental Actions*. Oxford: Oxford University Press.
Stoothoff, R. (1963), "Note on a Doctrine of Frege," *Mind*, vol. 72, no. 287: 406–8.
Strawson, G. (2003), "Mental Ballistics *or* the Involuntariness of Spontaneity," *Proceedings of the Aristotelian Society*, vol. 103: 227–56.
Travis, C. (2008), "Thinking About Thinking." Inaugural Lecture at King's College London, (online at http://www.kcl.ac.uk/content/1/c6/04/33/24/ThinkThink4-4.pdf).
Velleman, J. D. (2000), *The Possibility of Practical Reason*. Oxford: Oxford University Press.
Velleman, J. D. (2006), *Self to Self*. Cambridge: Cambridge University Press.
Williamson, T. (2000), *Knowledge and Its Limits*. Oxford: Oxford University Press.

Part III
Free Agency

7
The Revisionist Turn: A Brief History of Recent Work on Free Will

Manuel Vargas

7.1 The story and how it shall be told

I've been told that in the good old days of the 1970s, when Quine's desert landscapes were regarded as ideal real estate and David Lewis and John Rawls had not yet left a legion of influential students rewriting the terrain of metaphysics and ethics respectively, compatibilism was still compatibilism about free will. And, of course, incompatibilism was still incompatibilism about free will. That is, compatibilism was the view that free will was compatible with determinism. Incompatibilism was the view that free will was incompatible with determinism.[1] What philosophers argued about was whether free will was compatible with determinism. Mostly, this was an argument about how to understand claims that one could do otherwise. You did not need to talk about moral responsibility, because it was obvious that you couldn't have moral responsibility without free will. The literature was a temple of clarity.

Then, somehow, things began to go horribly wrong. To be sure, there had been activity in the 1960s that would have struck some observers as ominous. Still, it was not until the 1980s that those initial warning signs gave way to real trouble. The meanings of terms twisted. Hybrid positions appeared. By the late 1980s a landslide had begun, giving way to a veritable avalanche of work in the mid-1990s that continues up to now. Now, self-described compatibilists and incompatibilists make frequent concessions to each other, concessions that made little sense in the framework of the older literature. New positions and strange terminology appear in every journal publication. The temple of clarity is no more.

At any rate, that's what I've been told. I think this tale is mostly correct, but for reasons importantly different than those given by its usual tellers. I do think the terminology deployed in the contemporary literature can mislead in a way that hinders an easy grasp of the issues. However, I also think the infelicities of the current literature arose in no small part because the architects of the prior debates did not appreciate some subtle fault lines running under the old temple. It is those fault lines, and why they went unnoticed, and what we can do about them now that we see them, that constitute the principal subjects of this chapter.

Less metaphorically, what I wish to explain is *how* we came to our current place, what under-appreciated difficulties the recent history has given rise to, and what ways we have for extricating ourselves from these difficulties. I will begin somewhat elliptically: I wish to focus on some broad themes before I make the case that there are genuine difficulties with our current ways of framing the issues of free will and moral responsibility. This is partly because the problems I will ultimately focus on are harder to see if they are disconnected from broadly methodological issues in philosophy. So, I begin by discussing some broader philosophical currents, and their implications for the free will debate. I then focus on some important changes internal to the literature on free will over roughly the past 40 years. I argue that these changes—both internal and external to work on free will—have indeed left us with some underappreciated challenges. I conclude by outlining one way out of these difficulties.

7.2 From metaphysics to ethics and back again

Conventional wisdom is that there are two major clusters of interests on the free will problem reflected in two populations that approach matters with interests grounded in distinct sub-fields within philosophy. The two groups are the *metaphysicians* and the *ethicists*.[2] The former are more apt to focus on *free will* and the latter are more apt to focus on *moral responsibility*. And, the former are more apt to be incompatibilists and the latter seem more evenly split, perhaps even favoring compatibilism.

The distinction is not perfect, but it is useful for getting at two phenomena: distinct centers of gravity in the literature and the way in which these centers of gravity structure interactions between groups. For instance, concerns that are regarded as central to one cluster seem peripheral, at best, to the other. The divergence of concern is manifest in the frequency with which philosophers disagree about the fundamental terms of the debate, the invocation of burden of proof arguments, and the increasingly frequent discoveries of purported "dialectical stalemates."[3] However, to understand why ethicists and metaphysicians may be talking past each other, we have to look beyond the boundaries of work on specifically free will and moral responsibility.

Consider the following conventional story of mainstream Anglophone philosophy in the second half of the twentieth century. Around the mid-century, logical positivism and ordinary language philosophy had both collapsed because of internal and external pressure. In the aftermath, there was a synthesis of those elements that seemed most promising from the prior movements. On one side there was a logical constructionist tradition (think: Frege, Russell, Carnap) that grew out of concerns about ideal language and the aspirations to a logical foundation to mathematics. On the other, there were the puzzles that emerged from ordinary language philosophy's reflections on natural language. The synthesis was one where the methods of the logical constructionists were brought to bear on, among other things, the concerns suggested by natural language.[4] Two strands emerged from this synthesis. One was a broadly naturalistic strand that took its proximal inspiration from Quine and the idea of philosophy being on a continuum with the sciences. The other strand was broadly Strawsonian: conceptual analysis was central and distinctive of philosophy, and any postulated metaphysics were expected to be elucidations of implicit conceptual structures.

The Quinean strand was broadly revisionist in that it accepted the necessity of philosophical accounts departing from common sense, and indeed, it fully expected that such departures were in keeping with the general scientific spirit. Where philosophical work is continuous with the project of science, conceptual reform is inevitable, and usually a sign of hard-nosed progress. From Quine, we got a recommendation to pursue naturalized epistemology and to treat philosophical theorizing as engaged in some degree of paraphrasing away from ordinary usage. Above all, we were enjoined to cast a baleful eye on grandiose metaphysics.

In contrast to the naturalistic, paraphrasing predilections of the Quinean strand, the Strawsonian strand was much less given to conceptual revision. The Strawsonian strand took its metaphysics descriptively—we could uncover the ontology of our convictions, but advocating conceptual change was to be regarded with suspicion. If the ideal language tools of the logical constructionist carried the day, their success was to be put in service of illuminating our existing concepts and their relationship to one another. Of course, conceptual analysis of the old, bad sort was to be rejected—no hard and fast distinction between the analytic and the synthetic here—but the philosopher's task was nevertheless to map concepts, both their internal structure and their relationship to one another.[5]

By the early 1970s, this picture began to change in some important ways. In an effort to build roads from our minds to the world, the work of Saul Kripke, David Lewis, Alvin Plantinga, and many others paved over Quine's beloved desert landscapes of ontology. The result was a renaissance in metaphysics. A particularly interesting aspect of that early work in metaphysics was that much of it stayed close to the Strawsonian project of descriptive metaphysics. Intuitions were the arbiters of the limits of any piece of analysis, and counterintuitiveness was almost always taken as a sign that things had gone badly. It was not always clear why ordinary semantic intuitions were any guide to metaphysics, but the basic ground rules in play were the ones offered by Lewis:

> One comes to philosophy already endowed with a stock of opinions. It is not the business of philosophy either to undermine or to justify these

> pre-existing opinions, to any great extent, but only to try to discover ways of expanding them into an orderly system. [. . .] It succeeds to the extent that (1) it is systematic, and (2) it respects those of our pre-philosophical opinions to which we are firmly attached. In so far as it does both better than any alternative we have thought of, we give it credence.[6]

To be sure, this approach, when combined with the logical tools afforded by twentieth century philosophy—modal logic, especially—was famously capable of yielding some startling, even strongly counter-intuitive conclusions. Still, the basic strategy was modest in its conceptual ambitions and profound in its respect for our received ontological categories and commitments.

At least some contemporary metaphysicians have aspirations importantly different than those given by Lewis in 1973. Nevertheless, Lewis' characterization captures the tenor of its time. Importantly, it also describes the rules of the work on the metaphysics of free will, both then and (to a lesser degree) now. There are several reasons why this conception of method persisted. First, the work on free will in the 1970s remains the starting point for understanding the metaphysics of free will. Arguments developed and cemented in that period—whether counterexamples to the conditional analysis or the Consequence Argument and its successors or Frankfurt cases, and so on—have remained central to the debate.[7] The methodological presuppositions of that period were inherited by the contemporary literature. Second, for reasons unclear to me, the broadly Quinean strand had less direct influence in the metaphysics of free will.[8] To be sure, the general rise of naturalism in analytic philosophy helped to rein in the seriousness with which non-naturalistic libertarian accounts were regarded. And the importance of consistency with naturalism was a crucial spur in the development of contemporary libertarian accounts, most of which are now intended to be compatible with naturalistic presuppositions.[9] However, the emphasis on conceptual revision, whether as a response to pressures from science or as part of a more general strategy of paraphrasing commonsense, gained little obvious traction in the metaphysically-oriented literature.

Here, though, is where that other center of gravity—the ethics-oriented literature—matters. Ethical concerns have long had a central place in work on free will.[10] In the early 1970s it was perhaps at a low ebb, but its influence was restored in the late 1980s and 1990s. The important thing to keep track of here is how philosophical ethics diverged from metaphysics in some important methodological assumptions. At least since the end of the nineteenth century, much of the philosophical tradition in ethics was already committed to the idea that intuitions were not sacrosanct.[11] Few ethicists held on to the ambition of showing that all our divergent intuitions about ethics could be neatly explained by a single ethical theory. There were always some intuitions that needed to be explained away. The challenge was to articulate principled reasons for discounting the problematic intuitions.

Awareness of this situation permeates the teaching of even introductory ethics. We challenge Kantian theories with cases where innocents can only be protected by lying. We raise doubts about utilitarianism by asking students to imagine grabbing people off the street to harvest organs. We invite objections to virtue ethics on grounds of embracing a kind of moral narcissism that misses agent-neutral moral values. The challenge is typically to explain away such intuitions, to treat them as compromises in a theory that gets the core notions compellingly correct; the hard part is to get students to see this and to not simply treat these as decisive counterexamples.

This is not to deny the existence of an important tradition of ethical theorizing, construed as an enterprise whose aspirations are to illuminate the structure of the categories we already possess. Such strands can be found as far back as Aristotle, at least. But the dominant, intuition-ambivalent strand from the late nineteenth century onwards was solidified by the advent of the Rawlsian methodology of wide reflective equilibrium.[12] Rawls' idea was that any adequate normative theory was going to involve some compromise between our intuitions, our considered convictions, and the wider evidence we had for relevant suppositions. So, unlike descriptive metaphysics, ethics was already widely open to even substantial revision of its subject matter.

Here, then, is where we find the seeds for much of the talking past one another that occurs between various camps in the free will literature. Much of the debate, at least as it was conducted in the late 1960s and 1970s was structured by issues close to the metaphysician's heart: the Consequence Argument, debates about the conditional analysis of 'can', alternative possibilities. Perhaps atypically, at least for the late modern period in philosophy onwards, the moral issues receded into the background. For all that, though, the moral dimensions of the problem were never fully expunged. Inevitably, these issues attracted the interests of some ethics-oriented philosophers. Such philosophers stepped into debates where the extant literature and governing suppositions were set by the aims and methods of the metaphysicians. These suppositions tended to be at cross-purposes with the methodology familiar to ethicists, and the dominance of the metaphysical approach made otherwise natural questions harder to ask. (For example, if one approaches the problem of free will internal to concerns in ethics, it should seem easy to ask why there is so much concern about ordinary intuitions about free will: why should we suppose that an adequate account of moral responsibility and the condition of control it demands of agents should perfectly map on to the intuitions we already have about this matter? It would be a miraculous alignment between the justified norms and our existing practices.) But these questions were hard to ask in a climate where the norms in play where those of descriptive metaphysics. An unstable solution began to emerge: maintain the ethical concerns but adhere to the norms of description.[13]

Importantly, the difference between metaphysicians and ethicists working on free will was not and is not *just* a difference in metaphysical versus moral issues. More fundamentally, it is a difference in how one goes about building a philosophical theory and what role departures from intuition play in that theorizing. So, there is a difference in focus and a difference in method. However, I also think there is a third difference: a difference in *the aim* of theorizing.[14]

While there are certainly more, there have been at least two important conceptions of aim in the free will literature, one we can call *constructionist* and the other *descriptionist*.[15] The constructionist's aim is to build the most plausible picture possible with the best credentialed tools we have available to us. We begin by assessing what resources we have that are plausible or otherwise in good epistemic standing. The project of the descriptionists is related, but importantly distinct. Here, the chief aim is to say what it would take for us to have the kinds of things we, perhaps pre-philosophically, take ourselves to have. We begin with our stockpile of naive concepts and ask how we might make good on them.

These differences in theoretical aims are oftentimes connected to an under-appreciated element among philosophers: religious commitments. It is striking how few non-religious libertarians there are in philosophy. My speculation—and that is all that it is—is that the many religious philosophers who worry about free will do so because (1) they think that the powers of free will we need in order to get the traditional Christian conception of God off the hook for evil in the world must be pretty substantial and (2) only a radical species of freedom could suffice to ground the justifiability of eternal damnation. Indeed, I suspect that the variety (or varieties) of freedom apparently required for these tasks are more demanding than the conception of free will we need to do nearly everything else—for example, to justify praise and blame, to explain the relevant senses of 'can' in ordinary discourse, to make sense of deliberation, and so on. Given the decidedly secular ethos of mainstream analytic philosophy, this motivation is invisible in most discussions. Widespread acceptance of a standard of consistency with naturalism does not help, either. But the religious aspect is not limited to motivations in favoring one or another conception of free will. It is also connected to the point I have been making about the aim of theorizing. In the context of philosophy of religion—especially in connection with the problem of evil—philosophers have offered "defenses" or theodicies that endeavor to show how some or another thesis is possible, or how there could be sufficient reason for its obtaining.[16] In doing so, their task has been closely aligned to the descriptionist project: it begins with a stockpile of concepts (for example, human freedom, the existence of evil, the classical Christian conception of the deity, and so on) and attempts to determine whether and how it could exist. For philosophers familiar with, and sometimes operating internal to this sort of project, all-things-considered plausibility from the standpoint of a broadly scientific worldview is not the aspiration. Instead, we seek to explain how these commitments *could* be vindicated.[17] In many cases, then, religious convictions may be joining a bundle of mutually reinforcing commitments: descriptionist aims, intuition-celebrating metaphysics, theological concerns, and continuity with theodicy or "defense" of some possibility.

It goes almost without saying that this picture simplifies a good deal. And, as natural as some of these clusterings may be, we should not lose sight of the fact that the particular cocktail of methodological presumptions in any given account will surely vary.[18] This variation, though, makes disentangling confusions from mere cross-purposes a complicated task. Still, recognizing methodological and aspirational differences is important if we wish to get a firmer grip on the free will problem.

Unfortunately, until very recently there was virtually no sustained discussion of methodological differences in the work on free will, what ramifications these differences have had for particular proposals, debates about them, and so on.[19] What I hope to have made plausible is the possibility that there is some amount of talking past each other in the literature. We can, for example, explain the sometimes mutually dismissive attitude among philosophers in each camp, frustrated at the deafness of the others to their work. The metaphysicians set the terms of the debate but given the motivating concerns and conception of methods, ethicists have seldom produced accounts that satisfy the intuition-championing terms of the debate. Similarly, ethicists are often baffled why one should be concerned to defend a picture of agency as demanding as those offered by (inevitably, metaphysician) libertarians. And so the debate has gone on.

7.3 Rip van Inkle in the Philosophy Library: Terminology

In the previous section I discussed the effects various large-scale changes in philosophy had for work on free will. In this and the next section my focus is internal to the free will literature. In particular, I wish to consider some important ways in which the terrain of the free will problem has unfolded over roughly the past four decades, and why these changes have obscured some issues in the contemporary literature.

Suppose a dedicated inquirer into the problems of free will fell asleep in a philosophy library 35 years ago and awoke today with the aim of catching up on the current literature. This philosopher —let us call him Rip van Inkle— would surely be bewildered by the contents of the latest journals. Rip would, I think, object to at least two developments over the past several decades: (A) the current uses of 'compatibilism' and 'incompatibilism', and (B) the prominence of moral responsibility in debates about free will. Let us consider each in turn.

Compatibilist and *incompatibilist* have become slippery terms. In the good old days, these terms denoted the thesis that the theses of determinism and free will were compatible or incompatible, respectively. In today's literature, though, if someone self-identifies as a compatibilist, we need to know exactly what one is a compatibilist about, and what sort of compatibilism one is committed to. We need to know this because some philosophers use the term in connection with free will, but others use the term in connection with responsibility, and some use it in ways connected to both usages. So, for example, some philosophers are prepared to acknowledge that the thesis of determinism might be incompatible with some varieties of free will, even though moral responsibility is compatible with determinism.[20] Others, often in defense of libertarianism, have declared that there are varieties of genuine freedom that could still be had even if determinism is true.[21] Others have argued that they are both compatibilists and incompatibilists.[22] Some have said that they are neither, or that such views are partly right but incompletely so.[23] And others have pronounced themselves agnostic about the whole business and offered accounts of both.[24]

Rip van Inkle would surely think that these Young Turks have made a mess of things. And, if van Inkle were a publishing type, he might even craft an article admonishing today's philosophers of free will to return to former locutions. Back in the good old days, Rip might note, almost everyone was clear that free will was about the ability to do otherwise, and moreover, that without this ability no one could be morally responsible. The free will debate was about the compatibility of free will and determinism, and responsibility didn't much enter the picture. It was just obvious that people are morally responsible. Moreover, discussions about free will were comparatively tidy back then because they focused on a particular agential property—being able to do otherwise—and philosophers argued about what, exactly, that comes to. On this view, there was really only one debate in town: showing whether it was possible to do otherwise if determinism were true.

There were two ways one might try to motivate one's favored position in this debate. First, one could try to provide an account of 'can' or 'ability' to show that the ability to do otherwise was compatible with determinism or not. This was the work of those who proposed and attacked various conditional analyses of *can*, or the idea that all the word 'can' meant was that "if one had decided to do some action X, then one would have done X." Alternately, one could try to offer a more general argument about what determinism entailed and why that ruled out the ability to do otherwise. The most famous of this family of arguments is what is now widely called the Consequence Argument.[25]

In the intervening decades, things have changed in some important ways. For instance, the classic conditional analysis of 'can' has fallen into wide disfavor. Few, if any compatibilists, are willing to undertake a defense of it. (In very recent years there have been a few attempts to resurrect something like it, but with some important innovations.[26]) However, the failure of the conditional analysis proved to be less devastating to compatibilism than one might have thought. At about the same time the conditional analysis was put on life support, Harry Frankfurt's work opened up a different path for compatibilism, one that eschewed any requirement of an ability to do otherwise.[27] This development proved to be important for several reasons. First, it made it possible to persist in one's compatibilism even in the face of the failure to articulate a plausible conditional analysis of 'can'. Second, it broke apart the consensus that free will, the ability to do otherwise, and moral responsibility were a tightly integrated package of conceptual commitments. That is, Frankfurt came to be widely regarded as having offered an account of free will that made no appeal to the ability to do otherwise while also showing that moral responsibility did not require the ability to do otherwise. The latter conclusion was drawn by a class of examples commonly referred to as "Frankfurt cases." Frankfurt presented these cases as counterexamples to the Principle of Alternative Possibilities, which states that "a person is morally responsible for what he has done only if he could have done otherwise."[28] To some, this suggested a path whereby one could disconnect the requirements of (and thus, threats to) free will from the requirements of moral responsibility.[29] To many it suggested that the future of compatibilism hinged not on analyzing 'can' but on defending Frankfurt-style cases where an agent lacked alternative possibilities but was intuitively responsible.[30]

So, many of the chief suppositions that structured the dialectic between incompatibilists and compatibilists in van Inkle's day are no longer uniformly accepted by even the major partisans of the literature that came after his nap: free will is not obviously to be analyzed in terms of an ability to do otherwise, many have become convinced that moral responsibility does not require the ability to do otherwise, at least some went on to think that one could be responsible without having free will. If debates about the Consequence Argument remain consequential, the defense of a conditional analysis seems, to many, less so. Changing conceptions of the free will problem are not new, but we do well to recognize them.[31]

When turning to the contemporary literature, I think it is fair to say that the contemporary free will debate is not as overwhelmingly preoccupied with the compatibility of free will and determinism as it once was. It is an important issue, to be sure. And, very smart and thoughtful philosophers continue to focus on this issue. However, it is no longer the only significant axis on which most of the self-identified free will literature centers.

Recognizing the newly multi-polar world of work on free will is crucial if one wishes to understand why the vocabulary has shifted—and, admittedly, gotten messier—in the flood of post-1970s neologisms.[32] At least some philosophers have argued that this terminological tide should be resisted. For example, Peter van Inwagen "strongly recommend[s] that philosophers never use ['libertarianism' or 'hard determinism']—except, of course, when they are forced to because they are discussing the work of philosophers who have been imprudent enough to use them" (331).[33] To be sure, talk of libertarianism and other "-isms" offer new opportunities for confusion, but it also helps to make other matters clear for those less concerned about the compatibility debate. Many philosophers have sought to bracket the compatibility debate for the purpose of exploring those aspects of agency implicated in freedom and responsibility, aspects that are themselves neutral with respect to the compatibility debate. For example, suppose I am giving an account of rational, deliberating agency of the sort I take to be implicated in true ascriptions of responsibility. It may be useful for me to quickly identify what commitments, if any, my account has to an indeterministic form of agency. Rather than entangling myself in debates about what properly constitutes free will, I can simply say that my account does not presume libertarian free will. In saying this, I bracket the matter of free will's relationship to moral responsibility, and whether there are reasons apart from deliberative agency for requiring indeterminism in one's account of free will or moral responsibility. Inelegance is sometimes the price of efficient expression.

The proliferation of terminology van Inwagen objects to is a by-product of three things: (1) the fact of a much larger body of philosophers working on the subject matter, generating novel views, and consequently needing to label positions in ways that distinguish their own view from others, (2) disagreement that the central issue is the compatibility debate, and (3) the fragmentation of convictions concerning how to characterize free will. But, it seems to me, either of (2) or (3) is all we need to justify the terminology, even if it does introduce some confusions. However, I wish to say a bit more about (3), or the fragmentation of convictions concerning how to characterize free will, and why these changes should matter to vans Inkle and Inwagen.

7.4 Rip van Inkle, Again: The rise of responsibility-centrism

If Rip managed to keep reading despite his dissatisfaction with how 'incompatibilism' and the like are thrown about, it would not take him long to become distressed by the way in which moral responsibility has come to be in the foreground of discussions about free will. Compared to the literature Rip knew before his nap, where free will was often characterized in terms of the ability to do otherwise, the newer literature often explicitly appeals to a conception of free will that treats it as a kind of control that must be satisfied for an agent to count as a responsible agent.[34]

Let us suppose that we cannot talk Rip out of thinking of free will in terms of the ability to do otherwise. Rip has his reasons, and anyway, philosophers don't change their minds very easily.[35] Now I have already noted some reasons for thinking that attention to the larger historical record would show that the period prior to Rip's nap was atypical, at least in the modern period. But let us suppose that it was not. Even so, we would do well to understand why free will is no longer widely characterized in terms of alternative possibilities. As it turns out, there are some very good reasons for this change.

As we've already seen, one reason why philosophers stopped characterizing free will in terms of alternative possibilities was Frankfurt's work. If one could provide a plausible enough story about free will that did not appeal to alternative possibilities, then it was simply a mistake to characterize free will in terms of alternative possibilities. Note that one need not have been *convinced* by Frankfurt's account. Rather, all one had to think was that Frankfurt's proposal was recognizably an account of free will, even if one regarded it as false. That is, if one thinks that something is recognizably an account of free will without it obviously requiring alternative possibilities, then one is going to want some way of characterizing free will that does not appeal to a requirement of alternative possibilities. Characterizing free will in terms of a control condition on moral responsibility was the solution.[36]

Second, it is worth noting that much of the way philosophers have motivated the free will problem—both in Rip's time and now—is by appealing to its connection to moral responsibility. In undergraduate classrooms and in professional venues, it is common for philosophers to motivate the interest or importance of their work by appeal to the relevance of free will for moral responsibility. Indeed, the importance of free will for moral responsibility is a recurring theme among many philosophers in much of the modern period with Hume, Kant, and Nietzsche among them. It is beyond both my expertise and the scope of this paper to address the extent to which these figures thought of free will as something like a control or freedom condition on moral responsibility. Nevertheless, the widespread invocation—both historical and contemporaneously—of moral responsibility entailing free will is surely one reason why philosophers in the current literature widely appeal to a characterization of free will in terms of it.[37] If the philosophical and pedagogical interest in the matter turns on the relevance of free will to moral responsibility, and there is dispute about whether free will involves alternative possibilities, then it should be unsurprising that philosophers will characterize free will in terms of some condition on moral responsibility.[38]

One interesting consequence of thinking more systematically about moral responsibility and what its conditions require has been the development of a view that would surely strike Rip as startling, and something of an extreme view: that we lack moral responsibility and/or free will. In Rip's day, it was widely assumed by philosophers that we are morally responsible, and that this fact was obvious. Perhaps it really was obvious in Rip van Inkle's day that people are morally responsible.[39] Today, however, there has been a considerable amount of careful work done by philosophers to argue that it is not at all obvious that we are free and responsible.[40] I write this not to embrace the skeptical conclusion. Indeed, elsewhere I've argued against it.[41] Still, it is striking that what was widely regarded in Rip's time as a philosophical curiosity is now taken seriously by a number of philosophers firmly in the mainstream of the literature.

There is another element to the story. The possibility of Frankfurt-style counterexamples to the Principle of Alternative Possibilities suggested that moral responsibility might not require alternative possibilities. Since many philosophers were taken with the idea that free will was to be defined in terms of something like a control or freedom condition on moral responsibility, this suggested that free will need not require alternative possibilities. Out of this mix of ideas came the thought that perhaps what free will required was not alternative possibilities—as nearly everyone back in the 1960s might have thought—but instead a kind of "sourcehood" or "origination."[42] The idea here is that threats to free will are threats not because they rule out alternative possibilities, but rather, inasmuch as they undermine the possibility of us being the appropriate sources or originators of our actions. How, precisely, these accounts operate and the complexities they raise with respect to their connection to a broader theory of action, is something I will not try to detail in this paper. The important point, though, is that the development of these accounts closed off the possibility of simply characterizing free will as involving an ability to do otherwise. There are too many self-described accounts of free will that require no such thing. Thus, insisting on characterizing free will as an ability to do otherwise suggests either a willful disregard of recent developments or a deafness to how the terrain has shifted.

There has been a curious conceptual doubling back in the literature, where the old view of the free will problem gave birth to its own demise. By insisting on what was supposed to be an unremarkable and obvious entailment between moral responsibility and free will, the only way to accommodate the possibility of successful Frankfurt cases was to abandon the idea that free will requires alternative possibilities. Of course, one could resist Frankfurt cases and still hold on to the idea that free will requires alternative possibilities. There are both compatibilists and incompatibilists who have gone this route. Alternately, one could give up on the idea that moral responsibility entails free will.[43] However, given that many were persuaded by Frankfurt cases or their successors, the only way to recognize this fact in the literature is to abandon insistence on characterizing free will in a way that involves alternative possibilities.

Still, a number of philosophers would surely agree with Rip that the recent centrality of responsibility is a grave error. Some of these philosophers have argued that what is properly central to the free will problem is a kind of *deliberative agency*. On this conception of the problem, free will is a kind of capacity that is implicated in deliberation and threatened by beliefs that undermine the efficacy, utility, or necessity of freedom in deliberation, usually when considered against the backdrop of the natural causal order. There are also philosophers who have focused on the idea that free will is centrally about our ability to make a distinctive difference to the causal order, whether deterministic or not. Call this a *causal contributor conception* of free will. Moreover, there have been philosophers whose interest has been in what can be called *strong agency*, or the kind of agency required for robust self-control, and perhaps characteristically human powers such as creativity and originality in decision-making. For these latter philosophers, their interest in free will may intersect with concerns about moral responsibility but what is really at stake is to characterize some particularly complex or demanding form of agency, often identified as *autonomy*.[44]

Note that these conceptions I have just mentioned need not be "pure" or interrelated with alternative conceptions. You could, for example, think one or more of these notions are co-extensional, or that free will is an agential feature that combines several of these concerns.[45] Or, one could reject all of this and instead try to police the terminological shifts and related changes in foci that have occurred under the umbrella of work ostensibly on free will. Van Inwagen seems inclined to something like this, proposing that by "free will" we should only mean "the thesis that we are sometimes in the following position with respect to a contemplated future act: we simultaneously have both the following abilities: the ability to perform that act and the ability to refrain from performing that act" (330).[46] However, in light of developments tied to Frankfurt's work and the advent of "source" theories, such a proposal strikes me as a non-starter. Instead, we would be better served by recognizing the existing disagreements, and flagging our own interests and concerns in what—at least as matter of tradition—we might continue to call "the free will problem," even as we recognize that there is no single problem that has a unique and exclusive claim on being the problem of free will. It makes things less terminologically tidy, but it reflects the diversity of genuinely interesting philosophical puzzles that have a recognizable claim on being part of the philosophical tradition of reflection on free will. But it does leave us with a problem.

7.5 The revisionist turn

The confluence of methodological differences, blindness to them, and important shifts in terminology over time has impeded our understanding of each other and our grasp of the free will problem. The first step to solving this problem is to acknowledge that it exists. Then, we need to be clear about what it is that our own projects are endeavoring to do, and what we take to be the conditions of success or failure for that project. Here, I will briefly outline a new approach to walking out of this thicket of competing methodologies, priorities, and interests.

In my work the animating question is this: what are the conditions under which we rightly morally praise and blame agents for what they do? My interest in the free will problem, and in responding to alternative views (including views that deny we have free will and moral responsibility), is largely driven by a concern for determining whether these accounts provide the tools to answer that core question. So, I think about free will as a kind of power or capacity that is a distinctive requirement for being a responsible agent, and in this, I share the current responsibility-centric assumptions of the literature.[47] In framing the matter this way, I do not deny that there are other concerns that have and do motivate how philosophers have come to frame the free will problem, and it is an open question whether a responsibility-centric account will be able to satisfactorily address those concerns. However, I do challenge those who think about the free will problem differently to be clear about what the governing conception of free will is in their own work. Moreover, if they think it is the only philosophically appropriate way to think about free will, then they need to explain why we should think so.

Internal to my responsibility-centric approach to free will, I'm interested in pursuing a constructionist project. That is, I am interested in articulating what I take to be the most plausible and defensible account of the conditions on agency required for deserving moral praise and blame. And, importantly, I do not think that our best account of *that* will necessarily cohere with our pre-philosophical intuitions. It is important that we distinguish between an account that describes the contours of our ordinary thinking about freedom and responsibility (something we might think of as conceptual mapping of a sort), and an account of what we *ought* to believe about these things, given everything we know. The first I call a "diagnostic" or "descriptive" project. The latter I call a "prescriptive" project. The possibility that we get divergent theories from doing, respectively, description and prescription is what creates the possibility of revisionism. That is, revisionism, of the sort I recommend, is the view that the best prescriptive account will depart in important ways from our best diagnostic account.[48]

One might wonder how it could be possible that free will and moral responsibility might be anything other than what we think it to be. There are several paths to an answer. One is by reflecting on developments in philosophy of language from the mid-1970s and on.[49] The advent of externalist semantics—accounts of the meanings of terms, roughly—showed how it was plausible that the meanings of various terms are not settled by the contents of a speaker's thoughts. Putnam and Kripke made these points in the context of natural kind terms, but the basic strategy is not obviously dependent on natural kinds (indeed, it is not altogether clear what constitutes a natural kind). A second but related strategy is to make use of an externalist theory of reference. On this approach, even if you accept that there is some sense to be made of the idea that our thoughts about something fix the strict meaning of something, it is still another matter what the term refers to or "picks out" in the world. And, one might think, facts about usage or the world make a contribution in some way external to what is in our heads. So, for example, at one point in the mid-twentieth century, perhaps the U.S.-specific meaning of "race" in its social category sense was, roughly, a category of human kind distinguished by particular genetic features. Plausibly, however, the reference of "race" was groups of people marked *not* by shared genetic features (it has been extraordinarily difficult to isolate any that map onto our categories) but instead groups marked by malleable social categories and relations. Importantly, those social relations used a web of markers for identifying race, none of which were genetic. So, one might embrace externalism about meaning and/or reference in the case of free will and moral responsibility. A third path is to argue that even if the meaning of "free will" is fixed by our thoughts about it, this putative fact does not mean that we cannot change how we think about free will, thereby changing its meaning. In the face of new evidence, pressures to coherence, or changing patterns of usage, we can and have re-anchored references for any number of ideas—marriage, adultery, being a magician, quarterback sacks, and so on. There are, I suspect, other paths to the same basic point that concepts, meanings, and references associated with terms are not always fixed to an immovable firmament, discovered from the comfort of our armchairs. Of course, revisions of meanings, references, or concepts cannot be done indiscriminately. There are various constraints on any plausible revision, including preserving the general conceptual role of the term, adhering to standards of plausibility, and capturing the main normative burdens implicated in usages of the term. My point, though, is that there is no reason to think that, on this face of it, revisionism about free will and moral responsibility is closed off to us.[50]

So, we can and should distinguish between a descriptive and prescriptive account of free will. I think the best descriptive account is one that is tantamount to an incompatibilist conception of the free will problem. However, the best prescriptive account—the picture of agency we ought to believe is true—turns out to be compatible with determinism. Because it renounces a variety of incompatibilist intuitions—for example, a particularly robust conception of alternative possibilities, the demand for being the ultimate source of any free action, and some attendant ideas about the origin of one's responsibility-relevant capacities—this latter picture of agency will not be fully intuitive for many competent users of the concepts of free will and moral responsibility. This counterintuitiveness reflects the fact that for many of us, our default conceptual commitments in this domain are neither necessary nor advantageous.

Elsewhere, I have attempted to explain why I think it is extremely implausible to think that any acceptable account of freedom will cohere with our pre-philosophical intuitions. Here, I can only outline some of the details. First, I think that we have diverse intuitions on these matters. For many of us, there is a robust set of incompatibilist intuitions, but they are not uniformly or universally present in all of us.[51] We are better off acknowledging this and abandoning the dream of finding an account that is immune to counterintuitive results. Second, even if we did have these intuitions uniformly and universally, there is little hope of vindicating them. That is, I think that the best libertarian accounts, while coherent, describe a form of agency we are unlikely to have.[52] This is problematic, however, because if the only justification for moral praise and blame is the libertarian one, then all those moral and legal practices that depend on these things are untenable. This is, I think, an under-appreciated moral problem for libertarianism. Until libertarians can show that we have good reason to think that we are indeed agents of the sort described by their preferred accounts, then we are left in a position of holding people responsible on tenuous epistemic grounds, grounds that those subject to blame and punishment dependent on moral responsibility can justifiably object to.[53]

I also reject skepticism and eliminativism about free will and moral responsibility. I do so because there is a justification for praise and blame available to us that, while not capturing all of our intuitions about responsible agency, is sufficient to capture the bulk of our ordinary ascriptions, attitudes, and practices—albeit on grounds different than many of us previously supposed.[54] For this reason, I believe a revisionist project has something new to offer the free will debates: it provides us with a way to acknowledge the attractions of our concepts as we find them, while at the same time permitting us to bracket the attendant intuitions. Our task is then to grapple directly with the matter of what forms of agency are required to justify attributions of praise and blame. In doing so, the moderately revisionist approach provides a place for the method of concept-mapping that is important to those engaged in descriptive metaphysics. However, it also opens the door to re-writing our self-conception in light of a firmer grasp on what forms of agency are minimally required to justify the practices of praise, blame, and desert that have been central concerns for ethicists.

The categories of the compatibility debate, when combined with the diverse methodological aims, and the various conceptions of how to frame what is at stake, have too often obscured the more specific commitments and projects that philosophers can and do undertake. The moderate form of revisionism that I recommend is proposed partly with an eye toward clarifying some of these issues, but also with an eye toward recommending a kind of theory whose possibility has been under-appreciated and seldom developed. In reply to this latter aspiration, however, one might protest that the prescriptive element of the account is merely another form of compatibilism, and that revisionism is not a theory in its own right.

I do think it is fair to say that there are strands of revisionism floating around in the literature, especially in the compatibilist literature.[55] But such strands are caught on some thorny branches of commitments that favor disavowals of revisionism. As I have noted above and elsewhere, there is an ambiguity in many compatibilist accounts, and many of the norms imported from the project of descriptive metaphysics have put pressure on the ready acceptance of revisionism.[56] Moreover, there are a number of things that might count as revisionism, but many of these things turn out to be comparatively uninteresting forms of revisionism, as when, for example, an account suggests that we have misunderstood our own commitments and that we need to revise our theories to better track the commitments we already have.[57]

Let me say a bit more about this last issue. In practice, revisionism is importantly distinct from the projects of the mainstream of compatibilism. In a more conciliatory mode we might identify two varieties of compatibilists with distinct relationships to the form of revisionism I propose. Call one group *purebloods*. Purebloods see nothing interestingly revisionist about their project. These philosophers are, in keeping with the bulk of the compatibilist tradition, insistent that our concepts and meanings as we find them are indeed compatible with the thesis of determinism. They endeavor to tell us "what we mean, *all* we mean" by "free will" and "moral responsibility."[58] From the standpoint of purebloods, moderate revisionism will seem distinctive, but committed to unnecessary concessions to incompatibilists on the matter of the current meaning or concepts of free will and moral responsibility. Purebloods think that careful reflection on the matter shows that substantive revision is unnecessary. We might label a different group of compatibilists *mongrels*. Mongrels are more prone to slipping into the language of otherwise revision-tolerating ethicists—for example, speaking of varieties of free will worth wanting. And, if they held true to these ways of thinking and talking, we might rightly think that revisionism of the form I recommend is indeed a mongrel compatibilism. However, most existing mongrels have internalized norms of the literature expressed in the frequent citation of hoary accusations against compatibilism as "quagmires of evasion" (James) and a "wretched subterfuge" (Kant). So, these potentially revision-friendly compatibilists have had reason to disavow any suggestion of revision.[59] So long as that tension between pro- and anti-revisionist sentiment is present among them, revisionism will seem perhaps too uncomfortably familiar to be much of an alternative, even if—as I believe—it is what these self-identified compatibilists *ought* to espouse.

Given these considerations, and the tangled skein of commitments I described in sections 2–4, I am not much interested in arguing that the form of revisionism I advocate could not be assimilated under *some* construal of compatibilism or incompatibilism. I have no objection to my view being characterized as a moderately conceptually revisionist prescriptive form of constructionist compatibilism. My reluctance concerns the connotational baggage of the simple, unmodified labels of compatibilism and incompatibilism. Too often, that baggage pollutes the theorist's proposal and the interpreter's grasp of it. Thus, I have emphasized an idea that is not already widely a part of the literature: any plausible (constructionist) account of moral responsibility will depart from important strands of our commonsense thinking about moral responsibility. This is what is distinctive about the kind of view I favor, and this is what is missing in going accounts of free will, whether compatibilist or incompatibilist.[60] Skeptical or eliminativist incompatibilists are vulnerable to this complaint, too: they reject free will and moral responsibility precisely because they think it is either as we imagine it to be or it must not exist.[61] So, as long as this idea—the idea that that we will need to excise some aspects of ordinary thinking—is taken seriously, I do not have any investment in whether one treats my accounts as compatibilist or incompatibilist. My aim has been to re-focus our attention on explaining *why* some or another account would require this or that power for moral responsibility.

On this latter issue, the *why* of some stipulated power or condition on agency, appealing to its intuitiveness is not good enough for the revisionist. In contrast, it has been for most conventional compatibilists and incompatibilists. What I reject is the idea that we have done our work by simply illustrating the intuitiveness of, for example, agent causation, the idea that we must be responsible for what capacities we have, or that our intuitions about some case of responsibility attribution cut one way rather than another. What we need is some explanation of why these requirements are necessary for freedom and responsibility, and why we should take seriously intuitions that favor some or another reading of, for example, a Frankfurt case. The answers to these questions should invoke principles, arguments, and justifications which may themselves, eventually, bottom out in considerations that are intertwined with intuitiveness. That's fine. We cannot repair all of our ship simultaneously. Conceptual improvement is always piecemeal. Still, inasmuch as blame and punishment are visited on real people in light of our conceptions of responsibility, we must take seriously the normative pressure to articulate a justification that goes beyond a declaration that one's proposal coheres with our pre-philosophical prejudices.

To summarize, once we acknowledge the possibility of a revisionist approach to these matters, what is foregrounded is the need to explain why posited requirements on free will and moral responsibility should be taken seriously. Intuitiveness is a kind of virtue, but a limited one. We are only now beginning to take seriously that there are discreet families of intuitions at work in ordinary and philosophical cognition about the matter, and that such intuitional diversity may be found within individuals, and that it may even be pervasive across cultures. If there is a lesson here, it is that we must be clear about the aims and methods of our theorizing, and sensitive to the possibility that our interests are not always best met by the stockpile of assumptions and conceptual commitments we already possess. Indeed, this should seem especially plausible for concepts like free will, which have a long and complicated history with potentially diverse subject matters that have been bandied about under the same title. Even if we prefer to focus on some and not others of these subjects we should be careful to both recognize the diversity and respect the possibility of differing interests.[62]

Notes

1. This is a bit of shorthand. More precisely, we can say that *incompatibilism* is the view that the free will thesis is incompatible with the thesis of determinism. These locutions were introduced and made influential by Peter van Inwagen. See, for example, Peter Van Inwagen, *An Essay on Free Will* (New York: Oxford University Press, 1983); Peter Van Inwagen, "How to Think About the Problem of Free Will," *Journal of Ethics* 12 (2008): 327–41; Peter Van Inwagen, "The Incompatibility of Free Will and Determinism," *Philosophical Studies* 27 (1975): 185–99. However, I will depart from van Inwagen's recommendations on this and other matters, following standard practice in speaking of determinism, keeping the "thesis of" only tacitly present.
2. In the former camp, we find figures such as Peter van Inwagen, Carl Ginet, John Fischer, Kadri Vihvelin, Robert Kane, Derk Pereboom, Randolph Clarke, and Laura Ekstrom. In the latter camp, some of the notables include Gary Watson, T.M. Scanlon, R. Jay Wallace, and Susan Wolf. There are, of course, very influential figures who don't fit into this too-tidy story. This is partly because there is at least a third strand here: those who work principally in philosophy of action in its traditional conception. Harry Frankfurt, Al Mele, David Velleman, and Michael Bratman are in this group (Carl Ginet should be counted in this group as well), and the concerns of most of these authors has had to do with the metaphysics of agency. For my purposes, though, the methodological disagreements between the metaphysicians and the ethicists are the core of the difficulty I am concerned to identify.
3. My point is not that these things have no place in philosophical debates. Rather, my point is that the frequency with which these things occur in the contemporary literature suggests that there are deeper issues lurking than would appear from the surface-level play of arguments. Hence, the suggestion that these things are symptomatic of some degree of talking past each other. (And, for the record, in my callow youth I was not immune to the temptation of declaring dialectical stalemates, as Mele has rightly noted: see Alfred Mele, "Moral Responsibility and History Revisited," *Ethical Theory and Moral Practice* 12, no. 5 (2009): 463–75.
4. Whether one views this as a synthesis or instead as the triumph of the logical constructionist strand over ordinary language philosophy is something we need not settle here. For an instructive overview of these developments, and one that argues that there is a synthesis, albeit one favoring the logical constructionist approach, see Tyler Burge, "Philosophy of Language and Mind: 1950–1990," *The Philosophical Review* 101, no. 1 (1992): 3–51.
5. P. F. Strawson, *Analysis and Metaphysics* (New York: Oxford, 1992).
6. David Lewis, *Counterfactuals* (Cambridge: Harvard University Press, 1973).
7. Although I will discuss them in more detail later in this chapter, it may be useful to quickly characterize these bits of jargon. The *conditional analysis* of "can" is the idea that the correct analysis of "can" is one that identifies a conditional power, that is, to say that one can do something means, roughly, that *were* one to decide to do it, one would successfully do it. The *Consequence Argument* is the name for an influential version of an argument for incompatibilism. The central idea of the Consequence Argument is that if you can't control the past and you can't control

the laws of nature, then if determinism is true you cannot do otherwise than you in fact do (that is, there are no genuine alternatives to any course of action.) *Frankfurt cases* are a type of example, made famous by Harry Frankfurt, that purport to show that one can be responsible even if one cannot do otherwise. On a standard Frankfurt-style example, someone is deciding how to vote in some election, but unbeknownst to the voter there is a chip in his head that will force him to vote for candidate X if the agent doesn't vote for candidate X on his own. Crucial to the power of the example, though, the voter votes for candidate X without intervention from the chip—hence, the voter lacks alternative possibilities but decides on his or her own what to do.

8. Sometimes outsiders to the literature will project on to it Quinean impulses, especially if those impulses are central to their own project. For one example, see Frank Jackson, *From Metaphysics to Ethics: A Defense of Conceptual Analysis* (New York: Oxford University Press, 1998). There, Jackson interprets compatibilists as *not* defending the ordinary, folk concept of free will, but instead a reasonable extension of it. In doing so, they are "changing the subject, albeit in a strictly limited sense" (45). Although I think there are many virtues to the project Jackson describes, it substantially mischaracterizes what most compatibilists I know take themselves to be doing. Indeed, perhaps the biggest challenge for compatibilists has been to explain to incompatibilists how their proposals are precisely *not* instances of changing the subject.
9. Randolph Clarke, "Toward a Credible Agent-Causal Account of Free Will," *Nous* 27 (1993): 191–203; Laura Waddell Ekstrom, *Free Will: A Philosophical Study* (Boulder, Colorado: Westview Press, 2000); Robert Kane, *The Significance of Free Will* (Oxford: Oxford, 1996); Alfred Mele, *Free Will and Luck* (Oxford: New York, 2006); Timothy O'Connor, *Persons and Causes* (New York: Oxford University Press, 2000).
10. Sometimes philosophers claim otherwise, that, for example, a focus on ethical issues was an invention of the second half of the twentieth century, or that coupling free will to powers required for moral responsibility is a recent perversion in debates about free will. But these philosophers are just plain wrong. Even bracketing notable historical examples such as Kant and Nietzsche, in the early twentieth century, discussions of free will were commonplace in books on ethics, and worries about moral responsibility frequently propelled construals of free will. See, for example, chapters on free will in G. E. Moore, *Ethics* (Oxford: Oxford University Press, 1912); Moritz Schlick, *The Problems of Ethics*, trans. D. Rynin (New York: Prentice Hall, 1939).
11. The idea was present in Sidgwick, of course, but also in Nietzsche's more radical call for "a revaluation of values." See Friedrich Wilhelm Nietzsche, *Twilight of the Idols, Or, How to Philosophize With the Hammer* (Indianapolis, Ind.: Hackett Pub, 1997); Henry Sidgwick, *The Methods of Ethics*, 7th edn (Indianapolis, IN: Hackett, 1981).
12. Perhaps the right way to understand the influence of what I'm calling "the broadly Quinean strand" in the free will literature, beyond the influence of naturalist presuppositions, is through the role of reflective equilibrium in the ethics strand, as introduced by Rawls who gets the idea from Nelson Goodman. It may also be worth noting that the uptake of reflective equilibrium in normative ethics was not hindered by the fact that Rawls' students ended up in virtually every major philosophy department in the US by the end of the twentieth century.
13. The work of P.F. Strawson is absolutely critical to how this part of the history unfolded. At the risk of misleading by omission, I lack the space to say

much about the sizable influence of Strawson in cementing what I've called the "unstable solution." Nevertheless, it is clear that Strawson's approach in "Freedom and Resentment" inspired a very influential strand of compatibilism. For our purposes, Strawson's chief methodological contribution was to focus the free will debate on the centrality of praise, blame, and the attendant moral psychology while dismissing the need for revision of our practices or concepts. See P. F. Strawson, "Freedom and Resentment," *Proceedings of the British Academy* XLVIII (1962): 1–25. While I think there is much to be said for taking up the Strawsonian project along broadly revisionist lines, I do not think this is Strawson's own conception of his project in that article. See Manuel Vargas, "Responsibility and the Aims of Theory: Strawson and Revisionism," *Pacific Philosophical Quarterly* 85, no. 2 (2004): 218–41. For a different interpretation, however, see Jonathan Bennett, "Accountability," in *Philosophical Subjects*, ed. Zak Van Straaten (New York: Clarendon, 1980).

14. Thanks to Dan Speak for pointing this out to me.
15. These are homely labels, I know. But given the loaded meanings of "constructivist" and "descriptivist," neologisms seem to be the better alternative.
16. There is some dispute internal to the literature on these matters about how, precisely, to understand the term "theodicy" and whether it is distinct from a philosophical "defense." For example, Plantinga's conception of what constitutes a theodicy is very demanding, and this has led him to propose a less ambitious plan of "defense." See Alvin Plantinga, *God, Freedom and Evil* (Grand Rapids, MI: Eerdmans, 1977).
17. Compare the project of "clarification" articulated and defended in Scott MacDonald, "What is Philosophical Theology?" in *Arguing About Religion*, ed. Kevin Timpe (New York: Routledge, 2009).
18. Consider: Nozick's interest in free will is part of a larger project of providing "philosophical explanations," or explanations of how our stock of sometimes puzzling concepts could turn out to be true. To that extent, his project is in keeping with typical libertarian projects. However, his discussion is centrally concerned with free will's importance for human dignity. In short, for Nozick, the descriptionist project is entwined with a fundamentally normative concern, albeit not the usual one. For a useful discussion of Nozick on free will, see Michael Bratman, "Nozick on Free Will," in *Robert Nozick*, ed. David Schmidtz (New York: Cambridge, 2002).
19. Richard Double's work was an exception, but an isolated one. See Richard Double, *The Non-Reality of Free Will* (New York: Oxford University Press, 1991); Richard Double, *Metaphilosophy and Free Will* (New York: Oxford University Press, 1996). I suspect that many people outside the literature on free will, and perhaps a few people internal to it, think that Dennett's work—under the slogan of "the varieties of free will worth wanting"—made some groundbreaking contributions to the matter of methodology and free will. But Dennett's contributions were not those suggested by asking what varieties of free will are worth wanting, because his answer was "the variety that we actually do want." See Manuel Vargas, "Compatibilism Evolves? On Some Varieties of Dennett Worth Wanting," *Metaphilosophy* 36, no. 4 (2005): 460–75.
20. John Martin Fischer, and Mark Ravizza, *Responsibility and Control: A Theory of Moral Responsibility* (New York: Cambridge University Press, 1998); John Martin Fischer, *My Way: Essays on Moral Responsibility* (Oxford: New York, 2006); Nomy Arpaly, *Merit, Meaning, and Human Bondage* (Princeton, NJ: Princeton, 2006).

21. Robert Kane, *The Significance of Free Will*; Dan Speak, "Towards an Axiological Defense of Libertarianism," *Philosophical Topics* 32, no. 1&2 (2004): 353–69; Alfred Mele, *Free Will and Luck*.
22. Saul Smilansky, *Free Will and Illusion* (New York: Clarendon, 2000).
23. Ted Honderich, *A Theory of Determinism* (New York: Oxford, 1988).
24. Alfred Mele, *Autonomous Agents: From Self-Control to Autonomy* (New York: Oxford University Press, 1995); Alfred Mele, *Free Will and Luck*.
25. Early versions of something like the Consequence Argument can be found in Carl Ginet, "Might We Have No Choice?," in *Freedom and Determinism*, ed. Keith Lehrer (1966); David Wiggins, "Towards a Reasonable Libertarianism," in *Essays on Freedom of Action*, ed. Ted Honderich (London: Routledge & Kegan Paul, 1973). For canonical formulations of the Consequence Argument, see Peter Van Inwagen, "The Incompatibility of Free Will and Determinism"; Peter Van Inwagen, *An Essay on Free Will*.
26. It is difficult to see how compatibilists could get by without *something* like the conditional analysis. For a critical discussion of the recent work on this issue (for example, by David Lewis, Michael Smith, Michael Fara, and Kadri Vihvelin), see Randolph Clarke, "Dispositions, Abilities to Act, and Free Will: The New Dispositionalism," *Mind* 118, no. 470 (2009): 323–51.
27. See Harry Frankfurt, "Alternate Possibilities and Moral Responsibility," *Journal of Philosophy* 66, no. 23 (1969): 829–39; Harry Frankfurt, "Freedom of the Will and the Concept of a Person," *Journal of Philosophy* 68, no. 1 (1971): 5–20. Both are reprinted in Harry G. Frankfurt, *The Importance of What We Care About: Philosophical Essays* (Cambridge: Cambridge University Press, 1988). An influential alternative to Frankfurt's account, and one that similarly does not obviously appeal to alternative possibilities is Gary Watson, "Free Agency," *Journal of Philosophy* 72, no. 8 (1975): 205–20.
28. Harry G. Frankfurt, *The Importance of What We Care About*, p. 1.
29. While Frankfurt's work first came on to the scene in the late 1960s and early 1970s, it took a while for the literature to reshape itself around these claims. Indeed, the flourishing of Frankfurt-inspired work in the free will literature did not really get going until the late 1980s and early 1990s, due in no small part to the efforts of John Martin Fischer in exploring the ramifications and consequences of this work. Fischer's own view, which couples compatibilism about moral responsibility with openness to the possibility that free will is incompatible with determinism, has been developed in numerous places. See, for example, John Martin Fischer, *The Metaphysics of Free Will: An Essay on Control* (Cambridge, MA: Blackwell, 1994); John Martin Fischer, *My Way*; John Martin Fischer et al., *Four Views on Free Will* (Malden, MA: Blackwell, 2007); John Martin Fischer, and Mark Ravizza, *Responsibility and Control: A Theory of Moral Responsibility*.
30. To get a sense of the directions this literature went in, see the many excellent papers in David Widerker, and Michael McKenna, eds. *Moral Responsibility and Alternative Possibilities: Essays on the Importance of Alternative Possibilities* (Burlington, VT: Ashgate, 2003).
31. For a history of conceptual accretions to what we now think of as the free will debate, see Richard Sorabji, "The Concept of the Will From Plato to Maximus the Confessor," in *The Will*, ed. Thomas Pink, and Martin Stone (London: Routledge, 2003).
32. A hardly exhaustive list of '-isms' that immediately came to mind: semicompatibilism, hard incompatibilism, revisionism, soft libertarianism, broad/narrow

incompatibilism, neurotic compatibilism, attributionism, source incompatibilism, leeway incompatibilism, moderate libertarianism, event-causal libertarianism, agent causal libertarianism, illusionism, impossibilism, and mysterianism.

33. Peter Van Inwagen, "How to Think About the Problem of Free Will."
34. Van Inwagen seems to share Rip's distress. See Peter Van Inwagen, "How to Think About the Problem of Free Will." There, he writes "Whatever you do, do not define 'free will' this way: 'Free will is whatever sort of freedom is required for moral responsibility' (or 'Free will consists in having whatever sort of access to alternative possibilities is required for moral responsibility')" (329n). For some examples (among many) of explicit appeals to a conception of free will picked out by its role in responsibility or responsible agency: John Martin Fischer et al., *Four Views on Free Will*; Alfred Mele, *Free Will and Luck*; Derk Pereboom, "Defending Hard Incompatibilism," *Midwest Studies in Philosophy* 29, no. 1 (2005): 228–47.
35. Some have characterized van Inwagen's work as unresponsive in this sort of way, claiming that, for example: "Van Inwagen summed up his thought on free will in his book *An Essay on Free Will* (1983), and has pretty much avoided learning anything about the problem since—other than by sitting about and thinking it over" (215). See Peter Van Inwagen, "Van Inwagen on Free Will," in *Freedom and Determinism*, ed. Joseph Klein Campbell et al. (Cambridge MA: MIT Press, 2004). I reject that school of van Inwagen interpretation as both uncharitable and almost certainly false. Indeed, I can testify that van Inwagen read several books and articles on free will in the Fall of 1995, as he taught them in a graduate seminar I took from him that term. He had not previously read some of that material and (to my knowledge) he did not seek to avoid teaching that class. Collectively, these facts suggest that such a characterization of van Inwagen is wrong on both accounts: he didn't completely avoid learning anything, and what he did learn did not *only* involve sitting and thinking.
36. Notice, for example, that despite his rejection of defining free will in terms of the freedom required for moral responsibility, van Inwagen's presentation of what he calls "the problem of free will" goes on to invoke the idea that moral responsibility entails the existence of free will. This is not to say that van Inwagen does not have good reasons for insisting that free will not be defined in terms of a freedom required for moral responsibility. Rather, my point is that given a widespread sense of entailment between moral responsibility and free will, many philosophers thought it sensible to characterize free will in virtue of the role it plays in ascriptions of responsibility.
37. It may be tempting to think of *moral responsibility* as exclusively a philosopher's term of art, albeit an umbrella category for a range of things. Although it is surely used as something of a term of art, it is not purely a philosopher's invention. "Moral responsibility" has currency in ordinary discourse, sometimes referring to an agent's status ("is responsible" "being responsible"), sometimes picking out characteristic practices—blaming, sanctioning, praising, rewarding—as when we speak of "holding responsible," and sometimes being used to pick out a particular class of action (for example, when we speak of "the responsible thing to do"). The uses are interconnected, but perhaps not univocal in their uses and meanings of responsibility. Nevertheless, there is an anchor in ordinary discourse for philosophical talk of responsibility, an anchor sunk into our understandings of moral praise and blame, and the thought that there is a distinctive form of agency required to deserve those things.

38. Again, the influence of P. F. Strawson's "Freedom and Resentment" is surely a part of the more complete story. Strawson's work begins with the supposition that determinism is a threat to various moral notions, and that we can answer that threat by understanding how our interpersonal attitudes operate in a way that is insensitive to the truth or falsity of the thesis of determinism. Many philosophers were (and are) persuaded by his account, at least in general outline, and thus accepted that the principal philosophical issue concerning determinism and sophisticated agency was the threat to moral responsibility.
39. Van Inwagen has famously thought it obvious—his words—that we are morally responsible for what we do. (So much so, that he has signaled that he may be willing to give up his incompatibilism if he became convinced that causal determinism is true. See p. 219 of Peter Van Inwagen, *An Essay on Free Will*.) In a similar vein, a number of philosophers have tried to motivate the thought that responsibility is in some sense not "up for grabs" and used this as part of an argument for compatibilism. This element is present in, for example, P. F. Strawson, "Freedom and Resentment." It is also an important motivation for how John Fischer regards his own compatibilism about moral responsibility (what he calls "semicompatibilism"). See John Martin Fischer, *My Way*; John Martin Fischer et al., *Four Views on Free Will*.
40. Ted Honderich, *A Theory of Determinism*; Derk Pereboom, *Living Without Free Will* (Cambridge: Cambridge, 2001); Gideon Rosen, "Skepticism About Moral Responsibility," *Philosophical Perspectives* 18 (2004): 295–313; Saul Smilansky, *Free Will and Illusion*; Galen Strawson, *Freedom and Belief* (Oxford: Oxford University Press, 1986).
41. Manuel Vargas, "Libertarianism and Skepticism About Free Will: Some Arguments Against Both," *Philosophical Topics* 32, no. 1&2 (2004): 403–26; Manuel Vargas, "Desert, Retribution, and Moral Responsibility," (unpublished).
42. The language of "sourcehood" was, I believe, first introduced by Michael McKenna in Michael McKenna, "Source Incompatibilism, Ultimacy, and the Transfer of Non-Responsibility," *American Philosophical Quarterly* 38, no. 1 (2001): 37–51. Although it clearly has a number of antecedents, in the recent literature one of the first articulations of the idea in its current form can be found in John Martin Fischer, "Responsibility and Control," *Journal of Philosophy* 89 (1982): 24–40.
43. This view is rarely strongly embraced anywhere in the literature, although it is sometimes attributed to John Fischer. (Here I will simply bracket whether that attribution is correct, as matters are deceptively complicated on this point.) Arpaly explicitly detaches compatibilism about responsibility from compatibilism about freedom. See n.3, p. 6 of Nomy Arpaly, *Merit, Meaning, and Human Bondage*.
44. Searle is a notable example of someone who seems particularly interested in understanding free will as tied to conscious, deliberative agency and has at times contrasted this with accounts that focus on moral responsibility. See John Searle, *Freedom and Neurobiology* (New York: Columbia University Press, 2007). Robert Nozick also emphasized that his interest in free will was disconnected from moral responsibility. See Robert Nozick, *Philosophical Explanations* (Oxford: Clarendon Press, 1981). If one only read these authors—especially Searle—one might be led into thinking (erroneously) that there have been no philosophers in the past 50 years interested in free will detached from concerns about moral responsibility. But there is a lively literature on the relationship of freedom to deliberation that

often proceeds with little or no reference to moral responsibility, See, for example: Randolph Clarke, "Deliberation and Beliefs About One's Own Abilities," *Pacific Philosophical Quarterly* 73 (1992): 101–13; Richard Holton, "The Act of Choice," *Philosopher's Imprint* 6, no. 3 (2006): 1–15; Dana Nelkin, "Deliberative Alternatives," *Philosophical Topics* 32, no. 1–2 (2004): 215–40; Derk Pereboom, "A Compatibilist Account of the Epistemic Conditions on Rational Deliberation," *Journal of Ethics* 12 (2008): 287–306; J. David Velleman, "Epistemic Freedom," *Pacific Philosophical Quarterly* 70 (1989): 73–97. One philosopher whose interest in free will seems largely grounded in a concern for how we can be genuine contributors to the causal nexus is Thomas Nagel. See Thomas Nagel, *The View From Nowhere* (New York: Oxford University Press, 1986). I take it, though, that something like this concern has motivated a number of source incompatibilists and agent causationists, including N. Markosian, "A Compatibilist Version of the Theory of Agent Causation," *Pacific Philosophical Quarterly* 80, no. 3 (1999): 257–77; Timothy O'Connor, *Persons and Causes*; Kevin Timpe, *Free Will: Sourcehood and Its Alternatives* (New York: Continuum, 2008). A concern for strong agency is suggested in Alfred Mele, *Autonomous Agents: From Self-Control to Autonomy*; Gideon Yaffe, "Free Will and Agency At Its Best," *Philosophical Perspectives* 14 (2000): 203–29. An interest in strong agency, but with little or no appeal to free will, is central to much of Frankfurt's later work and to the recent work of Michael Bratman. See many of the essays in, respectively, Harry G. Frankfurt, *Necessity, Volition, and Love* (New York: Cambridge University Press, 1999); Michael E. Bratman, *Structures of Agency: Essays* (New York: Oxford University Press, USA, 2007).

45. I suspect that for anyone disposed to reject the centrality of a conception of free will bound up with moral responsibility, there are three main alternatives for conceiving the relationship between one's own favored conception of free will and the dominant responsibility-focused conception of free will. First, one could think there is a relation of dependence: free willx (reading for 'free willX' any of the non-dominant conceptions of free will previously mentioned) is prior to free willMR, (read: free willmoral responsibility) and that the latter depends on the capacities specified in one's account of free willX. Where there is no free willx there can be no free willMR (perhaps moral responsibility requires more than is required for free willx). Second, one could think there is a relation of independence: one could think that one's preferred conception and free willMR are altogether independent things with no substantive relationship, but that free willx is the true and proper meaning of the term "free will." On this second view, the current concern with free willMR represents a perhaps crass, moralized hijacking of a perfectly respectable and properly metaphysical or epistemological topic. A third possibility is a relationship of overlap: one could think that these notions imperfectly overlap without any hierarchy of dependence. On this latter view, the alternative form of agency that is of interest and responsible agency might both rely on set of shared characteristics, even if one or the other also requires some additional features to hold true as well. On this model, perhaps the most natural thing to say about the current focus on free willMR is just that it represents a natural and perhaps respectable confusion with the true and proper subject of free will.
46. Peter Van Inwagen, "How to Think About the Problem of Free Will."
47. Moreover, I expect that when the dialectical winds change, I will come to regard this period as the good old days of the literature. In philosophy, the good old days

are those days in which the prejudices of the literature reflect one's sense of what matters.

48. On at least one construal of wide reflective equilibrium, the revisionist approach I recommend is consistent with it.
49. I am puzzled why these developments did not make their way into the literature on free will earlier. Many of us who have been moved to adopting revisionism in name or in de facto commitments were driven by the thought that some important but familiar points in philosophy of language had failed to be taken seriously by people working on free will. See, for example, Mark Heller, "The Mad Scientist Meets the Robot Cats: Compatibilism, Kinds, and Counterexamples," *Philosophy and Phenomenological Research* 56 (1996): 333–37; Susan Hurley, "Is Responsibility Essentially Impossible?," *Philosophical Studies* 99 (2000): 229–68; Shaun Nichols, "Folk Intuitions on Free Will," *Journal of Cognition and Culture* 6, no. 1 & 2 (2006): 57–86; Manuel Vargas, "The Revisionist's Guide to Responsibility," *Philosophical Studies* 125, no. 3 (2005): 399–429.
50. An important recent development has been a body of experiments directed at probing ordinary intuitions about philosophically interesting cases. The initial results of these experiments suggest that non-philosophers have remarkably diverse intuitions about free will, and that any account that prescribes a consistently compatibilist or incompatibilist account of free will must revise away from a non-trivial set of ordinary judgments about the conditions of free will. See Eddy Nahmias et al., "Free Will, Moral Responsibility, and Mechanism: Experiments on Folk Intuitions," *Midwest Studies in Philosophy* XXXI (2007): 214–41; Shaun Nichols, and Joshua Knobe, "Moral Responsibility and Determinism: The Cognitive Science of Folk Intuitions," *Nous* 41, no. 4 (2007): 663–85; Shaun Nichols, "Folk Intuitions on Free Will"; Eddy Nahmias et al., "Is Incompatibilism Intuitive?," *Philosophy and Phenomenological Research* 73, no. 1 (2006): 28–53.
51. For some discussion of the relevant evidence, see Manuel Vargas, "Philosophy and the Folk: On Some Implications of Experimental Work for Philosophical Debates on Free Will," *Journal of Cognition and Culture* 6, no. 1 & 2 (2006): 239–54; Manuel Vargas, "Revisionism About Free Will: A Statement & Defense," *Philosophical Studies* 144.1 (2009): 45–62.
52. Although the details have changed a bit over time, see my discussions of libertarianism in John Martin Fischer et al., *Four Views on Free Will;* Manuel Vargas, "Libertarianism and Skepticism About Free Will: Some Arguments Against Both."
53. Manuel Vargas, "Revisionism About Free Will: A Statement & Defense."
54. My account focuses on the role these practices have in cultivating a special form of agency. See Manuel Vargas, "Moral Influence, Moral Responsibility," in *Essays on Free Will and Moral Responsibility*, ed. Nick Trakakis, and Daniel Cohen (Newcastle, UK: Cambridge Scholars Press, 2008).
55. Not exclusively, though. See Timothy O'Connor, *Persons and Causes*. One way to read O'Connor's rejection of Kane's event causal libertarianism is precisely as a rejection of a kind of revisionism internal to libertarianism (41–2). Indeed, I suspect Clarke took a similar view of event causal libertarianism, prior to his abandonment of libertarianism in Randolph Clarke, *Libertarian Accounts of Free Will* (Oxford: Oxford University Press, 2003).
56. See Manuel Vargas, "Compatibilism Evolves"; Manuel Vargas, "Revisionism About Free Will: A Statement & Defense."
57. Manuel Vargas, "The Revisionist's Guide to Responsibility."

58. Many of the recent "new wave" dispositionalist compatibilists fall in to this camp, I suspect. And, I take it that much of the work of Kadri Vihvelin, Dana Nelkin, Eddy Nahmias, and Joe Campbell is in this vein.
59. See Manuel Vargas, "Responsibility and the Aims of Theory: Strawson and Revisionism"; Manuel Vargas, "Compatibilism Evolves."
60. John Martin Fischer's "semicompatibilism" might be taken to represent a counterexample to this claim. However, I think there is something misleading in how many people think of semicompatibilism. First off, the kind of revisionary nature it suggests is much less dramatic that one might think, for it seems that the revisionary element is somewhat "meta"—it is not the idea that concepts, meanings, or references must be changed but simply that our self-understanding of these things is out of alignment with the commitments we already have. This is something I elsewhere call *weak revisionism*, and it is distinct from the moderate form of revisionism that thinks that (whatever our self-understanding of our concepts, meanings, or references) at least some of the first-order elements are themselves in need of change. Second, I think that despite the suggestion that semicompatibilism is an alternative to compatibilism, it is instead simply a species of compatibilism on most contemporary conceptions of compatibilism, and indeed, on nearly any historical conception of compatibilism in the modern period. For these arguments, see, respectively, Manuel Vargas, "Revisionism About Free Will: A Statement & Defense"; Manuel Vargas, "Taking the Highway on Luck, Skepticism, and the Value of Responsibility," *Journal of Moral Philosophy* 6, no. 2 (2009): 249–65.
61. Susan Hurley, "Is Responsibility Essentially Impossible?"; Manuel Vargas, "Libertarianism and Skepticism About Free Will: Some Arguments Against Both."
62. Several years ago, over lunch in Bloomington, Indiana, Al Mele convinced me that I should write a paper about these issues of methodology and how distinct conceptions of the philosophical project generate the peculiar structure of the free will debate. Without his encouragement I doubt I ever would have tried to make explicit many of these thoughts—he has my thanks. Thanks also to Andrei Buckareff, Al Mele, Michael McKenna, Jason Miller, and Kevin Timpe for feedback on an earlier version of this paper, and to Dan Speak for conversations about many of the ideas in this paper. Thanks too, to the material and financial support of the Radcliffe Institute for Advanced Study at Harvard, where I worked on this paper during a sabbatical from the University of San Francisco. Finally, I am grateful to Peter van Inwagen for having gotten me interested in the free will problem in the first place. We obviously disagree about what these matters come to and how they should be framed, but I have learned a good deal from him and his work.

References

Arpaly, N. (2006), *Merit, Meaning, and Human Bondage*. Princeton, NJ: Princeton.

Bennett, J. (1980), "Accountability," in Zak Van Straaten, ed., *Philosophical Subjects*, New York: Clarendon.

Bratman, M. E. (2002) "Nozick on Free Will," in David Schmidtz, ed., *Robert Nozick*, 155–74. New York: Cambridge.

Bratman, M. E (2007), *Structures of Agency: Essays*. New York: Oxford University Press, USA.

Burge, T. (1992), "Philosophy of Language and Mind: 1950–1990," *The Philosophical Review* 101 (1): 3–51.

Clarke, R. (1992), "Deliberation and Beliefs About One's Own Abilities," *Pacific Philosophical Quarterly* 73: 101–13.

———. (1993), "Toward a Credible Agent-Causal Account of Free Will," *Nous* 27: 191–203.

———. (2003), *Libertarian Accounts of Free Will*. Oxford: Oxford University Press.

———. (2009) "Dispositions, Abilities to Act, and Free Will: The New Dispositionalism," *Mind* 118 (470): 323–51.

Double, R. (1991), *The Non-Reality of Free Will*. New York: Oxford University Press, 1991.

———. (1996), *Metaphilosophy and Free Will*. New York: Oxford University Press.

Ekstrom, L. W. (2000) *Free Will: A Philosophical Study*. Boulder, Colorado: Westview Press.

Fischer, J. M. (1994) *The Metaphysics of Free Will: An Essay on Control*. Cambridge, MA: Blackwell.

———. (2006), *My Way: Essays on Moral Responsibility*. Oxford: New York.

———. (1982), "Responsibility and Control," *Journal of Philosophy* 89: 24–40.

Fischer, J. M., Kane, R., Pereboom, D., and Vargas, M. (2007), *Four Views on Free Will*. Malden, MA: Blackwell.

Fischer, J. M. and Ravizza, M. (1998), *Responsibility and Control: A Theory of Moral Responsibility*. New York: Cambridge University Press.

Frankfurt, H. (1969), "Alternate Possibilities and Moral Responsibility," *Journal of Philosophy* 66 (23): 829–39.

———. (1971), "Freedom of the Will and the Concept of a Person," *Journal of Philosophy* 68 (1): 5–20.

Frankfurt, H. (1988), *The Importance of What We Care About: Philosophical Essays*. Cambridge: Cambridge University Press.

———. (1999), *Necessity, Volition, and Love*. New York: Cambridge University Press.

Ginet, C. (1996), "Might We Have No Choice?" in Keith Lehrer, ed., *Freedom and Determinism*, 87–104.

Heller, M. (1996), "The Mad Scientist Meets the Robot Cats: Compatibilism, Kinds, and Counterexamples," *Philosophy and Phenomenological Research* 56: 333–7.

Holton, R. (2006), "The Act of Choice," *Philosopher's Imprint* 6 (3): 1–15.

Honderich, T. (1988), *A Theory of Determinism*. New York: Oxford.

Hurley, S. (2000), "Is Responsibility Essentially Impossible?" *Philosophical Studies* 99: 229–68.

Jackson, F. (1998), *From Metaphysics to Ethics: A Defense of Conceptual Analysis*. New York: Oxford University Press.

Kane, R. (1996), *The Significance of Free Will*. Oxford: Oxford University Press.

Lewis, D. (1973), *Counterfactuals*. Cambridge: Harvard University Press.

MacDonald, S. (2009), "What is Philosophical Theology?" in Kevin Timpe, ed., *Arguing About Religion*, 17–29, New York: Routledge.

Markosian, N. (1999), "A Compatibilist Version of the Theory of Agent Causation," *Pacific Philosophical Quarterly* 80 (3): 257–77.

McKenna, M. (2001), "Source Incompatibilism, Ultimacy, and the Transfer of Non-Responsibility," *American Philosophical Quarterly* 38 (1): 37–51.

Mele, A. (1995), *Autonomous Agents: From Self-Control to Autonomy*. New York: Oxford University Press.

———. (2006), *Free Will and Luck*. Oxford: New York.

———. (2009), "Moral Responsibility and History Revisited." *Ethical Theory and Moral Practice* 12, no. 5: 463–75.

Moore, G. E. (1912), *Ethics*. Oxford: Oxford University Press.

Nagel, T. (1986), *The View From Nowhere*. New York: Oxford University Press.

Nahmias, E. C., Justin, D., and Trevor, K. (2007), "Free Will, Moral Responsibility, and Mechanism: Experiments on Folk Intuitions," *Midwest Studies in Philosophy* XXXI: 214–41.

Nahmias, E., Morris, S., Nadelhoffer, T., and Turner, J. (2006),"Is Incompatibilism Intuitive?" *Philosophy and Phenomenological Research* 73 (1): 28–53.

Nelkin, D. (2004), "Deliberative Alternatives," *Philosophical Topics* 32 (1–2): 215–40.

Nichols, S. (2006), "Folk Intuitions on Free Will," *Journal of Cognition and Culture* 6 (1 & 2): 57–86.

Nichols, S. and Knobe, J. (2007), "Moral Responsibility and Determinism: The Cognitive Science of Folk Intuitions," *Nous* 41 (4): 663–85.

Nietzsche, F. W. (1997), *Twilight of the Idols, Or, How to Philosophize With the Hammer*. Indianapolis, Ind.: Hackett Pub.

Nozick, R. (1981), *Philosophical Explanations*. Oxford: Clarendon Press.

O'Connor, T. (2000), *Persons and Causes*. New York: Oxford University Press.

Pereboom, D. (2001), *Living Without Free Will*. Cambridge: Cambridge University Press.

———. (2005), "Defending Hard Incompatibilism," *Midwest Studies in Philosophy* 29 (1): 228–47.

———. (2008), "A Compatibilist Account of the Epistemic Conditions on Rational Deliberation," *Journal of Ethics* 12: 287–306.

Plantinga, A. (1977), *God, Freedom and Evil*. Eerdmans.

Rosen, G. (2004), "Skepticism About Moral Responsibility," *Philosophical Perspectives* 18: 295–313.

Schlick, M. (1939), *The Problems of Ethics*. Translated by D. Rynin. New York: Prentice Hall.

Searle, J. (2007), *Freedom and Neurobiology*. New York: Columbia University Press.

Sidgwick, H. (1981), *The Methods of Ethics*. 7th edn. Indianapolis, IN: Hackett.

Smilansky, S. (2000), *Free Will and Illusion*. New York: Clarendon.

Sorabji, R. (2003), "The Concept of the Will From Plato to Maximus the Confessor," in Thomas Pink and Martin Stone, eds, *The Will*, 6–28. London: Routledge.

Speak, D. (2004), "Towards an Axiological Defense of Libertarianism," *Philosophical Topics* 32 (1&2): 353–69.

Strawson, G. (1986), *Freedom and Belief*. Oxford: Oxford University Press.

Strawson, P. F. (1962), "Freedom and Resentment." *Proceedings of the British Academy* XLVIII: 1–25.

———. (1992), *Analysis and Metaphysics*. New York: Oxford University Press.

Timpe, K. (2008), *Free Will: Sourcehood and Its Alternatives*. New York: Continuum.

Van Inwagen, P. (1975), "The Incompatibility of Free Will and Determinism," *Philosophical Studies* 27: 185–99.

———. (1983), *An Essay on Free Will*. New York: Oxford University Press.

———. (2004), "Van Inwagen on Free Will," in Joseph Klein Campbell, Michael O'Rourke, and David Shier, eds, *Freedom and Determinism*, 213–30. Cambridge MA: MIT Press.

———. (2008), "How to Think About the Problem of Free Will," *Journal of Ethics* 12: 327–41.

Vargas, M. (2004), "Responsibility and the Aims of Theory: Strawson and Revisionism," *Pacific Philosophical Quarterly* 85 (2): 218–41.

———. (2005), "The Revisionist's Guide to Responsibility," *Philosophical Studies* 125 (3): 399–429.

———. (2005), "Compatibilism Evolves? On Some Varieties of Dennett Worth Wanting," *Metaphilosophy* 36 (4): 460–75.

———. (2006), "Philosophy and the Folk: On Some Implications of Experimental Work for Philosophical Debates on Free Will," *Journal of Cognition and Culture* 6 (1 & 2): 239–54.

———. (2008), "Moral Influence, Moral Responsibility," in Nick Trakakis and Daniel Cohen, eds, *Essays on Free Will and Moral Responsibility*, 90–122. Newcastle, UK: Cambridge Scholars Press.

———. (2009), "Revisionism About Free Will: A Statement & Defense," *Philosophical Studies* 144.1: 45–62.

———. (2004), "Libertarianism and Skepticism About Free Will: Some Arguments Against Both," *Philosophical Topics* 32 (1&2): 403–26.

———. (2009), "Taking the Highway on Luck, Skepticism, and the Value of Responsibility," *Journal of Moral Philosophy* 6 (2): 249–65.

———. (unpublished), "Desert, Retribution, and Moral Responsibility."

Velleman, J. D. (1989), "Epistemic Freedom," *Pacific Philosophical Quarterly* 70: 73–97.

Watson, G. (1975), "Free Agency," *Journal of Philosophy* 72 (8): 205–20.

Widerker, D. and McKenna, M. (eds) (2003), *Moral Responsibility and Alternative Possibilities: Essays on the Importance of Alternative Possibilities*. Burlington, VT: Ashgate.

Wiggins, D. (1973), "Towards a Reasonable Libertarianism," in Ted Honderich, ed., *Essays on Freedom of Action*, 31–62. London: Routledge & Kegan Paul.

Yaffe, G. (2000), "Free Will and Agency At Its Best," *Philosophical Perspectives* 14: 203–29.

8
Luck and Free Will

Neil Levy

Arguments that turn on questions of luck have been a staple of the free will literature for a very long time. Typically, these arguments have been aimed at libertarianism. The traditional luck objection against libertarianism turns on the claim that an undetermined event is merely a lucky event, and lucky events cannot enhance our freedom. At best, such events add nothing to freedom; on this view, libertarianism has no advantage over compatibilism. At worst, such lucky events would detract from our freedom; on this view, compatibilism has an advantage over libertarianism. Despite the centrality of arguments from luck to the free will debate, however, for the most part philosophers working on free will have been content to use an intuitive and rough conception of luck. In this paper, I shall defend a more precise conception; with this account of luck in hand, I shall argue that luck is a more serious problem than has formerly been recognized. It is not uniquely a problem for libertarianism, but for all accounts of free will.

8.1 What is luck?

It might be useful to begin defining luck by setting out some paradigms of luck-involving events; any adequate account of luck must yield the result that these events are luck-involving. Paradigm lucky (where an event is "lucky" if it is good or bad luck for an agent) events include: winning the lottery, being hit by lightning, walking away from a bad auto accident unharmed, finding a $50 bill. One thing all these events have in common is low subjective probability: these are events that antecedently seem very unlikely to the person who is their subject. They also seem to have a low objective probability. Should it be subjective or objective probability that matters so far as luck is concerned? Consider a case in which the two come apart. Suppose Joe stumbles across an ancient solid gold coin in the middle of a field in England. Joe will consider himself very lucky, and so shall we if we know nothing further about the event. But suppose we learn that Joe's fairy godmother has scattered solid gold coins everywhere she thinks that

Joe will walk. Now we are no longer disposed to think Joe lucky *to find the coin* (though perhaps he is lucky to have a fairy godmother). Thus it seems that it is the objective probability of the event that matters, so far as luck is concerned.

So lucky events have a low objective probability. But not all events that have a low objective probability are lucky. Schrödinger's cat is lucky to survive being placed in the sealed box with a lump of radioactive material if the probability of its surviving is low. But remove the cat from the picture and we remove the luck as well: it is not lucky that a lump of radium emits a radioactive particle at *t*, no matter how low the probability that the particle is emitted. Unless the low probability event is *significant* for a subject, it doesn't count as lucky.

How low need the objective probability be for an event to count as lucky? Coffman (2007) holds that the cut-off point is roughly 50 percent; though I can be lucky when the coin upon which I have bet comes down heads, I cannot be lucky to survive playing Russian roulette with a six-chambered revolver which has only one bullet in it. Instead, Coffman thinks that I am merely fortunate to survive playing Russian roulette. I think this is ad hoc, and ignores the fact that luck is plainly a function of *degree* of significance. Significance and probability seem to interact: the lower the degree of significance for an agent, the less likely it must be to count as lucky. Considering a variety of possible lottery wins makes this clear. Suppose my odds of winning are 45 percent - below the threshold Coffman sets for an event no longer to count as lucky. It would be strange to say that I was lucky to win if the payoff was two cents. But I am clearly *very* lucky if the payoff is $100,000. It would be even stranger to say that I was lucky to win two cents on a lottery, if my odds of winning were 75 percent. But I think we would say that I was lucky if the payoff was $250,000. Since significance and probability interact in this manner, we should not follow Coffman and set a probability threshold above which an event no longer counts as lucky; instead, we should recognize how the threshold shifts as a function of significance. Even an overwhelmingly likely event might be lucky if, say, the fate of the universe hangs on it.

The centrality of chanciness to an adequate account of luck can best be captured by analyzing luck in modal terms; that is, in terms of the proportion of nearby possible worlds in which an event that occurs in the actual world fails to occur (Pritchard 2005; Coffman 2007). In order to apply this modal account, we need two things: a means of determining which worlds are relevant, and a means of settling what proportion of such worlds must differ from the actual world for an event in the actual world to count as lucky. Which worlds are nearby in modal space (for the purposes of an account of luck)? Pritchard (2005) suggests we allow ourselves to be guided by intuition here, but such reliance should be a last resort. The purpose of advancing an account of luck is to have a standard to which we can refer in settling whether disputed cases are lucky or not; to the extent to which the account incorporates intuitions as an indispensable element, it will be less useful for settling disputed cases. Fortunately, we can do better. Following Coffman, I will define nearby worlds, for the purposes of the account, as those which differ from the actual world in only trivial respects. Slightly more formally:

> An event occurring in the actual world at *t* is lucky for an agent if it is significant for that agent and it fails to occur in a large enough proportion of nearby worlds, where a world is nearby iff it differs from the actual world in only trivial respects just prior to *t*.

Though this is not yet a full account of luck, it is a very promising foundation. It yields the right results in paradigm cases. I am lucky to win the lottery because winning the lottery is significant for me and because I fail to win the lottery in a large enough proportion of nearby possible worlds, where these worlds differ from the actual world in only trivial respects. Thus, in all those worlds in which the lottery occurred but in which (say), the balls were dropped into the barrel a millisecond earlier, or in which they spun slightly longer, or in which the surface properties of one of them was slightly different, my numbers did not come up. Given the odds in most actual lotteries, I am *very* lucky to win, because the proportion of nearby worlds in which I fail to win is extremely high, and the significance for me is very high too. Were either the odds better or the payoff worse, we would assess whether my winning was lucky by considering whether the other feature was sufficiently high to compensate.

Notice that the suggested account makes no reference to the causal structure of the universe. This, I claim, is appropriate. Despite the impression one might glean from reading the free will debate, luck is not confined to universes containing macro-level indeterminism (that is, indeterminism that is not confined to the quantum-level, but which affects events at the macro-level, which is, of course, the level at which events can have significance for agents, even if they have such a significance, as in the Schrödinger's cat thought experiment, *by* affecting the quantum level). Were this not so, settling certain disputed questions in physics would be much easier than it actually is. Since luck is so obviously a feature of this world—it is obvious, for instance, that you are unlucky if you are hit by lightning and that you are lucky if you win the lottery—if we knew that luck required indeterminism in the causal structure of the world, we could settle the dispute between physicists who hold that the universe is genuinely indeterministic and those who advance "hidden variable" explanations of apparent indeterminism *a priori*. But these questions cannot be settled so easily (nor is this the right way to do physics).

I said above that the modal account of luck offered here was not yet complete. In fact, the account just given begs the question against agent-causal libertarians. Agent-causal libertarians hold that low probability, significant events can be under the direct control of the agent (Clarke 2005). Of course, it is widely held that advocates of agent-causal accounts of free will are not entitled to this claim; that they are themselves vulnerable to the luck objection (Haji 2004; Mele 2006). However, if we are to make progress on settling this dispute, we had better not have the answer be a direct entailment of our account—not unless an account which does not have this result and which is equally plausible is unavailable. We can easily construct such an account by adding an absence of control condition to what we already have. That still leaves us with a problem, because an absence of control condition depends upon us having an adequate account of control, and I doubt that any such account is available. Rather than defend an account of control here, I leave "control" unanalyzed; a fully adequate account of luck must await a fully adequate account of control.

We can now define luck as follows:

> *Luck as chanciness*: An event occurring in the actual world at *t* is lucky for an agent if it is significant for that agent, beyond his or her direct control, and it fails to occur in a large enough proportion of nearby worlds, where a world is nearby iff it differs from the actual world in only trivial respects just prior to *t*.

The definition (which borrows heavily from Coffman 2007) speaks of *direct* control and not just *control* because agents can and often do influence the probability of lucky events, without thereby bringing it about that those events are not lucky if they occur. For instance, agents can influence the probability of their winning the lottery, by buying two (or more) tickets.

Though the above account is not without its critics (see Lackey 2008; Levy forthcoming replies), it is the best account of lucky events available. Call this kind of luck *present* luck (following Mele 2006). However, present luck does not seem to the only sort of luck there is. In his well-known paper "Moral Luck" Nagel (1979) identified several sorts of luck which are not captured by the above account. In particular, *constitutive* luck—luck in the traits, abilities and dispositions which make one the kind of person one is—is not chancy. That it, it is (plausibly) false that the traits which are constitutive of me are such that *I* do not have them in a large (enough) proportion of nearby worlds, or indeed, in *any* nearby worlds. Suppose some kind of Kripkean essentialism about identity is true, such that no being which does not trace its beginnings back to the same fertilized ovum as me is identical to me. In that case, it is widely believed, for a large number of traits, any world in which I lack those traits which are constitutive of me is a world from which I am simply absent (the locus classicus here is Parfit 1984). Take an agent who is born with congenital disability *D*. Since *D* is congenital, any being who traces its origin back to the same fertilized ovum will also have *D*, or so it is widely held.

Due to the belief that at least some of the traits that are constitutive of agents do not vary across possible worlds, the notion of constitutive luck is widely rejected as incoherent (Hurley 1993; Rescher 1995). I think this is too hasty. First, the argument from Kripkean essentialism is controversial; not all philosophers agree that the causal route back to a fertilized ovum fixes the reference of proper names across possible worlds. Second, even if the argument is accepted, it only applies to our essential traits, and most of our traits are not essential (Latus 2003). It is controversial how malleable our traits are, given our genome, but it is not controversial that almost all our traits could have been very different. Without knowing your genome, for instance, I can confidently predict that had you been severely malnourished as a child, your IQ would been significantly lower than it actually is.

Constitutive luck certainly *seems* to be luck; most people seem to have the intuition that, say, an infant who is born profoundly disabled is desperately unlucky. Any account of luck that ruled out constitutive luck strikes me as dramatically revisionist. We should revise so dramatically only if the best account of constitutive luck we can offer diverges from the best account of present luck too radically for the claim that they are accounts of the same kind of thing to be plausible. In fact, the best account of constitutive luck is remarkably similar to the account we have offered of present luck.

We can simply import the significance condition and the absence of control condition unaltered into our account of constitutive luck; it is the modal condition that is troubling, inasmuch (as we have seen) as it is apparently false that I might have lacked some of my intuitively constitutively lucky traits. However, though my constitutively lucky traits *might* not vary across possible worlds, they do vary across other kinds of reference groups; it is this fact, I suggest, that gives rise to the intuition that they are lucky. Constitutively lucky traits are traits that vary significantly across human beings (or other agents) and they are lucky only in those ways in which they vary. Thus, traits that do not vary significantly are not said to be constitutively lucky; it is good constitutive luck for an agent to be more intelligent than the average person, but it is not good constitutive luck for a human being to be more intelligent than a dog, because almost all human beings are more intelligent than dogs (this kind of asymmetry is characteristic of present luck too: I would be lucky to win the lottery, but I am not unlucky to lose).

With this in mind, we can advance the following account of constitutive luck:

> A trait manifested by an agent is constitutively lucky for her if it is significant for her, beyond her direct control, and it varies across a relevant reference group.

"Relevant reference group" is vague, but I doubt it is possible to be more precise. Sometimes the reference group will be local and sometimes it will be much broader. It might be, for instance, that thanks to improvements in nutrition, the average IQ of infants born in Western countries is much higher than the long-term human average. We might therefore want to relativize claims about constitutive luck to the local average, saying that a baby born with an IQ of 75 is unlucky, but for some purposes we will probably have in mind a much broader reference group when we make claims about constitutive luck.

8.2 Luck and libertarianism

Now that we have a relatively precise account of luck available to us, we can better assess the luck objection commonly leveled against libertarian accounts of free will. I will treat event-causal and agent-causal accounts of libertarianism separately (in Levy (2008), I sketch a luck objection to a non-causal account).

First, event-causal libertarianism (ECL). There are several different varieties of ECL on the market today; here I focus on the most influential, Robert Kane's sophisticated dual-control account (Kane 1996; 1999). On Kane's account, agents act with direct freedom only when it is causally open to them to perform one of at least two incompatible actions; this occurs when they experience a significant conflict concerning how they ought to act. In such circumstances, when they are genuinely torn about which course of action to pursue, sufficient chaotic activity in the brain may be generated to disrupt its thermodynamic equilibrium, thereby magnifying quantum level indeterminacy. It then becomes causally open to the agent to perform either action. Their efforts set in train two rival causal processes, each of which leads to one of the incompatible actions; which they actually perform depends upon which causal process goes to completion, and this is genuinely undetermined.

The luck objection has been repeatedly leveled at Kane's ECL. If it is causally open to the agent to perform either of two incompatible actions, but which they perform is settled by an indeterministic process, isn't it simply a matter of luck which they perform? Mele (2006), probably the single most influential proponent of the luck objection in the contemporary literature, develops the objection in terms of *differences* between possible worlds. Suppose an agent is torn between two actions, one selfish and the other altruistic, and the conflict is sufficient to disrupt the thermodynamic equilibrium in his brain and thereby render both courses of action causally open. Suppose, as it happens, the agent performs the selfish action. Is he blameworthy for so doing? Mele suggests that if it is a matter of luck alone that the agent performed the selfish act and not the altruistic act, he is not blameworthy. Mele asks us to focus on the difference between worlds in which the agent performs the selfish action and worlds in which he performs the altruistic action. This difference, he says, is *wholly* a matter of luck, but since it is this difference which makes a moral difference here, it is difficult to see how the agent can be blameworthy for the action.

I think Mele's case is persuasive, but I doubt that the cross-world difference upon which he focuses is relevant here. Mele highlights this difference because he wants to isolate the luck in the agent's action, distinguishing it from non-lucky aspects of the context. On Kane's view, agents act for reasons: they experience the conflict which renders incompatible actions causally open to them because they have reasons for both actions. These reasons, which reflect the state of their characters, their beliefs and their desires, entail that it is not *simply* a matter of luck that they choose as they do. But the cross-world difference *is* simply a matter of luck; hence Mele's decision to focus on it.

However, focusing on this cross-world difference is missing the target. First, the luck of which the agent is the subject, on Kane's view, is not luck in a cross-world difference: no one is ever the subject of such a difference, because one can only be the subject of an event or process that occurs *in* a world, not between worlds. Second, Mele's account fails to make sense of the asymmetry that is characteristic of luck. Recall: I am lucky to win the lottery but not unlucky to lose it. Yet in both cases we can isolate a cross-world difference that is, on Mele's view, a matter of luck. Suppose, for concreteness, the lottery is indeterministic, but that the probability of my winning is very low (say 0.00001%). In that case, I would be very lucky to win, but I am not unlucky to lose. However, there is a world in which I do win, nearby in modal space. Now consider the difference between the actual world and that world. That difference is *entirely* a matter of luck. Since the cross-world difference is entirely a matter of luck in both cases, we do not hone in on the luck in my winning the lottery by focusing on it. Instead, we hone in on luck by looking at the clustering of worlds. The world in which I win the lottery is nearby (that world differs—at most—only trivially from the actual world at *t*, where *t* is just prior to the winning numbers being drawn; given causal indeterminism, that world might be *identical* to the actual world at *t*). But that world is surrounded by a huge number of worlds that differ (at most) only trivially from the actual world at *t* and in which I do not win. The clustering of possible worlds is a function of how lucky I am to win or to lose: we measure the degree of luck by a formula that multiplies the proportion of nearby possible worlds in which the event that takes places in the actual world fails to occur, by the significance of that event for me.

Thus the modal account fares better than Mele's account. How does ECL fare, on this account? Whether actions that satisfy Kane's conditions for direct freedom are lucky depends upon whether they satisfy the modal condition; that is, on the proportion of possible worlds in which the action that is performed in the actual world fails to occur. The other two conditions seem straightforwardly to be satisfied: (1) agents who satisfy the conditions for direct freedom lack direct control over which of the actions causally open to them they perform and, (2) the action is significant for them (significance seems necessary to provoke the conflict that renders both courses of action causally open). Whether the modal condition is satisfied depends upon the probabilities: if there is large (enough) chance that the action performed in the actual world was not selected in nearby possible worlds, that action is lucky.

Kane claims that the probabilities of the competing options may vary anywhere between 0 and 1, "depending upon the *strength or weakness of the agent's will* with respect to the options" (1996: 177). However, there is a case for saying that he is not entitled to the claim that the probabilities can vary very significantly from parity. Recall the role that the experience of conflict plays on his account: such conflict would appear to be a consequence of the fact that the agent is genuinely torn, and it is difficult to see how an agent can be genuinely torn if the state of his "will" is such that his reasons or character make one option very much more likely for him than the other. Being torn, in the sense intended by Kane, occurs when the agent's will is such that more than one option is *all things considered* attractive enough to him or her to generate significant conflict for him or her; among the things that an all things considered judgment considers, of course, is our other options (how would we measure the value to us of our options if we did not take their opportunity costs into account?); it follows that being torn seems to require that we value each option more or less equally. If this is correct, then the proportion of possible worlds in which the option selected in the actual world is not chosen will be high, regardless of which option is selected, and the choice of option is therefore lucky.

Whether or not Kane is entitled to the claim that the probability of the competing options might depart very significantly from parity, however, an ECL that held that agents act with direct freedom when it is causally open to them to perform either of two incompatible actions, but which held that the probability of the actions might depart very significantly from parity is a conceptual possibility. On such an ECL, an agent would be *very* lucky to choose the low probability option, but would almost invariably choose the high probability option. On such an ECL, agents acting with direct freedom would very rarely be subject to luck. Hence the luck objection, in its traditional form, would be all but impotent against this kind of view.

The fact that such an ECL would be invulnerable to the luck objection is comforting to the libertarian, of course, only if an ECL that stipulated probabilities as suggested satisfies other libertarian desiderata. The obvious problem is that in corralling indeterminacy in the manner suggested, the account comes very close to rendering it too insignificant to play any genuine role in securing a degree of freedom greater than that available on an adequate compatibilism. Indeed, the suggested account looks very much like a compatibilism. Given the probabilities, it is difficult to see how such an ECL could satisfy the first libertarian desideratum, the alternative possibilities condition. The worry is that an alternative possibility so unlikely would not be what has come to be called *robust*, where a robust alternative is an alternative in virtue of the availability of which the agent is morally responsible for their actual action (Fischer 1994). But the envisaged account seems to do better in satisfying the other libertarian desideratum, sourcehood. On this theory, with regard to every directly free action, it is false that prior to the agent's decision there were sufficient conditions for the performance of that very action. The agent will have the kind of causal bearing on her actions that source incompatibilists seem to crave. I conclude, then, that given the adequacy of a compatibilist account of free will (which such an ECL so resembles), an ECL that could secure some kind of sourcehood condition would be invulnerable to the luck objection.

Let's now turn to agent-causal libertarianism (ACL). Proponents of ACL, who have been prominent among those levelling the luck objection at ECL, believe that it succeeds at avoiding this problem. Though it may be true that the modal condition is satisfied by the actions of agent-causes—that is, it is true that in many nearby worlds the option chosen by the agent would not be chosen—and the significance condition is satisfied, the absence of control condition is *not* satisfied, defenders of ACL claim. The exercise of the agent-causal power, the power to be an uncaused cause, is *essentially* an exercise of direct control (Clark 2005). If this claim is true, then standard luck objections to ACL fail. These objections focus on the wrong condition. They aim at establishing that the modal condition is satisfied; that is, that holding everything about the agent's belief, desires and character fixed, the action that was performed in the actual world would not have been selected in a wide class of nearby possible worlds (Haji 2004; Mele 2005). But it is open to the proponent of ACL to concede the point and yet insist that because the exercise of agent-causation is an exercise of direct control, agent-causation is invulnerable to the luck objection.

Of course, the success of this move depends entirely on the plausibility of the claim that the exercise of agent-causation is an exercise of direct control. This claim is, I shall argue, not very plausible: the agent-causal power cannot be exercised *for reasons*, and therefore is not an exercise of direct control. Control is a rational power: we cannot be said to control what we cause blindly or for no reason at all. But since agent-causation cannot give us control, and the other two conditions of my account of luck are satisfied, agent-causation, too, is vulnerable to the luck objection.

Defenders of ACL recognize that they must show that the agent-causal power can be exercised for reasons. They attempt to satisfy this demand in different ways. On Clarke's *hybrid* account, there are two, nomologically linked, causal routes to action. On one, actions are indeterministically event-caused by the agent's reasons; reasons-explanation is allegedly secured on this route. On the second route, actions are agent-caused; direct control is secured on this second route. The agent-causal power is exercised to select from among the options which the agent's reasons make available to her (Clarke 2003: 136–7), but only if she agent-causes a particular option will it be caused by her reasons. Thus, on Clarke's picture, the agent-causal power is always exercised for reasons.

However, in assessing the adequacy of Clarke's view as a response to the luck objection, we need to ask not whether the agent-causal power is exercised for reasons, in some broad sense, but whether agent-causation *itself* can be exercised for reasons. Reasons-explanation is satisfied, on Clarke's view, on the *event-causal* route to action. But, as we have already seen, the degree of control on this route is not sufficient to avoid the luck objection. On the agent-causal route to action itself, reasons do not operate. To be sure, the options between which the agent-cause selects are constrained by the agent's reasons, but once reasons have arrayed the options before the agent, their power is exhausted. An agent cannot select an option from the choices made available by their reasons *for those very reasons*; that would be double counting of reasons. Since reasons are deployed only event-causally, on one of Clarke's routes to action, and have no role other than constraining the options, the agent-causal power itself, the final selection from among the options, is exercised blindly. Clarke's version of ACL therefore fails to secure reasons-explanation over and above that available on ECL, and therefore fails to avoid the luck objection.

Let's turn, now, to the other major ACL available today, that developed by Timothy O'Connor (2000). O'Connor aims to secure reasons-explanation and therefore direct control by postulating a single causal route to action, integrating reasons and the agent-causal power. The agent-causal power causes an intention to act *for the sake of* some goal (2000: 86). On O'Connor's account, like Clarke's, the agent's reasons constrain the options between which the agent chooses, but because reasons are built into the agent-caused intention, the agent-causal power is then exercised for one (or more) of these same reasons.

It should be clear, however, that O'Connor's account fails to secure any greater degree of control than Clarke's, and for much the same reason. We cannot select from among the options our reasons make available for choice *for those very reasons*. That involves an illicit double counting of reasons. It might be that the agent-cause can select one of those reasons and increase its causal power, but this must be a selection that cannot itself be made for reasons. Thus, this power is exercised blindly. We can say that the agent-causal power is exercised for reasons, if we like, but this is true only insofar as the options between which the power selects are constrained by reasons: the final push—that is to say, the exercise of the agent-causal power *itself*—is not made for reasons. All the reasons the agent had took her up to the point at which her options were arrayed, as choiceworthy alternatives, before her.

She cannot now choose between those options for those very reasons. Yet those are all the reasons she has. Hence on O'Connor's account, as much as on Clarke's, she must exercise the agent-causal power by selecting from among those options for no reason at all. That is, there is no reason at all why she chose one of those options *rather than* any other.

Thus ACL has no better reply to the luck objection than does ECL. Neither can secure direct control for the agent. It should be noted that, like ECL, ACL can avoid this particular luck objection and secure one of the libertarian desiderata—the sourcehood condition—by modeling itself more closely on compatibilism; that is, by postulating that agential choices are near deterministic. If they were to adopt this suggestion, they could avoid the modal condition: if our choices are near deterministic it will rarely be true that the option selected in the actual world would not be selected in a wide class of nearby possible worlds. As we have seen, however, though such a libertarianism might satisfy the sourcehood condition, it is difficult to see how it might satisfy the alternative possibilities condition. I shall now argue, moreover, that any theory that escapes the luck version by modelling itself on compatibilism does so only to run into another serious version of the problem.

8.2.1 Luck and compatibilism

Obviously, libertarianism can avoid the luck objection by modeling itself on compatibilism only if compatibilism can avoid the luck objection. Some philosophers have argued that compatibilism is vulnerable to a problem concerning luck; that the problem of determinism can itself be understood as the problem of "remote deterministic luck" (Mele 2006: 77). Strictly, speaking, however, there is no such problem. There is a problem of constitutive luck, which is luck in one's traits inasmuch as these traits are significant and vary sufficiently from those in a relevant reference group, and there is a problem of circumstantial luck, which is closely analogous, but there is no problem of luck inherent in having one's traits and circumstances determined. My having two hands is (plausibly) determined, but I am not lucky to have two hands.

Most philosophers seem to think that if there is no problem of remote deterministic luck, compatibilism is not subject to luck objections at all; certainly there is no literature pressing a luck objection against compatibilism. Perhaps compatibilism is thought to be resistant to luck because it does not require indeterminism in the causal chain leading to action; perhaps it is thought that indeterministic processes are lucky in a way that deterministic processes could never be. But the fact that the account of luck offered here makes no mention of indeterminism should give philosophers tempted by this thought pause. Luck is a feature of deterministic universes, as well as indeterministic.

There is every reason to think that agents in deterministic worlds are subject to luck. Consider an agent deliberating about a significant choice in a deterministic world. Luck will infect every aspect of their deliberation process: it will be true (for instance) that the considerations that occur to them during deliberation will vary across nearby possible worlds. Had the weather been different, had environmental conditions (which might prime associated thoughts) been different, had they had slightly more, or slightly less, coffee, had stochastic events in the brains not occurred in the precise manner in which they did, different considerations would have occurred to them, or the same considerations would have struck them with different force. Indeed one (sometime) defender of libertarianism, Mele, refers to just this fact in defense of his account. Mele (2006) points out that though it is true that on his libertarianism (upon which the process of deliberation is indeterministic), the considerations that occur to agents are subject to luck, there is no reason to think that this is more the case than it would be in a similar deterministic world.

Mele believes that showing that his libertarian agents are no more subject to luck than are compatibilist agents suffices to show that his account is proof against the (standard) luck objection. But he is correct only if the degree of luck to which compatibilist agents are subject is not freedom-undermining. Mele is sanguine about luck in deliberation, no matter whether it effects his libertarian agents or compatibilist agents, because the considerations that happen, by chance, to cross the agent's mind are merely *inputs* into their deliberative processes. They have, "at most, an indirect effect on what the agent decides, an effect that is mediated by the agent's assessment of them" (Mele 2006: 12). We can read Mele as denying that (well-designed) agents subject to chance in deliberation are subject to responsibility-undermining luck, because the significance condition is not satisfied. The considerations that occur to the agent will not be decisive, because the agent will assess them and respond to them in ways that reflect their values and beliefs. By failing to be decisive, the chance fails to be significant enough to count as luck.

Mele is clearly right that often chance in deliberation fails to be significant enough to count as luck. Well-designed agents (like us) have failsafe mechanisms designed to compensate for failures to bring the most relevant considerations to mind. Moreover, even when considerations are uncompensated for by mechanisms such as these, how we respond to them is still within our control, such that the subsequent action is a good reflection of our practical agency. However, and equally clearly, chance in deliberation can sometimes be significant enough for the subsequent action to be infected with luck. Sometimes what considerations occur to an agent in deliberation will be decisive for her.

This will typically be the case when a decision is difficult; that is, when the agent takes the considerations on both sides to be approximately equally weighty. In these circumstances, a new consideration can tip the balance one way or another. This is especially likely when the new consideration is not just another independent reason in favor of one option or the other, but is seen as affecting a whole class of reasons. For instance, suppose I am deliberating between two vacation options. I am leaning toward the exotic destination, rather than the attractions of my old home town, friends and family. Then I recall that the travel guide upon which I am basing my information regarding the attractions of one destination has recently been involved in a scandal involving writers taking kickbacks from tourist boards in exchange for downplaying problems. My recalling this fact could tip the balance decisively against the exotic destination; my failure to recall it would probably result in my choosing that location. Thus chance in deliberation can be decisive, thereby satisfying the significance condition and counting as lucky.

Hence compatibilist agents are sometimes subject to precisely the same kind of luck that afflicts libertarian agents. However, given that compatibilists do not seek to satisfy the alternative possibilities condition (understood as libertarians typically do, such that an agent has alternative possibilities iff more than one action is causally open to her), compatibilists can, in good faith, seek to minimize their exposure to such luck. Nothing in typical compatibilisms requires compatibilists to see this kind of luck as anything more than a misfortune. Unlike traditional libertarians, who seek to retain alternative possibilities, compatibilists can seek to extirpate them. So while this kind of luck is a problem for the compatibilist, there is no need for it to be more than an occasional problem, one with which they, and we, can live.

The problem is really serious for one kind of compatibilist, however, those who are *history-sensitive*. A history-sensitive compatibilist maintains that responsibility and therefore free will are partially historical: agents who are exactly similar at a time, and act in precisely the same way in precisely the same circumstances, can differ in their degree of freedom (or even in *whether* they are free) because of their causal history. Historical considerations are commonly adduced by compatibilists in response to manipulation cases: though agents can be manipulated into satisfying all the non-historical conditions of compatibilist accounts, it is difficult to see how they can be manipulated into having the right history (though see McKenna 2008). Historically-sensitive compatibilisms hold that agents are responsible for their actions only if (inter alia) they have taken responsibility for their values, dispositions and beliefs.[1] In so doing, they might be seen as responding to the problem of constitutive luck, distancing the agent from the merely chancy effects of genes and environment in endowing them with a character. These compatibilisms are especially vulnerable to luck for the following reason: the actions whereby agents allegedly take responsibility for their values (and so on) will either themselves simply reflect their character or will be subject to the kind of luck which we just sketched.

Consider an agent reflecting on their character and deciding either to attempt to modify it or to endorse it (of course, agents do not typically think of their decisions in this way, but the kinds of actions that history-sensitive compatibilists regard as those by which we take responsibility for our characters can be described in this way). These decisions will range over a continuum from easy to hard for the agent. The difficulty of the decision will be a product of the extent to which the aspect of their character about which they are deliberating coheres with their other beliefs and values. If it is consistent with most or with their deepest dispositions, or if it is consistent with few or only their shallowest, the decision will be easy: in one case to endorse it, in the other to seek to alter it. The decision will be difficult when considerations are more evenly balanced, in favor and against alteration. When it is difficult, however, when things are finely balanced, the option that is chosen is subject to luck in deliberation, as we have seen. The considerations that occur to the agent, the force with which they strike her, her passing fancies—any of these might be decisive. Given that she must make the choice one way or another, there are only two possibilities: either she makes it for some reason or she makes it for no reason at all. On either disjunct, she is subject to chance (and therefore to luck). If she makes the choice for some reason, then she will be subject to luck in deliberation, because it is overwhelmingly likely that one or more consideration in the set that is on the winning side is there only by chance, but since things are evenly balanced, that entails that chance is decisive. But if she makes the choice for no reason at all (perhaps she has a tie-breaker mechanism in her brain), she is equally subject to chance.

When the actions by which we allegedly take responsibility for our characters are the product of easy choices, then they simply express those very springs: it is our existing character, beliefs and values that make the choice easy. But when the actions are the product of difficult choices, they are subject to luck in deliberation. On either disjunct, our actions cannot play the role that historically sensitive compatibilists demand of them: either our choices simply express the very endowment for which they are supposed to take responsibility, or they are unacceptably subject to luck.

It is illuminating to see historically-sensitive compatibilism as a response to the problem of constitutive luck: the requirement that we take responsibility for the springs of our action is motivated by worries that these springs are the product of a causal history over which we lack control and which results in our having dispositions, to good and to evil, that others who were not lucky in the same way do not have. One way to understand the lesson above is this: it is impossible to solve for constitutive luck and luck in deliberations simultaneously. It is only if we accept that constitutive luck is not a problem that needs solving that we can confront luck in deliberation, for it is only if are sanguine about the fact that the background against which we deliberate makes many choices easy for us that we can opt for the route taken by the libertarians I sketched above, who limit their exposure to luck by making most choices easy for the agent.

If responsibility is essentially historical, of course, then we cannot take this route. It is only if responsibility is not essentially historical that we can be sanguine about constitutive luck. Any theory of free will, compatibilist or libertarian, that holds that responsibility is historical must do the impossible: solve simultaneously for constitutive and present luck (see Levy 2009 for a more careful elaboration of these thoughts).[2]

Galen Strawson has said that luck swallows everything. This is, no doubt, an exaggeration, but luck does swallow free will, at least if free will is essentially historical. Whether a non-historical account of free will, libertarian or compatibilist, can escape from the jaws of luck remains to be seen.[3]

Notes

1. It should be noted that some historically sensitive compatibilists defend negative accounts: rather than holding that agents have a history with some positive component (for example, having taken responsibility for their values), they hold that a responsible agent must *lack* a history of a certain kind (Mele 1995; Haji and Cuypers 2007). These kinds of historicisms raise difficult issues, which I cannot satisfactorily address here. I am skeptical, however, that these views are stable. Mele's negative historicism is motivated by the thought that an agent might have values that are all practically sheddable, but I doubt an agent for whom all significant values were practically sheddable (in the sense Mele defines) would possess a deliberative standpoint at all. Haji and Cuypers' view seems to me to rest on an intuition that I doubt most people would share: that significant manipulation of an agent who has previously existed for even the briefest period of time necessarily brings it about that that agent is not suitably invested in her attitudes, but a time-slice identical duplicate who lacks a past at all might be so invested. Obviously, these brief remarks are inadequate; the subject deserves a fuller consideration than I can give it here.
2. As a referee points out, the picture of historically sensitive compatibilism which I sketch here does not fit Fischer and Ravizza's account (for which see Fischer and Ravizza 1998). For them, the historical element in responsibility has three features: the agent must see himself as the source of the behavior, as a fair target of the reactive attitudes on the basis of that behavior, and these views of himself must be based, in an appropriate way, on the evidence. However, I doubt that this account of the historical element adequately captures the concerns of people with deeply historical intuitions. We might best describe these concerns as centring around the ability of an agent to be the source of his or her own behavior, and not just a creature of circumstances and genes. As Mele (2006) shows with his case of Chuck, intuitively an agent becomes responsible for their actions by, as it were, becoming their own creature; not by taking responsibility for the mechanisms upon which they act, but—far more importantly—for the values which motivate them. Nothing in the Fischer and Ravizza account guarantees the satisfaction of this condition. I think it is no accident that though the Fischer/Ravizza account of moral responsibility plays a pivotal role in the free will debate generally, it is relatively peripheral to the debate over the degree to which responsibility is a deeply historical notion.
3. I would like to thank Randy Clarke, Michael McKenna, Manuel Vargas and an anonymous referee for helpful comments on an earlier draft.

References

Clarke, R. (2003), *Libertarian Accounts of Free Will.* New York: Oxford University Press.

Clarke, R. (2005), "Agent Causation and the Problem of Luck," *Pacific Philosophical Quarterly* 86: 408–21.

Coffman, E. J. (2007). "Thinking about Luck," *Synthese* 158: 385–98.

Fischer, J. M. (1994). *The Metaphysics of Free Will.* Oxford: Blackwell.

Fischer, J. M. and Ravizza, M. (1998). *Responsibility and Control: An Essay on Moral Responsibility.* Cambridge: Cambridge University Press.

Haji, I. (2004). "Active Control, Agent-Causation and Free Action," *Philosophical Explorations* 7: 131–48.

Hurley, S. (1993). "Justice Without Constitutive Luck," In A. P. Griffith (ed)., *Ethics.* Cambridge, Cambridge University Press, pp. 179–212.

Kane, R. (1996), *The Significance of Free Will,* New York: Oxford University Press.

Kane, R. (1999), "Responsibility, Luck, and Chance: Reflections on Free Will and Indeterminism," *Journal of Philosophy* 96: 217–40.

Lackey, J. (2008), "What Luck is Not," *Australasian Journal of Philosophy* 86: 255–67.

Latus, A. (2003), "Constitutive Luck," *Metaphilosophy* 34: 460–75.

Levy, N. (2008), "Bad Luck Once Again," *Philosophy and Phenomenological Research,* 77: 749–54.

Levy, N. (2009), "What, and Where, Luck Is: A Response to Jennifer Lackey," *Australasian Journal of Philosophy,* 87: 489–97.

Levy, N. (2009), "Luck and History-Sensitive Compatibilism," *Philosophical Quarterly* 59: 237–51

McKenna, M. (2008), "A Hard-line Reply to Pereboom's Four-Case Manipulation Argument," *Philosophy and Phenomenological Research* 77: 142–59.

Mele, A. R. (2005), "Libertarianism, Luck, and Control," *Pacific Philosophical Quarterly* 86: 381–407.

Mele, A. (2006), *Free Will and Luck.* New York: Oxford University Press.

Nagel, T. (1979), "Moral Luck," in *Mortal Questions,* New York: Cambridge University Press, pp. 24–38.

O'Connor, T. (2000), *Persons and Causes: The Metaphysics of Free Will.* New York: Oxford University Press.

Parfit, D. (1984), *Reasons and Persons.* Oxford: Oxford University Press.

Pritchard, D. (2005), *Epistemic Luck.* Oxford: Oxford University Press.

Rescher, N. (1995), *Luck: The Brilliant Randomness of Everyday Life.* New York: Farrar, Strauss and Giroux.

9

Experimental Philosophy on Free Will: An Error Theory for Incompatibilist Intuitions

Eddy Nahmias and Dylan Murray

9.1 Introduction

It's called "the problem of free will and determinism," but much depends on what determinism is taken to mean and entail. *Incompatibilists* claim that it is impossible for people to have free will and moral responsibility if determinism is true, and they often suggest that this is the natural position to take, supported by our pre-theoretical intuitions. Robert Kane, for instance, states that "ordinary persons start out as natural incompatibilists" (1999, 217), and Galen Strawson claims that "it is in our nature to take determinism to pose a serious problem for our notions of responsibility and freedom" (1986, 89). Sometimes people take "determinism" to *mean* "the opposite of free will," in which case incompatibilism is indeed intuitive, but at the cost of being an empty tautology. In philosophical debates, *determinism* has a technical meaning: a complete description of the state of the universe at one time and of the laws of nature logically entails a complete description of the state of the universe at any later time.[1] However, it is not obvious why determinism, defined in this way, is supposed to be incompatible with free will; rather, a further explanation of just why determinism precludes some ability associated with free will seems required. The explanations generally offered by incompatibilists are that determinism precludes either (i) the ability to choose among *alternative possibilities* for action, while holding fixed the actual past and the laws of nature (AP), or (ii) the ability to be the *ultimate source* of one's actions, such that one is ultimately responsible for some aspect of the conditions that led up to one's actions (US). To say that incompatibilism is intuitive, then, is presumably to claim that it is natural to find one or both of these conditions necessary for free will and to understand the condition in such a way that determinism precludes it.

Compatibilists, who believe that determinism does *not* preclude free will and moral responsibility, often develop arguments to show why AP and US, as defined by incompatibilists, are *not* in fact required for free will and responsibility, sometimes offering analyses of abilities meant to capture the attractive features of AP and US but in ways consistent with determinism. They often argue that certain premises and principles used in incompatibilist arguments are mistaken. Compatibilists have also attempted to *explain away* the intuitions incompatibilists appeal to, sometimes suggesting that these intuitions are based on mistaken interpretations of the implications of determinism. For example, determinism may *appear* to threaten free will because it is conflated with types of coercion or manipulation, which, the compatibilist argues, are importantly different from determinism.

These conflicting views about what determinism entails and which abilities are required for free will typically lead to stalemates, often bottoming out in disagreements about which view best captures our ordinary intuitions and conceptual usage. For instance, incompatibilists claim that it is widely accepted that free will requires the ability to do otherwise. Compatibilists respond that it is not obvious that this ability must be "unconditional" (as suggested by AP); rather, free action requires a "conditional" ability to do otherwise *if* relevant earlier conditions had been different, an ability that is consistent with determinism. Given such stalemates, it would help to gain a better understanding of people's pre-philosophical intuitions about free will, moral responsibility, and determinism, as well as the sources of these intuitions. This could help to elucidate which position in fact accords best with ordinary thinking about these issues, or whether some of the intuitions supporting one position are produced in systematically unreliable ways. Though such information certainly won't *resolve* the debate, it can suggest that one side needs to answer certain questions, motivate its views in new ways, or take on the argumentative burden of proof.

One might attempt to uncover such information about folk intuitions and their underlying psychological processes through armchair analysis, but empirical methods will often be required to supplement such analysis, especially when philosophers on opposing sides offer conflicting claims about what is intuitive. The recent movement of "experimental philosophy" does just this, drawing on the empirical methods of psychology to systematically examine people's intuitions about philosophical issues, and then carefully considering whether and how these results impact the philosophical debates. Below, we offer a brief history of experimental philosophy on free will before presenting results from our recent study. But first we jump ahead to the conclusion we take our results to support.

Our goal is to develop an "error theory" for incompatibilist intuitions—to show that, when ordinary people take determinism to preclude free will and moral responsibility, they usually do so because they *misinterpret* what determinism involves. In other words, we aim to explain why people *appear* to have incompatibilist intuitions, when in fact they do not. Whereas incompatibilists have suggested that "ordinary persons have to be talked out of [their] natural incompatibilism by the clever arguments of philosophers" (Kane, 1999, 217) and that "beginning students typically recoil at the compatibilist response to the problem of moral responsibility" (Pereboom, 2001, xvi), we believe that ordinary persons typically need help seeing the allure of incompatibilism. As suggested above, the proper conception of determinism needs to be given to them—without being presented in a misleading way—and then some explanation needs to be given for why determinism, so defined, is incompatible with free will and moral responsibility, perhaps by motivating the idea that they require AP and US. We suggest that in this process many ordinary persons (for example, beginning students) come to interpret determinism as entailing threats to free will that it does *not* in fact entail. We predict that laypersons often mistakenly take determinism to mean that everything that happens is inevitable—it will happen *no matter what*—or that agents' decisions, desires, or beliefs make no difference to what they end up doing, and that such mistakes then generate people's intuitions about agents' lacking free will and moral responsibility. Indeed, people may take determinism to preclude the sorts of abilities *compatibilists* associate with free will, such as the abilities to consciously deliberate about what to do and to control one's behavior in light of one's reasons. But if people's purportedly *incompatibilist* intuitions result primarily from mistakenly interpreting determinism to preclude what *compatibilists* require for free will, then these intuitions do not support incompatibilism.

Suppose laypersons are presented with scenarios that describe a deterministic universe, and suppose that some respond that agents in that universe do *not* have free will (FW) and are *not* morally responsible (MR) for their actions—they express "incompatibilist intuitions"—while others respond that agents in these deterministic universes can have FW and MR—they express "compatibilist intuitions." One explanation for such mixed results (see below for examples) is that different people simply have different intuitions about the relationship between determinism and FW or MR, perhaps because they have different conceptions of free will or attribute moral responsibility in varying ways (see Knobe & Doris, 2010). We think that this interpretation may explain *some* of the variations in people's intuitions and may even help to explain the intractability of the philosophical debates. It may also be that some people who express compatibilist intuitions do not understand the deterministic nature of the scenario or are not drawing the intuitive connections between it and factors like AP and US. Perhaps people fail to draw these purported implications of determinism due to an emotional bias (Nichols & Knobe, 2007; see below). This would suggest an error theory for compatibilist intuitions—that is, it would suggest that these people have only *apparent*, but not *genuine* compatibilist intuitions.

However, the conflicting results might also be explained with an error theory for the *incompatibilist* intuitions people seem to have. Our hypothesis is that many people who appear to have incompatibilist intuitions are interpreting determinism to entail what we will call "bypassing," and that they take *bypassing* to preclude FW and MR. While bypassing does preclude

FW and MR, determinism *does not* entail bypassing. So, if the reason people seem to express incompatibilist intuitions is that they mistakenly take determinism to entail bypassing, then those intuitions are not *genuine* incompatibilist intuitions, and do not in fact support the conclusion that determinism, properly understood, is incompatible with free will.

What is "bypassing"? The basic idea is that one's actions are caused by forces that bypass one's conscious self, or what one identifies as one's "self." More specifically, it is the thesis that one's actions are produced in a way that bypasses the abilities compatibilists typically identify with free will, such as rational deliberation, conscious consideration of beliefs and desires, formation of higher-order volitions, planning, self-control, and the like.[2] As such, bypassing might take the form of *epiphenomenalism* about the relevant mental states (that is, that deliberations, beliefs, and desires are causally irrelevant to action), or it might take the form of *fatalism*—that certain things will happen no matter what one decides or tries to do, or that one's actions *have to* happen *even if* the past had been different. Bypassing suggests that conscious agents have no control over their actions because they play no role in the causal chains that leads to their actions, and for our study discussed below, we "operationalized" bypassing in specific ways that we take to capture this intuitive idea.

The crucial point is that determinism, as defined by philosophers debating free will, simply does *not* entail bypassing (certainly not in the way we operationalize it below). The history of compatibilism might be caricatured as an attempt to drive home this point. Compatibilists have emphasized that determinism does not mean or entail that all events are inevitable, in the sense that they will happen no matter what we decide or try to do. They point out that determinism does not render our beliefs, desires, deliberations, or decisions causally impotent. Quite the contrary. So long as our mental states are part of the deterministic sequence of events, they play a crucial role in determining what will happen. Of course, incompatibilists generally agree with all this, but claim their arguments are not based on such mistakes. Nonetheless, the pre-philosophical *intuitive* appeal of incompatibilism may rest largely on such mistakes, and to the extent that it does, incompatibilists either need to abandon the appeal to wide-scale intuitive support as a motivation or a basis for their position, or they need to demonstrate that incompatibilism remains intuitive *even when* people properly recognize that determinism does not entail bypassing. Put another way, since incompatibilists generally allow that determinism is compatible with the abilities compatibilists associate with free will, "*genuine* incompatibilist intuitions" are those that do not involve misinterpreting determinism to involve bypassing of these compatibilist abilities (see Figure 9.1). If most people who take determinism to preclude FW and MR do so only on the basis of such a mistake, then, this should at least shift the burden of proof onto incompatibilists to formulate arguments for their position in a way that does not rely on the existence of *genuine* incompatibilist

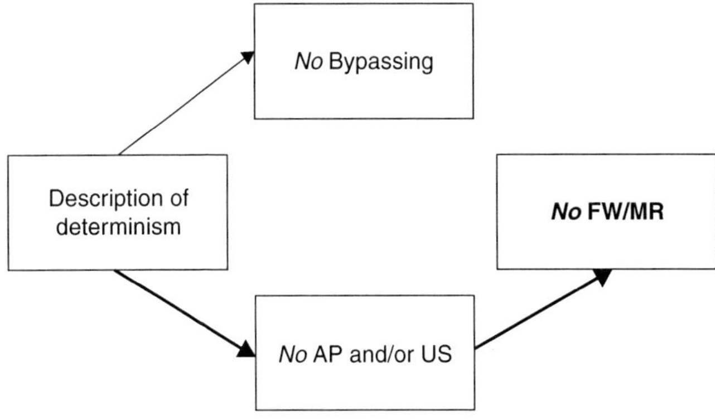

Figure 9.1 *Genuine* incompatibilist intuitions

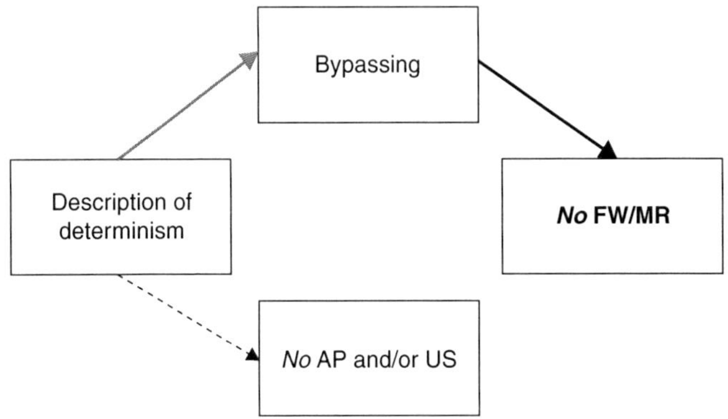

Figure 9.2 *Apparent* incompatibilist intuitions

intuitions. Our goal here is to offer evidence that most laypersons who respond that agents do *not* have FW and MR in deterministic universes are in fact expressing only "*apparent* incompatibilist intuitions" because they misunderstand determinism to involve bypassing (see Figure 9.2).

9.2 Experimental philosophy on free will

As we have seen, philosophers often appeal to ordinary intuitions and common sense about free will and moral responsibility. We think such appeals have a legitimate place in the philosophical debate. This debate, unlike others about more technical concepts, is about concepts that are intimately connected to ordinary people's beliefs about and practices concerning morality, agency, praise, blame, punishment, reward, and so on. The claim is not that ordinary intuitions or conceptual usage should *exhaust* the philosophical analysis of free will, much less that they will inform us about any extra-semantic facts about the nature of human decision-making. Rather, the claim is that folk intuitions provide important information about *which* extra-semantic facts we should be looking for when we want to know whether humans have free will and are morally responsible for their actions. Philosophical theories should systematize such intuitions as much as possible, revise them when they are inconsistent or when competing theoretical advantages (such as consistency with scientific facts) call for it, or explain the intuitions away—that is, offer an error theory for why they *appear* to support a particular position when in fact they do not. If, instead, philosophers end up mired in disputes about the proper analysis of a technical concept of "free will" that no longer connects with ordinary concepts and practices, then these debates risk being irrelevant.

We take it to be particularly important for incompatibilists to establish the intuitive plausibility of their position, primarily because incompatibilist theories of free will are generally more metaphysically demanding than compatibilist alternatives. Incompatibilist theories require indeterministic events in the agent at the right time and place, and often, additionally, agent causal powers. These conditions are typically required *in addition to*, rather than *instead of*, compatibilist conditions. Other things being equal, incompatibilists should motivate the need for these extra metaphysical conditions. Many incompatibilists have motivated their more metaphysically demanding theories, at least in part, by claiming that other things are *not* equal, because our ordinary intuitions, as well as our phenomenology of decision-making, support incompatibilist views. It is certainly unclear why, *without* wide-scale intuitive support for incompatibilism, the burden of proof would be on compatibilists.[3]

Motivated by these considerations and the lack of any empirical data on what intuitions laypersons actually have, Eddy Nahmias, Stephen Morris, Thomas Nadelhoffer, and Jason Turner (2005, 2006) developed the initial experimental philosophy studies on folk intuitions about FW, MR, and determinism. Using three different descriptions of determinism, they found that a significant majority of participants (typically 65–85%) judged that agents in a deterministic scenario act of their own free will and are morally responsible for their actions. One of the descriptions of determinism was the following "re-creating universe" scenario:

> Imagine there is a universe (Universe C) that is re-created over and over again, starting from the exact same initial conditions and with all the same laws of nature. In this universe the same initial conditions and the same laws of nature cause the exact same events for the entire history of the universe, so that every single time the universe is re-created, everything

> must happen the exact same way. For instance, in this universe a person named Jill decides to steal a necklace at a particular time and then steals it, and *every* time the universe is re-created, Jill decides to steal the necklace at that time and then steals it.[4]

After reading the scenario, participants were asked to judge whether Jill decided to steal the necklace of her own free will and whether "it would be fair to hold her morally responsible (that is, blame her) for her decision to steal the necklace." 66% of subjects judged that Jill acted of her own free will, and 77% judged her to be morally responsible. Similar results were found using two other scenarios describing determinism in different ways, which also included variations with agents' performing positive actions (for example, saving a child) or neutral actions (for example, going jogging).[5] These results offer evidence that a significant majority of laypersons are *not* in fact "natural incompatibilists" and thus call for an explanation as to why so many philosophers have assumed that most ordinary people begin with the intuition that determinism is incompatible with free will and moral responsibility.

In response to these results from Nahmias, Morris, Nadelhoffer, and Turner (NMNT), one might argue that people only *appear* to have compatibilist intuitions, when in fact they do not. Such judgments might be unreliable, or not reflect people's *considered* beliefs or folk theories about FW and MR. In part to provide such an error theory for people's compatibilist judgments, Shaun Nichols and Joshua Knobe (2007) developed experiments aimed at exploring the psychological mechanisms that generate intuitions about moral responsibility. In their studies, participants were randomly assigned to one of two groups, one of which was presented with a scenario in the "abstract" condition, and the other in the "concrete" condition. The scenario in the *abstract* condition read:

> Imagine a universe (Universe A) in which everything that happens is completely caused by whatever happened before it. This is true from the very beginning of the universe, so what happened in the beginning of the universe caused what happened next, and so on right up until the present. For example one day John decided to have French Fries at lunch. Like everything else, this decision was completely caused by what happened before it. So, if everything in this universe was exactly the same up until John made his decision, then it *had to happen* that John would decide to have French Fries.
>
> Now imagine a universe (Universe B) in which *almost* everything that happens is completely caused by whatever happened before it. The one exception is human decision making. For example, one day Mary decided to have French Fries at lunch. Since a person's decision in this universe is not completely caused by what happened before it, even if everything

> in the universe was exactly the same up until Mary made her decision, it *did* ***not*** *have to happen* that Mary would decide to have French Fries. She could have decided to have something different.
>
> The key difference, then, is that in Universe A every decision is completely caused by what happened before the decision – given the past, each decision *has to happen* the way that it does. By contrast, in Universe B, decisions are not completely caused by the past, and each human decision *does* ***not*** *have to happen* the way that it does.

In the *concrete* condition, this scenario was followed by another paragraph:

> In Universe A, a man named Bill has become attracted to his secretary, and he decided that the only way to be with her is to kill his wife and 3 children. He knows that it is impossible to escape from his house in the event of a fire. Before he leaves on a business trip, he sets up a device in his basement that burns down the house and kills his family.

In the abstract condition, participants were asked:

> In Universe A, is it possible for a person to be fully morally responsible for their actions?
> Yes No

and in the concrete condition:

> Is Bill fully morally responsible for killing his wife and children?
> Yes No

In the concrete condition, 72% of subjects gave the compatibilist response that Bill *is* fully morally responsible. In the abstract condition, however, 84% gave the purportedly *incompatibilist* response that it is *not* possible for a person to be fully morally responsible in Universe A.

Nichols and Knobe (N&K) claim that this disparity between participants' responses to the abstract and concrete cases is due to the psychological mechanisms driving people's intuitions. They suggest that the immoral action in the concrete case engages people's emotions in a way that leads them to offer compatibilist judgments, but that these judgments are the result of a performance error, or breakdown, in people's normal capacity to make correct attributions of moral responsibility. According to this *affective performance error model*, the emotions induced by high-affect scenarios, such as an agent's murdering his spouse and children, skew people's attributions of MR. Compatibilist responses are "performance errors brought about by affective reactions. In the abstract condition, people's underlying theory is revealed for what it is—incompatibilist" (2007, 672). The performance error model thus presents an error theory for compatibilist intuitions. Because they are the result of affect-produced error, these intuitions should not be assigned any real significance in a theory of moral responsibility. As N&K say, "if we could eliminate the performance errors, the compatibilist intuitions should disappear" (2007, 678). N&K are rightly tentative about the affective performance error model and discuss the possibility that an *affective competence model*, a *concrete competence model*, or some hybrid model might instead be correct. N&K note that "we don't yet have the data we need to decide between these competing models," but they claim that "the philosophical implications of the performance error model have a special significance because the experimental evidence gathered thus far [including NMNT's] seems to suggest that the basic idea behind this model is actually true" (2007, 678).[6]

We believe that there are several problems with Nichols and Knobe's (2007) study, as well as with their favored performance error model. For instance, N&K do not ask any questions about free will because, they say, "the expression 'free will' has become a term of philosophical art, and it's unclear how to interpret lay responses concerning such technical terms" (682, note 3). We do not think "free will" should be treated as a technical term nor that ordinary intuitions about free will are irrelevant to philosophical debates, so we continue to ask questions about it in our studies here. N&K instead use just one experimental question, asking whether it is possible for a person to be "fully morally responsible" for their actions. This phrase (itself somewhat technical sounding) is ambiguous and likely to be understood differently by different people. First, the "fully" may be contrasted either with being *partially* responsible or with being responsible in some *lesser* sense not involving moral desert. Indeed, attributions of MR are notoriously ambiguous between holding people responsible for forward-looking (for example, deterrent) reasons and holding them responsible for backward-looking (retributive) reasons. Thus, we think it is difficult to move directly from people's responses to questions about being "fully morally responsible" to their intuitions about the compatibility of determinism and the sort of MR (or FW) involved in philosophical debates. Though we're unsure how best to address these issues, we think questions about whether agents *deserve* blame (or praise) are more likely to elicit the relevant notion of moral responsibility, and we include questions using this language in our studies.[7]

We are more concerned with N&K's description of determinism. For instance, they write that in Universe A, "given the past, each decision *has to happen* the way that it does." This wording leaves the scope of the modal operator ambiguous. It may be interpreted as: "Given past events, it is necessary (or inevitable) that later events (for example, decisions) happen the way they do" rather than: "It is necessary that, given past events, later events (for example, decisions) occur."[8] The latter, correct reading allows that later events (effects) *could* be otherwise as long as earlier events (causes) were otherwise. The former reading, however, mistakenly conflates determinism with fatalism (that all actual events are necessary or inevitable), and it negates a compatibilist, conditional understanding of the ability to do otherwise (see above), because one's actions *have to* happen *even if* the past (for example, one's reasons) had been different (see Nahmias 2006 and Turner and Nahmias 2006). Furthermore, the concluding sentence of N&K's abstract scenario reads, "By contrast, in Universe B, decisions are not completely caused by the past, and each human decision *does* ***not*** *have to happen* the way that it does." Some participants may read this to mean that (by contrast), in Universe A, each human decision *does* ***have*** *to happen* the way it does (full stop). We suspect that this reading, perhaps along with the other issues we've raised, may lead people to interpret N&K's description of determinism to suggest one or more of the following: that agents' actions could not happen otherwise *even if* the past had been different; that agents' decisions, beliefs, and desires are not playing a role in influencing their actions; or that agents have no control over what they do. That is, we predict that N&K's scenario will lead many people to interpret determinism to involve bypassing.

N&K claim that "one cannot plausibly dismiss the high rate of incompatibilist responses in the abstract condition as a product of some subtle bias in our description of determinism. After all, the concrete condition used precisely the same description, and yet subjects in that condition were significantly more likely to give compatibilist responses" (670–71). This response, however, neglects the possibility that the description of determinism has potentially misleading features that imply bypassing in the abstract case but *not* in the concrete case. We do not dispute the idea that the high negative affect likely induced in N&K's concrete case—with Bill's selfish, premeditated, and wanton murder of his wife and three children—may bias many participants to judge Bill to be morally responsible, but it may also lead participants to neglect features of the scenario that might otherwise mitigate their responsibility attributions. Indeed, it may be that the high negative affect causes participants to neglect the *bypassing* features of the scenario. In other words, N&K's description of determinism may lead people to make a mistake, which is then "cancelled out" in the concrete case—but not in the abstract case—by high negative affect. Hence, we predict that most people will *not* read N&K's *concrete* scenario to involve bypassing, which may help to explain why they are generally willing to attribute MR to Bill.

While we agree with N&K that very high negative affect likely biases people to neglect potential responsibility-mitigating factors, we do not agree with the more general assumption that people are more competent in making judgments about FW, MR, and determinism when they consider *abstract* cases than when they consider *concrete* cases including specific agents performing specific actions. On the contrary, assuming all else is equal (such as degree of affect), we believe that concrete conditions likely *facilitate* participants' comprehension and capacity to make accurate attributions of responsibility (in N&K's terms, we advocate a type of "concrete competence model").

Specifically, we believe that judgments about responsibility—including whether agents deserve credit or blame for their actions—will be more reliable if they engage our capacities to think about the beliefs, desires, and intentions of agents (for example, our "theory of mind" capacities), which are presumably more likely to be engaged when we consider specific agents in specific circumstances. More generally, it may be that people's intuitions are more reliable when they have more details about a scenario, which is likely part of the reason why philosophers construct thought experiments with specific details to probe (or prime) our intuitions.[9] Hence, while we agree with N&K that concrete cases that *also* involve high affect may lead to errors, we do not believe this is a product of concreteness *per se*. Rather, we believe that, in general, concrete cases are more likely to reveal reliable intuitions about MR and FW than abstract cases. For instance, we believe that N&K's description of determinism is more likely to lead to interpretations of bypassing in the abstract case.[10]

Finally, some other explanation is required for why so many more participants express incompatibilist intuitions in N&K's abstract scenario than in NMNT's cases, since the performance error model simply cannot account for this difference. The majority of participants in NMNT's (2006) studies gave compatibilist responses, even for those scenarios that *did not involve high negative affect*—that is, those that involved positive actions, such as saving a child from a burning building or returning money one finds in a lost wallet, as well as those that involved neutral actions, such as going jogging. Moreover, no significant differences in responses were found between these cases and those that did involve negative actions—robbing a bank, stealing a necklace, and keeping the money one finds in a lost wallet (see note 5 above).[11] Thus, the performance error model does not provide an explanation for these previous results. Some other explanation for the difference in responses to N&K's and NMNT's cases is required. One possibility is that all of NMNT's scenarios describe *concrete* agents and actions and ask about those agents' FW and MR, whereas N&K's abstract scenario does not include or ask about specific agents or actions, but again, we believe there is no good reason to think concreteness alone leads to performance errors. Another (non-exclusive) possibility is that N&K's description of determinism primes bypassing judgments significantly more than NMNT's descriptions. Our new study explores these possibilities.

An initial attempt to explore the issue of bypassing was developed in Nahmias, Justin Coates, and Trevor Kvaran (2007). They found that, across several different scenarios, most people responded that MR and FW were possible in a deterministic universe *if* the scenario described the decisions of agents in that universe as being "completely caused by the specific thoughts, desires, and plans occurring in our minds." In contrast, most people responded that FW and MR were *not* possible in a deterministic universe *if* the scenario described agents' decisions as "completely caused by the specific chemical reactions and neural processes occurring in our brains."[12] The latter, reductionistic description seems to prime people to think that agents' mental states are not playing the proper role in their actions—that their conscious self is bypassed. Thus, even though determinism in the technical sense is equally present in both scenarios, people tend to think determinism is compatible with FW and MR unless they take determinism to involve bypassing.

We designed our current study in order to further explore the possible effects of bypassing on people's judgments of FW and MR, and to test our error theory for incompatibilist intuitions. We presented participants with different descriptions of determinism (N&K's scenario versus NMNT's "re-creating universe" scenario, with abstract and concrete versions of each), and then asked participants not only about FW and MR but also about bypassing. We predicted that:

1. In general, participants' judgments about bypassing would correlate significantly with their judgments about MR and FW. That is, when making judgments about agents in a deterministic universe, (a) most participants who respond that the agents do *not* have MR and FW would also respond that the agents' decisions, beliefs, and desires do *not* affect what happens—that is, such participants would interpret the deterministic nature of the scenario to involve bypassing—whereas (b) most participants rejecting the bypassing claims would respond that the agents *do* have MR and FW. That is, bypassing judgments would explain away most *apparent* incompatibilist intuitions, whereas most people who do *not* misunderstand determinism to involve bypassing would express *prima facie* compatibilist intuitions.[13]
2. Judgments of FW and MR would be *lower*, while judgments of bypassing would be *higher*, in N&K's abstract scenario compared to NMNT's abstract scenario. That is, N&K's description of determinism would, in the abstract case, lead more people to misunderstand determinism.
3. Judgments of FW and MR would be *lower*, while judgments of bypassing would be *higher*, in the abstract scenarios compared to the concrete scenarios, with this difference especially pronounced in N&K's high-affect scenario.

9.3 Methods

Participants included in the analysis were 249 undergraduate students at Georgia State University (Atlanta, GA) who were randomly assigned to complete one of four versions of the experimental task.[14] We used software from QuestionPro to develop and administer these surveys online. Using a 2x2 between-subjects design, four scenarios were generated by systematically varying (1) whether the deterministic scenario was *N&K's* or *NMNT's*, and (2) whether the scenario was *abstract* or *concrete*.

Participants began by reading a general description of the task, providing informed consent, and then reading one of the four scenarios. After reading the scenario, participants answered a series of experimental questions designed to probe their intuitions about FW and MR, as well as whether they interpreted the scenario to involve bypassing. N&K's abstract and concrete scenarios read exactly as they are presented above, as did NMNT's concrete scenario. NMNT's abstract scenario replaces the last sentence of the concrete version with:

> For instance, in this universe whenever a person decides to do something, *every* time the universe is re-created, that person decides to do the same thing at that time and then does it.

In order to replicate N&K's study, participants given those surveys were first asked:

> Which of these universes do you think is most like ours?
>
> Universe A
>
> Universe B

Participants who were given the NMNT surveys were first asked:

> Is it possible that our universe could be like Universe C, in that the same initial conditions and the same laws of nature cause the exact same events for the entire history of the universe?
> Yes No

Participants were next asked to indicate their level of agreement with each of a series of statements using a 6-point rating scale (strongly disagree, disagree, somewhat disagree, somewhat agree, agree, strongly agree). The first statement was always the *moral responsibility* (MR) question (replicating N&K's format). The remaining statements in each survey were randomized to decrease the likelihood of order effects. The most important experimental questions we asked read as follows (variations between scenarios are in brackets: *N&K abstract* scenario asks about Universe A; *NMNT abstract* asks about Universe C; *N&K concrete* asks about Bill; *NMNT concrete* asks about Jill):

9.3.1 The MR/FW questions

> **MR**: In Universe [A/C], it is possible for a person to be fully morally responsible for their actions.
> [Bill/Jill] is fully morally responsible for [killing his wife and children/stealing the necklace].
> **FW**: In Universe [A/C], it is possible for a person to have free will.
> It is possible for [Bill/Jill] to have free will.

Blame: In Universe [A/C], a person deserves to be blamed for the bad things they do.
[Bill/Jill] deserves to be blamed for [killing his wife and children/stealing the necklace.]

9.3.2 The Bypassing questions

(These questions represent our way of operationalizing "bypassing"; we take it that philosophers on all sides of the free will debate should agree that if one *properly* understands determinism, one should *not* agree with these statements.)

Decisions: In Universe [A/C], a person's decisions have no effect on what they end up being caused to do.
[Bill's/Jill's] decision to [kill his wife and children/steal the necklace] has no effect on what [he/she] ends up being caused to do.
Wants: In Universe [A/C], what a person wants has no effect on what they end up being caused to do.
What [Bill/Jill] wants has no effect on what [he/she] ends up being caused to do.
Believes: In Universe [A/C], what a person believes has no effect on what they end up being caused to do.
What [Bill/Jill] believes has no effect on what [he/she] ends up being caused to do.
No Control: In Universe [A/C], a person has no control over what they do.
[Bill/Jill] has no control over what [he/she] does.
Past Different: In Universe A, everything that happens *has to* happen, even if what happened in the past had been different.
Bill *has* to kill his wife and children, even if what happened in the past had been different.[15]

After providing responses to these questions, participants then answered two comprehension questions to ensure that they understood the scenario and several demographic questions (for example, gender, age, and religious affiliation).

9.4 Main results

In order to examine the relationship between participants' judgments about bypassing and their judgments about MR and FW, we created two composite scores which we used for the analyses below: an *MR/FW composite score*, which was obtained by computing the average of each participant's responses to the MR, FW, and Blame questions, and a *Bypassing composite score*, obtained by computing the average of each participant's responses to the Decisions, Wants, Believes, and No Control questions.[16] Initial inspection of the data suggested that, as we predicted, (i) *MR/FW* scores were lower and *Bypassing* scores higher in response to the abstract scenarios compared to the concrete scenarios, and (ii) *MR/FW* scores were lower, while *Bypassing* scores were higher, in response to *N&K's abstract* scenario compared to *NMNT's abstract* scenario (see Figure 9.3). Moreover, across conditions, (iii) the majority of participants who gave *apparent* incompatibilist responses (*MR/FW* scores less than the 3.5 midpoint) also gave *high* bypassing responses (*Bypassing* scores > 3.5), whereas (iv) most participants who gave *prima facie* compatibilist responses (*MR/FW* scores > 3.5) also gave *low* (< 3.5) bypassing responses (see Figure 9.4).[17] Given these findings, we employed a series of analyses in order to determine whether these results were statistically significant.[18]

To determine whether *MR/FW* scores were significantly lower in N&K's surveys than in NMNT's surveys and lower in the abstract conditions than in the concrete conditions, we ran a 2 (survey: N&K, NMNT) x 2 (condition: abstract, concrete) Analysis of Variance (ANOVA) on the mean *MR/FW* composite scores (see Figure 9.5). The ANOVA showed a significant main effect for survey: $F(1, 245) = 5.396$, $p = .021$, a significant main effect for condition: $F(1, 245) = 61.058$, $p < .001$, and a marginally significant interaction

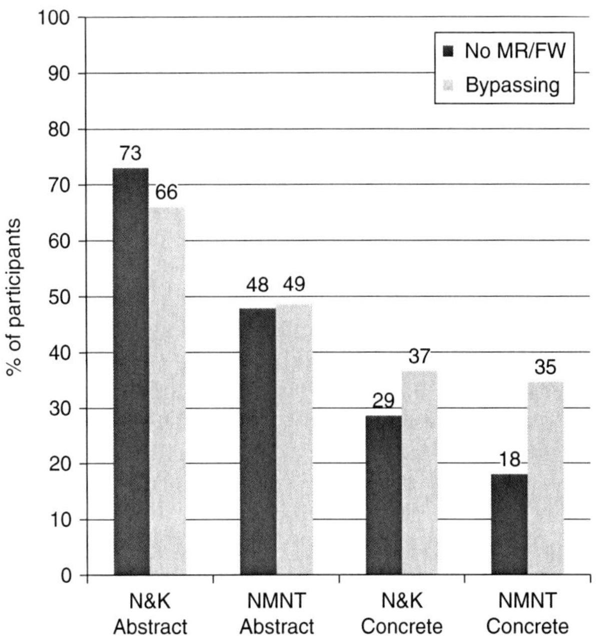

Figure 9.3 Judgments about MR, FW, and bypassing

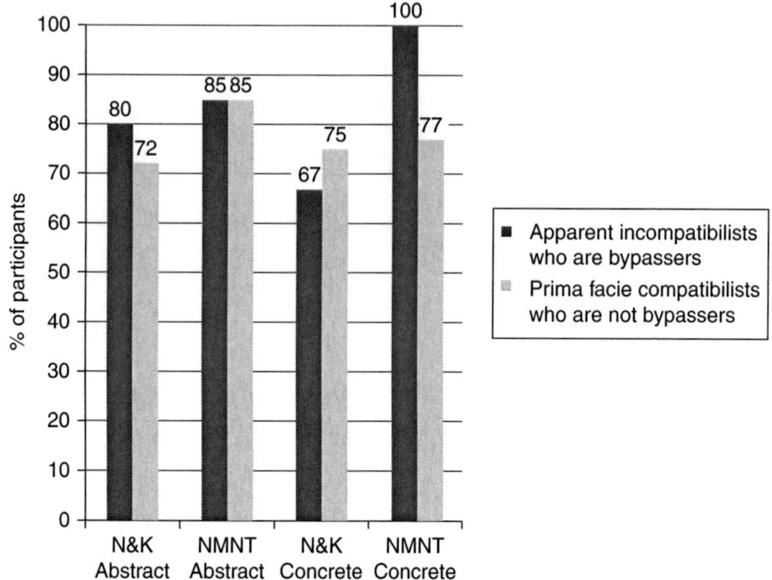

Figure 9.4 Apparent incompatibilists who are bypassers and prima facie compatibilists who are not

effect: $F(1, 245) = 3.297$, $p < .071$. We ran two additional pre-planned *t*-tests specifically comparing the mean *MR/FW* composite responses to *N&K abstract* vs. *NMNT abstract,* and to *N&K concrete* vs. *NMNT concrete.* We found that the mean *MR/FW* score was significantly lower in *N&K abstract* than in *NMNT abstract*: $t(1, 131) = -2.973$, $p = .004$, but was *not* significantly different between the two concrete conditions: $t(1, 114) = 2.346$, $p = .128$. Thus, the abstract scenarios received significantly lower *MR/FW* ratings than the concrete scenarios, independent of whether the survey was N&K's or NMNT's, and N&K's surveys received lower *MR/FW* scores than NMNT's in both the concrete and abstract conditions, but only significantly lower scores in the concrete condition. We believe that *MR/FW* scores are not significantly lower in *NMNT concrete* because of the very high affect involved in *N&K concrete,* which we suspect drives down participants' *Bypassing* scores, and thereby drives up their *MR/FW* scores compared to what those scores would be in the absence of high affect (see Section 9.2, p. 198 and notes 19 and 20).

To determine whether *Bypassing* scores were significantly higher in N&K's surveys than in NMNT's surveys and higher in the abstract conditions than in the concrete conditions, we ran a 2 (survey: N&K, NMNT) x 2 (condition: abstract, concrete) ANOVA on the mean *Bypassing* composite scores (see Figure 9.5). The ANOVA showed a significant main effect for condition: $F(1, 245) = 20.665$, $p < .001$, but only a near-significant effect for

			MR/FW		Bypassing	
Survey	Condition	N	Mean	Std. Dev.	Mean	Std. Dev.
N&K	Abstract	77	2.818	1.204	3.958	1.205
	Concrete	56	4.363	1.298	3.018	1.216
NMNT	Abstract	56	3.482	1.360	3.442	1.346
	Concrete	60	4.444	1.174	2.946	1.183

Figure 9.5 MR/FW and bypassing descriptive statistics

survey: $F(1, 245) = 3.463$, $p = .064$ (see note 20). There was no significant interaction effect. Thus, the abstract scenarios received significantly higher *Bypassing* scores than the concrete scenarios, independent of whether the survey was N&K's or NMNT's, and N&K's surveys received marginally higher *Bypassing* scores than NMNT's, independent of whether the condition was abstract or concrete. We ran an additional pre-planned *t*-test specifically comparing the mean *Bypassing* responses to *N&K abstract* vs. *NMNT abstract.* As hypothesized, we found that the mean *Bypassing* score was significantly higher in *N&K abstract* than in *NMNT abstract*: $t(1, 131) = 2.319$, $p = .022$.[19]

In order to statistically assess the relationship between these two variables of interest, we computed Pearson correlation coefficients between the *MR/FW* and *Bypassing* composite scores for each scenario. Consistent with our hypothesis, but even more dramatically than we expected, we found a strong inverse correlation between *Bypassing* and *MR/FW* scores—that is, the higher a participant's *Bypassing* score, the lower his or her *MR/FW* score, and vice versa—in each of the four scenarios (*N&K abstract*: $r(75) = -0.695$, $p < .001$; *N&K concrete*: $r(54) = -0.569$, $p < .001$; *NMNT abstract*: $r(54) = -0.803$, $p < .001$; *NMNT concrete*: $r(58) = -0.708$, $p < .001$). Collapsing across all four surveys, the correlation coefficient between *Bypassing* and *MR/FW* scores was strikingly high: $r(247) = -0.734$, $p < .001$.

Consistent with our hypothesis, then, average scores in response to the Bypassing questions were significantly *higher* in *N&K's abstract* scenario than in *NMNT's abstract* scenario, average scores in response to the MR/FW questions were significantly *lower* in *N&K abstract* than in *NMNT abstract*, and responses to the Bypassing and MR/FW questions were strongly inversely correlated across scenarios. Given these results, we further suspected that responses to the MR/FW questions were lower for *N&K abstract* compared to *NMNT abstract* precisely *because* participants interpreted N&K's abstract scenario to involve a higher degree of bypassing. We hypothesized that the degree to which one interpreted a scenario to involve bypassing would *mediate* the relationship between survey and *MR/FW* responses. That is, we hypothesized that the difference in *MR/FW* responses between the two *abstract* conditions of the surveys was *caused* largely by people's bypassing judgments. In order to test this causal hypothesis more directly, we used a mediation analysis.[20]

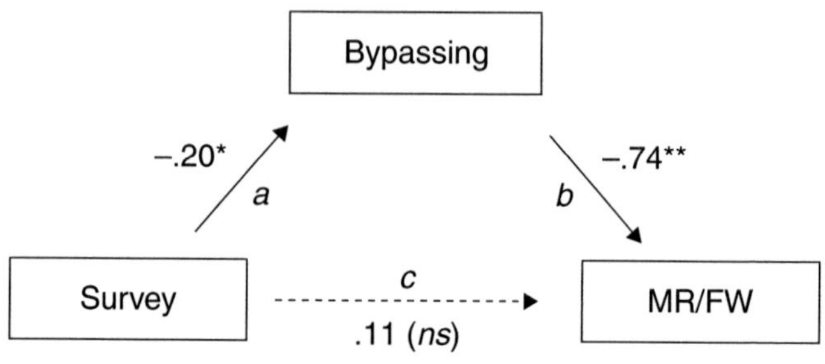

Figure 9.6 Mediation analysis

We conducted three regression analyses to test for mediation (see Figure 9.6), as outlined by Baron and Kenny (1986) and more recently by MacKinnon et al. (2002).[21] The first regression equation used survey type (*N&K abstract, NMNT abstract*) to predict *MR/FW* score (path c), and yielded a significant effect: $t(132) = 2.973$, $p = .004$, corroborating the above results showing that *N&K abstract* prompts participants to respond that agents do not have MR and FW more than does *NMNT abstract*. The second regression equation estimated changes in *Bypassing* score using survey type (path a) and also yielded a significant effect: $t(132) = -2.319$, $p = .022$, corroborating the above results showing that participants interpreted *N&K abstract* to involve bypassing more than they did *NMNT abstract*. The third equation estimated *MR/FW* score using both survey type and *Bypassing* score. The link between *Bypassing* and *MR/FW* scores (path b) was highly significant: $t(132) = -12.799$, $p < .001$, and the relation (path c) between survey and *MR/FW* score was reduced to *non-significance* once *Bypassing* was included in the model: $t(132) = 1.821$, *ns*; Sobel test = 2.286, $p < .022$. Thus, all the conditions of mediation were met: survey type was a significant predictor of *MR/FW* and of *Bypassing* scores, and *Bypassing* was a significant predictor of *MR/FW* scores while controlling for survey.[22]

Thus, as we hypothesized, the effect that survey type (that is, the description of determinism in the abstract scenarios) had on a participant's *MR/FW* responses was mediated by whether the participant interpreted the description to involve bypassing. That is, these results suggest that which survey participants read (*N&K* versus *NMNT abstract*) had *no significant causal effect* on their *MR/FW* responses *over and above* the effect it had in virtue of causing different interpretations of whether the scenario involved bypassing.

9.5 Discussion

We predicted that participants across surveys and conditions would be *more* likely to judge determinism to threaten free will and moral responsibility when they interpreted determinism to involve bypassing. We also predicted that participants would be *more* likely to interpret determinism to involve bypassing in *N&K's abstract* scenario than in *NMNT's abstract* scenario, and that this would help to explain why the description of determinism in N&K's scenario leads people to be *less* likely to attribute FW and MR to agents. Finally, we predicted that participants would be *less* likely to interpret determinism to involve bypassing in concrete scenarios, especially in N&K's high-affect case, and hence *more* likely to attribute FW and MR to the agents in those scenarios. Our results strongly support each of these predictions. Indeed, not only do our results show that (i) the vast majority of participants who express *apparent* incompatibilist intuitions interpret determinism to involve bypassing, while those who express *prima facie* compatibilist intuitions tend *not* to misinterpret determinism in this way, and that (ii) there is a dramatic correlation between the degree to which participants take a scenario to involve bypassing and the degree to which they attribute MR and FW to agents in that scenario, but the results also suggest that (iii) the difference in attributions of MR and FW between the abstract conditions is *caused by* people's bypassing interpretations.

We think it is safe to conclude from our results that there is an important connection between (a) whether people take a description of determinism to entail bypassing and (b) whether people take the scenario so described to preclude free will and moral responsibility. The most plausible interpretation of this connection is that when a person takes determinism to entail bypassing it generally *causes* him or her to judge that determinism precludes MR and FW, and hence to offer *apparent* incompatibilist intuitions. Conversely, when a person does *not* take determinism to entail bypassing, they are likely to offer compatibilist intuitions—they do not see any conflict between determinism and FW or MR (below we will further consider whether such intuitions should count as supporting compatibilism). This causal conclusion also draws support from Nahmias et al.'s (2007) study, which manipulated a type of bypassing directly—rather than measuring responses to it—and found that it significantly influenced participants' attributions of MR and FW. Thus, previous evidence supports the conclusion that bypassing judgments mediate attributions of MR and FW, rather than the other way around.

If these interpretations of the data are correct, then people's interpreting determinism to entail bypassing may be the best explanation for ordinary people's intuitions that *appear* to support the incompatibility of determinism and FW and MR. But these intuitions do *not* properly support incompatibilism because determinism does *not* properly entail bypassing as we have operationalized it here. Determinism, properly understood, simply does *not* entail that our decisions, beliefs, and desires have no effect on what we end up doing, nor that we have no control over what we do (see note 16), nor that our actions *have to* happen just as they do *even if* the past had been different (see below). When people do not misinterpret determinism in these ways, they usually do not take it to threaten FW and MR.

Furthermore, our results suggest that certain descriptions of determinism and certain conditions increase the degree to which people will misinterpret determinism to entail bypassing (and hence to lower their attributions of MR and FW). Specifically, Nichols and Knobe's (2007) description of determinism in the abstract condition has this effect, and this likely occurs because of the problems we pointed out earlier with their description of determinism, including the use of language that may suggest that decisions and actions in Universe A *have to* happen *even if* the past had been different. Indeed, 48% of participants in the *N&K abstract* condition responded (to the Past Different question) that, in Universe A, everything that happens has to happen the way it does even if the past had been different, and these responses were significantly correlated with participants' *MR/FW* scores.[23] The degree to which people interpret determinism to involve bypassing is also higher in the abstract conditions than in the concrete conditions, perhaps because descriptions of concrete agents and actions prime people to think about the effectiveness of agent's beliefs, desires, and decisions (for example, consider how difficult it is to agree with the statement: "What Bill wants has no effect on what he ends up being caused to do"—his desire to be with his secretary was precisely what led to his murderous actions!).

Again, we find it plausible that very high negative affect can induce biases in MR judgments; there is, after all, evidence of such biases (see Nichols & Knobe 2007, 672). But this does not suggest that, in general, people get things wrong in concrete cases and right in abstract cases. What *is* clearly a mistake is interpreting determinism to entail bypassing, and it appears that scenarios with abstract descriptions of unspecified agents performing unspecified actions may bias people toward making this mistake. This is unsurprising, since thinking in terms of the efficacy of agents' mental states—taking the intentional stance—is more likely to occur when one is thinking about specific agents performing specific actions.

Due to these considerations, we believe that, in general, concrete scenarios involving low affect are more useful for eliciting reliable intuitions about FW, MR, and (in)compatibilism than either abstract or high-affect scenarios. Indeed, fewer participants made the mistake of interpreting determinism to involve bypassing in *NMNT concrete* than in any other scenario. Furthermore, *every* one of the few participants who did respond as an apparent incompatibilist in *NMNT concrete* also interpreted the scenario to involve bypassing, while *every* participant who did *not* interpret the scenario to involve bypassing responded as a *prima facie* compatibilist. Thus, the scenario caused fewer participants to mistake the scenario to involve bypassing and less variability in responses among participants' who did not make this mistake. Future research should explore these issues. For instance, it would be useful to compare responses to bypassing and MR/FW questions in other concrete cases, such as N&K's low-affect concrete case of the tax cheat and NMNT's cases involving positive actions (for example, agent saving a child) and neutral actions (for example, agent mowing the lawn), and perhaps also to develop, if possible, high-affect *abstract* cases.

Hence, we conclude that the extant research in experimental philosophy on free will converges on the conclusion that most laypersons do *not* have *genuine* incompatibilist intuitions. They do have the intuition that bypassing undermines FW and MR, and they can be primed to judge that determinism entails bypassing. But the latter judgment is based on a mistaken interpretation of determinism. The judgment that bypassing undermines FW and MR does not support incompatibilism. If anything, it supports compatibilist theories of freedom and responsibility, since those theories emphasize that FW and MR require that our conscious, rational deliberative processes play the right role in producing our decisions and actions. So, folk intuitions that take bypassing of these processes to preclude FW and MR support compatibilist theories. People seem to be attending to compatibilist conditions for FW and MR—whether agent's actions are properly caused by their decisions, beliefs, desires, and so on. The more likely it is that people believe that these conditions are met, the more likely they are to attribute FW and MR; the more likely it is that people believe that these conditions are *not* met—for example, because of bypassing—the less likely they are to attribute FW and MR. These results support the claim that people have merely *apparent* incompatibilist intuitions—most people do *not* seem to think that determinism—*without* bypassing—precludes FW and MR (see Figure 9.2).

There are several ways in which incompatibilists might object to these interpretations of our results, but space limits us to consider only some of them briefly—we leave it to our critics to complete the task.

First, one might argue that even *after* recognizing that determinism does *not* involve bypassing, people would (or should) recognize that determinism threatens FW and MR, and that those who do not recognize this are likely failing to understand the deterministic nature of the scenario. This response, in effect, offers a debunking explanation for compatibilist intuitions by arguing that participants who express such judgments do so because they fail to understand determinism or its implications. Perhaps they do not recognize that determinism is incompatible alternative possibilities (AP) or ultimate sourcehood (US), but if they *did,* they would think it was incompatible with MR and FW (even while also recognizing that determinism does not involve bypassing).

This is an interesting objection, and we would be intrigued to see experiments to test for it. Recall that the vast majority of our participants who did *not* take determinism to involve bypassing also attributed FW and MR to agents in those scenarios, so this objection requires that most of these participants are failing to understand the deterministic nature of the scenario or failing to understand that these agents do not meet conditions *the participants themselves* take to be necessary for free will (for example, AP or US *in the incompatibilists' sense*). Future research should try to elicit whether people understand determinism to conflict with AP and US and whether people take AP and US—understood in ways that are incompatible with determinism—to be necessary for free will or moral responsibility. Unfortunately, it is difficult to properly describe what it means for an agent to be the ultimate source of her decisions, or to have an *unconditional* ability to do otherwise, without a good bit of explanation, which might verge on "intuition coaching." While we are inclined to think that this difficulty suggests that AP and US are not particularly "natural" or intuitive to non-philosophers, others may argue that they *are* intuitive once people properly understand the relevant ideas. This suggests a second objection to our interpretation of the data.

The incompatibilist might argue that untutored intuitions are simply *irrelevant* to the philosophical debates about free will and moral responsibility or, what is different, that the sort of studies carried out by experimental philosophers cannot uncover information about the relevant intuitions. These objections might be motivated by the belief that the issues are so complex that responses from untrained individuals reveal little to nothing about the truth, or by the conviction that philosophers can discern the relevant intuitions by considering their own intuitions or those adduced from their students and other folk, or by the belief that the methods employed by experimental philosophers simply cannot do the job they aim to do (see, for example, Kauppinen, 2007).

Extensive responses to such objections applied to experimental philosophy in general have been offered elsewhere (for example, Nadelhoffer and Nahmias, 2007; Nahmias et al., 2006; Knobe and Nichols, 2008; Weinberg, 2007). We reiterate that philosophical debates about free will and moral responsibility require an understanding of the way non-philosophers think about these issues in order to develop a theory that accords with folk intuitions, where possible, and to know what it is that we're revising (and why) where revision is advocated. We agree with David Lewis when he says that in developing philosophical theories "we are trying to improve *that* theory, that is to leave it recognizably the same theory we had before" (1986, 134). If the studies we have presented here or previous studies have design flaws, then attempts should be made to improve them, rather than abandoning the very idea of understanding folk intuitions in an empirically informed way. Part of this process might include making sure that participants understand the concepts involved as clearly as possible, but one of the motivations for surveying people untrained in the philosophical debates is the worry that philosophical training may end up shaping intuitions toward a certain theory. For instance, it is not uncommon for philosophy teachers to initially present determinism using metaphors that suggest fatalism or epiphenomenalism (or, on the other side, to present indeterminism as involving entirely random uncaused events). Finally, since professional philosophers writing about free will tend to have theoretical commitments and hence *post*-theoretical "intuitions," and since these "intuitions" (as well as reports about folk, for example, students' intuitions) tend to conflict with each other, it is appropriate to attempt, as best we can, to uncover information about *pre*-theoretical intuitions, their sources, and their reliability.

9.6 Conclusion

Incompatibilists suggest that free will and moral responsibility require conditions that are incompatible with determinism—conditions that are generally more demanding than those required by compatibilists. One way to motivate the claim that these conditions are indeed necessary is to argue that incompatibilism is intuitive, and that compatibilism is thus a "quagmire of evasion," a revision of the way ordinary people think about these issues—to suggest that "ordinary persons have to be talked out of this natural incompatibilism by the clever arguments of philosophers" (Kane, 1999, 217). Our evidence here suggests that people may instead need to be talked *into* incompatibilism by the clever arguments, or subtle thought experiments, of philosophers. We suggest that incompatibilism only *appears* to be intuitive, largely because determinism is misinterpreted. Indeed, it is misinterpreted such that it precludes the very conditions compatibilists identify with free and responsible agency. It may be that incompatibilism is intuitive even *after* this mistake is corrected—that people find determinism threatening even if they understand that it does *not* involve bypassing (for example, fatalism or epiphenomenalism). We await the evidence. And obviously, *some* people—for example, some philosophers—do have genuine incompatibilist intuitions. But if most people think that free will and moral responsibility can exist even if determinism (properly construed) is true, the argumentative burden shifts to these philosophers to explain why people's intuitions need to be revised so that they accept a more demanding theory of free will. We await the argument.[24]

Notes

1. This definition is drawn from van Inwagen (1983). Two less technical, though not quite equivalent, ways of stating determinism are: (1) In a deterministic universe, necessarily, re-creating identical initial conditions and laws of nature produces identical later events; (2) Determinism is the thesis that every event is *completely caused* by earlier events, such that, necessarily, *given* the earlier events and the laws of nature, the later events occur. These two descriptions are more similar to the ones used in the studies described below.
2. For compatibilist accounts of these abilities, see, for example, Fischer and Ravizza (1998), Frankfurt (1971), Watson (1976), and Wolf (1990). Even incompatibilists

generally take these sorts of capacities to be *necessary* for free and responsible agency—see, for example, O'Connor (2005). Related use of "bypassing" language is introduced in Blumenfeld (1988) and Mele (1995).

3. For further development of the points raised in this paragraph see Nahmias *et al.* 2006, 30–33. Moreover, if *revisionism* is called for (Vargas, 2005), it's unclear why philosophers should revise the concept of free will to be more metaphysically demanding than required by our ordinary intuitions.
4. The wording of the scenario as presented here is slightly altered from that used by Nahmias et al. (2006) in order to reflect the exact wording we used in our new study presented below.
5. In one scenario (Jeremy), affirmative responses for FW were 76% (negative action), 68% (positive), and 79% (neutral), and for MR they were 83% (negative) and 88% (positive). For the other scenario (Fred & Barney), affirmative responses for FW were 76% (negative action) and 76% (positive), and for MR they were 60% (negative) and 64% (positive) (see Nahmias et al., 2006, 39). All results were significantly different from chance, as determined by χ^2 goodness-of-fit tests.
6. Interestingly, Paul Edwards anticipated this model 50 years earlier: "The very same persons, whether educated or uneducated, use it [MR] in certain contexts in the one sense and in other contexts in the other. Practically all human beings ... use what [C.A.] Campbell calls the unreflective conception when they are dominated by violent emotions like anger, indignation, or hate, and especially when the conduct they are judging has been personally injurious to them. On the other hand, a great many people, whether they are educated or not, will employ what Campbell calls the reflective conception when they are not consumed with hate or anger—when they are judging a situation calmly and reflectively and when the fact that the agent did not ultimately shape his own character has been vividly brought to their attention" (1958, 111). Edwards goes on to suggest that the "reflective conception" is the right one because the "unreflective conception" is driven by emotional bias.
7. Moreover, some participants may interpret the MR question in the concrete case as: "Should Bill be punished for his action?" and even if they do *not* think he has free will or "full moral responsibility," they may think he needs to be punished for his multiple homicides. This interpretation might not be primed in the abstract case since there is no specific human action to be (potentially) punished. Finally, notice a subtle but important difference: Universe A does not mention *humans*, whereas Universe B explicitly mentions that the "one exception is human decision making," and it concludes: "each human decision *does **not** have to happen* the way that it does." This may prime some readers to think that Universe B is more like our universe, especially in the abstract condition, which is *not* then followed by the description of Bill, whose behavior suggests that he is human. In that case, some of the differences in results between N&K's abstract and concrete cases might also be explained by a difference in intuitions people have about moral responsibility when asked about an 'alternate universe' (A) vs. a 'real-world universe' (B), differences that have been demonstrated in Nahmias, Coates, and Kvaran (2007) and Roskies and Nichols (2008).
8. That is, the description suggests that determinism entails: $[(\text{Past \& Laws}) \rightarrow \Box(\text{Future})]$, rather than the proper: $\Box[(\text{Past \& Laws}) \rightarrow \text{Future}]$.
9. Consider, by analogy, linguistic surveys intended to elicit people's intuitions concerning grammaticality. These surveys generally ask people to consider specific

sentences rather than asking them to consider abstract questions about whether various constructions of sentences could be grammatical.

10. For more discussion of differences in judgments about FW and MR based on abstract/concrete differences, as well as real world/alternate world differences, see Nahmias, Coates, and Kvaran (2007) and Roskies and Nichols (2008).
11. Even NMNT's scenarios that do involve negative actions are not very "high-affect." Stealing a necklace, robbing a bank, and keeping $1000 found in a wallet seem more similar to N&K's (2007) *low-affect* condition, in which Bill cheats on his taxes, than N&K's *high-affect* condition, in which Bill murders his family.
12. For instance, in one version (the real world cases), when the agents were described with the psychological predicates, 89% of participants said that agents should be held morally responsible and 83% said they had free will, whereas when the agents were described with the "neuro-reductionistic" predicates, only 40% said they had MR and 38% said they had FW.
13. We call them "*prima facie* compatibilist intuitions" in part because we are not committed to the idea that ordinary people have the (positive) intuition that determinism is compatible with FW and MR—their intuitions may not be so theoretically rich. But we think that lacking intuitions that (genuinely) support incompatibilism is sufficient to say that people are "natural compatibilists." We also accept that there may be alternative explanations that suggest people are expressing only *apparent* compatibilist intuitions (see section 9.5).
14. Participants were 436 undergraduate students in critical thinking or psychology courses at Georgia State University who completed the entire survey. We excluded 187 participants prior to analysis who (a) responded incorrectly to either of two comprehension questions or (b) completed the survey too quickly (less than one half of one standard deviation from the mean time for completion), leaving 249 (42% male, 58% female) participants whose data we analyzed. Studies were carried out under previous approval of the University's Institutional Review Board.
15. This question was not asked in the NMNT surveys, though the following similar statements were used: "If Universe C were re-created with *different* initial conditions or *different* laws of nature, it is possible Jill would *not* [mow her lawn/steal the necklace] at that time." Because of these differences, however, the Past Different question was not used in the composite scores described below. (See note 23).
16. These composite scores provide a more robust measure of people's intuitions concerning MR, FW, and bypassing. Lest one worry about averaging these scores, and in so doing losing information about responses to each particular question, responses to all questions factored into each composite score were, with very few exceptions, highly positively intracorrelated with one another in all four survey conditions. Across conditions, reliability analyses produced a Cronbach's alpha of .807 among the questions used to compute the *MR/FW* composite score, and a Cronbach's alpha of .823 among the questions used to compute the *Bypassing* composite score, indicating that each composite score was strongly internally consistent. Some might worry that the "no control" question is an inappropriate measure to assess bypassing because they think that determinism *does* entail that one has *no* control over what one does. We believe that this is mistaken on philosophical grounds, but removing the "no control" question from the *Bypassing* composite score also lowers the Cronbach's alpha among the questions used to compute it from .823 to .797, which suggests that responses to the "no control"

question are accessing the same folk concept(s) as responses to the other questions about bypassing.

17. Data reported in Figures 9.3 and 9.4 do not include the composite scores for 20 of the 249 participants whose *Bypassing* composite scores were equal to the 3.5 midpoint.
18. While we did replicate N&K's overall findings, our results were slightly different than theirs. In our study, 68% of participants in the abstract condition gave the apparent incompatibilist response that it is *not* possible for a person to be fully morally responsible in Universe A, compared to the 84% in N&K's previous study. Also, 87.5% of participants in our present study responded that Bill is fully morally responsible in N&K's concrete scenario, compared to 72% in N&K's study.
19. A *t*-test comparing the mean *Bypassing* responses in *N&K concrete* and *NMNT concrete* was *not* significant, which explains why the ANOVA did not show a significant main effect for survey. We suspect that this lack of effect is due to the very high affect in the *N&K concrete* scenario driving down participants' *Bypassing* scores.
20. Because *N&K's concrete* scenario involves high affect in a way that *NMNT's concrete* scenario does not, we did not include either concrete scenario in the mediation analysis, as doing so would introduce another, potentially confounding, variable (high affect) in addition to condition (concrete vs. abstract) (see also note 19).
21. Mediation analysis involves the specification of a causal model between three variables. Suppose that an *initial variable*, X (in our case, survey type), is assumed to have a causal effect on an *outcome variable*, Y (in our case, MR/FW responses). Call c the direct effect of X on Y. A mediational model of the relationship between them, then, is one in which the causal effect of X on Y is *mediated* by an *intervening variable*, M (in our case, bypassing judgments). Call a the effect of the initial variable X on M, and b the effect of M on the outcome variable Y. *Complete mediation* obtains when variable X no longer has any direct effect on Y when M is controlled for, such that path c is zero. *Partial mediation* obtains when c is reduced if M is controlled for, but not to zero, because paths a and b account for some, but not all, of the overall causal effect of X on Y. Mediational models can be assessed statistically by mediation analysis, which uses multiple regression analyses to estimate the values of paths a, b, and c.
22. The mediating variable, *Bypassing*, explains 58% of the total effect of survey type on *MR/FW* score (see Kenny, Kashy, & Bolger, 1998, 260–1).
23. Pearson correlation coefficient between Past Different ($M = 3.66$, $SD = 1.57$) and *MR/FW* composite scores in *N&K abstract*: $r(75) = -.277$, $p = .015$. By comparison, in the *NMNT abstract* scenario only 7% disagreed with (that is, "missed") the following similar question ($M = 2.68$, $SD = 1.40$): "Suppose that in Universe C, a person named Jill decides to mow her lawn at a particular time and then does it. If Universe C were re-created with *different* initial conditions or *different* laws of nature, it is possible Jill would *not* mow her lawn at that time."
24. We would like to thank the following people for helpful comments on earlier drafts: Shaun Nichols, Al Mele, Jason Turner, Stephen Morris, Neil Levy, Tamler Sommers, George Graham, Dan Weiskopf, Joshua Knobe, Reuben Stern, Jason Shepard, Thomas Nadelhoffer, Trevor Kvaran, Fiery Cushman, David Blumenfeld, and especially Bradley Thomas. This chapter was completed in part with support from a grant (for E.N.) from the University of Chicago Arete Initiative and the John Templeton Foundation.

References

Baron, R. M. and Kenny, D. A. (1986), "The Moderator-Mediator Variable Distinction in Social Psychological Research: Conceptual, Strategic, and Statistical Considerations," *Journal of Personality and Social Psychology* 51: 1173–82.

Blumenfeld, D. (1988), "Freedom and Mind Control," *American Philosophical Quarterly* 25: 215–27.

Chalmers, D. (1996), *The Conscious Mind: In Search of a Fundamental Theory*. New York: Oxford University Press.

Edwards, P. (1958), "Hard and Soft Determinism," in S. Hook, ed., *Determinism and Freedom in the Age of Modern Science*, New York: New York University Press.

Fischer, J. and Ravizza, M. (1998), *Responsibility and Control: A Theory of Moral Responsibility*. Cambridge: Cambridge University Press.

Frankfurt, H. (1971), "Freedom of the Will and the Concept of a Person," in *The Importance of What We Care About* (Cambridge University Press, 1988), 11–25.

Kane, R. (1999), "Responsibility, Luck, and Chance: Reflections on Free Will and Indeterminism," *Journal of Philosophy* 96: 217–40.

Kauppinen, A. (2007), "The Rise and Fall of Experimental Philosophy," *Philosophical Explorations* 10: 95–118.

Kenny, D. A. Deborah. A. K. and Bolger, N. (1998), "Data Analysis in Social Psychology," in D. Gilbert, S. Fiske, and G. Lindzey, eds, *The Handbook of Social Psychology: Vol. 1* (4th edn). Boston: McGraw-Hill, 233–65.

Knobe, J. and Nichols, S. (2008), "An Experimental Philosophy Manifesto," in J. Knobe and S. Nichols, eds, *Experimental Philosophy*, New York: Oxford University Press: 3–14.

Knobe, J. and Doris, J. (2010), "Responsibility," in J. Doris, ed., *The Handbook of Moral Psychology*, New York: Oxford University Press: 321–354.

Lewis, D. (1986), *The Plurality of Worlds*. Oxford: Blackwell Publishers.

Lycan, W. (2003), "Free Will and the Burden of Proof," in Anthony O'Hear, ed, *Proceedings of the Royal Institute of Philosophy for 2001–02*, Cambridge: Cambridge University Press, 107–22.

MacKinnon, D. P. Lockwood, C. M. Hoffman, J. M. West, S. G. and Sheets, V. (2002), "A Comparison of Methods to Test Mediation and other Intervening Variable Effects," *Psychological Methods* 7: 83–104.

Mele, A. (2005), *Autonomous Agents*. New York: Oxford University Press.

Nadelhoffer, T. and Nahmias, E. (2007), "The Past and Future of Experimental Philosophy," *Philosophical Explorations* 10.2: 123–49.

Nahmias, E. (2006), "Folk Fears about Freedom and Responsibility: Determinism vs. Reductionism," *Journal of Cognition and Culture* 6: 215–37.

Nahmias, E. Morris, S. Nadelhoffer, T. and Turner, J. (2005), "Surveying Freedom: Folk Intuitions about Free Will and Moral Responsibility," *Philosophical Psychology* 18: 561–84.

Nahmias, E. Morris, S. Nadelhoffer, T. and Turner, J. (2006), "Is Incompatibilism Intuitive?" *Philosophy and Phenomenological Research* 73: 28–53.

Nahmias, E. Coates, J. and Kvaran, T. (2007), "Free Will, Moral Responsibility, and Mechanism: Experiments on Folk Intuitions," *Midwest Studies in Philosophy* 31: 214–42.

Nichols, S. and Knobe, J. (2007), "Moral Responsibility and Determinism: The Cognitive Science of Folk Intuitions," *Nous* 41: 663–85.

O'Connor, T. (2005), "Freedom With a Human Face," *Midwest Studies in Philosophy*, 29, 207–27.

Pereboom, D. (2001), *Living Without Free Will*. Cambridge: Cambridge University Press.
Roskies, A., and Nichols, S. (2008). "Bringing Responsibility Down to Earth," *Journal of Philosophy* 105: 371–388.
Strawson, G. (1986), *Freedom and Belief*. Oxford: Clarendon Press.
Turner, J. and Nahmias, E. (2006), "Are the Folk Agent Causationists?" *Mind and Language* 21: 597–609.
van Inwagen, P. (1983), *An Essay on Free Will*. Oxford: Clarendon Press.
Vargas, M. (2005), "The Revisionist's Guide to Responsibility," *Philosophical Studies* 125: 399–429.
Watson, G. (1975), "Free Agency," in G. Watson, ed., *Free Will*, Oxford University Press, 96–110.
Weinberg, J. (2007), "How to Challenge Intuitions Empirically Without Risking Skepticism," *Midwest Studies in Philosophy* 31: 318–43.
Wolf, S. (1990), *Freedom within Reason*. New York: Oxford University Press.

Part IV
Action and Agency in Context

10 Agentive Experiences as Pushmi-Pullyu Representations

Tim Bayne

10.1 Introduction

Experiences of agency—or "agentive experiences" as I shall call them—have not received the attention from either philosophers of action or philosophers of consciousness that they deserve. Philosophers of action have tended to ignore the questions raised by the phenomenology of agency in favor of those that concern the identity conditions of actions or the logical structure of action-ascribing sentences, and philosophers of mind have tended to ignore the phenomenology of agency in favor of that of perception and bodily sensations. However, this unhappy state of affairs is beginning to change, and there is now a burgeoning literature dedicated to exploring various aspects of the phenomenology of agency.[1]

This chapter contributes to that literature by examining the intentional structure of agentive experience. Some theorists take agentive experiences to have a thetic (or descriptive) structure. According to this view, agentive experiences are in the business of representing what the world is like. Other theorists take agentive experiences to have telic (or directive) structure. According to this view, agentive experiences are in the business of making it the case that the world is a certain way. I examine the case for each of these views before presenting an alternative account that draws on Millikan's (1996) notion of a pushmi-pullyu representation. The pushmi-pullyu account holds that agentive experiences—or at least *some* agentive experiences—have both thetic and telic structure. The chapter concludes with some brief reflections on the implication of the pushmi-pullyu analysis for representationalist accounts of phenomenal character.

10.2 Agentive experience

Consider what it is like to engage in a mundane action, such as waving goodbye to a friend. In addition to experiencing one's body as moving in a certain way, one will also experience oneself as acting and, indeed, as carrying out a particular kind of action (say, waving). One will experience the movements of one's arm as intentional and as goal-directed; one will experience oneself as the agent of the action. One may also experience oneself as having a certain degree of control over both the initiation and execution of the action; one may experience the action as "up to oneself." The action might be experienced as involving a certain amount of effort. It might also be experienced as an action that one performs freely or voluntarily. Each of these types of mental states is, I assume, familiar to you from your own experience. I will group these states together under the heading of "agentive experiences."

Within the class of agentive experiences we can distinguish between core and non-core elements. The core elements of agentive experience are elements that must be possessed by any agentive experience whatsoever. As the name suggests, the core elements of agentive experience lie at the heart of the phenomenon. We might think of the core as "the feeling of doing" or "the sense of agency." A minimal construal of this core would identify it with nothing more than a bare experience of oneself as acting—what Ginet (1990) refers to as "actish phenomenology." A richer conception of the agentive core might identify it with the experience of acting on the basis of a particular aim or goal. We need not decide between these two conceptions of the agentive core here.

By the "non-core" elements of agentive experience I mean to identify those elements of agentive phenomenology that need not be present within an experience of agency. It is something of an open question just what phenomenal features might qualify as non-core elements of agentive experience, but I would include experiences of effort and experiences of freedom in this category. Although many of our actions involve a sense of effort or a sense of freedom, these elements are not essential to the sense of agency as such. Arguably, one can experience a movement as an action without experiencing it as something in which one is investing effort or as something that one is executing freely. At any rate, the focus of this chapter is on the core aspects of agentive experience—the basic experience of acting. Exactly how the analysis of the agentive core might apply to the non-core elements of agentive experience is a question that I will leave largely to one side.

As with other forms of experience, our most fundamental grip on agentive experiences is in terms of what it is like to enjoy them—that is, in terms of their phenomenal character. The phenomenal character associated with acting might be less impressive or striking than is the phenomenal character associated with certain perceptual episodes (seeing red; tasting strawberries) or bodily sensations (pains and orgasms), but it is no less real for that. In addition to having phenomenal character agentive experiences also have intentional content—indeed, their phenomenal character is intimately related to their intentional content. Just as we can distinguish various perceptual experiences from each other on the basis of their intentional content, so too we can distinguish various agentive experiences from each other on the basis of their intentional content.

There are various ways in which we can think of the contents of agentive experience. On the one hand, one can think of agentive content in terms of objects and properties. In acting, one is often aware—or at least seems to be aware—of oneself as instantiating certain properties, such as the property of (say) raising one's arm or trying to remember a phone number. Alternatively, we can think of agentive content in propositional terms. On this view, the content of the experience of moving one's arm might be given by the proposition <I am now moving my arm in such-and-such a way>. I will assume here a propositional account of agentive experience, but much of what I say can be translated into talk of objects and properties. Note that in adopting a propositional account of agentive content I am *not* suggesting that the contents of agentive experience are—or even could be—conceptual (*pace* Bach 1978). In fact, I suspect that the contents of agentive experience are largely non-conceptual (whatever exactly the contrast between conceptual and non-conceptual content might amount to). At the very least, one can experience oneself as the agent of one's actions without possessing either the concept of an agent or the concept of agency Pacherie (forthcoming).

The intentionalist approach to agentive experience that I have adopted here is less demanding than it might at first appear. I am not committed to the claim that the phenomenal character of agentive experiences can be exhaustively captured by appeal to intentional notions, nor am I committed to the claim that all agentive experiences have intentional content. Moreover, even if all agentive experiences have intentional content, those contents might be "carried" by a more primitive layer of phenomenal properties—properties that could in principle carry intentional contents of another kind. On this view, the phenomenal character of agentive experience would function as a kind of 'mental paint' (Block 1996). Furthermore, the intentionalist approach to agentive experience need not be *reductive*. It is one thing to hold that the phenomenal character of agentive experience can be fully captured by appeal to intentional content, but it is quite another to hold that the intentional content of such states is more primitive than their phenomenal character. I take no position here on the question of whether intentionalism might provide us with either an exhaustive or a reductive analysis of the phenomenology of agency. All I assume here is that agentive experiences—in particular, the core elements of agentive experience—have intentional content. My concern is with the intentional structure of that content. To that topic I now turn.

10.3 The intentional structure of agentive experience

What is the relation between agentive experiences and their contents? In order to answer this question we need the notion of a propositional attitude (or "mode"). The idea is a familiar one from discussions of thought. Thoughts are individuated on the basis of their content and their attitude. We distinguish <believing that p> from <desiring that p>, and we distinguish both of these states from the state of <entertaining that p>. Just how to construe the attitudinal component of propositional attitudes is a far from straightforward matter, but a useful starting point is provided by Anscombe's (1957) influential distinction between two directions of fit. Anscombe points out that a list of items might be used in two quite different ways: it might be used descriptively to represent what someone has bought, or it might be given a directive function—it might tell someone what they ought to buy. As with lists so too with mental states: some are in the business of describing the world while others are in the business of shaping the world. Following Searle (1983) we can say that the former have a *mind-to-world* direction of fit whereas the latter have a *world-to-mind* direction of fit. These terms are somewhat cumbersome, and I will follow Humberstone (1992) in calling states with a mind-to-world direction of fit *thetic* states and states with a world-to-mind direction of fit *telic* states[2].

Although direction of fit talk is most naturally applied to thoughts there is no reason why it cannot be extended to experiences. Indeed, insofar as experiences have intentional content they *must* have something akin to an attitude (or mode), for intentional content cannot occur "bare," as it were. Intentional contents, as such, have no satisfaction conditions, and their ascription can serve no purpose. So, what intentional attitude might agentive experiences have?

The literature provides two rather different answers to this question. The first answer is suggested by Horgan and colleagues, who describe agentive experience—what they call "the phenomenology of doing"—as "an aspect of sensory-perceptual experience, broadly construed" (Horgan et al. 2003: 324; Horgan 2007). This suggests a thetic conception of agentive experience, a reading that is vindicated by the fact that Horgan and colleagues go on to identify one of the central questions facing the analysis of agentive experience as that of identifying its veridicality (or accuracy) conditions. For example, they ask what must the world be like in order for one's experience of free will to be veridical.[3]

The second account of the intentional structure of agentive experience to be found in the literature is that defended by Searle, who contrasts the structure of agentive experience—what he calls "the experience of acting"—with that of perceptual experience (see also O'Shaughnessy 2003). Searle holds that whereas perceptual experiences have a mind-to-world direction of fit, experiences of acting have a world-to-mind direction of fit.

> As far as Intentionality is concerned, the differences between the visual experience and the experience of acting are in the direction of fit and in the direction of causation: the visual experience stands to the table in the

> mind-to-world direction of fit. If the table isn't there, we say that I was mistaken, or was having a hallucination, or some such. And the direction of causation is from the object to the visual experience. If the Intentional component is satisfied it must be caused by the presence and features of the object. But in the case of the experience of acting, the Intention component has the world-to-mind direction of fit. If I have this experience but the event doesn't occur we say such things as that I *failed* to raise my arm, and that I *tried* to raise my arm but did not succeed. And the direction of causation is from the experience of acting to the event. Where the Intentional content is satisfied, that is, where I actually succeed in raising my arm, the experience of acting causes the arm to go up. If it didn't cause the arm to go up, but something else did, I didn't raise my arm: it just went up for some other reason.
>
> (Searle 1983: 88, emphasis in original; see also 1983: 123f.)

These comments suggest a telic analysis of agentive experience.[4] On this model, experiences of acting are in the business of making things happen rather than saying how they are—they are *directives* rather than *descriptions*. If Searle is right, it makes no more sense to ask whether experiences of acting are correct than to ask whether desires or intentions are correct. Such states might be satisfied, but they are not satisfied in virtue of the fact that their veridicality conditions are met for they have no veridicality conditions.

Although the contrast between the thetic and telic views is a stark one it is not always clearly appreciated, and some authors appear to hover between the two approaches. Consider Peacocke's recent discussion of what he calls "action-awareness." On the one hand Peacocke's account appears to qualify as a version of the thetic view, for he says that action-awareness "is representational in the sense that in enjoying action-awareness, it seems to the subject that the world is a certain way" (Peacocke 2007: 247). At the same time Peacocke contrasts action awareness with perceptual awareness:

> One of the most distinctive features [of conscious mental actions] is that such mental actions as judging, deciding, and the rest have the phenomenology of doing something, rather than involving the phenomenology of something being *presented* as being the case, as in perception, or as of something occurring to one, as in unintended imagination, in which cases the subject is passive. ... The action-awareness of raising one's arm is equally not that of being presented with some fact, but is rather a phenomenology of one's doing something.
>
> (Peacocke 2007: 365; emphasis in original).

This passage sits uneasily with the thetic analysis, for on the thetic view action-awareness does involve the presentation of facts—namely facts about what one is doing (or trying to do). Peacocke seems to be concerned that a "perceptual" conception of action-awareness would make such states "too passive," but this worry dissipates once one appreciates that agency is contained within the content of the state. Given this, there is no need to attempt to build it into the structure of such states as well.

I have contrasted the thetic account with the telic account, but it is possible that an account of agentive experience will need to draw on both models. In fact, there are at least two ways in which a full analysis of agentive experience might need to be pluralistic. Firstly, it is possible that agentive experiences with certain contents are thetic whereas agentive experiences with other contents are telic. Secondly, it could even be the case that there is no uniform structure for agentive experiences even when they are typed according to propositional contents, and that some *tokens* of a particular type of agentive experience have thetic structure while others have telic structure. For ease of exposition I will proceed by contrasting the thetic analysis with the telic analysis as such, but the possibility of a pluralistic approach to the analysis of agentive experience should not be ignored.

10.4 The thetic and telic analyses

How might we decide between the telic conception and thetic account of agentive experience? Some theorists seem to have thought that the thetic account can be dismissed on the grounds that genuinely agentive content could not be experientially encoded. Korsgaard appears to have this idea in mind when she claims that 'to experience something is (in part) to be passively receptive to it, and therefore we cannot have experiences of activity as such' (1996: 204). (Perhaps something akin to this worry lies behind Peacocke's rejection of the perceptual approach in the passage quoted above.) I find this worry puzzling. Why should the passivity of experience prevent agentive content from being experientially encoded? After all, the passivity of belief does not prevent us from having beliefs about activity as such. The thetic model might be wrong, but it cannot be dismissed on a priori grounds.

A rather more attractive thought is that we might appeal to introspection in order to decide between these two models. After all, introspection reveals not only the contents of one's thoughts but also their attitude (or "mode"). One can tell from the first-person perspective whether one is *judging* that it is snowing in Budapest or *hoping* that it is snowing in Budapest. And if introspection can reveal the attitudinal component of one's *thoughts* why shouldn't it also be able to reveal the attitudinal component of one's *experiences*?

At this point we need to consider the so-called transparency (or diaphanousness) of experience (Harman 1990; Tye 2002). According to what we might call the strong version of transparency, introspection can reveal to us only the contents of experience; we are introspectively blind to the properties of experiences themselves. Since the debate between the telic and thetic accounts concerns non-contentful features of experience, strong transparency would suggest that it is not resolvable by appeal to introspection, even in principle.

Of course, strong transparency is controversial and there are at least two reasons for thinking that it might need to be weakened (Kind 2003; Siewert 2004; Stoljar 2004; Thompson 2008). Firstly, we can introspectively distinguish perceiving that *P* from imagining that *P*, even though these two kinds of states differ only in attitudinal type. A second challenge for transparency is provided by the contrast between experiences in different modalities. The contrast between seeing that a surface is flat and feeling that it is flat is introspectively discernable, despite the fact that the two types of experiences share the same content. Neither of these two challenges to strong transparency is decisive—in fact, I suspect that the introspectable differences between these states will always involve subtle differences in content—but they certainly put the view under pressure. And were transparency to be weakened so as to allow introspective access to a state's intentional structure, then the debate between the telic and thetic accounts might be resolvable by appeal to introspection.

Whether or not introspection has the ability to rule on the debate between the thetic and the telic accounts in principle, it certainly doesn't seem to have made much of an impact on the debate in practice. Presumably both telic theorists and thetic theorists enjoy agentive experiences with the same structure, and yet the two parties do not see eye-to-eye. Although it is possible that the disagreement between them might be resolved on the basis of additional—or simply more careful—introspection, that seems to me to be a rather improbable scenario. So, how might we resolve the debate between these accounts?

In order to make progress here we need to consider again the notion of a direction of fit. Although there is no consensus as to precisely how this notion ought to be understood, it is widely acknowledged that the contrast between thetic and telic states is at least partly functional.[5] The status of a state as thetic or telic depends on the functional role that it plays within the cognitive economy in which it occurs.

Consider first the functional role of thetic states. The paradigm thetic states are beliefs and perceptual states. These states are in the business of tracking states of the world. This obviously does not require that all beliefs and perceptual states *do* track states of the world, for we need to make room for beliefs and perceptual states that are non-veridical. Rather, it requires that the creature *takes* its beliefs and perceptual states to track the world (unless it has reason to think otherwise). For example, a subject with a visual experience (as) of a cat on a mat has a defeasible reason to think that there is a cat on a mat, a reason that it can and should employ in its practical and theoretical deliberations.

The attractions of the thetic analysis should now be manifest. Agentive experiences of various kinds provide one with information—or at least apparent information—about one's agency. We can and do appeal to our agentive experiences in determining just what we are doing and how we are doing it. In the absence of information to the contrary experiences of acting will lead one to believe that one is acting; experiences of effort will lead one to believe that one is exerting effort; experiences of freedom will lead one to believe that one is acting freely; experiences of mental causation will lead one to believe that there is mental causation, and so on.

What about the functional role of telic states? Telic states are in the business of making the world a certain way—of bringing about particular states of affairs. Under this heading we can include desires, intentions, and tryings, together with executive representations (Bach 1978), motor representations (Pacherie 2000) and volitions (Israel et al. 1993). Again, we should not assume that all telic states will succeed in bringing about those states of affairs to which they are directed; in fact, it is arguable that most desires go unsatisfied and most intentions unrealized. The point is that telic states are the sorts of states that directly initiate and govern an agent's action. Because of this, it is appropriate to evaluate telic states with respect to whether the states of affairs that they are in the business of bringing about are realized, rather than in terms of how well they describe the world. Telic states have satisfaction conditions but their satisfaction conditions are not veridicality conditions. To the best of my knowledge there is no term that picks out the satisfaction conditions of telic states in the way that "veridicality conditions" picks out the satisfaction conditions of thetic state. We might, however, use the term "realization conditions" for this notion.

In light of this brief sketch of telic states what reasons do we have for thinking of agentive experiences as telic states? The passage from Searle quoted above suggests two lines of argument for the view. The first line of argument appeals to what we would (ought to?) say in contexts in which an agent experiences herself as *A*-ing—or at least trying to *A*—but fails to *A*. Suppose that an agent experiences herself as raising her hand but her hand fails to move. As Searle suggests, in such a case we would say that there is a frustrated trying (or intention-in-action). This, in turn, suggests that we think of the agentive experience itself as a trying (or intention-in-action). Searle's second argument appeals to a claim about the causal role of experiences of acting. Searle assumes that experiences of acting are themselves causally implicated in those movements that they take as their intentional objects. On this view, an agent's experience of herself as raising her hand initiates and guides the movement of her hand, and hence it should be identified with an intention-in-action for this is precisely the functional role of intentions-in-action.

Neither of these two arguments is beyond challenge.[6] The advocate of the thetic account might respond to the first argument by pointing out that if experiences of agency are thetic then an agent's experiences of herself as trying could be non-veridical. Not only might an agent misrepresent herself as doing such-and-such, she might even misrepresent herself as *trying* to do such-and-such. This suggestion may sound incoherent to some ears, but I see no reason to dismiss it out of hand. For its part, the second argument is clearly hostage to fortune, for it could turn out that agentive experiences play only a minor role—or even no role at all—in initiating and guiding an agent's actions. Contrary to what is often assumed, Libet's work on the readiness potential fails to show that agentive experience plays no role in action control, but it is conceivable that future work in the cognitive neuroscience of agency might establish this claim. But although neither of Searle's arguments is decisive, taken together they clearly go some way toward justifying the appeal of the telic model.

So, we have two accounts of agentive experience: a thetic account and a telic account. Each of these two accounts appears to be supported by our intuitive conception of the functional role of agentive experiences, and yet they appear to be at odds with each other. What should we do?

10.5 The pushmi-pullyu account

I suggest that agentive experiences might have both thetic and telic structure. By this I don't simply mean that some agentive experiences have thetic structure while others have telic structure—although that might indeed by true—but that *particular* agentive experiences might have both thetic and telic directions of fit. Following Millikan (1996) I will call such states "pushmi-pullyu representations"—or "PPRs" for short. Like Dr. Doolittle's mythical animal, PPRs face in two directions at once: they both describe how the world is and they direct how it ought to be.

Among the examples of PPRs that Millikan gives are primitive animal signals such as bird songs, rabbit thumps, and bee dances. These states describe what the world is like (for example, "there is nectar at such-and-such a location") and they direct the creatures concerned to engage in a certain kind of behavior ("fly in such-and-such a direction"). Millikan also argues that certain speech acts, such as performatives, can be regarded as PPRs. When uttered by an appropriate authority the statement "This meeting is open" both makes it the case that the meeting is open and represents the meeting as open.

Because PPRs have two directions of fit there are two ways in which they can fail. On the one hand a PPR might fail insofar as its *descriptive* satisfaction conditions are not met. A forgetful bee might misrepresent the location of a food source and a chairperson without the requisite authority might falsely declare a meeting to be open. On the other hand, a PPR might fail insofar as its *directive* satisfaction conditions are not met. A bee's dance might fail to guide the hive to the source of nectar if someone has moved it, and a chairperson's attempt to open a meeting might be unsuccessful if the quorum has not been met.

It is useful to distinguish between two types of PPRs: *monadic* PPRs and *dyadic* PPRs. Monadic PPRs have a single intentional content with both thetic and telic structure. An utterance of "this meeting is open" qualifies as a monadic PPR for the single content <the meeting is open> has both a mind-to-world and a world-to-mind direction of fit. Dyadic PPRs have dual contents, one of which has telic structure and one of which has thetic structure. A bee's dance would qualify as a dyadic PPR, for the descriptive content of the dance differs from its directive content.

If agentive experiences are PPRs then we would have an attractive account of why some theorists regard them as thetic states while others regard them as telic states. Thetic theorists latch onto the fact that agentive experiences have veridicality conditions but ignore the possibility that they might have realization conditions, while advocates of the telic approach make precisely the opposite mistake. Of course, the fact that the pushmi-pullyu model can do justice to the motivation behind both thetic and telic accounts falls short of establishing that it is true. A full-defence of the model requires a detailed account of the role played by agentive experiences within our cognitive architecture. We do not yet have such an account, but let me sketch some of the ways in which current approaches to agentive experience within cognitive science might bear on this question.

Discussions of agentive experience within cognitive science typically contrast "retrospective" or "inferential" models on the one hand with "predictive" or "non-inferential" models on the other (see Bayne & Pacherie 2007). Retrospective models take agentive experiences to be generated subsequent to the movement in question as a post-hoc interpretive reconstruction of the action (Wegner 2002; Lau et al. 2007). Experiences of acting arise out of "central-systems" processes that are concerned to make sense of the agent's behavior. As such, they play little to no role in the on-line control of action itself. By contrast, predictive models take agentive experiences to be generated by the motor control system. In particular, such models focus on the predictions made by the forward model component of the motor control system (Blakemore et al. 2002; Haggard 2005). These predictions are not passive bystanders in the processes responsible for action control, but play an essential role in ensuring that the subject's intentions are realized.

Prima facie, the retrospective account of agentive experience suggests a purely thetic conception of agentive experiences, for on this approach agentive experiences are generated only after the initiation of the action in question, and thus arise too late in the processing chain to be able to direct the execution of the target action. By contrast, predictive models point towards a telic analysis, for such accounts suggest that agentive experiences play an essential role in ensuring that the intention in question is realized.

The debate between predictive models and retrospective models is a complex one, and each side can point to evidence in favor of its approach.

However, one proposal that has quite a bit going for it is that agentive experiences are produced by a complex set of processes that contain both predictive and retrospective elements. Moore and Haggard present one version of this proposal:

> We suggest that awareness of action switches from a predictive to an inferential source as the action itself occurs, and as sensory information becomes available. This time-varying mixture of predictive and inferential information may ensure that our experience of our own action is an optimal reflection of the actual relation between our voluntary motor system and the outside world.
>
> (Moore & Haggard 2008: 143)

According to this dynamic conception of agentive experience, we might think of agentive experiences as having an overall pushmi-pullyu structure, with the telic components predominating early in the representational process and thetic components coming to the fore later in the representational process. The *overall* experiential state, however, can be assigned both realization and veridicality conditions.

If agentive experiences are PPRs what kind of PPRs might they be? I suspect that they are most plausibly regarded as monadic PPRs. Consider the experience of doing—the "sense of agency"—that one enjoys when (say) reaching for a cup. This state has content—roughly, "that I am reaching for this cup"—which both directs and describes the agent's activities. As a directive state it guides the trajectory of the subject's hand in moving thus-and-so and can be evaluated on the basis of how successful it is in this respect, and as a descriptive state it represents (to the agent) that she is engaged in a particular action. When this state fails it fails both as a directive state and as a descriptive state: not only will the agent's goals not be realized, she will also enjoy a non-veridical representation of her own agency.

A critic might grant that although agentive experiences are PPRs they are best thought of as dyadic PPRs rather than monadic PPRs. This is because their directive and descriptive contents are agentive in quite different senses. The descriptive content of an agentive experience is agentive in the sense that it includes an explicit reference to agency in its content: it represents the agent as executing an action of a certain type. By contrast, the directive content is agentive only in the sense that it *realizes* an action. And—this line of thought runs—the content of intentions do not normally contain any reference to agency as such. Instead, the content of an intention is typically focused on the realization of a certain (non-agentive) state of affairs. For example, one's intention is that there be a cup in one's hand, it is not that one grasp a cup. Arguably this content could be realized even if the movement of one's hand toward the cup fails to constitute an act of grasping (perhaps because of its deviant cause). This account would suggest that agentive experiences are dyadic PPRs, because it suggests that their directive content is subtly different from their descriptive content.

I'm not persuaded. Although there may be a class of actions that fail to contain any self-referential content, it seems to me that most intentional content is implicitly self-referential and hence is robustly agentive. The satisfaction conditions of the typical intention-in-action requires that it itself play a role in bringing about the target state of affairs. This is one respect in which intentions differ from desires, for desires do not represent themselves as causally efficacious in the way that intentions do. So if agentive experiences are intentions of a certain kind then their directive content will be no less truly agentive than their descriptive content.

If agentive experiences are monadic pushmi-pullyu states, then there is a sense in which their telic structure will be more fundamental than their thetic structure. This is because the descriptive satisfaction conditions of monadic PPRs are satisfied only when their directive satisfaction conditions are satisfied. If the agent's hand moves toward the cup without being appropriately guided by their agentive experiences, then the descriptive element of the agentive experience has not been satisfied, for the agent has not reached for the cup (even if his or her hand has followed the appropriate trajectory). In short, the kinds of PPRs that might characterize the phenomenology of agency are more akin to performatives than they are to the bee's dance: their descriptive conditions of satisfaction are met in virtue of their directive conditions of satisfaction being met.

Might forms of agentive experiences other than the core "experience of doing" qualify as pushmi-pullyu states? Possibly. Consider the experience of effort. Such states are thetic insofar as they provide one with evidence about how effortful one's actions are, but they are arguably also telic insofar as the experience of effort may be constitutively involved in making it the case that an action is effortful. Similar claims can be made about the experience of free will. As we mentioned in §10.4, experiences of free will have veridicality conditions; indeed, there is a lively debate about just what those veridicality conditions are. Some theorists take them to be incompatibilist in nature; others hold that they are compatibilist (Nahmias et al. 2004). But might experiences of free will also have realization conditions? Perhaps. It is often suggested that experiences of free will are implicated in the possession of free will itself—that one couldn't have free will without experiencing oneself as having free will. The justification for this claim is far from clear but there is certainly something to be said on its behalf. At any rate, if this claim can be defended then experiences of free will might also turn out to be pushmi-pullyu states.

10.6 Representationalism and phenomenal character

One of the central questions in the philosophy of mind concerns the relationship between phenomenality and intentionality. Do the phenomenal aspects of the mind float free of its intentional aspects, or are a subject's phenomenal states determined by—or perhaps even identical to—their intentional states? In this concluding section I briefly consider how the pushmi-pullyu account might bear on this question.

An influential conception of the relationship between the phenomenal mind and the intentional mind goes by the name of "representationalism." Representationalism comes in a variety of forms, but at its core is the claim that a subject's phenomenal states supervene on its representational states: there can be no difference in phenomenal character without a difference in intentional content.[7]

Is the pushmi-pullyu analysis at odds with representationalism? That depends on how the notion of a representational state is understood. Let us distinguish between representational states narrowly conceived and representational states broadly conceived. Representational states narrowly conceived are thetic states: states that represent that things are thus-and-so. Representational states broadly conceived are states with intentional content irrespective of their attitudinal structure or direction of fit.

Most discussions of representationalism—whether friendly or hostile—appear to assume that representationalism should be understood in terms of representational states narrowly conceived. Consider, for example, the opening paragraphs of Tye's entry on representationalism in the *Oxford Handbook of Philosophy of Mind*:

> It is obvious that some mental states have representational content. Take the case of beliefs, for example. Beliefs are either true or false. They are true if the world is as their subjects believe it to be and false otherwise. Each belief, thus, has accuracy conditions—it is accurate in certain circumstances and inaccurate in others—and any state with accuracy conditions has representational content. It is also obvious that some mental states are conscious. Recent representationalist theories of consciousness hold that there is a deep and important connection between the sort of consciousness that has most puzzled philosophers—phenomenal consciousness, as it is often called—and representational content.
>
> (Tye 2009: 253)

Although Tye does not explicitly say that he is working with the narrow notion of a representational state the tenor of this passage certainly points in that direction. But if agentive experiences are pushmi-pullyu states then representationalism needs to be understood in broad terms if it is to have any plausibility. Although such a view would involve a departure from the letter of many versions of representationalism it would be firmly within their spirit. Perhaps the most fundamental motivation for representationalism is what Lycan (1996) has dubbed "the hegemony of representation"—the claim that the mind has no special properties over and above its representational properties. The notion of "representation" in play here is clearly not one that need be restricted to thetic states.

Representationalists might be tempted to insist on a narrow version of representationalism if the only plausible examples of pushmi-pullyu states were agentive experiences, but this turns out not to be the case. Consider pain experiences. Intentionalist treatments of pain typically construe pains as thetic states: representations of (say) bodily damage (see for example, Tye 1995; Bain 2003). Although it is certainly plausible to suppose that pain experiences do contain descriptive content, a strong case can be made for thinking that they are not purely descriptive. Pains tell us what to do—or, perhaps more accurately, what *not* to do. A pain in the foot tells one to take care in how one moves one's foot; a pain in the neck tells one to take care in how one moves one's neck. In this vein, Hall (2008) suggests that pains should be thought of as having a compound intentional structure that is partly descriptive and partly imperative (see also Klein 2007). Hall provides a similar account of tickle experiences: they both represent that the skin is being lightly touched and contain an imperative to laugh. To the list of viable candidates for a pushmi-pullyu analysis we might add the various bodily sensations associated with thirst, hunger and other bodily functions, together with affective experiences of various kinds. The domain of pushmi-pullyu experiences might turn out to be a rather broad one.

The contrast between these two conceptions of representationalism is no mere technical nicety but has important implications for how representationalism might be developed. Let me conclude by mentioning one such implication. Given that not all representational states play a role in fixing a subject's phenomenal states, representationalists need an account of why some representational states play a role in fixing phenomenology while others do not. Representationalists typically address this challenge by looking at the functional roles of representational states. The idea, roughly speaking, is that we can isolate a functional role that is distinctive of precisely those representational states that determine phenomenal character. But note that the theorist's search for this functional role will crucially depend on whether she adopts a position of broad representationalism or narrow representationalism, for the kinds of functional roles available to non-thetic states might be rather different to those available to thetic states.

10.7 Conclusion

This chapter has focused on the intentional structure of agentive experiences. Some theorists hold that agentive experiences have thetic structure, while others hold that agentive experiences have telic structure. I have suggested that both views contain a grain of truth insofar as agentive experiences have both thetic and telic structure. Like Dr. Doolittle's pushmi-pullyu, experiences of acting face in two directions at once: they both describe how the world is and they direct how it ought to be.

Although I have suggested that certain agentive experiences are pushmi-pullyu states I have not argued that this is a conceptual truth. Instead, my case for the pushmi-pullyu account was made on empirical grounds: it accords with our current understanding of the role that agentive experiences play within our cognitive architecture. In this respect it is instructive to consider the contrast between agentive experiences and other kinds of mental states. The intentional structure of many types of mental states is built into our concepts of them. Beliefs are necessarily thetic states, and no one who has failed to grasp the fact that a belief has a mind-to-world direction of fit could be said to know what a belief is. Similarly, desires are necessarily telic states, and no one who failed to grasp the fact that desires have a world-to-mind direction of fit could be said to know what a desire is. By contrast, the intentional structure of agentive experiences is not internal to the concept that we have of them. Our notion of an agentive experience leaves open the question of whether such states have thetic structure, telic structure—or, as the pushmi-pullyu analysis has it—both telic and thetic structure. Indeed, if the analysis presented here is correct then it is possible that agentive experiences as a class have no single intentional structure, but vary in structure depending on the cognitive architecture of the creature in question. Experiences of agency might play a telic role within some cognitive economies, a thetic role within others, and a pushmi-pullyu role in yet others. I have suggested that the core components of our experiences of agency have a pushmi-pullyu structure, but the case for this proposal is very much a prima facie one and the final verdict on it will require a more detailed account of the structure of agency than that which we currently possess.[8]

Notes

1. See Bayne 2008 and Pacherie 2008 for reviews of the recent literature on the phenomenology of agency. Useful anthologies include Roessler & Eilan (2003), Pockett, Banks & Gallagher (2006) and Sebanz & Prinz (2006). Although philosophers of action have tended to overlook the phenomenology of agency, O'Shaughnessy (1963) and Bach (1978) are notable exceptions to this rule.
2. Although I assume that all intentional states have an attitude I do not assume that all intentional states have a direction of fit. For example, the state of entertaining a thought appears to have no direction of fit as such. Not all propositional attitudes can be understood in terms of direction of fit.
3. Other treatments of agentive experience that adopt a thetic approach include Bayne 2010; Prinz 2007; Nida-Rümelin 2007 and Proust 2003.
4. It is unclear whether Searle thinks that the intentional content of experiences of acting exhausts, or even fixes, their phenomenal character. In one place he describes experiences of acting as actions that are "accompanied by certain phenomenal properties" (Searle 1983: 92), which suggests that he would resist the thought that the phenomenology of agency can be fully captured by appeal to intentional notions.
5. For discussion of the notion of direction of fit see Humberstone 1992, Smith 1994 and Zangwill 1998.

6. The following borrows on material that is developed more fully in Bayne (2010).
7. For discussions of representationalism (although not always under this label) see Byrne 2001, Chalmers 2004, Tye 1995, Dretske 1995 and Lycan 1996.
8. I am very grateful to Joëlle Proust and Terry Horgan for a helpful set of comments on this paper. This paper was presented to the Thumos seminar of the Départment de Philosophie at the Université de Genève, and I am grateful to the audience on that occasion for their comments. I would particularly like to thank Kevin Mulligan and Olivier Massin. I have also benefited a great deal from conversations on these matters with Elisabeth Pacherie, Frédérique de Vignemont, Michael Schmitz and Nicholas Shea.

References

Anscombe, E. (1957), *Intention*. Oxford: Blackwell.

Bach, K. (1978), "A Representational Theory of Action," *Philosophical Studies*, 34: 361–79.

Bain, D. (2003), "Intentionalism and Pain," *The Philosophical Quarterly*, 53: 502–23.

Bayne, T. (2008), "The Phenomenology of Agency," *Philosophy Compass*, 3: 1–21.

Bayne, T. (2010), "The Sense of Agency," in F. Macpherson ed., *The Senses*. Oxford: Oxford University Press.

Bayne, T. and Pacherie, E. (2007), "Narrators and Comparators: The Architecture of Agentive Self-Awareness," *Synthese*, 159: 475–91.

Blakemore, S-J., Wolpert, D. M., Frith, C. D. (2002), "Abnormalities in the Awareness of Action," *Trends in Cognitive Science*, 6/6: 337–42.

Block, N. (1996), "Mental Paint and Mental Latex," in E. Villanueva ed., *Philosophical Issues 7*, Atascadero, CA: Ridgeview, pp. 19–49.

Byrne, A. (2001), "Intentionalism Defended," *Philosophical Review,* 110: 199–240.

Chalmers, D. (2004), "The Representational Character of Experience," in B. Leiter ed., *The Future for Philosophy*. Oxford: Oxford University Press, pp. 153–81.

Dretske, F. (1995), *Naturalizing the Mind*. Cambridge, MA: MIT Press.

Ginet, C. (1990), *On Action*. Cambridge: Cambridge University Press.

Haggard, P. (2005), "Conscious Intention and Motor Cognition," *Trends in Cognitive Sciences* 9(6): 290–5.

Hall, R. J. (2008), "If it Itches, Scratch!" *Australasian Journal of Philosophy*, 86 (4): 525–35.

Harman, G. (1990), "The Intrinsic Quality of Experience," in J. Tomberlin ed., *Philosophical Perspectives 4*, Atascadero, CA: Ridgeview, pp. 31–52.

Horgan, T. (2007), "Mental Causation and the Agent-Exclusion Problem," *Erkenntnis* 67: 183–200.

Horgan, T., Tienson, J., and Graham, G. (2003), "The Phenomenology of First-Person Agency," in S. Walter and H-D Heckmann eds, *Physicalism and Mental Causation: The Metaphysics of Mind and Action*. Exeter, UK: Imprint Academic, pp. 323–40.

Humberstone, L. (1992), "Direction of Fit," *Mind*, 101: 59–83.

Israel, D., Perry, J. and Tutiya, S. (1993), "Executions, Motivations, and Accomplishments," *The Philosophical Review*, 102: 515–40.

Kind, A. (2003), "What's So Transparent about Transparency?" *Philosophical Studies* 115 (3): 225–44.

Klein, C. (2007), "An Imperative Theory of Pain," *Journal of Philosophy*, 104 (10): 517–32.

Korsgaard, C. (1996), *Creating the Kingdom of Ends*. Cambridge: Cambridge University Press.

Lau, H., Rogers, R., and Passingham, R. (2007), "Manipulating the Experienced Onset of Intention after Action Execution," *Journal of Cognitive Neuroscience*, 19/1: 1–10.

Lycan, W. (1996), "Layered Perceptual Representation," in E. Villanueva ed., *Philosophical Issues*, 7, Atascadero, CA: Ridgeview, pp. 81–100.

Millikan, R. G. (1996), "Pushmi-Pullyu Representations," in J. Tomberlin ed., *Philosophical Perspectives IX*, 185–200. Reprinted in *Mind and Morals*, L. May and M. Friedman eds. Cambridge, MA: MIT Press, pp. 145–61.

Moore, J. and Haggard, P. (2008), "Awareness of Action: Inference and Prediction," *Consciousness and Cognition*, 17: 136–44.

Nahmias, E., Morris, S. Nadelhoffer, T., and Turner, J. (2004), "The Phenomenology of Free Will," *Journal of Consciousness Studies*, 11/7–8: 162–79.

Nida-Rümelin, M. (2007), "Doings and Subject Causation, *Erkenntnis*, 67: 255–72.

O'Shaughnessy, B. (1963), "Observation and the Will," *Journal of Philosophy*, LX: 367–92.

O'Shaughnessy, B. (2003), "The Epistemology of Physical Action," in J. Roessler and N. Eilan eds, *Agency and Self-Awareness*. Oxford: Clarendon Press, pp. 345–57.

Pacherie, E. (2000), "The Content of Intentions," *Mind and Language*, 15: 400–32.

Pacherie, E. (2008), "The Phenomenology of Action: A Conceptual Framework," *Cognition*, 107/1: 179–217.

Pacherie, E. (forthcoming), "Nonconceptual Representations for Action and the Limits of Intentional Control," *Social Psychology*.

Peacocke, C. (2007), "Mental Action and Self-Awareness (I)," in B. McLaughlin and J. Cohen eds, *Contemporary Debates in Philosophy of Mind*. Oxford: Blackwell, pp. 358–76.

Pockett, S., Banks, W. P., and Gallagher, S. eds (2006), "Does Consciousness Cause Behavior?" Cambridge, MA: MIT Press.

Prinz, J. (2007), "All Consciousness is Perceptual," in B. McLaughlin & J. Cohen eds, *Contemporary Debates in Philosophy of Mind*. Oxford: Blackwell, pp. 335–57.

Proust, J. (2003), "Perceiving Intentions," In J. Roessler and N. Eilen eds, *Agency and Self-Awareness: Issues in Philosophy and Psychology*. Oxford: Clarendon Press, pp. 296–320.

Roessler, J. and Eilan, N. eds (2003), *Agency and Self-Awareness: Issues in Philosophy and Psychology*. Oxford: Clarendon Press.

Searle, J. (1983), *Intentionality*. Cambridge: Cambridge University Press.

Sebanz, N. and Prinz, W. eds (2006), *Disorders of Volition*. Cambridge, MA: MIT press.

Siewert, C. (2004), "Is Experience Transparent?" *Philosophical Studies*, 117: 15–41.

Smith, M. (1994), *The Moral Problem*. Blackwell: Oxford.

Stoljar, D. (2004), "The Argument from Diaphanousness," in M. Ezcurdia, R. Stainton, and C. Viger eds, *New Essays in the Philosophy of Language and Mind*. Supplemental volume of the *Canadian Journal of Philosophy*. Calgary: University of Calgary Press, pp. 341–90.

Soljar, D. (2007), "The Consequences of Intentionalism," *Erkenntnis* 66: 247–70.

Thompson, E. (2008), "Representationalism and the Phenomenology of Mental Imagery," *Synthese*, 160: 397–415.

Tye, M. (1995), *Ten Problems of Consciousness*. Cambridge, MA: MIT Press.

Tye, M. (2002), "Representationalism and the Transparency of Experience," *Noûs*, 36: 137–51.

Tye, M. (2009), "Representationalist Theories of Consciousness," in B. McLaughlin and A. Beckermann eds, *The Oxford Handbook of Philosophy of Mind*. Oxford: Oxford University Press, 253–67.

Wegner, D. (2002), *The Illusion of Conscious Will*. Cambridge, MA: MIT Press.

Zangwill, N. (1998), "Direction of Fit and Normative Functionalism," *Philosophical Studies*, 91/2: 173–203.

11

Double Bookkeeping in Delusions: Explaining the Gap between Saying and Doing

Lisa Bortolotti

11.1 Introduction

Delusions are usually regarded as irrational belief-like states that are symptoms of a variety of psychiatric disorders, among which are schizophrenia, dementia and delusional disorders. The doxastic account of delusions is the view that delusions are genuine instances of belief. One powerful objection to the doxastic account is that delusions are not beliefs because, differently from beliefs, they do not lead to action in the relevant circumstances. For instance, people with schizophrenic delusions may fail to manifest commitment to the content of their delusions either verbally or behaviorally. They may endorse attitudes that conflict with their delusions, provide bad reasons or no reasons at all for endorsing their delusions or fail to act on their delusions. This is also known in the literature as the phenomenon of "double bookkeeping."

In this chapter, I shall defend the doxastic account of delusions by arguing that people may fail to act on their delusions even if they genuinely believe their content. I shall attempt to explain the gap between reporting a state with apparent conviction and behaving in a way that is not consistent with the report by appealing to two kinds of considerations. First, as people with delusions are not perfectly rational agents, they suffer from attitude-behavior inconsistencies. Second, people with delusions may fail to acquire or to maintain the motivation to act on their beliefs. Both explanations of the gap between saying and doing apply not just to delusional states, but to belief states more generally, although in people with delusions rationality of beliefs and motivation to act may be compromised to a greater extent than in people without.

11.2 An anti-doxastic argument

According to the *Diagnostic and Statistical Manual of Mental Disorders* (DSM-IV 2000, p. 765), delusions are irrational beliefs:

> **Delusion.** A false belief based on incorrect inference about external reality that is firmly sustained despite what almost everyone else believes and despite what constitutes incontrovertible and obvious proof or evidence to the contrary. The belief is not one ordinarily accepted by other members of the person's culture or subculture (e.g., it is not an article of religious faith). When a false belief involves a value judgment, it is regarded as a delusion only when the judgment is so extreme as to defy credibility.

There is a lively debate on whether delusions should be characterized as beliefs at all (Bayne and Pacherie 2005). Although some of the alternative accounts of delusions are critical toward standard doxastic conceptions, they do not necessarily deny that the phenomenon of delusions involves the formation of normal or abnormal beliefs. Rather, the central idea seems to be that, even if people with delusions report false or irrational beliefs, paying attention only to their first-order cognitive states and to the doxastic dimension of their pathology can lead to a partial and potentially misleading view of the phenomenon of delusions.

Some authors emphasize the experiential and phenomenological character of delusions over the doxastic one (for example, Sass 1994; Gold and Hohwy 2000), and others conceive of delusions not as mere representations of a person's experienced reality, but as attitudes toward representations (for example, Currie 2000; Currie and Jureidini 2001; Stephens and Graham 2006). Gallagher (2009) argues that an explanation of the delusion as a mere cognitive error would be inadequate, and introduces the terminology of delusional realities, modes of experience which involve shifts in familiarity and sense of reality and encompass cognition, bodily changes, affect, social and environmental factors. Fulford (1989, p. 218) argues that a delusion is not necessarily a belief, or not exclusively a belief, but a defective reason for action. It could be the negative evaluation of an event, or the result of a misplaced sense of guilt. Thus, as reasons for action, delusions are not false, but *unreasonable*.

The thesis that delusions are not beliefs is justified on the basis of the view that beliefs have core features which delusions do not share. For instance, one may argue that beliefs are distinctive from other intentional states because they are formed and revised on the basis of evidence, they are generally consistent with other beliefs, and they are action guiding in the relevant circumstances. The anti-doxastic argument has a simple structure: if delusions do not share the defining or constitutive features of beliefs, then they are not beliefs. Possibly the most powerful argument against the claim that delusions are beliefs is that delusions lack the capacity to guide action.

- It is constitutive of beliefs that they guide action in the relevant circumstances.
- Delusions do not guide action in the relevant circumstances.
- Thus, delusions are not beliefs.

In order to assess this argument, we need to answer three questions:

(a) Is it really true that delusions do not guide action?
(b) Is action guidance a constitutive feature of beliefs?
(c) When delusions do fail to guide action, is it because people do not genuinely believe the content of their delusions, or because they lack the motivation to act on their beliefs?

I shall address (a) in section 11.3, (b) in section 11.4 and (c) in section 11.5.

11.3 Delusions and action guidance

Are delusions action guiding? Answers to the question whether delusions guide action need to rely on the available empirical evidence. They differ widely, partly because there are conflicting views about what counts as action guidance, and partly because the evidence pulls in different directions. First, acting on a belief is only one way of manifesting commitment to the content of that belief, and a distinction should be made between general behavioral manifestations and action guidance *proper*. Some of the behavioral effects of having a belief do not amount to leading to a *specific* action in the *relevant* circumstances given the content of the delusion. All clinical delusions are minimally manifested in behavior, that is, they are reported and they probably wouldn't be diagnosed as delusions unless they had negative consequences for the well-being of the people reporting them. These consequences are often detectable in people's general health and lifestyle (in terms of stress, depression, preoccupation, social withdrawal).

Action guidance seems to require more than the presence of these general behavioral manifestations, as it hinges on there being some causal or explanatory connection between the content of the delusion and the action performed. A (delusional) belief guides action if the person's behavior can be explained on the basis of the person's having that (delusional) belief—together with other cognitive or motivational states and within a given context. An example of action guidance is when a person with delusions of passivity wears a cap because she wants to prevent her neighbor from inserting thoughts into her head.

Even if we agree on what action guidance requires, clinical vignettes and empirical evidence offer a heterogeneous picture of action guidance in delusions. Some support for action guidance in delusions comes from the observation of safety behaviors in people with persecutory delusions: they avoid specific situations or certain individuals because they perceive them as threatening (Freeman et al. 2001).

> Individuals believe that they are to suffer physical, social, or psychological harm. Many instances of acting on persecutory delusions may be anxious attempts to seek safety and prevent the perceived threat from occurring.
>
> (Freeman et al. 2007)

Some people with delusions are found to commit acts of violence motivated by their delusion (Junginger et al. 1998, Förstl et al. 1991, Bourget and Whitehurst 2004, Broome et al. 2010). Nielssen and colleagues who studied rates of homicide in New South Wales between 1993 and 2002 found that the risk of violence in people with psychotic symptoms is particularly high during their first serious episode of mental illness. In the ten years studied by the authors, 88 people were charged with 99 homicide offences, where the targets were primarily family and friends and only occasionally strangers.

> The offences themselves were largely secondary to frightening delusional beliefs in which the victim was perceived to present an immediate threat, and because of delusional beliefs about evil deeds or a duty to act.
>
> (Nielssen et al. 2007, p. 304)

Capgras patients often act on their delusions by showing hostile or aggressive behavior toward the alleged impostors. One often reported case is that of Ms. A., who killed her mother after having suffered for five years from the delusion that her parents were impostors (Silva et al. 1994). Affected by perceptual delusional bicephaly, the delusion that one has two heads, a man who believed that the second head belonged to his wife's gynecologist attempted to attack it with an axe. When the attack failed he attempted to shoot it and as a consequence he was hospitalized with gunshot wounds (Ames 1984). A woman who believed that people were trying to harm her by occult powers assaulted her parents and her sisters and then went to the police to complain that they had been using diabolic powers (Wessely et al. 1993). Self-inflicted eye injury and self-mutilation are common in people who believe that they deserve punishment due to their delusions of guilt (Buchanan and Wessely 1998).

The life of a woman with Frégoli delusion, the belief that people the patient sees are actually the same person in disguise, was dominated by her conviction that her adulterous neighbor was following her to prevent her from telling others about his extra-marital relationship.

> Betty allowed herself little time either to sleep or to eat: instead she constantly watched the street, noting the time and the number plates of passing cars. She sometimes confronted the drivers, demanding that they reveal their true identities and intentions.
>
> (Ellis and Szulecka 1996, pp. 40–1)

Cases of Cotard delusion have been reported where people stop eating and bathing themselves as a consequence of believing that they are dead.

> Patients not only claim that they are dead or non-existent and that their bodies have been replaced by corpses, but they might also act dead. They may be mute or speak in sepulchral tones. Along with saying that they have no feelings, they might not respond to obnoxious stimuli and threatening gestures [...]. They are akinetic and often refuse to eat.
>
> (Weinstein 1996, pp. 20–1)

However, since the early 20s, Bleuler had noticed that people with schizophrenia sometimes behave as if their delusion were to be taken metaphorically.

> They really do nothing to attain their goal; the emperor and the pope help to manure the fields; the queen of heaven irons the patients' shirts or besmears herself and the table with saliva.
>
> (Bleuler 1924, p. 392)

To explain this phenomenon, Bleuler (1950) introduces the notion of *double awareness* in schizophrenia: people with schizophrenic delusions may fail to act in accordance with their delusions and behave in a way that reflects how things really are, not how they say they believe things to be. Sass (1994, 2001, 2004) and Gallagher (2009) re-elaborate Bleuler's notion of double awareness, and call the phenomenon *double bookkeeping*. They suggest that people with delusions are at least implicitly aware that their delusions are not accurate representations of reality.

> A [...] feature of schizophrenic patients is what has been called their 'double-bookkeeping'. It is remarkable to what extent even the most disturbed schizophrenics may retain, even at the height of their psychotic periods, a quite accurate sense of what would generally be considered to be their objective or actual circumstances. Rather than mistaking the imaginary for the real, they often seem to live in two parallel but separate worlds: consensual reality and the realm of their hallucinations and delusions.
>
> (Sass 1994, p. 21)

> A patient can view doctors and nurses as poisoners (in delusional reality) but happily eats the food they give her (in everyday reality).
> (Gallagher 2009, p. 260)

In the light of the evidence on action guidance in delusion and the appeals to double bookkeeping, let's revise the second premise of the argument we started with, to recognize that *some* delusions are action guiding in the relevant circumstances, or that delusions are action guiding in *some* of the relevant circumstances:

- It is constitutive of beliefs that they guide action in the relevant circumstances.
- Some delusions do not guide action in the relevant circumstances.
- Thus, *those* delusions *that* do not guide action in the relevant circumstances are not beliefs.

Or:

- It is constitutive of beliefs that they guide action in the relevant circumstances.
- Delusions do not *always* guide action in the relevant circumstances.
- Thus, delusions are not *always* beliefs.

Now we have a more modest attack on the doxastic status of delusions. Some delusions, those that are not followed up in behavior, are not beliefs. In the alternative formulation, delusions are not beliefs when they are not followed up in behavior. The generality of the anti-doxastic argument has been undermined, but we are still in search of an explanation why delusions may fail to guide action. The traditional explanation for double bookkeeping is that people are not fully committed to their delusions because they do not genuinely believe the content of their delusions.

In the rest of the paper, I want to offer you some reasons to resist this type of explanation. The first challenge invites us to reject the first premise of the anti-doxastic argument: it is not constitutive of belief states *in general* that they are action guiding. Only some beliefs reliably and consistently lead to action in the appropriate circumstances. The second challenge offers an alternative explanation of the second premise in the anti-doxastic argument: when people don't act on their delusions it is because they have failed to acquire or to sustain the motivation to act on those delusions.

11.4 Double bookkeeping and rationality

Is action guidance a constitutive feature of beliefs? In the philosophical literature on delusions action guidance is often regarded as a constitutive feature of beliefs. That is why many identify double bookkeeping as a potential problem for the view that delusions are beliefs. For instance, Currie and Jureidini (2001) argue that delusions are more plausibly imaginings than beliefs, partly because they are not action guiding.

> It is usual to think of beliefs both as the source of action and as thoughts that carry a certain kind of conviction for the subject. We say that these two features can come apart to this extent: When imaginings masquerade as beliefs, you can have conviction without action-guidance. Assuming that belief can guide action without being explicitly available to the subject's awareness, this gives us a double dissociation.
>
> (Currie and Jureidini 2001, pp. 160–1)

Frankish (2009a) convincingly argues that there are two main functions played by the states to which the folk-psychological notion of belief applies. Accordingly, there are two types of beliefs: level-1 beliefs are nonconscious, passive, graded, dispositional states which are ascribed to others on the basis of rationality constraints; level-2 beliefs are conscious, controlled, binary, functional states that are subject to failures of activation and are not ascribed on the basis of rationality constraints. Level-1 beliefs are consistent with behavior and action guiding, whereas level-2 beliefs may not be.

In the account developed by Frankish, if delusions are beliefs at all, they are level-2 beliefs, in that they behave as general policies that people consciously adopt and not as pre-conscious behavioral dispositions. The apparently anomalous features of delusions are accounted for by the claim that delusions are level-2 beliefs: delusions are consciously reported, they are available to reflection, they have limited influence on behavior, and they are more often ascribed on the basis of verbal reports than on the basis of a rationalization of observable behavior.

> [The actions of deluded patients] are understandable qua manifestations of the premising policies in which those states consist, and interpreting a deluded patient will involve forming and testing hypotheses as to the character of these policies.
>
> (Frankish 2009a, p. 281)

In response to examples and arguments by Sass, Gallagher, Currie and Jureidini, I developed elsewhere (see Bortolotti 2009a, chapter 4) a more detailed argument against the second premise of the anti-doxastic argument and maintained that (i) delusions are typically manifested not just in verbal reports, but in other forms of observable behavior, and that (ii) delusions do not fare much worse than ordinary beliefs with respect to their action-guiding potential. I have also resisted the suggestion that beliefs can be neatly divided into the categories of level-1 versus level-2 beliefs. Frankish is fully aware of the limitations of a sharp dichotomy and has proposed ways of making it more psychologically realistic (see Frankish 2009b, pp. 102–05). That said, as it will soon become clear, I agree with Frankish that we have to distinguish between types of beliefs when we consider the question whether beliefs are action guiding.

Let me focus here on the first premise of the anti-doxastic argument. Is it constitutive of beliefs that they guide action in the relevant circumstances? *Some* beliefs guide action: I go to the seminar room at 4pm, because I believe that the seminar will start at that time. Other beliefs can have a number of behavioral manifestations, but do not necessarily lead people to act in a way that is explicable by reference to the content of those beliefs. There may be no *specific* action of mine that is explicable by my belief that humans are bipeds, although I would certainly assent to the claim that humans are bipeds if asked. These differences depend on the content of the beliefs, not just on their form.

The more controversial cases are those in which a reported belief that can have behavioral consequences fits badly with my actions (such as in cases of cognitive dissonance). I may report that I believe that people should donate ten percent of their salary to their preferred charity, but then fail to do so myself. In similar instances, when I state a general principle but fail to apply it to myself, one is entitled to doubt my sincerity and ask whether I *really* believe that people should donate ten percent of their salary to their preferred charity, or whether I just say it to look good (*hypocrisy*).

In cognitive psychology, evidence of the relationship between intentions and goal-directed behavior (Sheeran 2002) and evidence for the causal efficacy of the unconscious mind (Wilson 2002) suggest that it is difficult to predict people's behavior on the basis of their self-reported beliefs and intentions. In the psychological studies, attitude-behavior inconsistency is established on the basis of prediction. Typically, a person's attitude is measured, her future behavior is also measured, and then consistency is assessed on the basis of the correlation between reported attitude and behavior. When inconsistencies are found, self-reported attitudes and explanations are regarded as largely confabulatory.

The history of empirical evidence on attitude-behavior inconsistencies seems to have started in the thirties. The sociologist LaPiere found in 1934 that restaurants and hotels around the US had an explicit policy not to serve Asian people but would actually serve an Asian couple in the great majority of circumstances. In a similar vein Corey in 1937 found that knowing students' attitudes about cheating in an exam did not help predict whether they would actually cheat given the opportunity. In the study, the great majority of students who had expressed a very disapproving attitude toward cheating did actually cheat when asked to self-assess their exam papers, especially if the exam papers were difficult.

The vast philosophical literature on attitude-behavior inconsistency and cognitive dissonance continues to offer convincing examples of beliefs that are endorsed with conviction but are not acted upon in the relevant circumstances. In the light of this body of evidence, and restricting our attention exclusively to the type of belief-like states that can guide action, we should reformulate the first premise of the argument. Consistency between beliefs and behavior should be seen as a precondition for having beliefs, but as a requirement for rational agency.

- One of the conditions for rational agency is that beliefs guide action consistently in the relevant circumstances.
- Some delusions do not guide action consistently in the relevant circumstances.
- Thus, when delusions do not guide action consistently in the relevant circumstances one of the conditions for rational agency is not met.

The conclusion of this argument is much weaker and unsurprising. More important to us, the argument is no longer an anti-doxastic argument. It leaves it open that some delusions are beliefs held by non-rational agents.

The message is that we should not adopt double standards. In normal as in abnormal cognition, consistency between attitudes and behavior should not be taken for granted. It is certainly a mark of rational agency, but it should not be seen as a condition on having beliefs at all. The behavior of people with no known psychiatric disorders is rarely rational, in the sense that it is not guided by the relevant attitudes reported by those people. Why should we expect the behavior of people with delusions to fare better in that respect?

One could reply that delusions often concern events of great significance to the person reporting them, and if they were beliefs, they would be beliefs that one would be unlikely to insulate from action. For this reason, the double-bookkeeping objection to the belief status of delusions is hard to kill. People with delusions don't always show the commitment to the content of their delusions that we would expect given the content of the delusions, and this phenomenon deserves an explanation, especially when the topic of the delusion involves a self-defining event ("God spoke to me," "I'm disembodied," "I'm a famous musician"); an event with great emotional implications ("My wife has been replaced by an impostor," "Richard Gere is in love with me"); or possible threats to one's safety and well-being ("The FBI is having me followed and wants me dead"). Failing to be behaviorally responsive toward a belief that has wide-ranging consequences for one's self-concept or for one's life is more puzzling than failing to be behaviorally responsive toward a belief that is peripheral to one's image of oneself and to one's perception of how one's life is going. However, these considerations are not sufficient to support a disanalogy between attitude-behavior inconsistencies in the general population and in people with delusions.

Wilson (2002) reviews evidence showing that discrepancies between attitudes and behavior in normal cognition can extend to beliefs about oneself, to beliefs about the success of one's romantic relationships and to one's moral attitudes, which are arguably invested with great personal significance and play a crucial role in the construction of one's self-narratives.

Even if a disanalogy between double bookkeeping in normal and abnormal cognition were found, it would be useful to make a distinction between instances of double bookkeeping observed in the acute phases of mental illness, and instances of double bookkeeping observed as part of the gradual process of recovery, where people with, say, schizophrenia start questioning their delusional beliefs and are more willing to engage in reality-testing. As we read in the first-person report of a man who wanted to manage his delusions and prevent them from controlling his life, "the key is to be able to detect these beliefs and reinforce them as fiction" (Fleshner 1995, pp. 705–6). If recovering patients in Fleshner's situation are consciously trying to distance themselves from their delusions, and regard these delusions as implausible beliefs possibly caused by their mental illness, then it is not surprising that they will be less inclined to act on them. One exception is when acting on the delusion is done *experimentally*, as an attempt to "test" whether the delusion is true, and thus it is done when confidence in the truth of the delusion has already been significantly undermined.

To sum up the discussion so far, I have suggested that we should see consistency between beliefs and behavior not as a constitutive feature of beliefs, but as a mark of rational agency. Ordinary beliefs can fail to be acted upon even when they are significant to the person reporting them and when they are self-defining. People with delusions can present similar failures of consistency without coming to doubt that the content of their delusions is true. One exception to this is when double bookkeeping is manifested in the phase of recovery, when the person is open to the possibility that what she used to believe is an effect of her being mentally unwell.

11.5 Double bookkeeping and motivation

The strength of the first premise in the simplified anti-doxastic argument has been undermined. But suppose that my opponent is not persuaded, and wants to hang on to the idea that it is a constitutive features of (maybe some?) beliefs that they are action guiding. There is another move that we can make to resist the anti-doxastic conclusion of the argument. When a delusion does not lead to action, this is not necessarily due to a failure of commitment toward the content of the delusion. Rather, it may be due to the fact that the person reporting the delusion is unable to acquire or sustain the motivation to act on it.

The hypothesis I wish to consider now is that people with schizophrenic delusions are guilty of double bookkeeping when they fail to acquire or sustain their motivation to act on their delusions. In order to analyze the role of motivation in double bookkeeping, we need to rely on an account of how motivation is thought to work in normal cognition. In cognitive psychology it is believed that one's motivation to act is affected both by the perceived likelihood of achieving one's goals, and by the surrounding environmental and social context (see Allport 1937, Ford 1992, Austin and Vancouver 1996, Armitage and Christian 2004, and Kuhl and Beckman 1985).

Suppose that I believe that there are spies in the bus that I usually catch to get to work. Suppose that I also believe that they are following me because they intend to cause me harm. One goal I may form as a consequence of having these beliefs is to stop catching the bus and to start driving my car to work instead. In order for me to act on my beliefs, I need to have an intention to achieve the goal, and I need to have a positive attitude toward the goal. That is, I must think that it would be good for me to achieve the goal. The desirability of the goal may depend on other individual beliefs and aspirations, on social pressure, and on contextual factors. In addition to intention and attitude toward the goal, other criteria that need to be met are: (1) the perception of *behavioral control*, that is, a representation of the goal as something that can be achieved given its intrinsic features; and (2) the perception of *self-efficacy*, that is, a representation of the self as able to perform the action successfully and achieve the goal. The likelihood to achieve the goal thus depends on characteristics of the goal and on the agent's sense of her own competence in pursuing it.

Contextual factors play a crucial role too: it is important to determine whether the surrounding environment is responsive to the newly formed intention and whether the social structure supports it. Going back to our example, I am more likely to acquire and sustain my motivation to start driving to work if it is possible for me to drive to work (for example, if I obtained a valid driving license and I own a car), if I can drive safely and confidently, if there is available, inexpensive parking close to my office, and so on.

This (admittedly simplified) analysis suggests that when an agent fails to act on her beliefs, a number of explanations for such failure are plausible, and many of them involve failure to acquire or sustain motivation. For instance, the agent may never acquire the necessary motivation to act because she believes that she has no genuine control over her own behavior. Thus, her intention does not translate into action. (I may believe, for instance, that external forces are compelling me to catch the bus to work, and that I am not really free to alter my routine in the way I wish to do.) Alternatively, the agent may fail to sustain her own motivation to act, if she acquires a new attitude which is in conflict with her finding the original goal desirable. Such a situation would lead the agent to abandon a previously formed intention to act. (If I realized that it would be easy for the evil spies to follow my car when I am driving, then I could reason that altering my routine would be a wasted effort, as it would not deliver the desired outcome.)

Considerations in favor and against the intention of an agent can of course be seen as evidence to be weighed up in an ongoing process of deliberation, rather than factors affecting motivation alone. When the agent acquires a new conflicting attitude, for instance, it is possible for her to change her mind as a result, and withdraw her prior intention. But when the agent comes to think that she has no genuine control over her action, her thought is not supported by evidence that speaks against the original intention. Rather, it undermines the agent's confidence in the success of her attempt to convert intention into action.

In cognitive evaluation theory and action theory one key notion is that social and contextual factors which lead agents to see themselves as competent in performing an action (for example, by providing rewards) can support their motivation to act (Ryan and Deci 2000). This is especially the case when agents have a sense of *autonomy* (intended as the belief that the action is actually caused by them) and a sense of *relatedness* (intended as support from close personal relationships). Thus, in this theoretical framework, beliefs about lack of competence and beliefs about isolation could also be responsible for undermining motivation. It may not be a coincidence that some of the conditions responsible for lack of motivation are also among the causal factors contributing to psychopathology (Ryan and Deci 2000, p. 76), such as the impression that there is excessive external control on one's thoughts and actions, which compromises the agent's sense of autonomy, and the absence of supportive personal relationships, which negatively affects the sense of relatedness.

> In normal subjects, the drive and inclination to act are closely linked to the affective and emotional aspects of a belief. It seems possible that the likelihood of a delusional belief being acted upon will be influenced by similar factors.
>
> (Buchanan and Wessely 1998, p. 251)

The simplified anti-doxastic argument should be reformulated again in order to succeed in challenging the belief-status of delusions and in identifying a relevant difference between ordinary beliefs and delusions.

This is one proposal:

- It is constitutive of beliefs that they guide action in the relevant circumstances *when the agent is motivated to act on them.*
- Some delusions fail to guide action in the relevant circumstances *even when the agent is motivated to act on them.*
- Thus, those delusions that fail to guide action even when the agent is motivated to act on them are not beliefs.

But can we safely assume that, when people fail to act on their delusions, they satisfy the second premise and are motivated to act on their delusions?

We have reasons to doubt that motivation is intact in psychiatric disorders characterized by delusions (and especially in schizophrenia). Some argue that in schizophrenia and delusional disorders the capacity to act spontaneously on one's intentions is negatively affected by a problem with metarepresentational capacities. Moreover, there are affective aspects of pathologies such as schizophrenia and delusional disorders which arguably compromise motivation (flattened affect, avolition, emotional disturbances). I shall briefly explore these ideas in the rest of this section.

11.5.1 Poverty of action

Frith (1992) endorses a cognitive neuropsychological explanation of the negative and positive symptoms of schizophrenia. Negative symptoms are social withdrawal, flattened affect and inability to initiate action, whereas positive symptoms are thought disorders, hallucinations and delusions.

> I propose that the various behavioural abnormalities associated with schizophrenia are best understood in terms of a fundamental defect in the generation of willed action.
>
> (Frith 1992, p. 53)

The basic observation is that when action is not externally driven (for example, driven by a stimulus) but is supposed to be self-initiated, then people with schizophrenia are less likely to engage in the action, even if it does match their own goals. Given Frith and colleagues' description of how agency is affected in schizophrenia (see also Jahanshahi and Frith 1998), this dysfunction seems relevant to the failure of acting on delusions. The agent successfully identifies goals that are suitably related to her beliefs, but her goals fail to generate an intention to act (so-called poverty of action). This may be due to the incapacity to access the identified goals at a later time.

> Frith suggests that poverty of action is due to an inability to produce self-willed (as opposed to stimulus-elicited) action, that this is in turn due to an inability to access one's goals and that it is failure of metarepresentation which is responsible for this lack of access to goals.
>
> (Currie 2000, pp. 170–1)

11.5.2 Flattened affect

Another reason for doubting that people with delusions are motivated to act on their delusions is that they may suffer from flattened affect. Bleuler, who identifies schizophrenia with a "breakdown of the emotions" notices that people affected by schizophrenia often appear *indifferent* (such "indifference" would now be considered as a negative symptom):

> Indifference seems to be the external sign of their state. [...] The patients appear lazy and negligent because they no longer have the urge to do anything either of their own initiative or at the bidding of another.
>
> (Bleuler 1950, p. 70)

Can lack of motivation be explained by the flattening of affect? People set a goal for themselves but do not find the goal attractive and thus are not moved by their desire to pursue it. Evidence that seems to support a positive correlation between affect and motivation emerges from the observation that, when there are strong emotional reactions relevant to a person's delusions, such as anger and anxiety, the person is more likely to act on her delusions. If these emotions associated with the content of the delusions are prevented from manifesting themselves, as in flattened affect, then the motivation to act may be undermined.

11.5.3 Avolition

> Individuals with schizophrenia exhibit deficits in their ability to couple their behavior to the motivational properties of a stimulus despite equivalent subjective in the moment pleasantness and arousal ratings for these stimuli compared with healthy controls. Furthermore, significant correlations were noted between these deficits and working memory impairment, particularly for those situations requiring the maintenance of an internal representation for the stimulus. The authors conclude that motivational deficits in schizophrenia reflect impairment in the ability to translate experience into action.
>
> (Foussias and Remington 2008, pp. 6–7)

In the passage above, the authors suggest that people with schizophrenia are not necessarily impaired in the appreciation of the pleasantness of their goals, but find it harder than controls to act in such a way as to enjoy those pleasant emotions and channel them into action. So, at a first glance, it would seem that they do not necessarily suffer from flattened affect, but experience problems with volition, and fail to convert experience into goal-directed action.

Studies reviewed by Kring and Bachorowski (1999) seem to confirm this hypothesis. They find that people suffering from psychopathologies report less pleasure than controls when asked to self-report their emotional responses to potentially pleasurable activities. In the authors' terminology, there are two emotional components to the enjoyment of pleasant experiences, the *appetive* and the *consummatory*. The appetive component concerns the pleasure derived from the imagination or the expectation of a rewarding experience. The consummatory component concerns the pleasure derived from the actual pursuit of and engagement in the desired activity.

People with psychopathologies report that they experience fewer positive emotions than controls. One hypothesis is that their capacity to imagine future outcomes is impaired and this prevents them from anticipating the pleasure they may derive from an activity. Another hypothesis is that they are able to enjoy pleasurable activities as much as controls, but they actually engage in the pleasurable activities less frequently, probably because they have fewer opportunities for social interaction. Both these obstacles to the enjoyment of pleasant experiences could affect motivation by undermining the desirability of the goals that people set for themselves.

In the following two passages, we find references to *avolition* in people with schizophrenia. Barch argues that the poor performance of people engaging in cognitive tasks may be partially explained by their lack of incentives. Corlett and colleagues observe how lack of motivation contributes not only to people failing to commit to the content of their delusions, but also to the decreased conviction in their delusional beliefs.

> [S]tudies of cognition function in healthy individuals often rely on the assumption that people are motivated in some way to do well on the cognitive task, either because of some intrinsic drive to do well or because of the external reinforcement provided by praise or even money. However, such assumptions may not necessarily hold true for individuals with schizophrenia, if the illness itself may impair either intrinsic motivational drives or responsivity to extrinsic reinforcers. If so, then it could be that poor performance on cognitive tasks reflects a lack of engagement or motivation to do well rather than an inherent difficulty with the cognitive process tapped by the task.
>
> (Barch 2005, pp. 875–6.)

> Some more chronically ill patients appear to show another kind of double-awareness, known as double bookkeeping (Sass 2004). Here, patients appear to regain a modicum of insight: delusions persist but the patient does not consistently act upon them. This may be because chronically ill patients experience severe negative symptoms including avolition and emotional blunting, with the consequence that delusional beliefs cannot maintain their previously high degree of salience. Thus, they no longer feel the compulsion to act or ruminate upon the beliefs, though the memory of how salient the belief used to be is sufficient to maintain it.
>
> (Sass 2004). (Corlett et al. 2009, pp. 4–5)

11.5.4 Emotional disturbances

In cognitive neuro-psychological approaches, the accepted view is that emotional disturbances are not a direct cause of psychotic symptoms, but contribute to the maintenance and severity of symptoms. For instance, in people with schizophrenia, negative self evaluation is correlated with more severe positive symptoms (Barrowclough et al. 2003). In people with delusions, distress is correlated with the severity of the delusions (Lysaker et al. 2003) and high levels of anger are often recorded (Siris 1995; Cullari 1994).

More recently, the accepted view has been challenged. For instance, Freeman and Garety (2003) have suggested that emotions can *directly* cause delusions. This is not just because emotions badly affect reasoning strategies and are partly responsible for reasoning biases (Garety et al. 2005), but because anxiety contributes to delusional conviction, in a way that is quite independent of reasoning.

> It is proposed that delusional explanations are a direct reflection of pre-existing beliefs about the self, world and others, and that these beliefs are intimately linked to emotion.
>
> (Freeman and Garety 2003, p. 931)

Moreover, Broome and colleagues (2005), who conducted seminal work on the developmental and epidemiological factors influencing prodromal symptoms (that is, the symptoms indicating the onset of a disease), observe how people at high risk of psychosis experience distress, decreased motivation and poor socialization from an early age. Those in the "high-risk" sample who make the transition to "psychotic" are often depressed and anxious before suffering from positive symptoms.

The widespread co-morbidity between schizophrenia and depression deserves a special mention, as it constitutes an independent argument for both the view that emotional disturbances contribute to the formation of delusions, and the hypothesis that people with delusions lack motivation. Individuals with low self-esteem who tend to attribute to themselves evil intentions and actions may also come to believe (delusionally) that they are sinful, that they are the devil, or that they are responsible for the death of others (Beck 1967, p. 37). These delusions are then more or less likely to be acted upon depending on the persistence of the emotional reactions that allegedly triggered them. This observed co-morbidity helps us see the reason why people with delusions may find it harder than controls to acquire or sustain their motivation to act. They feel hopeless and pessimistic about the probability of achieving their goals, they expect to fail, and thus they do not even engage in the pursuit of their goals.

To sum up, in this section I explored different routes to undermining motivation in psychopathology and I briefly examined the role of metarepresentation, volition and emotions in the formation and maintenance of positive psychotic symptoms. The literature on poverty of action, flattened affect, avolition and emotional deviance in schizophrenia and other psychiatric disorders characterized by delusions can be invoked in the explanation of the phenomenon of double bookkeeping. The reason why some people may not consistently act on their delusions is not that they do not genuinely believe the content of their delusions, but that they fail to acquire or sustain their motivation to act.

11.6 Conclusions

According to Lincoln (2007), there is strong continuity between delusional and non-delusional samples with respect to the likelihood that people act on their beliefs, with the major discriminating factor being distress. I have offered another take on double bookkeeping in delusions which also emphasizes the continuity between normal and abnormal cognition. Double bookkeeping affects both ordinary and delusional beliefs. Although the reasons why people may not act on their beliefs are of the same type (that is, attitude-behavior inconsistencies and lack of motivation), people with schizophrenic delusions may exhibit more inconsistencies between attitudes and behavior than other agents, and may find it harder to acquire or maintain their motivation to act on their beliefs.

In this paper my aim was to suggest that we do not need to give up the doxastic conception of delusions when faced with the phenomenon of people who do not act on their delusions. I examined three objections to a simplified anti-doxastic argument based on the phenomenon of double bookkeeping:

(a) many delusions *are* action guiding at least some of the time;
(b) the fact that some delusions are not action guiding does not show that they are other than beliefs – at most, it shows that they are not the type of belief that is acted upon and that agents endorsing such delusions do not satisfy the conditions for rational agency;
(c) the fact that some delusions are not action guiding some of the time may be due to the agent experiencing an absence or loss of motivation.

Considerations about the role of metarepresentation, affect, volition and emotions in psychopathologies suggest that many controversial assumptions need to be accepted before the anti-doxastic argument can succeed.

But the present investigation has significant limitations. First, more work needs to be done in order to examine both the soundness of the conceptual arguments and the plausibility of the empirical evidence for and against the role of motivation and emotions in the generation of action. Second, some additional hypotheses that could account for double bookkeeping have not been explored here. For instance, it may be that people fail to act on their delusions because conviction in the content of the delusions "comes and goes" or because people lack the opportunity to act on their delusional beliefs, given the bizarre content of some delusions. These are both interesting suggestions which need to be addressed in future research.

Acknowledgements

I would like to thank Matthew Broome, Keith Frankish, Iain Law, Heather Widdows and Kirk Surgener for extensive comments on a previous version of this paper.

References

Allport, G. (1937), "The Functional Autonomy of Motives," *American Journal of Psychology* 50: 141–56.

Ames, D. (1984), "Self Shooting of a Phantom Head," *British Journal of Psychiatry* 145 (2): 193–4.

Appelbaum, P., Clark Robbins, P. and Vesselinov, R. (2004), "Persistence and Stability of Delusions Over Time," *Comprehensive Psychiatry* 45(5): 317–24.

Armitage, C. and Christian, J. (eds) (2004), *Planned Behavior: the Relationship between Human Thought and Action*. New Brunswick: Transaction.

Austin, J. and Vancouver, J. (1996), "Goal Constructs in Psychology: Structure, Process and Content," *Psychological Bulletin* 120 (3): 338–75.

Barch, D. (2005), "The Relationships among Cognition, Motivation, and Emotion in Schizophrenia: How Much and How Little We Know," *Schizophrenia Bulletin* 31(4): 875–81.

Barrowclough, C., Tarrier, N., Humphreys, L. et al. (2003), "Self-Esteem in Schizophrenia," *Journal of Abnormal Psychology* 112(1): 92–9.

Bayne, T. and Pacherie, E. (2005), "In Defence of the Doxastic Conception of Delusion," *Mind & Language*, 20 (2): 163–88.

Beck, A. (1967), *Depressions: Causes and Treatment*. Philadelphia: University of Pennsylvania Press.

Bentall, R., Howard, R., Blackwood, N. and Kinderman, P. (2001), "Persecutory Delusions: A Review and Theoretical Integration," *Clinical Psychology Review* 21(8): 1143–92.

Bleuler, E. (1924), *Textbook of Psychiatry*. Transl. by A. Brill. New York (NY): Macmillan.

Bleuler, E. (1950), *Dementia Praecox or the Group of Schizophrenias*. New York: International Universities Press.

Bortolotti (2009a), *Delusions and Other Irrational Beliefs*. Oxford: Oxford University Press.

Bortolotti (2009b), "Delusion," in E. Zalta (ed.), *The Stanford Encyclopedia of Philosophy*, URL: http://plato.stanford.edu/entries/delusion/ 19 August 2010.

Bourget, D. and Whitehurst, L. (2004), "Capgras Syndrome: A Review of the Neurophysiological Correlates and Presenting Clinical Features in Cases Involving Physical Violence," *Canadian Journal of Psychiatry* 49(11): 719–25.

Breen, N., Caine, D., Coltheart, M., Hendy, J. and Roberts, C. (2000), "Toward an Understanding of Delusions of Misidentification: Four Case Studies," in M. Coltheart and M. Davies (eds), *Pathologies of Belief*. Oxford: Blackwell: 74–110.

Broome, M., Woolley, J., Tabraham, P., Johns, L., Bramon, E., Murray, G., Pariante, C., McGuire, P. and Murray, R. (2005), "What Causes the Onset of Psychosis?" *Schizophrenia Research* 79(1): 23–34.

Broome, M., Bortolotti, L. and Mameli, M. (2010), "Moral Responsibility and Mental Illness: A Case Study," *Cambridge Quarterly of Healthcare Ethics* 2 (19): 179–187.

Buchanan, A., Reed, A., Wessely, S., Garety, P., Taylor, P., Grubin, D. et al. (1993), "Acting on Delusions. II: The Phenomenological Correlates of Acting on Delusions," *British Journal of Psychiatry* 163: 77–81.

Buchanan, A. and Wessely, S. (1998), "Delusions, Action and Insight," in X. Amador and A. David (eds), *Insight and Psychosis*. Oxford: Oxford University Press: chapter 12.

Corlett, P., Krystal, J., Taylor, J. and Fletcher, P. (2009), "Why Delusions Persist?" *Frontiers in Human Neuroscience* 3 (12): 1–9. doi: 10.3389/neuro.09.012.2009.

Cullari, S. (1994), "Levels of Anger in Psychiatric Inpatients and Normal Subjects," *Psychological Reports* 75: 1163–8.

Currie, G. (2000), "Imagination, Delusion and Hallucinations," *Mind & Language* 15(1): 168–73.

Currie, G. and Jureidini, J. (2001), "Delusion, Rationality, Empathy," *Philosophy, Psychiatry and Psychology* 8 (2–3): 159–62.

Ellis, H. and Szulecka, T. K. (1996), "The Disguised Lover: A Case of Frégoli Delusion," in P. Halligan and J. Marshall (eds), *Method in Madness*. Exeter: Psychology Press: 39–50.

Fleshner, C. (1995), "Insight from a Schizophrenic Patient with Depression," *Schizophrenia Bulletin* 21(4): 703–07.

Ford, M. (1992), *Motivating Humans: Goals, Emotions and Personal Agency Beliefs*. Newbury Park (CA): Sage.

Förstl, H., Almeida, O. P., Owen, A. M., Burns, A. and Howard, R. (1991), "Psychiatric, Neurological and Medical Aspects of Misidentification Syndromes: A Review of 260 Cases," *Psychological Medicine* 21(4): 905–10.

Foussias, G. and Remington, G. (2008), "Negative Symptoms in Schizophrenia: Avolition and Occam's Razor," *Schizophrenia Bulletin*, doi: 10.1093/schbul/sbn094

Frankish, K. (2009a), "Delusions: A Two-Level Framework," in M. R. Broome and L. Bortolotti (eds), *Psychiatry as Cognitive Neuroscience: Philosophical Perspectives*. Oxford: Oxford University Press (chapter 14).

Frankish, K. (2009b), "Systems and Levels: Dual-System Theories and the Personal-Subpersonal Distinction," in J. Evans and K. Frankish (eds), *In Two Minds: Dual Processes and Beyond*. Oxford: Oxford University Press, (chapter 4).

Freeman, D., Garety, P., Kuipers, E., Fowler, D., Bebbington, P. and Dunn, G. (2007), "Acting on Persecutory Delusions: The Importance of Safety Seeking," *Behaviour Research and Therapy* 45(1): 89–99.

Freeman, D. and Garety, P. (2003), "Connecting Neurosis and Psychosis: The Direct Influence of Emotion on Delusions and Hallucinations," *Behaviour Research and Therapy* 41: 923–47.

Freeman, D., Garety, P. and Kuipers, E. (2001), "Persecutory Delusions: Developing the Understanding of Belief Maintenance and Emotional Distress," *Psychological Medicine* 31(7): 1293–306.

Frith, C. (1992), *The Cognitive Neuropsychology of Schizophrenia*. Hove: Psychology Press.

Fulford, K. (1989), *Moral Theory and Medical Practice*. Cambridge: Cambridge University Press.

Gallagher, S. (2009), "Delusional Realities," in M. R. Broome and L.Bortolotti (eds), *Psychiatry as Cognitive Neuroscience: Philosophical Perspectives*. Oxford: Oxford University Press, chapter 13.

Garety P., Freeman, D., Jolley, S. et al. (2005), "Reasoning, Emotions, and Delusional Conviction in Psychosis," *Journal of Abnormal Psychology* 114(3): 373–84.

Gold, I. and Hohwy, J. (2000), "Rationality and Schizophrenic Delusion," *Mind & Language* 15 (1): 146–67.

Jahanshahi, M. and Frith, C. (1999), "Willed Action and its Impairments," *Cognitive Neuropsychology* 15 (6/7/8): 483–533.

Junginger, J., Parks-Levy, J. and McGuire, L. (1998), "Delusions and Symptom-Consistent Violence," *Psychiatric Services* 49 (2): 218–20.

Kring, A. and Bachorowski, J. (1999), "Emotions and Psychopathology," *Cognition and Emotion* 13(5): 575–99.

Kring, A. and Moran, E. (2008), "Emotional Response Deficit in Schizophrenia," *Schizophrenia Bulletin*. Doi: 10.1093/schbul/sbn071.

Kuhl, J. and Beckman, J. (eds) (1985), *Action Control: From Cognitions to Behaviors*. New York: Springer.

Lincoln, T. (2007), "Relevant Dimensions of Delusions: Continuing the Continuum Versus Category Debate," *Schizophrenia Research* 93(1–3): 211–20.

Lysaker, P., Lancaster, R., Nees, M. and Davis, L. (2003), *Psychiatry Research* 119: 287–92.

Myin-Germeys, I., Nicolson, N. and Delespaul, P. (2001), "The Context of Delusional Experiences in the Daily Life of Patients with Schizophrenia," *Psychological Medicine* 31:489–98.

Nielssen, O., Westmore, B., Large, M. and Hayes, R. (2007), "Homicide during Psychotic Illness in New South Wales between 1993 and 2002," *Medical Journal of Australia* 186 (6): 301–04.

Ryan, R. and Deci, E. (2000), "Self-Determination Theory and the Facilitation of Intrinsic Motivation, Social Development, and Well-Being," *American Psychologist* 55(1): 68–78.

Sass, L. (1994), *The Paradoxes of Delusion: Wittgenstein, Schreber, and the Schizophrenic Mind*. New York (NY), Cornell University Press.

Sass, L. (2001), "Self and World in Schizophrenia: Three Classic Approaches," *Philosophy, Psychiatry, & Psychology* 8 (4): 251–70.

Sass, L. (2004), "Some Reflections on the (Analytic) Philosophical Approach to Delusion," *Philosophy, Psychiatry, & Psychology* 11(1): 71–80.

Sheeran, P. (2002), "Intention-Behavior Relations: A Conceptual and Empirical Review," in W. Strobe and M. Hewstone (eds), *European Review of Social Psychology*, vol. 12. Chichester: Wiley.

Silva, J. A., Leong, G. B., Weinstock, R. and Boyer, C. L. (1994), "Delusional Misidentification Syndromes and Dangerousness," *Psychopathology* 27 (3–5): 215–19.

Siris, S. (1995), "Depression and Schizophrenia," in S. R. Hirsch and D. Weinberger (eds), *Schizophrenia*. Oxford, Blackwell: 128–45.

Stephens, G. L. and Graham, G. (2006), "The Delusional Stance," in M. Cheung Chung, W. Fulford, G. Graham (eds), *Reconceiving Schizophrenia*. Oxford: Oxford University Press: 193–216.

Weinstein, E. (1996), "Reduplicative Misidentification Syndromes," in P. Halligan and J. Marshall (eds), *Method in Madness*. Exeter: Psychology Press: 13–36.

Wessely, S., Buchanan, A., Reed, A., Cutting, J., Everitt, B., Garety, P. and Taylor, P. (1993), "Acting on Delusions: (I) Prevalence," *British Journal of Psychiatry* 163(1): 69–76.

White, R. (1959), "Motivation Reconsidered: The Concept of Competence," *Psychological Review* 66 (5): 297–333.

Wilson, T. (2002), *Strangers to Ourselves: Discovering the Adaptive Unconscious*. Cambridge (MA): Harvard University Press.

12
The Limits of Rationality in Collective Action Explanations

Sara Rachel Chant

12.1 Introduction

Most analyses of collective action proceed by citing a set of rationalizing reasons why each individual agent in the group would participate in the action. This explanatory strategy is appropriate for an important class of collective actions, deserving detailed study. However, there is another important class of collective actions that is necessarily overlooked by what I shall call "rational choice accounts." These are cases in which a collective action is performed despite the fact that there are structural reasons why the individuals cannot rationally justify their contributory actions. In this paper, I discuss varieties of collective action, focusing on those which cannot be explained by appealing to the rationality of the individuals involved. I go on to suggest some ways in which we might profitably study this important class.

12.2 Background

Collective action has been the subject of an increasing number of analyses in recent years. Although these analyses differ in important ways, the vast majority share some central methodological assumptions. For our purposes, two of these assumptions are important. First, analyses aim to increase our understanding of the nature of collective actions by giving an etiological account of their origins. Specifically, they trace token collective actions back to the beliefs, desires, and other mental states of the individuals who compose the group. When we have an account of how and why an individual will decide to take part in a collective action, we will thereby have a satisfactory analysis of collective action.

The second methodological assumption is that collective action can be understood by way of an extended analogy to individual action.[1] That is, just as we understand individual action by employing such concepts as desire, belief, and intention, so too, collective action can be understood in terms of the collective's desires, beliefs, and intentions. Specifically, they proceed by thinking of collective actions as brought about in some way by the collective analogues of individual psychological states. Thus, the task of giving an account of collective action comes down to identifying the processes that culminate in the formation of these "collective states,"[2] which bring about the collective action.

Indeed, as I have argued at length elsewhere (2006, 2007, 2007a, 2007b, 2008, forthcoming), most analyses of collective action depend upon an assumption that the behavior of groups can be understood by employing an analogy to explanations of the behavior of individuals. Just as we deploy a folk psychological theory of mind in our explanations of individual behavior, explanations of the behavior of groups are often couched in the same terms. Whether such analyses succeed will ultimately depend upon whether the analogy between individual and group behavior is sound; but for now, the jury is still out.

Of course, when we explain an individual's behavior in terms of her beliefs and desires, we favor explanations that rationalize her behavior. Accordingly, writers on collective action also favor analyses that rationalize each individual's decision to participate in the collective action.

Given the analogy between individual and collective action and the desire to rationalize an individual's behavior when explaining individual action, it is to be expected that analyses of collective action are tightly focused on cases in which the rationality of the individual does not conflict with the collective rationality of the group. The core set of cases discussed in the literature are ones in which each individual's participation in the collective action benefits herself, as well as the group as a whole. Thus, whatever pressure there is to reduce collective action to the actions of individuals also leads naturally—although not logically—to an explanation that rationalizes each individual's behavior in terms of her own self-interest.

A particularly clear example of this strategy is provided by Raimo Tuomela's "bulletin board view" of collective action (Tuomela 2005), which I shall focus upon here.[3] Tuomela's account of (what he calls) "joint intentions" is based upon a metaphorical example, which he takes to represent the central cases of joint intention and cooperative activity. In this example, a group of agents must coordinate their individual intentions to collectively clean a park together. One of the agents proposes a plan for cleaning the park on a certain date, and posts this proposal on a public bulletin board. Other agents read the proposal and signal their acceptance of the plan by signing their names on the bulletin board. Thus, as the group of agents comes to collectively accept the plan, each agent learns that the other agents have also agreed to it. At the predetermined time, the agents show up and clean the park together, their individual intentions having been rationalized by their beliefs that the others will also do their parts.

The bulletin board example is supposed to represent a paradigmatic case of collective action. Accordingly, it is worthwhile to point out some of the key features of the example that are relevant here. First, the bulletin board quite properly emphasizes the central importance of so-called "interactive knowledge" in the generation of collective action; this is the knowledge that one person has about the knowledge of others in the group (Aumman1999a and 1999b, Koessler 2000). As Tuomela and others are right to point out, it often makes little sense for an agent to intend to take part in a collective action without possessing interactive knowledge as reassurance that the others in the group also intend to participate. For example, suppose that I would like for us to meet at a particular place and time. Obviously, in order for it to be rational for me to go to our meeting place at that time, I require some reason to believe that you will be there. Similarly, you will also require this interactive knowledge about my beliefs and intentions. As I have argued elsewhere (Chant and Ernst 2007a, 2008), this need for interactive knowledge is especially pressing when a participant in the collective action will incur some penalty if the others do not do their parts; for example, my need for interactive knowledge about your intentions is quite pressing if you have agreed to drive the getaway car after I run out of the bank with the money.

Second, interactive knowledge is especially helpful for generating the collective action because the individuals have similar reasons and incentives for participating in the collective action, at least insofar as they will benefit if the collective action is successfully carried out. Returning to Tuomela's example, it is an important feature of the situation that all of the people who sign their names on the bulletin board have the same goal in mind, and have similar criteria for determining whether they will participate. Thus, whatever conclusion I draw about my own participation in the collective action can also be drawn about your participation, and vice-versa. In other words, if my own participation is contingent upon some condition being met—for instance, that there are enough names on the bulletin board—then I may safely infer that when I judge that the condition has been met, others in the group will also judge that the condition has been met.

12.3 Levels of interactive knowledge

Although one might take issue with certain details of Tuomela's account, it is hard to deny that the features Tuomela identifies in the bulletin board example are crucial for a satisfactory account of collective action. Yet, there is an important element of the situation that is not figured into Tuomela's analysis—and this is a gap shared by many current analyses of collective action. Specifically, it is standard for writers on collective action to disregard the relative costs and benefits of doing one's part of a collective action. However, as I shall argue, these costs and benefits play an important role in determining the conditions under which the collective action will be performed.

Consider the following example. Suppose Mark and Bob need to arrange a clandestine meeting in a parking garage. Their arrangement is for Mark to put a flag outside his apartment window in order to signal that he wishes to meet. If the flag is present, then they are to meet at the garage at a preappointed time. Now suppose that Mark wants to meet, and so he places the flag outside his window. Just as planned, Bob notices the flag right away. We now consider the question of whether they will successfully meet.

As the story has been told so far, it is impossible to answer the question, even if we grant very strong assumptions about the rationality of both Mark and Bob. This is because we have not considered the relative costs and benefits for each of them to go to the garage. For instance, suppose that the benefits accrued to each of them are very large if they successfully meet, and that each man takes no risk and incurs no significant cost in going to their meeting place. Under these conditions, it is obviously rational for each of them to go the garage.

But if we change the example in a small, but realistic way, it is no longer clear that they can successfully meet. Suppose that if Mark goes to the garage but Bob does not, then Mark risks drawing unwanted attention to himself, which is very bad. With this new condition added to the story, it should be clear that Mark may rationally decide not to go to the garage, even though he has successfully signaled to Bob. For Mark does not have any assurance that Bob saw the flag—so as far as he is concerned, there is some positive probability that he will end up at the garage, alone. So in order for Mark to rationally decide to go to the garage as planned, he may require some assurance that his signal was received by Bob.

At this point, some terminology will make the point clearer. Following standard use in economics, I will say that a proposition is "mutual knowledge" when everyone in a group knows it. When a piece of knowledge is mutually known, and everyone knows that it is mutually known, then I shall say that the group has "second-order knowledge." If the previous statement can be iterated indefinitely, then the group has "common knowledge" of that fact (Lewis 1969).

What the previous example shows is that mutual knowledge may not be enough to guarantee collective action, even when the collective action is in the best interest of everyone in the group, and everyone knows that it is. For suppose that Mark and Bob are both aware of the flag; still, it may not be rational for them to go to the garage at the appointed time. They may require second-order knowledge (or higher) in order to justify taking relevant risks.[4]

12.4 A slippery slope

Unfortunately, it is reasonable to fear that the considerations I have raised in the previous section give rise to a kind of slippery slope argument ending in skepticism about the possibility of collective action. To see this, let us return to the simple case from above.

Suppose for the sake of discussion that Mark and Bob do require some reassurance that the signal has been sent and successfully received. For instance, let us assume that they have agreed that Bob is to move a certain flowerpot when he sees the flag, and that this flowerpot can be observed by Mark. Again, let us consider what happens when everything goes exactly as planned—Mark puts up the flag, Bob sees the flag and moves the flowerpot, and finally, Mark sees that the flowerpot has been moved. With this confirmation, we now consider whether they will meet.

Unfortunately, Bob may rationally reason as follows: "We both know that Mark requires confirmation in order for us to meet. Accordingly, I have confirmed—by moving the flowerpot—that I saw the flag. However, I don't know for certain that Mark has seen the flowerpot, and Mark knows this. So he doesn't have any assurance that I know he has received the confirmation. Accordingly, he doesn't know that I will go to the garage as we had planned. And because he will incur a large cost if he shows up at the garage alone, he will not go to the garage. So I shouldn't go to the garage, either."

Although Bob's line of reasoning may strike us as unusually cautious, it is not irrational, provided that the penalty for showing up at the garage alone is great enough. And obviously, Bob's reasoning can be iterated indefinitely. So it will not help to give Mark another flag to put up to indicate that he has seen the flowerpot. To put the point another way, once we have granted that Mark and Bob might require second-level interactive knowledge in order to act, we find that whatever reason they had for not acting upon first-order knowledge can be reiterated.

This discussion is not meant as a skeptical argument that collective action is impossible—rather, it is a demonstration that something crucial is missing from rational choice accounts of collective action. Binmore and Samuelson (2001) have suggested, in a different context, that this kind of regress argument can be headed-off by being sensitive to the fact that information typically comes at a cost. After all, there is typically a cost of time and resources for acquiring information—and this applies to information in the form of interactive knowledge. So to return to the example, suppose that everyone knows that Bob has to pay a hefty taxi fare every time he needs to go past Mark's apartment. After a certain number of iterations—that is, after a particular level of interactive knowledge has been reached—it may be rational for Bob to simply stop seeking more reassurances and simply go to the garage. This could happen, for instance, when the total cost of his cab fare is about to exceed the combined costs and benefits of the meeting. Knowing this fact about Bob, it is also rational for Mark to do the same. How many assurances and reassurances are necessary will depend upon the ratio between the cost of acquiring information, and the potential downside risk of showing up at the garage alone.

12.5 Intentions as conditional

Another way of approaching the problem of a vicious regress has been taken by David Velleman (1985) in a response to the account of collective action offered by Michael Bratman (1992, 1993). According to Velleman, we cannot explain the origins of collective action by reconstructing the individuals' intentions as "conditional," by which he means that the intention is to perform an action only on the condition that others perform their parts. For if, as most accounts allegedly require, a collective action is generated by the actions of many individuals whose contributions are contingent on the others' doing their part, then there is an obvious vicious regress. Suppose, for example, that Abe will do his part only if Betty does hers, and vice-versa. Then there are two ways in which their conditional intentions can be satisfied, namely, if both of them act, or if neither of them do.

It is important to note that the regress is not solved by citing any particular set of beliefs either Abe or Betty might have, even if those beliefs are about the other's beliefs.[5] So long as each one has only an intention in which the action is conditional upon the other, no set of beliefs will be sufficient to discharge that conditional intention.

In his response to Velleman, Bratman gives an interesting example of a case in which two agents have only conditional intentions to act, and yet they manage to act. In his example, Abe and Betty want water to be pumped from a well. In order to pump the water, Abe must pump the water while Betty turns a valve. Both want the water to be pumped, but each has only a conditional intention to do their part; that is, Abe will only pump if Betty turns the valve, and Betty will only turn the valve if Abe pumps.

In Bratman's example, Abe and Betty can see each other. Recognizing that Betty can see him, and that she wants the water to be pumped, it is now rational for Abe to simply start pumping without first having to communicate anything further to Betty. For as soon as he starts pumping the water, it is now completely up to Betty whether the water is successfully pumped or not; after all, given that Abe is already doing his part, the water will be pumped if and only if she turns the valve. Because she wants the water to be pumped, it is not mysterious at all how Betty can rationally decide to turn the valve. Furthermore, Abe already knows that Betty will reason in this way if he starts pumping, so it is also perfectly rational for him to do his part initially. Bratman puts the point more generally:

> . . . I can "frame" the intention that we J in part on the assumption that you will, as a result, come also so to intend. While I confidently predict you will come so to intend, I also recognize that you remain a free agent and this decision is really up to you... Second, even after I have formed the intention that we J, in part because I predict you will concur, I can recognize that you still need to concur: It is just that I am fully confident that you will.
>
> (1997 p. 59)

Bratman's response is perfectly sound—at least, for a particular class of cases. After all, Abe has changed the payoffs that Betty can reasonably expect were she to do her part of the collective action. For prior to her seeing Abe pump the water, it was (by hypothesis) not known to her whether her effort to turn the valve would be wasted. Thus, we can think of the payoff she should expect from turning the valve to be diminished in proportion to her uncertainty about Abe's likely action. But once she sees that Abe is in fact pumping the water, this uncertainty is eliminated and she can expect her full payoff when she turns the valve.

This is a very plausible and realistic story about an important class of collective actions. When one person can actually observe the others perform their parts of the collective action, it can happen that this observation prompts that person to act. Indeed, this may be why certain risky, cooperative ventures often require a high level of "transparency" among the members of the group.

But it is equally important to note that this explanation clearly does not apply to a wide range of other cases. For if we cannot observe each other, then my unilateral performance of my part of the collective action does not justify my prediction "that you will concur." Returning to the example, if Abe and Betty have to stand on opposite sides of a house, then Betty cannot tell whether Abe is pumping the water or not, so the payoff she can expect from turning the valve remains uncertain.

Thus, like the case in which Mark and Bob want to meet, the explanation of the collective action depends crucially upon the structure of the individuals' payoffs. Just as Mark and Bob will go to the garage only if they have sufficient reassurance that the other will, Abe and Betty will successfully pump the water only if each believes the other will do their part. The only salient difference between the cases is that Abe and Betty each have the power to affect the other's expectations of their own payoff.

What we might call a "degenerate" case of collective action—in the sense that no particular explanation of it is necessary—is one in which performance of the collective action has positive value, but no negative downside risk whatsoever. For example, suppose that my friend and I want to meet at the local coffee shop. If we successfully meet, that will benefit both of us. And suppose also that neither of us would be worse off in any way if we were to go to the coffee shop and end up there alone. That is, in making the decision whether to stay home or attempt to meet, staying home is no better than going, even if the other person fails to show up.

Obviously, we do not need any complicated explanation of how we both rationally decide to go to the coffee shop. Indeed, even if I were fairly confident that you will not show up, it is still perfectly rational for me to go to the coffee shop; and of course, the same is true of you. Given this fact, we certainly do not need for our plans to be common knowledge, or even mutual knowledge.

12.6 The difficult remainder

The difficult cases are not like the one Bratman describes, nor are they like the "degenerate" case I mentioned above. Rather, they are cases in which there is a positive benefit for coordinating our actions, but in which there is also a penalty for anyone who does their part of the collective action when others do not. These form a remainder of cases for which interactive knowledge seems a necessary part of their explanation.

I have already argued above that—as in the case of Mark and Bob—rational agents may justifiably decide not to take part in a collective action, even if they have successfully signaled their desire that the collective action take place, and even if everyone prefers that the collective action be performed. In the example, this stumbling block to collective action is the fact that there can be a significant downside risk to "doing one's part" of the collective action if the others do not.

If this were the only kind of situation in which a difficulty remained, then our task would be more straightforward than it is. But it turns out that a qualitatively similar problem occurs over a wide range of cases. Consider an extremely simple example. Suppose that you and I have decided to meet for lunch at one of two restaurants, but we have forgotten in our conversations to decide which one. Restaurant A, let us say, is clearly better than restaurant B and we both know this. But we would prefer to meet even at the inferior restaurant B rather than not meet at all.[6] Further, suppose we have no way of communicating prior to the appointed meeting time.

In this simple situation, it is easy to predict what we will do; if we are at all normal, and no unspecified circumstances arise, then we will meet at restaurant A. Indeed, we may safely make the general observation that in a coordination problem in which one action is superior to the other for all parties involved, people will have no difficulty coordinating on that collective action.

But the obviousness of this fact obscures a difficult question, namely, *how* do we so easily coordinate our actions? To bring out the difficulty of answering this question, we have to ask whether I can *infer* that I should go to restaurant A. Suppose I am undecided about which restaurant to choose. Given the facts of the situation, it is rational for me to go to restaurant A only if I believe that you are going to restaurant A; and I should similarly go to restaurant B only if I believe that you are going to restaurant B (for although A is better than B, going to A alone is worse than successfully meeting at B). So the question of whether I can infer that I ought to go to restaurant A comes down to the question of whether I can infer that you are going to be there.

Following some common terminology, let us say that the beliefs I have about the probability of your performing particular actions are my "conjectures" about you. So I will go to restaurant A just in case my conjecture is that you will do so. In this way, coordination will depend on whether I can infer which restaurant you will choose.

Of course, one might suspect that, given how easy it is for real-world agents to coordinate in this kind of situation, it must be similarly easy for me to infer that you will go to restaurant A. However, this is not the case. For if we both prefer meeting over not meeting, then you will go to restaurant A only if you conjecture that I will; and similarly, if you were to conjecture that I would go to restaurant B, then you would prefer to go to restaurant B. In fact, each of us has only conditional preferences; that is, each of us prefers to go to a particular restaurant only if the other will go there, too. So if I am to infer that you will go to restaurant A, then this comes down to the problem of transforming my knowledge of:

(1) If you believe that I will go to restaurant A, then you will go to restaurant A.

into knowledge that:

(2) You will go to restaurant A.

Given the form of proposition (1), I can infer (2) only if you can infer:

(3) I will go to restaurant A.

Unfortunately, all you know is that

(4) If I believe that you will go to restaurant A, then I will go to restaurant A.

So we are left with (4), which is the exact analogue of (1). So no progress has been made; any attempt to infer what either of us will do leads only to the conclusion that she will do whatever it is that she believes the other will do. Thus, the inferences necessary for action fall into a vicious regress.

Of course, simply because a particular decision problem *can* be represented as intractable does not entail that it is *impossible* to represent it in such a way that it can be solved. But if one were to argue that in this case, I am somehow able to infer that you will go to restaurant A, then one would face a difficult problem. For one would have to find a way of inferring proposition (2) in a simple way, without making recourse to complex models, overly strong assumptions about the calculating ability of the individuals, and so on. The reason for this is that people coordinate so *easily* that it is unreasonable to suppose that there is highly abstract, complex reasoning underlying coordination that is so simple and common. It is not as if we are able to meet in restaurants and coffee shops only because we are all highly sophisticated game theorists and experts in decision theory!

To put the point another way, there are common cases in which people do successfully coordinate their actions, and they do so based upon the belief that other people will "do their part." However, if we suppose that such a conjecture is the result of an inference, then we are faced with a dilemma. Such an attempt to infer what other people are going to do either falls prey to a vicious regress such as we saw in (1)—(4) above, or otherwise it would have to be so sophisticated that it is unrealistic to suppose that it is commonly deployed.

However, one might be suspicious of the claim that some collective actions cannot be explained by citing any inferences made by individuals in the group. For there is a large literature in economics, decision theory, and game theory in which models are proposed in which coordination is achieved through the inferential powers of ideally rational agents. Thus, one might suspect that the above regress argument is too fast—for if it were sound, this large and well-established literature would be mistaken.

I agree with this observation, and it is certainly not my contention that there is any such flaw in the economics, game theory, or rational choice literature. However, no such models undermine the regress argument. The reason why they do not is simple. Rational choice models of decision making and coordination are based upon the assumption—often called the "Harsanyi Doctrine"—that an individual's choice of which action to perform is based only upon the information available to them (Harsanyi 1985). If rational decision making is a deterministic process, agents with the same information, and who are in the same situation, will necessarily perform the same action.[7] Or, to put the point as John Harsanyi put it, any differences in choice must be the result of differences in information.

In the most trivial coordination problems, there is very little information available to the agents, except perhaps which actions are available, and what the resultant payoffs will be if those actions are performed. Furthermore, in these trivial situations, the information available is identical for both agents. So it is little wonder that coordination is easy to achieve in these rational choice models.[8] For the presence of identical information simply *entails* identical choices.

Of course, it is possible to dispense with the Harsanyi Doctrine and allow for the possibility that two agents with identical information may settle on different actions. However, upon closer examination, it turns out that some other tendency to coordinate is assumed—either implicitly or explicitly—in the discussion. For example, in Binmore and Samuelson's (2001) discussion of the so-called "Coordinated Attack Problem" it is notoriously difficult for two agents to coordinate under almost any condition. However, Binmore and Samuelson note that in order for coordination to be achieved at all, the agents must have a tendency to coordinate with each other under simplified conditions; furthermore, this tendency to coordinate must be mutually known by everyone.

And it also turns out that the Harsanyi Doctrine—and even those strong assumptions in the economics literature—do not guarantee coordination on the obvious choice; they only guarantee coordination on some Nash equilibrium or other.[9] Most do not attempt to account for why individuals will coordinate on the obvious (or "salient") equilibrium. So, as in the discussion above, we conclude that even if such a model were to explain coordination in simple cases, it would not accurately describe the exact nature of the coordination that real human beings so easily achieve in those cases.

12.7 Possible approaches

At this point, I have presented a motley of arguments concerning different varieties of explanation for collective action. It is worthwhile to sum them up briefly.

In many cases, the traditional accounts of collective action—such as those offered by Tuomela—are basically correct. We form individual "we-intentions" to participate in a collective action, contingent upon our having good enough reason to believe that others similarly intend. These accounts correctly place primary importance on the mechanism by which we come to learn of each others' we-intentions. A sufficient level of (what I have called) "interactive knowledge"—which has also been called "joint knowledge" or "loop beliefs"—is taken as a central component of any account of collective action.

However, the appropriateness of such explanations depends upon the payoff structure of the situation. By this, I mean that the costs of attempting to participate in the collective action must be appropriately related to the potential benefits of successfully pulling off the collective action. If the risks are too high relative to the potential benefits, then there will be additional conditions which must be met in order for the collective action to take place. These may include the necessity of achieving higher levels of interactive knowledge, as we saw in the case of Mark and Bob's clandestine meeting. But on the other hand, if there is very little downside risk to attempting one's part of the collective action, and the potential payoffs are sufficiently high, then interactive knowledge might not even be necessary.

In cases that are non-trivial, and in which interactive knowledge is not explanatory—as when the individuals coordinate without being able to communicate—a regress problem looms. For if no individual can conspicuously and publicly initiate the collective action by unilaterally doing her part, and thereby prompt the others into doing their parts, then it may be impossible in principle for any agent to provide a rational choice explanation justifying their participation.

Let's call the cases that are subject to a regress, the "difficult cases." These are cases in which it is impossible for one person to unilaterally begin the collective action, thereby signaling to others that their contribution is likely to succeed. And yet, even in the difficult cases, real-world human beings are often able to successfully coordinate their actions straightaway.

One way to think about the difficult cases is that they are ones in which agents are more or less spontaneously inclined toward a particular action (out of a range of possible actions) that is particularly "salient." Following the seminal work of Lewis (1969), it has been recognized that there are cases ranging from spontaneous, everyday situations to highly complex and artificial situations, in which there exists one option that seems to "stand out" from the rest. In such situations, agents are able to coordinate their actions—and usually do so—despite the fact that there does not seem to be an obvious rational choice argument available to justify that choice.

One conclusion that can be drawn from this paper is that we should give up the search for a unified etiological account of collective action. That is, if collective action is to be given an analysis consisting of an explanation of the steps leading up to the successful performance of the collective action, then we will wind up with at best a motley of different explanations. In particular, we will need to understand the difficult cases; there are four obvious strategies for doing so.

First, one might hope that additional resources beyond the typical epistemological considerations would justify an individual's participation in a collective action in subtle ways. However, I think this is unlikely for one important reason. Real-world cases of collective action—even the difficult cases—usually do not call upon each individual to engage in complex, abstract reasoning. The phenomenology of collective action is that we often act "straightaway," without any awareness of the difficult arguments that might be needed to justify our action. We might make an analogy to language acquisition. Even if it were possible to give a detailed rational framework that an idealized child could use to figure out the grammar of her native language, we would be suspicious of any attempt to explain her acquisition of language this way. After all, it is clear that children are not reasoning as if they were very small linguists when they learn a language. Similarly, when we act together collectively, we are not thinking through the situation as if we were economists or game-theorists.

Second, it might be possible to explain difficult cases of collective action by supposing that there is a core set of cases in which collective action is rationally justified. Then, one might suppose that individuals behave cooperatively in other situations because of some perceived similarity to those core cases; the explanation might be couched in terms of certain "framing effects" influencing the individuals, and which are responsible for their propensity toward cooperation. To return to Bratman's example, we might reasonably suppose that Abe and Betty successfully coordinate their collective action of pumping water when they can see each other, just in the way Bratman supposes. Then, if they are called upon to accomplish the same task when they cannot see each other, they revert back to whatever behavior they displayed in similar circumstances. In this way, they accomplish their collective action, even in the face of a vicious regress of justification.

I think it is reasonable enough to suppose that something like this scenario does play out in many cases. However, merely citing the alleged fact that people have a tendency to coordinate their actions when certain "framing effects" are present does little to explain. Note that I said that Abe and Betty might coordinate their actions when they are faced with a situation that is "similar" to one they have seen before. This idea cannot be counted as an adequate explanation unless we can get some idea of what counts as a "similar" situation. Clearly, Abe and Betty's current situation may resemble different prior situations in different ways. Perhaps in some of those situations, they coordinated their actions, and in others they did not. Although it is certainly plausible that a person's choice of action will be informed—perhaps unconsciously—by the situations they have faced in the past, the real explanation of her coordination will lie in developing an account of how these framing effects work. Furthermore, I think this possible strategy is vulnerable to the same worry as the first strategy. That is, if it were a good general account, then it would have to be the case that for every "difficult case" in which coordination occurs, there exists for each agent some past situation relevantly similar to the present one, in which she successfully coordinated her actions. Although it is possible that this is the case in some situations, the proponent of this strategy for a general account faces a heavy burden of proof in that she must argue for the universal claim.

So I believe we are left with one last option, and that is to take seriously the possibility that humans have an innate tendency to engage in cooperative behavior. If true, this has an important effect upon philosophical action theory, namely, that we would have to divide what we normally call "collective action" into subclasses, and give up the search for a unified etiological explanation. At its most coarse, the division would be into two categories—the first consisting of those actions for which a rational choice explanation is available, and the second consisting of those for which no rational choice explanation is available. Of course, this latter set is just what I have been calling the "difficult cases."

But one might reasonably wonder whether we have any positive reason for suspecting that the difficult cases are, indeed, ones which would defy any rational choice explanation. Here, I think we have an interesting set of parallels to more familiar problems. In particular, the task of explaining these recalcitrant cases is closely related to the problem of explaining what economists call "anomalies."

Anomalies, as economists use the term, are cases in which people defy a rational choice prediction in favor of behavior that is likely to yield lower payoffs for them than they could otherwise achieve. The most famous examples of this phenomenon are Prisoner's Dilemma problems. These are cases in which each of two players has a choice between cooperating with the other player, or defecting. It is a dilemma because whatever choice the other player makes, defection always yields a higher payoff. But if both defect, then they each receive a lower payoff than they would have received had they cooperated. Because defection always yields a superior payoff, the rational choice model predicts mutual defection. But in many instances, that is not what real-world agents do. We frequently cooperate, and we frequently engage in other behaviors that we know will yield lower payoffs for ourselves.

Philosophical reactions to anomalous behavior in the Prisoner's Dilemma closely mirror efforts to explain collective action in action theory. First, we have a large number of failed attempts to rationally justify cooperation as a self-interested behavior; but all such efforts fail for the simple reason that, by definition, defection will always lead to the highest payoff.[10] Second, the experimental economics literature is filled with examples of experiments which attempt to identify the framing effects that promote cooperation and other forms of anomalous behavior. However, although many of these framing effects are compelling, this research has not yielded anything close to a general account of cooperation. And third, there is a parallel research effort dedicated to explaining how an innate tendency to perform anomalous behavior might have evolved by natural selection.

Of course, we are considering cases which are much weaker, in a sense, than the Prisoner's Dilemma. For as a rule, philosophers of action are not typically concerned with cases in which individuals act against their own self-interest when they take part in a collective action. Rather, typical cases are ones in which there is some benefit to successfully pulling off a collective action.

12.8 Conclusion

If the arguments in the paper have been correct, then we must abandon the search for a monolithic account of collective action, for the rational choice explanations that are standardly deployed will fail to account for collective action in at least two different ways. The first failure is that *contra* standard accounts, the level of interactive knowledge needed for rational agents to successfully coordinate their actions will depend crucially upon the agents' assessments of the potential risks and rewards involved. As I have argued elsewhere, the way to fill this theoretical gap is to take into account at least an informal theory of interactive epistemology. The second, and perhaps more interesting failure, is that in many cases, a rational choice model will not suffice to explain the performance of collective action at all.

If, as I have argued, there is no sound rational choice explanation of this large class of collective action, then something besides rationality must account for them. The situation is somewhat analogous to other research programs in which people's behavior seems impossible to justify on rational grounds. A possibility worth exploring is that individuals have an innate propensity to cooperate in particular kinds of circumstances. An argument for this possibility would proceed by way of an analogy to the well-known "poverty of the stimulus" arguments for innateness in language acquisition. In that context, we learn that children have an innate propensity to learn particular kinds of grammatical constructions because their environment does not provide nearly enough stimulus for them to infer the correct grammatical patterns. To put the point another way, the inferences that children seem to make—and their remarkable linguistic behavior—are perfectly sound and well-suited for interaction with other human beings in their environment, despite the fact that there are no rational principles that could possibly underwrite their language capacities.

Of course, what typically drives the poverty of stimulus argument is that the relevant inferences about the structure of grammar cannot be rationally justified because grammar is far too complex, given the paltry amount of information in the child's environment. In the case of collective action, it is probably not the case that the environment is too limited to underwrite the correct inferences; rather, the problem is that there is no possible rational justification for an agent's cooperative behavior. And yet it does occur. Therefore, something besides rationality must play an important role in collective action.

Thus, if this sketch is correct, we should approach certain problems of collective action from a standpoint similar to that taken in research on cooperative and altruistic behavior, such as in Prisoner's Dilemmas. For typically, we place cooperative behavior in coordination problems in a category that does not include Prisoner's Dilemmas and other instances of pro-social behavior. The reason for this is that one kind of behavior—coordination—results in higher payoffs for everyone, whereas other-regarding or altruistic behavior results in a lower payoff for the individual who displays that behavior. But as I have argued, it may turn out that for the purpose of providing as unified as possible a theory of collective action, this difference—which looms large in other contexts—may be unimportant. What they share is the unavailability of a rational choice explanation for the collective action, and that fact should guide further research.

Notes

1. John Searle's proposal is the major exception to this generalization.
2. For lack of a better term. I am emphatically not endorsing or assuming any view which attributes psychological states to a group (or worse yet, to a 'group mind').
3. Other analyses of collective action are relevantly similar, insofar as they follow the two assumptions I have outlined here. In addition to other work by Tuomela 1989, 1991, 2002, 2004, 2005, see Christopher Kutz, Miller 2001, Natalie Gold and Robert Sugden 2007, Michael Bratman 1993, and Jennifer Hornsby 1997. The only account I am aware of which thoroughly avoids these assumptions is offered by John Searle 1990, 1995, 1997.
4. It is easy to construct cases in which higher-order knowledge is required for collective action. Indeed, it is possible to construct a case in which rational agents will act only if all of the relevant information has been elevated to a state of common knowledge among them. See Binmore and Samuelson 2001, Rubinstein 1989.
5. Unless, of course, one of them has the belief that the other will act; but as this assumption cannot be given a rational choice explanation—on pain of the regress—I will disregard that possibility here. But I shall discuss it in more detail below.

6. This is just a so-called 'Hi-Lo' coordination game.
7. Of course, even such an idealized rational agent might decide to flip a coin, or otherwise randomize her behavior, particularly if her potential payoffs are uncertain. But I will not address such a possibility, since it does not arise in this simple example.
8. This observation explains why so-called 'common knowledge' assumptions are so pervasive in the economics literature on coordination, convention, and social contract theory.
9. Where we understand Nash equilibrium in the usual way, as a set of strategies having the property that no player can benefit by unilaterally switching strategies (Nash 1950, 1951).
10. For an excellent discussion of these attempts at a rational choice explanation of cooperation in Prisoner's Dilemma situations, see Ken Binmore's (1994).

References

Aumman, R. (1999a), "Interactive Epistemology I: Knowledge," *International Journal of Game Theory*, 28: 263–300.

Aumman, R. (1999b), "Interactive Epistemology II: Probability," *International Journal of Game Theory*, 28: 301–14.

Binmore, K. (1994), *Playing Fair*. MIT Press, Cambridge, Mass.

Binmore, K. and L. Samuelson. (2001), "Coordinated Action in the Electronic Mail Game," *Games and Economic Behavior*, 35: 6–30.

Bratman, M. (1992), "Shared Cooperative Activity," *The Philosophical Review*, 101: 327–41.

Bratman, M. (1993), "Shared Intention," *Ethics*, 104: 97–113.

Bratman, M. (1997), "I Intend that We j," vol. 2, pages 49–63. Kluwer Academic Publishers.

Chant, S. (2006), "The Special Composition Question in Action," *Pacific Philosophical Quarterly*, 87: 422–41.

Chant, S. (2007), "Unintentional Collective Action," *Philosophical Explorations*, 10(3): 245–56.

Chant, S. (2010), "Two Composition Questions in (Collective) Action," in Alan Hazlett, ed., *New Waves in Metaphysics*, New York: Blackwell.

Chant, S. and Z. Ernst (2007a), "Collective Action as Individual Choice," *Studia Logica*, 86: 415–434.

Chant, S. and Z. Ernst (2007b), "Group Intentions as Equilibria," *Philosophical Studies*, 133: 95–109.

Chant, S. and Z. Ernst (2008), "Epistemic Conditions for Collective Action," *Mind*, 117: 549.

Gold, N. and R. Sugden (2007), "Collective Intentions and Team Agency," *Journal of Philosophy*, 104: 109–137.

Harsanyi, J. (1985), "Does Reason Tell Us What Moral Code to Follow and, Indeed, to Follow Any Moral Code at all?" *Ethics*, 96: 42–55.

Hornsby, J. (1997), "Collectives and Intentionality," *Philosophy and Phenomenological Research*, 57: 429–34.

Koessler, F. (2000), "Common Knowledge and Interactive Behaviors: A Survey," *European Journal of Economic and Social Systems*, 14: 271–308.

Lewis, D. (1969), *Convention: A Philosophical Study*, Harvard University Press, Cambridge, Mass.

Miller, S. (2001), *Social Action: A Teleological Account*. Cambridge University Press, Cambridge.
Nash, J. (1950), "The Bargaining Problem," *Econometrica*, 18: 155–62.
Nash, J. (1951), "Non-Cooperative Games," *Annals of Mathematics*, 54: 286–95.
Rubinstein, A. (1989), "The Electronic Mail Game: Strategic Behavior Under 'Almost common knowledge'," *American Economic Review*, 79: 385–91.
Searle, J. (1990), "Collective Intentions and Actions," in Philip R. Cohen and J. Morgan, eds, *Intentions in Communication*, pp. 401–16. MIT Press, Cambridge, Mass.
Searle, J. (1995), *The Construction of Social Reality*, The Free Press, New York.
Searle, (1997), "Responses to Critics," *Philosophy and Phenomenological Research*, 57: 449–58.
Tuomela, R. (1989), "Actions by Collectives," *Philosophical Perspectives*, 3: 471–96.
Tuomela, R. (1991), "We Will do it: An Analysis of Group-Intentions," *Philosophy and Phenomenological Research*, 51: 249–77.
Tuomela, R. (2002), *The Philosophy of Social Practices: A Collective Acceptance View*, Cambridge University Press, Cambridge.
Tuomela, R. (2004), "Joint Action," *Workshop on Holistic Epistemology and Theory of Action*.
Tuomela, R. (2005), "We-Intentions Revisited," *Philosophical Studies*, 125: 327–69.
Tuomela, R. and Miller, K. (1988), "We-Intentions," *Philosophical Studies*, 53: 367–90.
Velleman, D. (1985), "Practical Reflection," *The Philosophical Review*, 94: 33–61.
Velleman, D. (1997), "How to Share an Intention," *Philosophy and Phenomenological Research*, 57: 29–50.

Index